VAX/VMS

P9-CAZ-400

Operating System Concepts

David Donald Miller

digital

DIGITAL PRESS

Printed in the United States of America.

9 8 7 6 5 4 3 2

Order number EY-F590E-DP

Design: Outside Designs

Production: Editorial Inc.

Composition: Modern Graphics, Inc.

CDC is a registered trademark of Control Data Corporation. CP/M is a registered trademark of Digital Research Incorporated. DEC, DECnet, DECsystem-10, DECUS, DECwriter, the DECtape, the Digital logo, IAS, MicroVAX, PDP, PDP-11, Rdb, RSTS, RSX, RT-11, ULTRIX, UNIBUS, VAX, VAX RMS, VM, and VT are trademarks of Digital Equipment Corporation. IBM, IBM PC, OS/2, and VM are trademarks of International Business Machines Corporation. Intel is a registered trademark of Intel Corporation. Motorola is a registered trademark of Motorola, Incorporated. MS-DOS is a registered trademark of Microsoft Corporation. UNIX is a trademark of AT&T Bell Laboratories.

Views expressed in this book are those of the author, not of the publisher. Digital Equipment Corporation assumes no responsibility for any errors that may appear in this book.

Library of Congress Cataloging-in-Publication Data

Miller, David Donald.
    VAX/VMS Operating system concepts
by David Donald Miller.
      p. cm.
    Includes index.
    ISBN 1-55558-065-3
    1. VAX/VMS. I. Title.
QA76.76.063M562 1991   91-25752
005.4'44—dc20   CIP

Contents

Preface

The first twenty years of my career were spent in various software engineering positions within the aerospace industry. During that time, I was involved with many application projects, yet I rarely found myself writing application programs. Instead, I supported the application programmers as the unofficial in-house operating system and compiler guru. "What does this error message mean?" "How do I tell the system to . . . ?" "How do you read this dump?" "Why didn't my program link?" "How do overlays work?" "How do I make this faster?"

I enjoyed this role because I was able to learn about applications in the context of the language and operating system. Whenever possible, I also taught about the operating system and the compiler and showed how they were a part of the application. Often, I participated in design reviews to make certain that the application was using the operating system to the best possible advantage.

My work during those years was consuming, but there were times when I asked myself why the tasks I performed were necessary. The application programmers' questions were not particularly difficult, or deep; in fact, 90 percent of them I considered to be trivial. Even so, whatever project I worked on, no matter what application, language, operating system, or company, I was drawn into the same role of operating system interpreter. And I began to realize that just as I had benefited from an understanding of applications, application programmers would benefit from an understanding of the operating system.

In familiarizing myself with operating systems, I read all the vendor documentation. Like a cookbook, it listed functions and features, but it rarely provided a meaningful description of a certain function's design or implementation or explained how it fit into the system as a whole. To complicate the situation further, users' manuals sometimes were (and still are) obscure. On one project, I found that the only useful information was contained in the minds of the operating system designers, and as a result, over the course of the project, I came to know them on a first-name basis. On other projects, when the designers were unavailable, I had to resort to trial-and-error programming to respond to certain questions.

When I "retired" from industry and turned to teaching, I was naturally drawn to the operating systems course. In searching for a text that dealt with questions I had spent years answering, I was surprised to find that none was available. This book, then, is an outgrowth of nearly thirty years' experience and a response to the need for a book that views the operating system as a problem-solving aid for a programmer to master, just as a programming language must be mastered.

APPROACH

Currently available texts take one of two approaches to the presentation of operating systems concepts. The first approach deals primarily with the theoretical aspects of operating systems. I do not believe a theoretical treatment alone, however, is sufficient for most software engineers. The second approach, rather than delving deeply into the theory, has the programmer design, code, and test parts or all of a small operating system. Studies of this kind also are inadequate because programmers generally lack time to probe many of the operating systems' issues to the depth of actual code. The programmer who implements parts of an operating system will learn a tremendous amount, but only about those parts. I find both of these presentation approaches unsatisfying. After all, we do not teach Pascal by discussing LR parsers and writing compilers; we teach it by applying it to problem solving.

A full-service, multi-user, interactive operating system is intended for use by application programmers. This book will not only show the programmer what an operating system is expected to provide, it will also give him or her a hands-on opportunity to use it. My approach includes theoretical discussions, but it emphasizes the application so that the software engineer can exploit the services provided by a working operating system, in this case the VAX/VMS system. Once the text introduces the purpose of a particular service, it will discuss how this service is provided and how the VMS operating system makes use of it.

ACKNOWLEDGMENTS

First, I wish to thank the many reviewers of this book: Paul Anagnostopoulos; Jack Beidler, University of Scranton; Richard Eckhouse, University of Massachusetts—Boston; Hank Levy, University of Washington; Phillip Ollapally, Tennessee State University; James Peters, Kansas State University; Susan Rossellet, Bemidji State University; Charles Shub, University of Colorado at Colorado Springs; Harold Schultz, Digital Equipment Corporation and Tennessee State University; Thomas Scott, Western Illinois University; James Silver, Indiana University, Purdue University at Fort Wayne; and David Teague, Western Carolina University.

Next, I wish to thank Michael Meehan of Digital Press for sticking by me and encouraging me through this project, and my local Digital representative, Rich Lynn, who supplied me with technical sales information.

I also wish to thank Sarah Lemaire, whose thorough technical edit improved the accuracy and consistency of the material presented. Her experience with VMS was invaluable in pinpointing errors, omissions, and inconsistencies in my presentation.

The ARGOSystems management and staff and the Bemidji State University staff also deserve my thanks for their support and constant encouragement. Without these two organizations, I would not have had either the time or the financial support necessary for such an endeavor.

Finally, my family, Kari, Serri, Maarit, and Ekren, deserves recognition too; without their cooperation, this task would have been impossible. They were willing to do without their husband and father for over a year, sacrificing fishing trips, concerts, plays, bike rides, vacations, walks, and quiet moments together so that I could write this book.

David Miller
June 1991

DMILLER @ MSUS1.BITNET

About This Book

This book introduces operating systems concepts and tools through examples implemented on the VAX/VMS operating system. For instance, Chapter 3 presents a program that mimics an alarm clock and describes how it runs within the context of the operating system. Chapter 4 shows how the statement order of a small program changes execution time from a few seconds to several minutes because thrashing is introduced. Chapter 5 presents two programs that impersonate Romeo and Juliet, illustrating how two processes can communicate; and Chapter 6 presents two programs that share data in a single critical region. Lastly, Chapter 8 presents an example program illustrating the use of asynchronous system traps (ASTs).

ORGANIZATION

Each chapter is organized so that its central concept is introduced by one or more diagrams together with its theoretical aspects and variations, including generally recognized solutions and algorithms. These preparatory sections are not directed at a particular operating system. Next, the chapter provides a detailed Pascal example using the concept and illustrating implementation details—the algorithms and data structures—employed by the VMS operating system. Each chapter concludes with a section outlining additional issues that are related to the central concept. This section briefly discusses alternate approaches that could be used by the operating system designer. Each chapter is accompanied by short answer exercises (with solutions), programming projects, and suggestions for research papers.

Chapter 1 is an introduction centering on one visible aspect of any interactive operating system—terminal input and output. This introductory material will lay the groundwork for future chapters.

Chapter 2 introduces the notion of a process, showing in particular how a process is created and destroyed by the VMS system and some of the data structures that it maintains. Exercises include developing experiments to time process creation and deletion. This chapter serves as an introduction to scheduling, which is the topic of Chapter 3.

Chapter 3 shows the reader how a process alternates between I/O and execution, which leads to the notion of time-sharing and process states. It also introduces a primitive, generic scheduling algorithm, describes several classical scheduling algorithms, and explains the VMS scheduler. A Pascal program—an alarm clock—is used to illustrate state changes in real time, and projects include developing the alarm clock program and observing its operation. Chapter 3 justifies the need for co-resident processes, and Chapter 4 explains how they are provided.

Chapter 4 addresses memory management of co-resident processes. It describes the classical solutions—overlays and partitions—and introduces the page as an intuitive solution to the difficulties inherent with classical approaches. Development of a behavior model introduces the working set concept and the VMS memory manager is shown to support the working set. The chapter also develops the VAX paging mechanism in detail to show how the hardware must support this concept, and it concludes with an overview of the VMS database introduced to this point.

Chapter 5 deals with process synchronization by illustrating three VMS techniques—forcing process state changes, event flags, and using mailboxes—to coordinate the activities of two processes on adjacent terminals. The VMS data structures required to implement these techniques are also developed.

Chapter 6 is an extension of synchronization into the realm of common data sharing. Where Chapter 5 dealt with processes exchanging one bit of information, Chapter 6 deals with unlimited data sharing. It develops the idea of an execution thread and with it the need for mutual exclusion. Once again, it presents practical solutions using VMS services. The consumer-producer problem is treated as a special case requiring no operating system support but, rather, careful attention to coding details.

In contrast to the sharing aspects developed in Chapter 6, security and privacy are the subject of Chapter 7, with the emphasis on privacy. System reliability is closely related and therefore discussed, again with VAX/VMS as the illustrative model to show how the theory has been successfully implemented. This chapter describes how the VAX maintains its levels of security and how some specifically designed instructions work. It also introduces the interrupt structure, although this is developed more fully in the next chapter.

Chapter 8 is devoted to the complex subject of input/output, again using the VAX for illustration. The Interrupt Priority Level (IPL) is described in detail because IPL is pivotal in understanding the VMS system in its totality and I/O operations in particular. The merging of hardware and software interrupt priority is at the very heart of the VMS design. Once again, issues such as mutual exclusion and data sharing are illustrated in a practical and complex application. Chapter 8 is by far the most intricate in the book. The programming projects include developing a primitive interrupt processor using the Asynchronous System Trap (AST) feature of VAX/VMS.

Chapter 9, which discusses disk file organization, is more generic than its predecessors. It first describes what the disk is, how it works, and what its limitations and strengths are. It then illustrates some methods of logical data storage, explains the concept of the directory, and defines the three file structures: sequential, direct, and indexed. The chapter closes with an overview of VMS disk files, including a directory, header, and data, and describes how to use and interpret VMS tools that deal with file structures.

Chapter 10 presents a brief history of operating systems produced by Digital Equipment Corporation.

TO THE INSTRUCTOR OR STUDENT

Most modern interactive operating systems have become too complex for a person with only a one-course exposure to comprehend, even in general terms. In fact, the study of operating systems is rapidly becoming a graduate-level, multi-course subdiscipline within computer science. Nevertheless, undergraduates must be introduced to the basic principles that are at the heart of today's systems. There is some middle ground between the operating system expert and the novice user, and the purpose of the undergraduate course is to prepare the student for this middle ground.

I have designed this text for college seniors with extensive design and programming experience in Pascal or, possibly, FORTRAN or C. The student should be familiar with computer architecture and an assembly language, preferably on the VAX, and should have some competence in data structure designs. I view this course as a capstone because it integrates many of these seemingly independent studies.

As an undergraduate text, this book is too long for a single ten-week quarter if the student implements the exercises. The first seven chapters alone would fill a quarter, but all ten chapters could be reasonably covered in a fourteen-week semester. If the book is used as a graduate text, its instructional emphasis should be on the papers, not on the programming projects.

TO THE PROFESSIONAL

Rather than present the application as subordinate to the operating system, I first introduce the software engineer to theory and then encourage hands-on practice in a time-sharing environment. This approach gives the professional some insight into and an intuitive "feeling" for the theory. An experiment in page thrashing, for instance, can be easily implemented and monitored under the VMS system. The programmer can then experimentally derive paging curves offered in other operating system texts. Unlike most books that stop the thrashing discussion at a theoretical level, this book allows the programmer working with a real system to further observe thrashing whether the system is busy or idle. Both the process and global system performance can be observed under varied conditions, which will lead naturally into a discussion of the philosophy behind the scheduler algorithm and topics related to guarding users from a thrashing process.

Few software engineers will ever design and code an operating system. Even in the mid-1960s, operating systems like OS/360 were over a million lines of assembly code. Short of implementing operating systems, however, most programmers will be called upon to use their operating system in every way possible; and the applications they design will not be trivial, one-page BASIC programs but large, highly involved applications, like Space Station, Star Wars, Advanced Tactical Fighter (ATF), and assembly line automation. Programmers will also be called on to synchronize processes, share data with

other processes, and evaluate and improve application program performance. Some theoretical understanding of operating system algorithms is necessary in understanding how to design the application programs, and a
guided experience, such as this book, will make it easier for programmers
to apply the theory to the application. A further benefit to the professional
using the VMS system is that he or she will be using one of the most versatile
operating systems available.

SOURCES AND LIMITATIONS

I must be honest and identify three subjects I did not cover in this book:
computer networks, distributed operating systems, and ULTRIX. To those
familiar with the "VAX Strategy" stated by Gordon Bell, DECnet will be
missed. Likewise, though Digital has pioneered multiprocessor systems, I
did not discuss the effect multiprocessors have on operating system design.
Finally, I avoided ULTRIX, Digital's version of UNIX for the VAX architecture. I don't mean to imply that these three subjects are not worthwhile;
they were omitted here because they cannot be adequately covered in a one-
quarter or semester presentation together with the other topics included in
this book.

In planning and writing this book, I struggled to identify a sensible
balance between a general introductory text containing VMS-related examples and a strictly VMS tutorial text. I had difficulty presenting a particular
concept without biasing the presentation toward the VMS implementation.
Furthermore, I often found it difficult to decide when to gloss over a VMS
detail and when to explore it. Acknowledging these difficulties, I expect
there will be objections to my final conclusions. Some readers will find too
many VMS details, and others will feel that there are not nearly enough.

To the former group, I apologize and point out that the marketplace
contains many excellent operating systems texts. To the latter group, I recommend *VAX/VMS Internals and Data Structures.*[1] I used this resource exten-
sively in researching my material, but I was careful not simply to reincarnate
it in developing this book. Instead, I deliberately suppressed its detail in
some places and combined sections in others. My goal is to provide a survey
for each of my subjects.

VAX/VMS Internals is probably too difficult material for readers who

---

1. Ruth E. Goldenberg and Lawrence J. Kenah, *VAX/VMS Internals and Data Structures:
Version 5.2* (Digital Press, 1991).

lack an understanding of the fundamental responsibilities and capabilities of an operating system. It is not preparatory, nor was that the intention of its authors. My intent, on the other hand, is to supply the necessary introductory material—the big picture—without presenting the elaborate detail. I can be persuaded to change my emphasis in various areas in future editions, and I encourage and solicit your comments—professionals, students, and instructors. That is why I included my BITNET address at the end of the Preface.

Now, a word to readers who are familiar with other Digital Press books that deal with VAX and VMS topics. I have aimed this text somewhere between *Computer Programming and Architecture*[2] and *VAX/VMS Internals.* Levy and Eckhouse have given their book an assembly and architecture orientation, and they cite the VAX/VMS operating system primarily to show how the hardware is utilized. As I said, *VAX/VMS Internals* does not pretend to be a textbook, but those well versed in operating systems can gain much insight by the depth of its discussions, which do a marvelous job of justifying the approach made in certain areas of the VMS system. I encourage professionals, instructors, and students to use both books as references to accompany this text.

A third Digital reference I used often for architectural details is the *VAX Architecture Reference Manual;*[3] many of these details are found nowhere else. A fourth book I recommend is *Writing VAX/VMS Applications Using Pascal.*[4] Because of our conflicting publication schedules, I was unable to use this book when developing mine. But now that it is available, I see that de Klerk has expanded on several of my examples in ways I would not have been able to, and he added other examples as well.

Finally, every reader who is interested in Digital Equipment Corporation should read *Computer Engineering*[5] for historical reasons alone. I only wish there were such a book that deals with Digital software in the same depth. The reader will find *Computer Engineering* interesting because it discusses the practical, technical, cost, and profit issues involved in designing and building a computer and supporting software. Granted, the machines described have returned to sand for the most part, but the principles extolled will live on.

2. Henry M. Levy and Richard H. Eckhouse, *Computer Programming and Architecture: The VAX,* 2d ed. (Digital Press, 1989).
3. Richard Brunner, ed., *VAX Architecture Reference Manual,* 2d ed. (Digital Press, 1991).
4. Theo de Klerk, *Writing VAX/VMS Applications Using Pascal* (Digital Press, 1991).
5. C. Gordon Bell, J. Craig Mudge, and John E. McNamara, *Computer Engineering: A DEC View of Hardware Systems Design* (Digital Press, 1978).

An Introduction to Operating Systems

1

GOALS

Why study operating systems?

Terminal input and output

Serial data transmission

Overview of a multi-user system

Overview of the hardware interrupt

Although you may often hear computer specialists say that operating systems rely largely on black magic, there is really nothing magical about them. An operating system is a collection of programs intended to help the user make the best use of the computer hardware. It is a layer of software between the user and the computer that simplifies the computer's functions, hiding its true operation from the user and replacing it with a more friendly interface. For instance, the user does not have to consider the numerous details required to perform terminal operations because this interface has been simplified by the operating system.

If there is any mystery to the operating system, it is in how so many actions seem to take place automatically, without any apparent guidance by you, the user. And only by studying the operating system will you be able to appreciate how much drudgery it is saving you. Rather than viewing the operating system as black magic, think of it as a service that eases the burden of using the hardware.

What this book will do is demystify the operating system so that you can understand it and, more important, use it most effectively. The operating system is not an obstacle to overcome or to do battle with when programming. On the contrary, it is an aid that will help you solve problems.

You probably think about the operating system in the same way you think about programming languages: have you ever asked yourself what the purpose of a programming language is? Do you think it was a diabolical brainchild of some sadistic professor? Students express this opinion from time to time, and their teachers have to correct them. The language processor you have become familiar with (Pascal in the examples in this book) is a tool you use to communicate your problem to the computer hardware, a tool much like a carpenter's hammer or a secretary's word processor. Any laborer must know how to wield the tools of the trade, and no matter what the trade, the more expert you become with its tools, the more efficiently you can solve the tasks before you. The same is true for the operating system—you have to master it to get the most out of it.

As you may know, an application that supports the Space Station or controls a paper mill or sequences an assembly line is actually a collection of programs designed to run only when necessary, and programs exchange information with one another as it becomes available. The applications being described are not a simple set of subroutines; that is, program A does not simply call program B. Instead, programs A and B are run as data arrives, as data is required to be reorganized in some way, or as data leaves the system—they are run on demand. Application programs run independently, yet they depend on one another for their input and output data.

This concept can be illustrated with the example of a fully instrumented automobile, which includes one or more computers[1] supporting advanced software applications like those we are considering. As illustrated in Figure 1.1, readings of the driveshaft rotation period are collected periodically and made available to programs for several different purposes, the most obvious being to display the car's speed. Combining successive readings produces the odometer value display, which is closely related to the trip odometer value, another display. Fuel efficiency is calculated by combining the driveshaft rotation period with the fuel consumption rate, and it too is displayed. Finally, the cruise control mechanism, also dependent on the driveshaft rotation period, works by comparing the actual driveshaft period to a reference value so that the fuel delivered to the carburetor can

---

1. The computers are embedded within the automobile, as they are in many high-technology products such as VCRs, microwave ovens, and FAX machines. The computer in these cases is a microprocessor, and the application programs cannot be modified by the user.

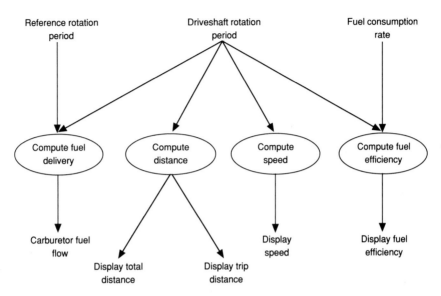

Figure 1.1. Part of an automobile instrument system

be adjusted to maintain a constant speed. The point of this illustration is that these several displays and calculations are derived from physical measurements that are presented to various software components for the necessary computations. The corresponding results are then displayed.

The data flow in such a system is not trivial. The collection rate of a measurement probably does not match the rate of the corresponding display. The speedometer display, for instance, is updated only when it changes, not whenever there is driveshaft data available, and the collection rate for driveshaft data is much higher than its display rate. Likewise, fuel efficiency may be displayed only on user demand, and then only when it changes. This input/output data independence results in several independent software functions: driveshaft rotation period measurement, speed calculation, speed display, fuel consumption rate measurement, fuel efficiency calculation, and fuel efficiency display. Thus, when designing an involved application, two of the most important aspects to consider are how to direct the data flow in the application and how to activate the programs that process that data.

A third aspect to consider when designing an application is its response time. You have probably considered the performance of certain algorithms, such as the various sorting techniques that have different execution times.

The choice of a specific algorithm, however, depends on more than simply the raw timing. If your application always sorts three variables, a "quick sort" algorithm is probably not very fast compared with a simple IF structure. Furthermore, specific algorithm designs are only a single aspect of an application's performance. A fast, efficient, yet complicated data structure may be inappropriate for a program that is activated only once a day. What you should consider are ways to measure the overall operational characteristic of the application system, not merely one or two algorithms buried deep within it. Moreover, global application operation should be measured in a *multi-user* environment. The VMS operating system includes some very convenient performance tools; you will be taught how to use them and how to interpret their results.

This introductory chapter presents a few simplified scenarios that show what takes place within the operating system when you are using it. As you advance through later chapters, you may want to review these scenarios to see if you understand them better after the detail is presented.

Some of you will be able to skim this introductory material because you are already familiar with it. Others of you will find it helps with questions you have asked yourselves in the past for which you never knew where to look for answers. Do not expect it to be overly technical; my intent is to familiarize you with some of the fundamental concepts, without elaborate definitions and algorithms, giving everyone an equal initial footing. The details will come in succeeding chapters; here you will get an intuitive feeling for commonly performed operating system functions.

1.1. Terminal Input and Output

The first scenario illustrates the activity that takes place between a single terminal and the computer, even though this book is about multi-user operating systems, the VMS system in particular. A multi-user system has many terminals attached to the computer, but for this illustration, consider only a single terminal and refer to Figure 1.2 while you are reading.

In the figure, there are two distinct paths between the terminal and the computer: one is the data path from the keyboard to the computer, and the other is a data path from the computer to the screen. A terminal is actually two devices—the keyboard and screen—that seem to be connected, but the connection takes place only at the computer—the devices themselves

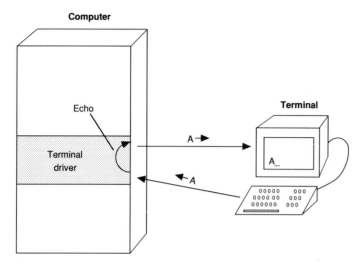

Figure 1.2. Terminal input and output

are independent. Observe what takes place when a user strikes the A key on the keyboard. That character is transmitted from the keyboard to the computer and then routed back out of the computer to the screen, where it is displayed. This rerouting is called an *echo*.

At first glance, it seems overly complicated, doesn't it? Why not just have the keyboard send data directly to the screen and to the computer at the same time? The basic reason for implementing an echo system is to guarantee to the user that the key struck is in fact the same one received by the computer. In the days of less reliable hardware, this was a very important consideration, but since hardware has improved over the years, there are now other, more pragmatic reasons to perpetuate the echo.

One reason is that the echo may be different from the key struck. For example, consider what must happen when the DELETE key is struck on a VT100: three characters are echoed, BACKSPACE, SPACE, BACKSPACE, as illustrated in Figure 1.3. Initially, the cursor, indicated by the underbar "_", is located to the right of the last character entered. To change the character B (Figure 1.3a), the DELETE key is struck, sending the DELETE key code (7F hexadecimal) to the computer. In response, the BACKSPACE code (8 hexadecimal) is the first character echoed, moving the cursor one position left, under the character to be removed (Figure 1.3b). Next, a SPACE (20 hexadecimal) echo is sent to overwrite that character, which

Activity	Results
a. The SHOW TIME line is entered, misspelled.	$ SHOW TIB_
b. The DELETE key is struck, the first echo character is BACKSPACE.	$ SHOW TI<u>B</u>
c. The second echo character is SPACE. That moves the cursor right.	$ SHOW TI _
d. The third echo character is another BACKSPACE which moves the cursor left to the correct position.	$ SHOW TI_

Figure 1.3. Activity of the DELETE key.

moves the cursor right once more (Figure 1.3c). The final BACKSPACE echo moves the cursor left again, to the newly vacated position (Figure 1.3d). In this example, cursor positioning is automatically performed by the terminal itself, not by the computer echo.

The echo concept is a very powerful one and is used in the same way by most operating systems. It is controlled by an operating system program called the *terminal driver*. All operating systems have drivers to deal with terminal I/O, as well as drivers to deal with all other I/O devices. A second function of the terminal driver is to generate an echo character sequence consistent with the terminal's display device. For instance, if the terminal is a hardcopy device (like a DECwriter), a BACKSPACE is not a reasonable action and instead an echo that prints the deleted character will be generated. A different terminal could interpret a DELETE request to mean "remove the character to the left of the cursor," so the DELETE echo sequence in Figure 1.3 would be inappropriate for it.

The most general approach to servicing multiple terminal types is to include an adaptable terminal driver. The VMS operating system has chosen this option, allowing the user to examine and change the characteristics the driver has assumed for a given terminal. The VMS command that permits the user to examine the current setting is SHOW TERMINAL. A typical output of this command is presented in Figure 1.4 and corresponds to a dial-up VT100 terminal. (Some of these settings will not be discussed now.)

```
Terminal: _TTD3:        Device_Type: VT100         Owner: The Perfesser
                                                   Username: DMILLER

    Input:    300     LFfill:  0     Width:  80     Parity: None
    Output:   300     CRfill:  0     Page:   24

Terminal Characteristics:
    Interactive       Echo                Type_ahead       No Escape
    No Hostsync       TTsync              Lowercase        Tab
    Wrap              Scope               No Remote        No Eightbit
    Broadcast         No Readsync         No Form          Fulldup
    Modem             No Local_echo       No Autobaud      Hangup
    No Brdcstmbx      No DMA              No Altypeahd     No Set_speed
    Line Editing      Overstrike editing No Fallback      Dialup
    No Secure server  Disconnect          No Pasthru       No Syspassword
    No SIXEL Graphics No Soft Characters No Printer Port   Numeric keypad
    ANSI_CRT          No Regis            No Block_mode    Advanced_video
    No Edit_mode      DEC_CRT             No DEC_CRT2      No DEC_CRT3
```

Figure 1.4. Typical output of command $ SHOW TERMINAL

The label "Device_Type:" at the top of the listing indicates terminal type. The terminal indicated determines how the terminal driver responds. Changing terminal characteristics is done with the SET TERMINAL command, which requires that you specify the characteristics you wish to change. For instance, to notify the terminal driver that the terminal is a hardcopy device, use the following command:

```
$ SET TERMINAL /DEVICE_TYPE=LA36
```

The VMS operating system will recognize a large variety of terminal types. To see which ones are legal, use the HELP command:

```
$ HELP SET TERMINAL /DEVICE_TYPE
```

Figure 1.5 shows the output of this command.

HELP output will not be presented regularly in these pages, but is included this first time since it may be unfamiliar to you. If you do not know about HELP, take some time to learn its basic capabilities. Start with the HELP HELP command.

Here is one more variation showing the versatility of the SET TERMINAL command. In Figure 1.4, notice the word "Tab" in the right column, second from the top. This means that the terminal driver will send the horizontal tab character (9 hexadecimal) to the terminal with the understanding that the tabs on the terminal are set correctly and that the terminal

```
SET

  TERMINAL

    /DEVICE_TYPE
     /DEVICE_TYPE=terminal-type

      Informs the system of the terminal type and sets characteristics
      according to the device type specified. You can specify any of the
      following terminal types:

              UNKNOWN            LA34
              FT1 - FT8          LA38
              LA12               LA100
              LA36               LQP02
              LA120              VT125
              LN03               LN01K
              VT05               VT131
              VT52               VT132
              VT55               VT173
              VT100              VT200
              VT101              PRO_SERIES
              VT102              LA210
              VT105              VT300

      The default characteristics for the VT100, VT102, and VT125 series
      terminals are as follows:

         /ADVANCEDVIDEO     /CRFILL=0      /LFFILL=0      /SPEED=9600

         /NOALTYPEAHD       /ECHO          /LOWERCASE     /TAB

         /ANSI_CRT          /NOEIGHT_BIT   /NODMA         /TTSYNC

         /NOAUTOBAUD        /NOESCAPE      /PAGE=24       /TYPE_AHEAD

         /NOBLOCK_MODE      /NOFORM        /NOPARITY      /WIDTH=80

         /NOBRDCSTMBX       /FULLDUP       /NOPASTHRU     /WRAP

         /BROADCAST         /NOHOSTSYNC    /NOREADSYN
```

Figure 1.5. Typical output
of the command $ HELP SET
TERMINAL/DEVICE TYPE

will insert the necessary number of blanks. The tab logic can be turned off with the command:

```
$ SET TERMINAL /NOTAB
```

which will tell the terminal driver to send spaces (20 hexadecimal) instead of the tab character, thus making the screen appear correctly formatted even when the terminal tab settings have been lost.

1.2. Serial Communication

Now we look at how data is transmitted between the terminal and the computer in more detail, because the more a programmer knows about hardware, the more effective he or she will be. If the terminal fails, a hardware technician usually has to be called in to fix it. This causes frustration and schedule delays because without the terminal, the programmer cannot complete the programming task. Instead of waiting for help, he or she might locate a screwdriver, disconnect the data cable from the terminal, remove its cover, and examine the connections. Doing so will often uncover a broken or poorly soldered wire. At the very least, this small effort will aid the repairman, and with only a little additional skill, the programmer can make a temporary or even permanent fix to the connection.

Look behind your terminal to identify the data cable (not the power cord) that attaches to it. It should be easy to locate because the plug is long and narrow and quite unlike the kind used for normal electrical appliances. This data connection is most often associated with a type of communications standard called *RS232C*, and it is the most common method of hooking a dumb[2] terminal to a computer. RS232C has many other applications—for instance, to hook up a terminal to a modem. There are other communications standards besides RS232C. An exercise at the end of the chapter is aimed at a more thorough investigation of the many data transmission techniques.

Unlike the power cord with its 3 *pins*, the RS232C plug contains either 9 or 25 pins, but often only 3 or perhaps 4 pins are actually used. The

---

2. A dumb terminal is one with the minimum amount of internal logic necessary to connect to a computer. A VT52 or VT100 class terminal is dumb. The VT200 and VT300 series terminals are smarter—they all use the RS232C data connection. In contrast, the VT1000 terminal is intelligent and requires a much more elaborate connection to the host computer.

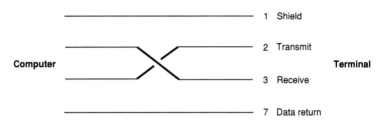

Figure 1.6. Common RS232C connections

function of each of the pins is explained in other references; the concern here is with the 3 pins in the 25-pin configuration.

Those 3 pins are numbers 2 (transmit), 3 (receive), and 7 (ground or data return), as depicted in Figure 1.6. The lines that run between the pins on the computer and the pins on the terminal represent cable connections; these connections are symmetrical. The optional fourth pin is pin 1, which acts as an electrical *shield* and carries no information. Rather, it protects the data from external and stray electrical fields such as "noise" generated by the buzz of fluorescent lights or by air conditioner compressors turning on or off.

Notice particularly the connection between pins 2 and 3: pin 2 from one end links to pin 3 on the other. This is a peculiar connection, since usually a cable is constructed so that corresponding pins are connected to each other. But such a configuration, called a *null modem* cable[3], has a logical explanation: data "transmitted" by the terminal must be "received" at the computer and vice versa. Since this is a very uncommon way to build a cable, occasionally the novice cable builder neglects to cross pins 2 and 3, instead connecting pin 2 on one plug to pin 2 on the other plug and likewise with pin 3 on each plug. When corresponding pins are connected, the result is a *point-to-point* cable. Whether to use a point-to-point or a null modem cable can be a source of confusion when connecting computer components because there are no error messages or hints to help the user if the connection does not work.

Figures 1.2 and 1.6 indicate that the terminal is capable of sending and receiving data simultaneously, since the two devices, keyboard and display, are independent. This mode of data transfer is called *full duplex.* Another

---

3. This term is misleading but convenient to use. A true null modem also involves several other pins.

data transmission mode is called *half duplex*, meaning that data can be transmitted in only one direction at a time—for instance, if the terminal is sending data, it cannot receive any. Theoretically, a half duplex cable only requires two wires, but in practice, it uses a four-wire cable, as in Figure 1.6. A *simplex* data path is used when data travels in only one direction. A joy-stick and a mouse are two examples of device-computer data simplex devices.

DATA TRANSMISSION

An ASCII character is represented by seven bits but, sometimes, an eighth bit is included to extend the character set for foreign letters and other special characters. The seven bits are "placed" on a pair of wires, one bit at a time. This is called *serial* data transmission because one bit follows another. *Parallel* data transmission requires a wire for each bit; in parallel mode, all the bits are sent simultaneously. Parallel data transmission is normally faster than serial transmission, but parallel transmission requires a more complex and expensive cable.

Here is how serial data transmission takes place. Each bit, starting with the least significant one, is represented by a voltage. A binary 1 is represented by a voltage between -15 and -5 volts, a binary 0 a voltage between $+5$ and $+15$. This electrical protocol was developed prior to computers, dating back to teletype machines; historically, logical 1 is called a *space* and logical 0 is called a *mark*. The length of time that the voltage remains constant is determined by the inverse of the *baud* rate. For example, a 2400-baud data transmission means that for each data bit, the voltage remains constant for 1/2400 or about 0.000417 second (417 microseconds). The voltage levels are referred to as the electrical or *physical protocol*.

A character is transmitted by changing the voltage levels corresponding to its 0-1 pattern. These changes for the ASCII character "j" are shown in Figure 1.7. The hexadecimal value of ASCII "j" is 6A (binary 1101010). Notice that this binary number appears backwards in the figure because the least significant bit is the first data bit transmitted.

In addition to the data, some synchronizing information or protocol must be sent with each character. We have identified the five parts of *logical protocol* below the bit pattern in the figure. In RS232C protocol, if no data is being sent, the data line is set to binary 1, a voltage between -5 and -15, as indicated on the left of Figure 1.7. The first bit transmitted is not part of the character itself; rather, it serves to alert and synchronize the receiver

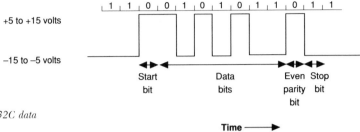

Figure 1.7. RS232C data for "j"

for the data that follows. This bit is called the *start bit*, and it is always a binary 0. Following the start bit, the next seven bits are data. In the example, this is 0-1-0-1-0-1-1, the reversed binary code for "j."

Next, a parity bit is transmitted. *Parity* is not data either; instead, it is an attempt to ensure that the data sent is the same as the data received, that no bits were reversed during transmission. The computation of the parity bit is discussed below.

The final protocol bit transmitted is the *stop bit*, and it is always a binary 1. The stop bit is necessary to give the receiver enough time to recover and reinitialize itself for the next character, which could follow immediately. It also serves to separate consecutive characters. In some cases, two stop bits are used. After the stop bit is transmitted, if there is no other data to be sent, a binary 1 is transmitted to indicate this.

Returning to the parity bit discussion, programmers are accustomed to thinking, incorrectly, that computers are deterministic. By deterministic we mean that when a software program is repeatedly executed, identical input produces repeatable output. But hardware is nondeterministic; it does not always produce repeatable output in response to the same input. It is not 100 percent reliable, just nearly so. Over the history of computers, great strides have been made in increasing hardware reliability, but transporting data over large distances will never be as reliable as is transmitting data within the computer itself. Thus, to increase reliability when transmitting data—within the computer, from computer to terminal, or within a network of computers—some form of a check is made on the transfer. The transmitter adds something to the data, and the receiver checks that additional information. Parity is the simplest method of checking data.

Even parity means that the parity bit is adjusted to make the number of 1's in the eight-bit field—data and parity—an even number. This implies that the parity calculation includes the parity bit as well as the data. The

Number of ones in the data bits	For even parity, set parity bit to:	For odd parity, set parity bit to:
even	0	1
odd	1	0

Figure 1.8. The four cases of
the parity bit

parity bit is a binary 0 in Figure 1.7 because there are already four 1's in "j." If there happens to be an odd number of bits in the data, the parity bit will be set to 1 so that the full eight bits have an even number of 1's. *Odd parity* is similarly defined: the total eight bits must have an odd number of 1's. Since these two definitions are confusing, we have summarized the four parity cases in Figure 1.8.

There is no advantage to either type of parity over the other, and most terminals support both. The transmitter computes the parity bit as it sends the data bits and then appends the parity bit to the end of the data stream. The receiver recomputes the parity upon receipt of the data bits, and then compares it with the received parity bit. If the two parity bits differ, the receiver assumes the data was bad. It can then ignore the error, flag the data with an error indication, or attempt to rectify the situation by requesting a character retransmission. (Details of these algorithms are beyond the scope of this discussion.)

To conclude this discussion, parity scheme has two notable limitations: the receiver cannot tell which bit was bad, and it cannot detect multiple bit errors. A two-bit error is undetectable, and a three-bit error looks like a one-bit error, and so forth. Since parity is not a very good indicator of transmission quality, parity checking may be disabled. Parity may also be disabled to increase the character transmission rate because one bit fewer per character needs to be transmitted.

More advanced data check codes contain more bits that can be used to detect and then correct certain classes of errors. Data correction codes can be applied to a group of characters as well as to only one. Again, these more elaborate schemes only enhance the reliability of the transmission, but they can never guarantee correct data delivery.

The point of this discussion is that there are more bits transmitted than simply the data bits: a minimum of 9 transmitted bits per character (1 start, 7 data, 1 stop) and a maximum of 12 transmitted bits per character (1 start, 8 data, 1 parity—either odd or even—and 2 stops). At 2,400 baud, it takes $9/2400 = 3,750$ microseconds per character for a 9-bit transmission, and it takes $12/2400 = 5,000$ microseconds per character for a 12-bit transmission.

The RS232C transmission protocol is *asynchronous*, meaning that a character can be transmitted at any time and that any length of time between characters is valid. In contrast to asynchronous data transmission, *synchronous* data transmission means that data must be sent only at prescribed times. Synchronous protocols do not require character start and stop bits; data is usually sent as blocks of characters and normally includes some advanced form of parity checking called *checksum* or *cyclic redundancy checks* (CRC). These two methods are more likely than parity to detect multiple errors, but they may not be able to correct them. More elaborate schemes can both detect and correct certain classes of single and multiple errors.

In the VMS operating system, most of the RS232C protocol variations are under the user's control through the SET TERMINAL command. Again, refer to Figure 1.4 to find the fields "Parity: None", "Input: 300", "Output: 300" (the baud rate), and "No Eightbit" (meaning seven bit). These can all be modified with a SET TERMINAL command. On the other hand, notice that there is no entry in the figure to indicate the number of stop bits. This means that there is no way to select either one or two stop bits and one stop bit is assumed.

The user must be careful in making arbitrary changes with the terminal SETUP feature because doing so can cause complete loss of computer-terminal communications. Keep in mind that hardware at both ends of the cable, the terminal and the computer, must use the same protocol—whatever protocol the transmitter adds to the data, the receiver must remove. It is possible, for example, to change the speed of your terminal with the terminal SETUP feature, but unless you also enter the corresponding SET TER-MINAL/SPEED= command, only one-half of the communication link (the terminal) will have been modified and data transmission will not be successful.[4] Some SET TERMINAL commands that change protocol affect only the computer. Other SET TERMINAL commands, such as SET TERMI-NAL/WIDTH, change both the computer and the terminal.

---

4. Some computer centers do not permit their users to change the baud rate.

1.3. A WRITE Example

The second scenario is a high-level representation of the activity that takes place when a language such as Pascal executes a WRITE statement. WRITE is simpler than READ, which is treated later. Figure 1.9 represents a Pascal program containing a WRITE statement followed by a WRITELN statement, and the following discussion refers to that figure. Chapter 8 is devoted to the I/O details introduced here.

In the compiled program, the WRITE operations are directed to a utility subroutine associated with the compiler rather than the terminal driver. For instance, the WRITE ('mumble') statement causes Pascal to produce a subroutine call, a CALLG, to its utility PAS$WRITE_STRING. When executed, this utility saves or *buffers* the character string (circle 1) until the line is completed. No data is passed to the terminal until the WRITELN statement is executed.

The WRITELN call in the program signals output line completion (circle 2), and when it is executed, another utility, PAS$WRITELN2, is called, which sends the entire line in the buffer to the terminal driver via the *system service* $QIOW (circle 3). This acronym means "Queue an input/output operation and wait for its completion." The $QIOW system service inhibits program execution until the terminal driver reports that the line has been sent to the screen. We will have more to say about what it means for a program to stop later in the chapter and examine the concept in detail in chapter 3.

The VMS operating system is a collection of subprograms that are executed at the user's request, most of which can be called by an application program. These subprograms are called *system services*, and many of them will be illustrated throughout the book. A larger collection of subprograms that are not part of the operating system are contained in the Run-Time Library (RTL), and they are also intended for use by application programs. We will illustrate some of these too.

$QIO—Queue an input/output operation—is the primary system service used to perform data I/O. Normally, I/O is performed with $QIOW to ensure that the data to be processed is synchronized with the program instructions. When the program requests the $QIOW system service, the request is queued and performed when the device is available, and only when the I/O operation is complete does the program continue.

$QIOW *queues* the I/O operation to the terminal driver and signals

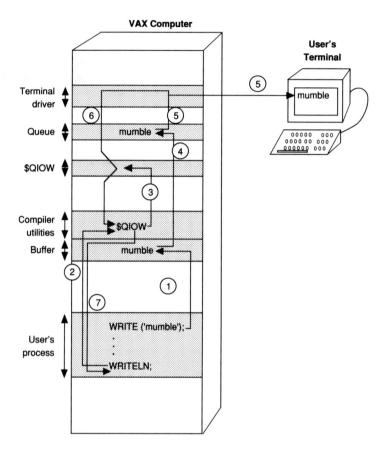

Figure 1.9. A program write operation

the driver that there is I/O ready to be performed (circle 4). It operates this way because, generally, the terminal driver is working on some other user's data stream when this new request appears. The new request must be saved until the terminal driver becomes available.

The terminal driver sends the string to the terminal character by character (circle 5), and after it sends the final character, signals the compiler utility (circle 6) that the $QIOW operation is complete. This action causes the program to restart. The compiler utility then returns to the statement following the WRITELN in the program (circle 7).

1.4. Multi-Users

Up to this point we have considered what happens to a single user on the system. How is your system physically set up? Are you in a large room filled with terminals all connected to the same computer? Are you sitting by yourself in your office, connected to the computer through a modem and telephone? Whatever your situation, when you are at the terminal, it appears that you are the only one using the system. You have no direct evidence that others are accessing it unless you are able to look at your neighbor's screen. Of course, you do not have the entire system to yourself; you are sharing it with many other users. This section discusses how a single computer is able to serve multiple users "simultaneously" while maintaining the illusion that each user is logged onto a system that is dedicated to her or his terminal.

Each terminal is connected to the computer and assigned a unique address. There are a variety of ways to do this; for example, the terminals may be directly connected to the computer, or they may be routed to it through some form of switch. When the computer connection is made to the terminal, the computer records this fact. Refer back to the upper left corner of Figure 1.4: the "Terminal:" field indicates the terminal address, in this case, "_TTD3:". In Figure 1.10, in the terminal column at the far right, note that the terminal name indicates the controller type (TT is a DZ11), the next letter indicates which controller (A,B,C, etc.), and the final digit is the address on that controller (0,1,2, etc.). In effect, the system maintains a *translation table* that contains the user name, process name, process id, and terminal address. To display this information, use this command:

```
$ SHOW USER/FULL
```

Figure 1.10 contains sample output from the SHOW USER command. Depending on how it is configured, the VMS system may also indicate where a particular user is located. With this display as input, it is possible to write a program that translates the terminal address into a room number. The system uses the translation table to direct a keyboard-entered character to the proper program and to direct a program's output to the proper display, as depicted in Figure 1.11. In the figure, user GOLDWING types at his keyboard and the terminal driver reads the translation table to determine which physical terminal to echo the output to. This figure indicates that all

```
        VAX/VMS User Processes at 23-JUL-1990 19:58:20.19
        Total number of users = 3, number of processes = 3

    Username      Process Name     PID      Terminal
    DMILLER       The Perfesser    00001314 TTD4:
    FESTUS82      Lets go golfin   00001395 TTB0:
    IHS           IHS              0000124C TTA1:
```

*Figure 1.10. Typical output of
the command $ SHOW USER/
FULL*

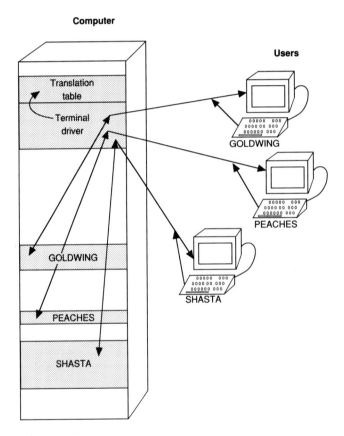

Figure 1.11. Multiple users

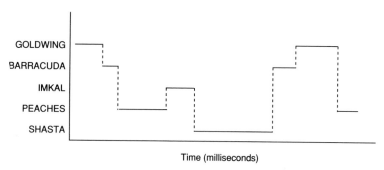

Time (milliseconds)

Figure 1.12. Time-sharing
processes

terminals are controlled by a single driver and the driver must associate the user with the proper terminal and vice versa.

Using a single-terminal shared driver is a VMS design decision. This design localizes all terminal functions into a subroutine, so the same software driver controls a VT100 (an alphanumeric terminal), a VT240 (a color graphics terminal), and many other terminal types. The result is a complex driver that is relatively easy to maintain. Other operating systems provide a separate driver for each terminal type supported by the system. This requires several drivers, which may be simpler, but many of the drivers may contain replicated code and the wide variety of drivers can make maintenance more laborious. The choice facing designers is thus between driver complexity and maintenance difficulties.

Figure 1.11 does not explain the apparent simultaneous operation of multiple users; it only shows how they are attached to the computer. Sharing the computer is accomplished by each user's program executing only for a fraction of a second. In this way, each of the programs takes a turn using the computer and a very short time is allotted to each. This is the *time-sharing* concept, which is illustrated in Figure 1.12. GOLDWING executes a little while, then BARRACUDA, PEACHES, IMKAL, and so forth. The programs do not necessarily execute for the same amount of time (although they could) or in any specific order. Note that Figure 1.12 shows that BARRACUDA, PEACHES, and IMKAL resume execution after the computer has completed executing the intervening programs.

Consider what will happen if the computer lets GOLDWING's program execute until it is finished, blocking the others from executing. To be more precise, consider the possible interpretations of the phrase "until finished." Does it mean session login to logout? If it does, then only one user at a time will have access to the machine. Why have multiple terminals at all when one terminal will do nicely? The users can simply queue up on that terminal and wait their turn, just like at the supermarket checkout line.

Clearly this is not a desirable system. The alternative is to divide a user's turn into finer increments than an entire session. Can "until finished" mean until the user is done with an editor session? Or maybe done with a compilation? This is obviously not desirable either. How long do you think you spend in an editor session? 15 minutes? An hour? Do you really expect everyone else to wait for you to finish?

In the VMS operating system and most other time-shared operating systems, programs are executing in the range of 10 to 50 milliseconds at a time. The selection of this time unit is important; it relates to the amount of time it takes a character to be transmitted from the terminal to the computer. In a previous example, it was 3,750 microseconds or 3.750 milliseconds, which seems like a very short period of time. However, electronically, within the computer, it allows a great deal to be accomplished.

Illustrating a typical computer operation will give you a better feeling for these time units. A simple, well-known example is the 8088 microprocessor, which is the heart of the IBM PC. The earliest 8088 versions have a 4.77-*megahertz* (MHz) clock, which ticks 4.77 million times per second. If you invert 4.77 MHz, you have the period or length of a *cycle*, about 0.21 microseconds. The fastest 16-bit integer ADD instruction on an 8088 takes three cycles—that is, 0.63 microseconds—to execute when the operands are located in registers and memory is not accessed. If all the operands access memory, the ADD can slow down to 40 cycles—8.4 microseconds. The 8088 is a relatively slow computer by today's standards. Newer processors in the 8088 family run much faster. For example, a 20-MHz clock is not at all unusual, meaning that the three-cycle ADD becomes 0.150 microseconds. Computer manufacturers are announcing even faster clocks and more powerful instruction sets all the time.

More complex computer architectures—the so-called midis and mainframes—are designed to optimize execution time for commonly used instructions and/or commonly referenced memory locations. Therefore, clock rate is not a very good way to determine the speed of the computer when it executes an actual program. The more common measure for these larger

---

5. A personal computer contains several "chips," including the processor, memory, graphics processor, I/O controllers, and others.

machines is a unit called *MIPS* (million instructions per second). This is a measure of the average execution speed of a specific mix of instructions that gives the customer a better way to compare computers. Inverting the MIPS value yields the average instruction execution time. For example, the execution speed of an instruction with an average number of memory references on a 10-MIPS computer is 0.1 microseconds. Therefore, for a 10-MIPS computer, 37,500 instructions can be executed during the 3,750 microseconds that it takes to transmit a single 9-bit character at 2400 baud.

Another computer performance measure is called *MFLOPS* (million floating point [or real] operations per second). This unit is designed for the scientific community, which uses real arithmetic more often than integer arithmetic. The difficulty with floating point operations is that they are much more complex than their integer counterparts are. So a machine like the 8088, which may have a reasonable integer performance, is very slow with real operations because these cannot be done in hardware at all but instead must be emulated with software.

What is the conclusion to this discussion? A computer is much faster than your intuition tells you it is. In what seems like a very short time, 3,750 microseconds, it can execute tens of thousands of instructions. The time-sharing system takes advantage of the relatively slow transmission time by allowing other programs to run while one program is waiting for data to be transmitted to the display or to be received from the keyboard. Note that personal computer operating systems like MS-DOS do not have to deal with time-sharing because there is only one process competing for the processor.

1.5. The Instruction Cycle

Now that we have discovered that programs run only for a fraction of a second at a time, it is important to examine how a program can be stopped and restarted without any disruption. The execution discontinuity must take place without the program's permission or knowledge of what has taken place. This section defines the *instruction cycle* and examines what takes place in the computer when an *instruction* is executed. The VAX instruction cycle is used to illustrate this activity.

The VAX architecture is known as a complex instruction set computer (*CISC*). A reduced instruction set computer (*RISC*) is similar, but its instruction cycle is simplified. The relative merits of CISC and RISC architectures are a controversial subject, and there is no clear "best" one (although currently, there is more interest in RISC machines). This brief discussion is an introduction to the issues.

CISC architecture contains a much larger variety of primitive instructions than does RISC architecture. Compare, for example, VAX's 304 instructions to the typical RISC machine's fewer than 100. This means that the RISC hardware is simpler and can be implemented to execute its instructions faster than can a CISC machine. However, the richer instruction set of the CISC machine means that it can execute many software functions more quickly. For example, the VAX includes a single instruction to convert a number from integer to real, but to do the same thing on a RISC machine takes more than 100 instructions.

A second difference between the two architectures is the variety of data types supported by hardware. The VAX includes instructions that manipulate three integer types, four real types, two queue types, and four character and string types. A typical RISC architecture supports only byte, integer, and perhaps two real types, so additional types must be supported by software subprograms on RISC machines.

RISC architecture puts a greater burden on software than CISC architecture does, and to compare the two is very difficult. While it is true that a MIPS rating will always favor the RISC architecture, this does not necessarily indicate actual performance in the user environment. To continue the conversion example above, a particular program that does numerous integer-to-real conversions may run faster on a CISC machine, but one that does no conversions may run faster on an RISC machine. That is, the exact nature of the application program is extremely important in determining the computer's performance. It may be that in a general interactive environment, where the users' applications are diverse, CISC is better. In a limited, single-user application, however, like a graphics workstation, the software engineer can optimize the application such that the RISC is a better choice.

A typical VAX instruction is composed of three elements: the *operation code*, zero or more *input operands*, and zero or more *output operands*. Figure 1.13 shows that the execution cycle begins when the operation code is read or *fetched* from memory, transferred to the *instruction register*, and then decoded to determine how many input and output operands are required. Next, the input operands are fetched either from memory or registers and the instruction is executed. Finally, the results, if any, are stored in either registers or memory according to the output operands.

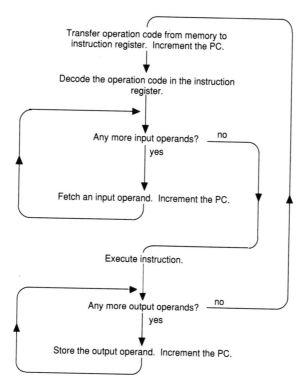

Transfer operation code from memory to instruction register. Increment the PC.

Decode the operation code in the instruction register.

Any more input operands? — no

yes

Fetch an input operand. Increment the PC.

Execute instruction.

Any more output operands? — no

yes

Store the output operand. Increment the PC.

Figure 1.13. The instruction cycle

Throughout the instruction cycle, the *program counter* (PC) is incremented after each step so that it always points to the next element of the instruction to be referenced, either operation code or operand. This cycle is repeated until the HALT instruction is encountered. These steps are performed in roughly the 0.1-microsecond (100-nanosecond) time frame mentioned earlier, depending on how fast operands can be fetched and stored. Incidentally, one reason to talk about average instruction time is the variable number of fetches and stores in an instruction.

To discontinue a program while it is executing means, in effect, to place a bookmark at the currently executing instruction. The bookmark is the program counter (refer again to Figure 1.13). Theoretically, the bookmark can be placed anywhere in the instruction cycle, but to minimize the amount of information that must be saved, the program is discontinued at the top of the cycle, between instructions.

As the program is executing additional information makes it unique; the *context* of the program changes as it executes. The context is defined by the PC and the contents of the computer's registers. When a program's execution is discontinued, its context is saved in memory, and another program is brought out of discontinuation by restoring *its* context. This is called a *context switch*. Notice that the program's code and data need not be saved explicitly because they are already preserved either in memory or on disk.

On the VAX, the context consists of the 16 general registers and other information. In the VMS operating system, the context of a program is saved in a data structure called the process header (*PHD*), which is described in detail in Chapter 4.

1.6. Interrupts and Operating System Cycle

This section introduces a model of the basic cycle of a time-sharing operating system. Throughout the book, this model will be refined as new terms and concepts are introduced. It is defined now so that you can view the entire picture before the details are added.

Begin by assuming that program A is executing; that is, the processor, also called the CPU, is executing A's instructions. A executes until any one of several events occur. For example:

- The program encounters an error, such as division by zero or a subscript bounds violation.
- It runs until it requests a system service such as an I/O operation.
- It may be *preempted* by a more important program. That is, a higher-*priority* program may become ready to execute.
- All instructions in A are executed and the program terminates.

Any one of several other events may occur also, in which case the operating system regains control of the CPU via a hardware mechanism called an *interrupt*. Interrupts demand the attention of the operating system; hence, A must relinquish the CPU. When the operating system completes the action indicated by the interrupt, A may or may not be permitted to use the CPU again depending on the type of interrupt.

Before the operating system cycle discussion goes any deeper, it is important to look at interrupts more systematically. In the most general sense an interrupt is a signal produced by either hardware or software.

To better understand a computer interrupt, consider the following analogy. In human relations, we tap someone on the shoulder and say "Excuse me" or clear our throat before attempting to say something. These actions are acceptable protocols for gaining attention in our society. It is the same with hardware; an interrupt is a tap on the computer's shoulder by a hardware device with something to communicate to the CPU. In more precise terms, it is a signal to the CPU's control unit, generated by some peripheral hardware device such as a terminal or disk drive (specifically, the peripheral's control unit or *controller*), requesting immediate attention by the computer.

The way the hardware implements the interrupt logic varies widely throughout the computer industry. Normally, in what amounts to a context switch, the interrupt stops the currently executing program and transfers control to that portion of the operating system called an *interrupt service routine* (ISR). An interrupt service routine must be provided for each possible interrupting device. A generic ISR is impossible because every hardware device operates differently and requires recognition by special purpose codes and protocols.

The interrupt service routines are considered part of the operating system, although most operating systems permit privileged users to add new devices to the system and to support them by writing new interrupt service routines. When the ISR has completed, in the simplest case, another context switch takes place and the previously executing program is permitted to continue.

Figure 1.14 provides a view of the computer hardware and interrupt path. When a device signals an interrupt, the CPU's control unit first saves the current program counter in a special part of memory (circle 1) and then accesses memory to find a new value for the program counter associated with the ISR (circle 2). There is one ISR for each hardware device, so a vector of PC addresses is required. This interrupt operation switches the CPU context from the currently executing program to the specific ISR. The most straightforward way to store ISR PC vector is to dedicate a memory location to each possible device. When the operating system is initialized, each interrupt location (also called *interrupt vector*) is loaded with the address of the corresponding ISR.

Once the PC has been changed, execution continues in the ISR. When complete, the ISR signals the control unit by executing a special instruction.

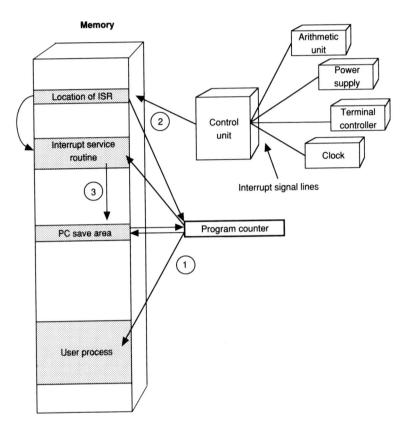

*Figure 1.14. A general view of
the interrupt mechanism*

This instruction (circle 3) restores the saved PC value to the PC, in effect making another context switch, and execution continues in the interrupted program.

Figure 1.15 provides a simplistic illustration of the operating system cycle. Assume that program A is running when an interrupt occurs. An interrupt can occur at any time but usually not until the completion of the current instruction. (This decision can vary with different computers, of course, and is not even true for all instructions in the VAX architecture.[6])

6. In the VAX, character string instructions that execute using registers—for instance, MOVC5, can be interrupted during execution but not during operand fetching.

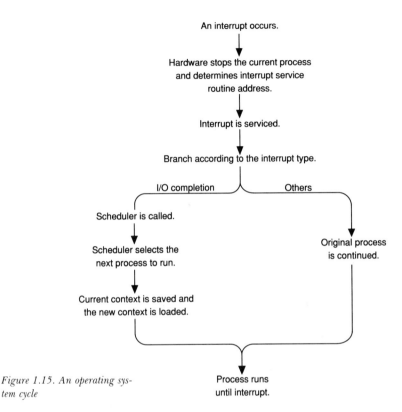

Figure 1.15. An operating system cycle

A hardware interrupt is considered more important than the running program, so program A is stopped temporarily and its PC is saved. Then, as previously described, the appropriate interrupt service routine is located in memory, its address is placed in the PC, and it is executed. After the interrupt has been serviced, depending on the interrupt type, the ISR restarts program A by restoring its PC. However, some types of interrupts are not so easily *dispatched*.

Consider a more complex case, such as the one illustrated in the left branch of Figure 1.15. Assume program A is running and the input data for program B for a READ instruction arrives. Data arrival causes an interrupt. The I/O ISR signals completion of the READ operation, thus making B ready to run again, so instead of A resuming, the *scheduler* is called to decide which program is to run next. Assume that program B, whose context was saved previously, is selected to run rather than program A.

Before program B can run, A's context must be saved in its PHD, then B's context is loaded from its PHD and restarted, resulting in a context switch.

An operating system design variation is to save the context of the program whenever an interrupt occurs. This approach has the advantage of permitting the interrupt service routine full access to all of the CPU's resources, in particular, all of the registers. However, depending on the size of the program context, saving it in memory can be a time-consuming operation.

The user program is executing whenever there are no interrupts to service. The interrupt concept permits temporary discontinuation of a program so that the CPU can be used for more important tasks. There is a difference between a context switch of two programs and a context switch caused by the interrupt mechanism. The interrupt is a much less time-consuming operation that involves fewer bytes than does a full context switch. This feature was designed into the VAX to facilitate rapid interrupt processing. When it switches to an interrupt service routine, the ISR's starting address is in a known location of memory. The control unit retrieves this starting location, places it in the program counter, and thus affects a context switch to the ISR. When the ISR is completed, control returns to the previously executing program.

1.7. A READ Example

This section describes a user program's READ operation, as implemented on the VMS operating system. At first glance, it may appear that the READ operation is identical to the WRITE operation; however, the two are quite different.

The terminal driver is responsible for echoing keystrokes such as DELETE (to delete a character) and LINE FEED (to delete a word), so it must be selective about which data it passes on to the program. Only the final, edited line ever reaches the program because the driver has made the corrections as the user enters the data.

As in the WRITE operation, the READ data is first buffered and then transferred into the requesting program only when the RETURN key is struck. Before then, the user may want to cancel an input line altogether (using the CTRL-U). Cancellation is performed by the driver within the system buffer, and the user program is never passed the data.

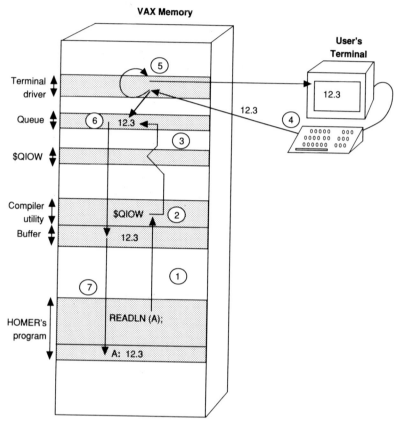

Figure 1.16. A program read operation

Figure 1.16 contains a Pascal program that executes a READLN instruction. The user strikes keys at the terminal, and the data is sent to the computer and echoed back to the screen by the terminal driver. The data is collected in the buffer until the RETURN key is struck, at which time the entire line is passed to the user's program for processing by Pascal's utilities. Figure 1.16 calls the user HOMER.[7] Naturally, many other users' activities are taking place during HOMER's keyboard entry.

7. Bemidji State University permits its students to choose their own user names. These accounts are entered once into the system and remain active for the student's career.

The program written by HOMER begins by executing a Pascal READLN command (circle 1). The compiler creates a CALLG to a compiler utility called PAS$READLN2, which makes a $QIOW system service call (circle 2). This terminal input request waits for keyboard data (circle 3). Since HOMER's program is waiting for input from the keyboard, it can no longer run. When HOMER strikes a key (circle 4), the terminal converts the keystroke to a stream of bits and transmits those bits to the terminal controller, one at a time, as described earlier in this chapter. When the last bit arrives, the controller creates the appropriate interrupt to get the attention of the terminal driver. Some other program is likely to be running, so the interrupt causes a context switch from that program to the terminal driver and the terminal controller passes the character to the terminal driver.

The terminal driver examines the character (circle 5). If it is an edit character, the appropriate echo is sent to the terminal and the buffer is likewise modified. For example, a DELETE must remove the previous character from the buffer as well as modify the display. Data entries are *buffered* in an array reserved for HOMER's data (circle 6). When the terminal driver is done processing HOMER's keystroke, the previously running program is restarted. HOMER continues to key data into the computer, editing it as necessary. Each time a key is struck, an interrupt occurs and the terminal driver buffers and echoes the character.

At some time, HOMER will strike the RETURN key. When the terminal driver detects the RETURN, the data line is copied from the $QIOW buffer into a buffer within HOMER's compiler utility, and HOMER's program is ready to execute again. But this does not guarantee that HOMER's program *will* execute immediately; it is only *ready* to execute now because it has the input data it needed.

Eventually, HOMER's program will be selected for execution. When that happens, the compiler utility converts the ASCII character string into a binary number suitable for computation (circle 7) and moves that data into the appropriate data area of the program. At this point, the READLN statement has completed execution and the next line of the program is then executed.

Each program, such as HOMER's, has various attributes, for example, its name and terminal number. Although the database maintained by the VMS operating system for the benefit of the program is large and complex, the most important information is stored in a data structure called the process control block (*PCB*).

An important attribute of a program is the *execution state.* This is a dynamic value and may change many times a second, unlike a program's

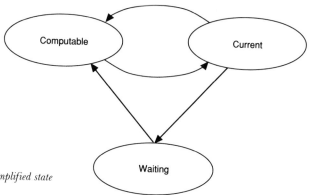

Figure 1.17. A simplified state diagram

terminal number, which is static throughout a terminal session. The VMS operating system assigns one of more than a dozen states to each program, but for now, the list will be simplified. Generally, a program is in one of three states:

- Currently executing
- Computable (able to execute)
- Waiting (for I/O)

On a system with a single CPU (a single-processor system), only one program is in the "currently executing" state. But if a system has multiple processors, a program can be "currently executing" on each processor. Additionally, on most systems, several programs are "computable" (although during off-peak hours, like two to five in the morning, this may not be true). Therefore, several programs—the "currently executing" one and the "computable" ones—are taking turns as the "currently executing" program, but the majority are in the "waiting" state; in fact, most of them are waiting for input, just like HOMER was.

Figure 1.17 illustrates execution state changes. Each bubble contains one of three execution states, Computable, Current, and Waiting, and the arrows indicate valid state transitions. Notice that some state transitions are not permitted.

In the Pascal READLN example, HOMER's program would be in the "currently executing" state to issue the READLN. It would then be transferred to the "waiting" state until HOMER hit the RETURN key at the terminal. The arrival of characters other than the RETURN would not cause HOMER's program to change states. This is a subtle point; the fact that the device driver is doing work for a particular program does not change the program's state because the device driver is part of the operating system. Once the input line was completed, however, HOMER's program would be moved from "waiting" to "computable" and, once again, take its turn on the processor. If it were chosen to begin execution, its state would become "currently executing" and the data would be available to the program.

1.8. Related Issues

All operating systems and supporting hardware do not function the same way. This section will outline some common variations in operating systems and hardware structure. As we will see, the hardware structure dictates much of the design of the operating system.

Although they are the exception, some computers have been built with no interrupts at all. Instead, the equivalent of the terminal driver program resides in a separate, *peripheral* computer, which the main processor *polls* occasionally to see if there is any data available. Polling performs the interrupt function. This permits the main processor to spend a greater portion of its time working on the computational section of the problem, and it allows the I/O part to be handled by a (usually) less expensive, less sophisticated machine. This concept was prevalent in the CDC 6000 series machines of the late 1960s.

A basic area of difference in operating system design is the handling of the *interactive* user. Historically, the first systems were designed only to support noninteractive programs in which all the data was prepared ahead of time and then fed in a single *batch* to the target computer. The batch program wrote all of the output on tape rather than displaying it, and the data was printed at a later time. Display devices were expensive and, if used at all, were employed only in graphics applications.

As personal computers become more popular in the business arena, so too do interactive systems. Even so, batch systems are still popular for a very good reason: *turnaround*, the time it takes to run the program, is much more flexible in batch because there is no user sitting at a terminal expecting output. This flexibility translates into running some programs late at night when there is little demand on computational facilities, which has the effect of averaging the computer load across time. The VMS system supports the batch concept, but only as a secondary feature.

The implementation of a device driver differs among operating systems. Most modern operating systems are designed to run on a particular computer or closely related class of machines; they are not normally very portable. (UNIX is a notable exception to this rule.) However, even if the operating system functions only in a specialized environment, it should be able to accommodate a variety of user terminal types simultaneously: hardcopy, paperless (or dumb), and semi-intelligent. The older, limited graphics "language" on a VT52 is different from that on the VT100, and the REGIS standard has little in common with its predecessors. In order to accommodate this diversity, the terminal driver should adapt to a variety of terminals, the operating system should supply multiple drivers, or all terminals on the system should be identical. The first approach, accommodating a variety of terminals, is the most preferable.

1.9. Summary

Looking at the operating system is like the blind men describing an elephant in the childhood fable. One man, holding the tail, describes the elephant as rope-like. Another, flapping an ear, thinks it is like a tent. A third, trying to embrace the elephant's leg, thinks a better analogy is a tree. So it is with the operating system, especially in these introductory descriptions: the whole is a composite of the bits and pieces.

In this chapter, we examined the hardware connection between the terminal and the host computer, and we described the terminal I/O function twice to give you a more complete understanding of its total function. We also detailed the RS232C protocol, the most common method of connecting a terminal to its host computer. This was so the software engineer, who is rarely exposed to the details of this communication method, might be well-informed concerning common hardware concepts as part of the software education process.

The primary method of user access to an interactive system is from a terminal; since there is a wide variety of terminals available, the operating system must be capable of communicating with them all, not just those sold by the computer manufacturer. Normally, most terminal communication protocols are under user control. The VMS system allows the user to display what the system is assuming about the terminal, and the user can change these assumptions if required.

We discussed the READ and WRITE operations in some detail. The examples illustrated how a Pascal program can use the VMS system service routine $QIOW to write to and read from a user's terminal, and they showed how the VMS operating system performs those two operations.

The hardware interrupt concept is the key to understanding most operating systems. We call the operating system interrupt-driven because the interrupts return the processor from the user's program to the operating system and thus give the operating system control. Each device has its own interrupt service routine.

An operating system model illustrated the part an operating system plays when a program is executed. The operating system is a collection of services, each one of which can be isolated and examined in detail. In discussing this high-level view of the operating system, we touched on the concept of time-sharing among all of the users in the system, and we introduced the notion that a program is represented by a collection of data maintained by the operating system. The program's execution state is only one element in this database.

We introduced two important terms in this chapter: the "terminal driver," meaning a software program, and the "terminal controller," meaning hardware that connects the terminal to the computer. The more general terms are the "device driver" and "device controller." Thus, a system has a printer (hardware), a printer controller (hardware), and a printer driver (software). Often, a device controller can be connected to more than one device. For example, the typical disk controller can be connected to eight or more disk drives. There may be multiple terminal controllers as well, and each controller can' have multiple terminals. The interrupt service routine is actually part of the driver.

ACRONYMS

$QIOW	Queue I/O and Wait system service
ASCII	American Standard Code for Information Interchange
CDC	Control Data Corporation
CISC	Complex Instruction Set Computer
CPU	Central Processing Unit
CRC	Cyclic Redundancy Check

DEC	Digital Equipment Corporation
EBCDIC	Extended Binary Coded Decimal Information Code
I/O	Input/Output
IBM	International Business Machines
ISR	Interrupt Service Routine
MFLOPS	Million Floating Point Operations Per Second
MHz	Megahertz
MIPS	Million Instructions Per Second
MS	Microsecond
MS-DOS	Microsoft Disk Operating System
PCB	Process Control Block
PC	Personal Computer. Program Counter
PHD	Process Header
REI	Assembly instruction to Return from Exception or Interrupt
RISC	Reduced Instruction Set Computer
ULTRIX	A UNIX-like operating system that runs on the VAX
VAX	Virtual Address Extension
VMS	Virtual Memory System

SHORT ANSWER EXERCISES

1. Obviously, striking an alphabetic or numeric key on the keyboard will result in an echo of that same character, but not all keys behave that way. What keys produce other than a trivial echo?

2. Why is it unreasonable to echo a backspace on a hardcopy device like the DECwriter?

3. This exercise deals with the parity computation logic of your terminal. If your terminal is able to detect a parity error, what does it do when it finds one? This is not an easy question to answer because you cannot write a program to create a parity error—this is strictly a device function. But you might be able to fake it by loosening the RS232C cable at your terminal and then wiggling it while the VAX is responding to a TYPE 'file' command. If the file you are displaying is quite long, chances are that a parity error can be induced into the data flow. This may cause your system to log you off. When you are done with this exercise, be sure to firmly reconnect the RS232C connector.

4. Draw a diagram in the style of Figure 1.7 for the character (indicated below) sent with one start bit, seven data bits, odd parity, and two stop bits.
   a. W
   b. *
   c. m
   d. 7

5. Draw a diagram in the style of Figure 1.7 for two consecutive characters (indicated below) sent with one start bit, eight data bits, even parity, and one stop bit.
   a. Wj
   b. %$
   c. 36
   d. /\

6. If you have a display-type terminal such as a VT100 or VT220, enter the command:

   ```
   $ SET TERMINAL /DEVICE_TYPE=LA34
   ```

   This command directs the terminal driver to assume that your terminal is a hardcopy device instead of a display terminal. Discover which echos change because of this command and how.

7. What is the minimum amount of time necessary to transmit an 80-character line from the computer to a terminal? Assume 4,800 baud, one start bit, seven data bits, odd parity, and one stop bit.

8. At what baud rate can a typist who is able to key 100 five-character words per minute generate characters? Assume that there is a space character between each word. Further assume one start bit, seven data bits, no parity, and one stop bit.

9. Why is there no arrow from "Computable" to "Waiting" in Figure 1.17?

10. Several VMS utilities do not echo consistently, for instance the up-arrow key in EDIT and MAIL work differently. Summarize the similarities and differences in the various utilities.

11. Enter the command:

    ```
    $ SET TERMINAL /NOECHO
    ```

    Describe what happens to entries that you make and to system responses. Do not forget to enter $ SET TERMINAL /ECHO when you complete this exercise.

12. Enter the command:

```
$ SET TERMINAL /NOTYPE_AHEAD
```

Describe what happens to entries that you make and to system responses. Do not forget to enter $ SET TERMINAL /TYPE_AHEAD when you complete this exercise.

PAPERS

1. Research the development of one of the electronic codes such as Morse, Baudot, BCD, EBCDIC, or ASCII. Write a paper presenting your findings.
2. "Conversational" computation was researched in detail at M.I.T. in the early 1960s. It was then called Compatible Timesharing System (CTSS). Write a paper that examines only the terminal communications aspect of this research project.
3. The computer language BASIC was originally developed for a time-sharing system in the mid 1960s. It was part of a project called Dartmouth Timesharing System (DTSS). Write a paper that examines only the terminal communications aspect of this research project.
4. This assignment is for those who have a good background in electronics. The RS232C communications standard is primarily concerned with hardware characteristics, such as voltage levels, waveforms, and so forth. Locate a copy of this standard and write a paper that describes the essential points in terms that software people can understand.
5. The RS232 standard has been changed three times; we are currently using version C. Write a paper tracing these changes and the reasons behind them in terms that software students with little or no electronics background can understand.
6. There are several other important serial computer transmission standards in use today. Find one of them and write a paper that compares that standard to RS232C, for instance, IEEE 488 or RS 449.
7. In order to measure the power of a machine in MIPS, a standard set of benchmark tests are run on the machine. Research the standard benchmarks and describe what they do and why they were chosen.
8. There is a controversy over the validity of the MIPS benchmark

programs because Digital uses another measurement called VUPs (VAX unit of processing). One VUP is approximately equal to one MIP. Research this controversy to find out why there are two different units.

9. Workstations that are devoted to graphics have an entirely different computational rating. Determine what is used to compare graphics workstations and explain why it is necessary to define still another standard.

The Process

GOALS

Process definition and database

Process creation and destruction

Command language interpretation

Image activation and rundown

VMS system services

2

The previous chapter used the term "program" throughout to minimize the number of new terms being introduced. Most software engineers feel comfortable with "program." However, in the strict sense, the accurate term is "process." The *process* is the smallest software unit managed by the operating system, and since it is the prime unit with which the operating system must deal, the user should attain a good understanding of the concept as soon as possible.

2.1. The Process and Operating System

A software engineer writes a program to perform a function; then the program is compiled, linked, and executed. Once the program is executing, it becomes part of the user's process. The user's process is represented in the operating system by a collection of data elements. These include the user's program and where it is located, accounting information, privilege

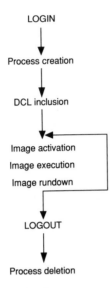

Figure 2.1. An overview of a process's lifetime

flags, information about current files, performance statistics, and so forth. This chapter outlines and develops the VMS process database. It also follows a process's lifetime shown in Figure 2.1 beginning with process creation at the user login time and continuing with the activation of DCL (Digital Command Language), which is the code that prompts, reads, and executes commands from the terminal. DCL works in conjunction with a subroutine called *image activation.* An image is a user program that executes as part of the process. ("Program" and "image" are used synonymously for the rest of the book.) Many images are activated, the most familiar being the activation of a user's program. Then when the program is finished, the image is *rundown.* Image activation and rundown can take place often during the lifetime of a process. Finally, this chapter will show how the process is destroyed at LOGOUT time. That is, process creation is reversed to release all of the various data elements that comprise the process.

This chapter also introduces the reader to some of the system displays that provide process metrics. In the exercises at the end, the reader will closely examine the LOGIN-LOGOUT activities by measuring the amount of time it takes to perform the various parts of the creation and deletion operations. In this way, he or she will learn to use investigative tools and examine units of measurement available in a time-sharing environment.

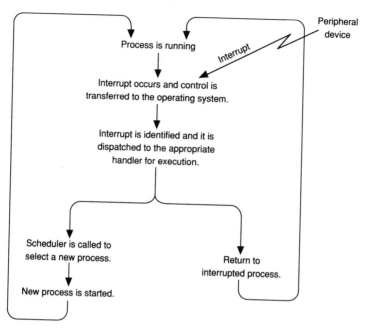

Figure 2.2. An operating system model

OPERATING SYSTEM MODEL

Chapter 1 introduced some of the functions of an operating system by looking at two common operations, reading and writing characters on the terminal. This chapter presents a more general view that will exhibit the larger structure and action of the system to see how the process and the operating system relate to each other. Figure 2.2 presents an initial working model of the operating system, depicted as an *interrupt dispatcher* and a collection of *interrupt handlers*. An *interrupt* is a signal from a peripheral device, such as a disk, printer, or user's terminal, to the central processing unit (CPU). It means that data is either available for the CPU to process or has been processed by the peripheral.

Figure 2.2 is cyclic. At the top, the process is executing, and directly below, an interrupt is received from a peripheral device. The operating system associates the interrupt with a particular interrupt handler, and whichever process is executing is discontinued in order for the CPU to respond to the interrupt. This discontinuation is made in such a way that the process can be restarted. In this model, after the specific handler executes

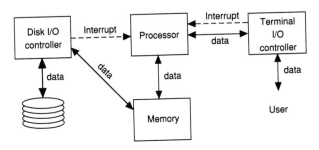

Figure 2.3. A computer system model

its assigned task, it decides to either return to the process that was interrupted or execute another process. The reason for this dichotomy is that the interrupt may have signaled an event requiring a more important process to execute. The determination of which process to execute next is the responsibility of the *scheduler,* a major subsystem of the operating system. The scheduler applies a complex algorithm to select the next process to be executed from a pool of eligible processes. Scheduling is examined in detail in Chapter 3.

Figure 2.3 illustrates a traditional computer system model. Note that data can travel in either direction to and from the processor. However, interrupts only travel from a peripheral device to the processor.

The same model of interrupts applies to system services initiated by the process, for example, $QIOW. The system service request initiates an interrupt-like signal called an *exception,* which differs from an interrupt in that it is synchronous to the execution flow of the process. Regardless of the origin, a handler must act upon the exception also. What distinguishes system services from ordinary utilities, like SQRT, is that they perform privileged operations that the ordinary user is not allowed to perform. The operating system uses the identical subroutine any time it needs that service. For instance, all I/O operations throughout the system use $QIOW. Likewise, a user is permitted to execute the system service $QIOW, and the Pascal command WRITELN also uses $QIOW, indirectly. Since system services are an important tool, this book will explain and demonstrate several of them.

Figure 2.4 expands the central section of Figure 2.2 labeled "Dispatched to the appropriate handler for execution." For instance, $QIOW is executed via a system service request made by a user's program. It must validate the I/O request, identify the physical device involved, and then add it to that device's execution queue; then it must alert the device handler that a new entry has been placed on its queue as indicated in the figure, and the

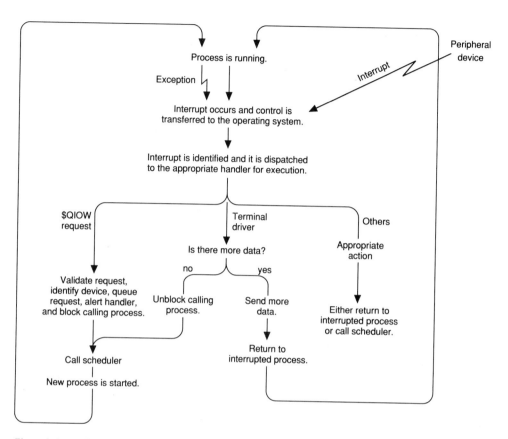

Figure 2.4. Another operating system model

device handler acts upon the request when it has an opportunity. The requesting process must be put into a blocked state to wait for completion of the I/O request. Finally, the scheduler is called by $QIOW to select another process to run because the process making the $QIOW request cannot continue until the request is completed.

Another example is shown in the figure. The terminal driver executes in response to a hardware interrupt rather than at the user's request. First, the terminal interrupt handler must determine if the I/O request has completed. If so, the requesting process is ready to execute once again and must be unblocked. If not, the handler will continue the I/O operation, and the interrupted process (not the requesting process) will be continued from the point that the interrupt took place.

A user's process is central to the operating system. Every model of the operating system shows it is manipulated either as a result of an interrupt or on the command of the process. As the following sections will illustrate, the process is represented internally by a complex database.

The material that follows is a summary of VMS activities related to processes. This approach was chosen for two reasons. One, the reader has not yet had a sufficient introduction to operating systems in general, and the VMS system in particular, to appreciate the details. Two, as stated in the preface, this book does not replicate *VAX/VMS Internals and Data Structures.*

2.2. Process Definition

Up to this point, the word *process* has been used as if it were well defined and understood, which, of course, it is not. This section defines and exemplifies this term to give a better feeling for the underlying concept. Without a good understanding of the process, you will not be able to grasp the intricacies of the operating system or appreciate its full influence on the process.

A process is a dynamic entity; it is a combination of the user's program and the operating system during execution. A process changes over time, not only because its data changes but because the user's images also change. In VMS, a process is larger than the user's program because it includes the operating system itself. In other operating systems, for example, Digital's operating system for the PDP-11 series called RSX-11, the program and the process are equivalent—the operating system is separate. In any case, this dynamic entity, the process, can be stopped at any time, usually between instructions, and execution is discontinued for an indefinite period. There are several reasons for discontinuing the process; interrupt processing is just one of the reasons.

A process is defined by six items. Four of them—the program, its data, an input source, and an output sink—are straightforward; the remaining two—the status of the CPU registers and memory—are less apparent. These six change as a consequence of process execution: that is, as it executes, the process changes and uses internal data variables to record intermediate values, to save results of computations, and to perform comparisons.

There are two ways to view a process. The first is from the user's terminal, since the process is an *environment* created and maintained by the operating system for the benefit of the user. The process may or may not include a user program at any given time. For instance, when editing a file, the process is composed entirely of operating system code and user data, but when running a user-specified program, the process includes that program. In the user view, the environment is primarily composed of memory and a processor. However, a process normally also needs a file that contains the program to be run and a terminal to control the program and to receive the output.

PROCESS DATABASE

The second view of the process is a collection of data blocks that form a database. Consider this analogy: the editor function is straightforward. It treats every file as data without distinguishing between a Pascal program, payroll data, and a personal letter. It has no understanding of what kind of data it is working with, but merely maneuvers characters according to the user-entered commands. Similarly, a user's process is part of a database that the operating system manipulates. For instance, on command it creates, initializes, and connects elements in its database to create the process. But, to the user sitting at the terminal, this activity has meaning; system LOGIN has been successfully completed.

Thus, much of the operating system's code is concerned with the manipulation of thousands of database details. The database is quite intricate and is designed to minimize execution time and space requirements. For example, queues and lists are used to minimize search time. They are linked together with either pointers or indexes to minimize insertion and deletion time. Much of the data involve variable-length structures, based on specific process parameters to minimize memory utilization.

Because of its complexity, the VMS database is designed to be self-checking so that system programmers can more easily locate and isolate design and implementation errors effectively. For instance, every data structure contains a unique identifier. Before any data structure is modified, the operating system code confirms that the modification is valid for that particular structure. Improper operations are recorded whenever they occur and, if required, execution is terminated.

Operating systems programmers are not immune to making errors, nor are they super-coders who write programs that always work the first time. Operating systems programming is probably one of the most demanding jobs in the industry, because an operating system is the most used software on any computer. Unlike utility programs such as compilers or editors, the operating system is in constant use by every user logged into the system. Thus, it must contain far fewer errors than any other software product. Moreover, if an error in the operating system were to go undetected, it could reduce a computer to a useless stack of metal and silicon. Without the operating system, the computer cannot function.

Consistent with the book's practical approach, we will examine the VMS process database in some detail throughout. This chapter concentrates on a process's creation and destruction, and succeeding chapters will show how a process is manipulated. There is a reason for this emphasis: if the process database is not well designed, overall system performance may be sluggish because the operating system is too busy attempting to locate the data necessary to fulfill its various functions. It is important to first understand the data structures and organization that define a process.

2.3. User LOGIN

There are several steps an operating system must perform to log in a user. Normally, the first step is validating that the user is permitted to use the machine, although in some *trusted* systems, this security measure is unnecessary. Besides performing the security function, the login operation places the user in a particular portion of the file hierarchy where he or she has access to personal files. System login is performed via a user dialogue, in which the system usually asks for a user name and password (or two).

Because of this login dialogue, the operating system designer is faced with an implementation decision: should a special system process direct the dialogue, or should the dialogue originate in the user's process? The VMS operating system uses the second alternative: a process is created that prompts for the user name and password, validates these data, initializes the user specific data variables, and performs the final user control of the process. Process creation is signaled to the user by the "$" prompt.

PROCESS CREATION

The only way a process can be created is by the action of another process; only a running process can create a new process. There are several per-

```
VAX/VMS V5.2    on node BSU 8-AUG-1990 14:04:50.48   Uptime   21 00:42:02
   Pid     Process Name      State  Pri    I/O         CPU      Page flts Ph.Mem
00000081 SWAPPER           HIB   16     0   0 00:00:01.66        0        0
00000084 ERRFMT            HIB    8   781   0 00:00:07.37       70       91
00000085 OPCOM             HIB    8   368   0 00:00:03.09     1805      125
00000086 JOB_CONTROL       HIB    9  2968   0 00:00:15.89      190      312
00000087 SYMBIONT_0001     HIB    6   135   0 00:00:03.05     1255       48
00000088 NTR               HIB   11 57850   0 00:00:57.90      184      276
0000008A NETACP            HIB   10  2302   0 00:00:09.90      314      205
0000008B EVL               HIB    6   109   0 00:00:02.54    22079       44 N
0000008C PSIACP            HIB   10   174   0 00:00:03.00      867      600
0000008D REMACP            HIB    8     7   0 00:00:00.14       67       33
000000A4 Monitor           LEF   15   586   0 00:00:05.56      901      322
000000DE Sir Dracut.       LEF    5  1242   0 00:00:08.32     1265      321
000000E1 The Perfesser     CUR    4   262   0 00:00:05.27     1209      233
```

Figure 2.5. Typical display of the command $ SHOW SYSTEM

manent system processes active and waiting to run. They are created during system startup and are never deleted from the system. All of the current processes in the system, permanent and user, are summarized in a display with the command:

$ SHOW SYSTEM

as seen in Figure 2.5. The top line of the display is self-explanatory except for the time format on the right: the "Uptime" units are the number of days, hours, minutes, and seconds since the system was started. In this example, the system has been up for slightly more than 21 days.

Next, the display shows several attributes of each process, indicated by the label at the top of each column. Starting at the left, "PID" (Process Identification) is an integer carried throughout the database that identifies the process to the operating system. "Process Name" is initially assigned as the user name by the system, but the user may redefine it at any time. "State" identifies the execution state of each process. The common state abbreviations used are COM for computable, HIB for hibernating, LEF for waiting for a local event flag, and CUR for the currently running process. In the figure, "The Perfesser" is the currently executing process. In terms of the state diagram presented in Figure 1.17, HIB and LEF are waiting, or blocked, states. Next to "State" is "Pri," the process priority: 0 is the lowest and 31 is the highest. Notice that the priority of "The Perfesser" is 4, which is a common value for an interactive process.

The remaining four columns have to do with process performance measurements. "I/O" records the number of I/O operations performed by the process since login. "CPU" means the actual CPU time (in days, hours, minutes, seconds, and hundredths of seconds) used by the process. This number has nothing to do with how long the process has been logged in but with how much of the CPU's resource has been consumed since login. "Page flts" means "page faults," and "Ph.Mem" means "physical memory." They deal with the memory utilization of the process and are fully discussed in Chapter 4. The rightmost column is unlabeled and may contain a single-letter code for the process type: a "B" means batch process, "N" means a network process, and "S" means a subprocess. In the figure, the process named EVL shows an "N."

As mentioned, several processes are permanent: SWAPPER controls several memory management functions; ERRFMT periodically records on disk hardware errors encountered during system operation; and OPCOM is the operator communications process. There could be several SYMBIONT processes that control the queues for printers and batch streams. Any system process ending in the letters "ACP" (Ancillary Control Process) assists device drivers in processing I/O requests. For instance, NETACP aids in DECnet controls, and REMACP helps with remote terminals. A system process can usually be identified by its elevated priority, but there are exceptions to this rule. Interactive user process priorities normally range between 4 and 9.

Notice in Figure 2.5 that JOB_CONTROL is waiting; it is in HIB (hibernate) state. Whenever a terminal device reports (via an interrupt) that a key has been struck, and if there is no other process performing a READ operation on the terminal, the input is directed to the permanent system process named JOB_CONTROL. This is done by the terminal driver. It attempts to associate a keystroke to an existing process using the translation table. But if there is no process connected to the terminal, JOB_CONTROL is notified instead. The login sequence is summarized in Figure 2.6. Normally, the terminal driver echoes the key, but not in this case (circle 1). JOB_CONTROL validates the keystroke because, for security, only certain keys are permitted to start the login sequence. The system manager may decide to make the BREAK key the only valid key or may permit the RETURN key to start the login sequence.

JOB_CONTROL then executes a system service routine called $CREPRC (Create Process) (circle 2), which creates another process that will eventually become the user's. Within the new process, an image called LOGINOUT is activated. LOGINOUT is responsible for prompting and reading the Username and Password (circle 3) and confirming their validity. If the user responds with a legal account, LOGINOUT starts the Digital Command Language (DCL) image, which is part of the process too, and writes the

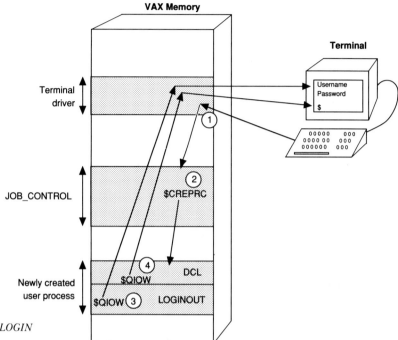

Figure 2.6. The LOGIN overview

welcoming message on the user's screen. DCL makes the LOGINOUT image rundown, and the LOGIN sequence is complete when DCL executes a $QIOW to the terminal driver and the DCL prompt "$" is displayed on the terminal (circle 4).

If the account is invalid, LOGINOUT destroys itself and the process in which it is executing. In effect, it automatically performs an immediate logout operation. This is the reason for combining the two functions into the single image, and it explains how the image received its name.

SYSTEM MANAGER

It is advisable to assign the numerous responsibilities of computer center operations to one person, *the system manager,* who is normally supported by several people depending on the center's size. The manager and support staff's responsibilities include:

- Hardware procurement, installation, and maintenance
- Software procurement, installation, and maintenance

- Procurement of expendables—tapes, paper, disk packs, etc.
- Maintenance of authorized user access information
- Regular data backup and restoration of data on demand
- Daily operations such as hanging user tapes, loading paper into printers, and performing data backup
- Determination and implementation of operational policy
- Maintaining acceptable facility performance levels
- Ensuring system security

2.4. Process Data Structure

To create the new user's process, JOB_CONTROL creates a generic dummy process using the system service $CREPRC (Create Process). $CREPRC, like other system services, is a sharable, privileged subroutine residing within the operating system that is callable from any process. In the LOGIN example, $CREPRC creates a skeleton process, which is identified by the terminal name, _TTD4: in Figure 2.7, since the user's name is not yet known. Because there is no user initially, JOB_CONTROL creates a dummy process with the same full privileges and quotas as it has. This dummy process also defaults to a system file structure. In other words, it is a fully privileged system process, at least temporarily.

When called, $CREPRC creates three blocks, depicted in Figure 2.7: the process control block (PCB), the job information block (JIB), and the process header (PHD). These blocks are located in an area dedicated to processes in the *kernel,* or central portion, of the VMS operating system, which is called the scheduler database.

The process control block (PCB) is paramount in the structure of the process, since all other data structures depend on it. (Its format is summarized in Figure 2.8.) The PCB and other blocks like it are allocated dynamically, as the need arises, from a data pool. The first three fields, forward link, backward link, and housekeeping, are found in almost all VMS data blocks. All blocks of a given type—for instance, the PCB—are double-linked together with a backward and forward pointer. The housekeeping field contains two informational fields: (not shown in figure) an integer identifier for the block type and the length of the block. These fields aid the system programmers in finding system errors.

The PCB includes data values, pointers, and links to other blocks. The ACB (asynchronous system trap (AST) control block) is discussed in Chapter

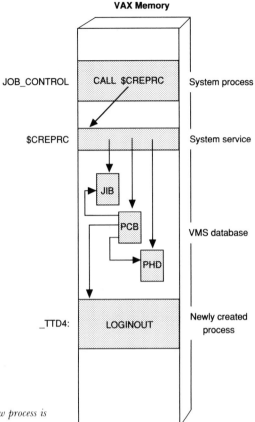

VAX Memory

JOB_CONTROL | CALL $CREPRC | System process

$CREPRC | | System service

JIB

PCB | VMS database

PHD

_TTD4: | LOGINOUT | Newly created process

Figure 2.7. A new process is created

8. The physical PCB, which is included in the PHD, is discussed in Chapter 3. Quota limits are described shortly, and event flags (EF) and event flag clusters are investigated in Chapter 5. The PID is the unique process identification number. The PHD (process header) is detailed in Chapter 4. The JIB (job information block) is shown later in this chapter. Privileges are investigated in Chapter 7, although they are elaborated on later in this chapter. The PCB also contains the process state, priority, and name. Figure 2.9 illustrates the relationships between these data blocks. Some of the links are permanent, but other connections are transitory because they are created only when requested by the user's image.

The PCB vector shown in the figure is an array of pointers to all PCBs

PCB
Process Control Block

Forward link
Backward link
Housekeeping
ACB links
Physical PCB pointer
Quota limits
Local event flags
EF cluster pointers
PID
PHD pointer
JIB pointer
Privileges
ACL links
State
Priority
Name

Figure 2.8. Overview of the
PCB structure

in the system, and the PID (Process Identification) is derived from the location of the PCB pointer in this vector, that is, part of the PID is the index
into the PCB vector. The remainder has to do with the location of the PCB
in the network of computers. The SHOW SYSTEM command uses the PCB
vector to identify and locate the PCB to determine name, state, and priority.
From the PCB, the PHD is accessed to read the essential accounting data.
The JIB (Job Information Block) contains additional information about the
process and is detailed later in the discussion of subprocesses.

The PHD (Process Header) is part of the permanent VMS database
structure and thus has an entirely different structure from those blocks
already discussed. It contains information to locate the process's instructions,
its memory utilization information, and the physical (or hardware) control
block. The PHD also contains accounting data.

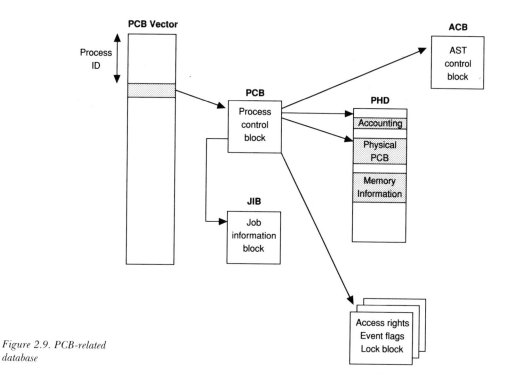

*Figure 2.9. PCB-related
database*

The description of process creation now continues. If there is room
for the new process in the PCB vector, $CREPRC informs the VMS system
of the new process, which cannot execute yet because its instructions and
data are still on disk. The new process is initially in an execution state called
computable outswapped (COMO), and when there is room in memory, its
state will be changed to computable (COM). When it is selected to execute
by the scheduler, the new process will be copied into memory as required.

Thus, when the $CREPRC system service returns to JOB_CONTROL,
a new process has been created. In its data structure, specifically, in the
PHD, is information indicating that the image, LOGINOUT, can be executed whenever the scheduler determines that CPU and memory space are
available. Since JOB_CONTROL is not part of this new process, it sends
itself back to a hibernate state using another system service called $HIBER.

When selected by the scheduler, the new process containing LOGIN-
OUT can be executed. Once LOGINOUT begins to execute, the default
values initialized in the JIB, PCB, and PHD are replaced by values pertaining
to the user who logged in. It is LOGINOUT that prompts for Username

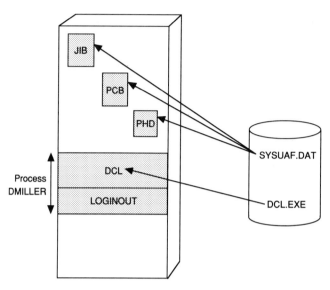

Figure 2.10. LOGINOUT
activities

and Password, and using these two items, it searches a file called SYS-UAF.DAT (User Authorization File) that contains information about all valid accounts. If this file indicates that the account is valid and active, LOGIN-OUT extracts information from it required to define the process, including:

- Process name, usually the user name
- Default disk drive and directory
- User privileges
- User quotas
- Run-time restrictions such as the time of day or the day of the week that the user is permitted to log in
- Process priority
- Default command language interpreter (CLI)

This activity is shown in Figure 2.10, in which the evolving process has now been renamed from _TTD4: to DMILLER.

A second major responsibility of LOGINOUT is to initialize the command language interpreter (CLI). The SYSUAF.DAT indicates which CLI is to be used, the most common one being Digital's Command Language, DCL. LOGINOUT makes room in memory for the CLI and, when it is finished, turns control over to it. If, however, the SYSUAF.DAT indicates an error in user name or password, LOGINOUT will destroy the process instead of starting the CLI.

For relating process creation to what can be experienced at the terminal, there is a command that displays many important process database parameters. Figure 2.11 is a display resulting from this command.

```
$ SHOW PROCESS/ALL
```

There are several sections in the display in Figure 2.11. Each depicts a different part of VMS's process database. The top two lines identify the user, and the next four lines show the terminal and files associated with that user. The limits or quotas of this process are listed next. The accounting section is used to compute user charges. Notice the two time entries: connect time is computed from LOGIN to the time this command was executed; CPU time is the actual execution time in terms of computer resources since LOGIN. The privileges and rights shown are available to everyone; they are the default values. The final section displays the job structure, a topic we will consider later in this chapter. Each section of this display can be requested individually as well as together. SHOW PROCESS/QUOTA,[1] for instance, will display just the "Process Quotas" section.

2.5. The DCL Cycle

Some part of an operating system must be delegated the responsibility to read, interpret, and execute commands entered by the user. Digital calls this part a Command Language Interpreter (CLI). The most commonly used CLI in the VMS system is the Digital Command Language (DCL).

When LOGINOUT has completed execution, the newly created process continues by starting DCL. The first thing DCL must do is eliminate LOGINOUT. It does this by simulating a user and assuming that the command previously entered was RUN LOGINOUT; that program has now finished. This causes the LOGINOUT image to be removed as described in the section on image rundown later in this chapter. Next, DCL prepares to execute the system manager's system-wide login procedure (called SYLO-

---

1. In order to reduce confusion between DCL commands and system services, the "$" is omitted from DCL commands in the prose. The "$" is part of the system service names and so will appear with them.

```
   8-AUG-1990   12:41:33.46   User: DMILLER        Process ID: 000000CF
                                                   Process name: The Perfesser

Terminal:            TTD4:
User Identifier:     [FACULTY,DMILLER]
Base Priority:       4
Default file spec:   DUA1:[FACULTY.DMILLER]

Devices allocated: TTD4:

Process Quotas:
 Account name: 1613DD6B
 CPU limit:                       Infinite Direct I/O limit:        18
 Buffered I/O byte count quota:      8192 Buffered I/O limit:        18
 Timer queue entry quota:              10 Open file quota:           20
 Paging file quota:                  3159 Subprocess quota:           5
 Default page fault cluster:           64 AST limit:                 22
 Enqueue quota:                        30 Shared file limit:          0
 Max detached processes:                0 Max active jobs:            4

Accounting information:
 Buffered I/O count:         300 Peak working set size:       671
 Direct I/O count:           126 Peak virtual size:          1321
 Page faults:               1404 Mounted volumes:               0
 Images activated:            11
 Elapsed CPU time:      0 00:00:06.77
 Connect time:          0 00:11:54.46

Process privileges:
 TMPMBX              may create temporary mailbox
 NETMBX              may create network device

Process rights identifiers:
 INTERACTIVE
 LOCAL

Process Dynamic Memory Area
    Current Size (bytes)       25600  Current Total Size (pages)      50
    Free Space (bytes)         22016  Space in Use (bytes)          3584
    Size of Largest Block      21888  Size of Smallest Block           8
    Number of Free Blocks          5  Free Blocks LEQU 32 Bytes        2

There is 1 process in this job:
 The Perfesser (*)
```

*Figure 2.11. Typical display
of command $ SHOW
PROCESS/ALL*

GIN.COM). After that is done, the user's LOGIN.COM file is executed. Figure 2.12 shows that executing login files actually requires several trips around the DCL loop, one for every command in the file. Finally, the initial VMS prompt is displayed on the user's terminal and the process creation and login function is completed; the user may now enter commands.

The reader must realize that there is a significant difference between VMS—the operating system—and DCL—the command language. The VMS operating system is a collection of processes (like JOB_CONTROL) and system services (like $CREPRC) used by any command language interpreter and by the user. DCL is an interface between the user and VMS. The commands used in the examples, like SET and SHOW, are entered by the user and executed by DCL. DCL makes use of system services whenever necessary to execute a particular command. For instance, the SET TERMINAL command is performed in part by $QIOW, and the SPAWN command is one way a user has to access $CREPRC to create a process.

DCL is not normally considered part of the operating system any more than the compilers and editors are, although they are all supplied and supported by Digital. Rather, DCL is a level of abstraction above VMS, a shell around VMS that makes the system easier for the user to access.

Even though DCL is not directly related to the process discussion, it is part of the process. Since it is used so much, it is important to understand it well. Once initialized, DCL cycles until the user logs out and the process is deleted. At the top of the loop, the prompt and read are executed. Once a command is entered and read, there are two distinct paths DCL can take. In Figure 2.12, the left-hand path shows that most commands are executed internally by DCL, without the aid of an image. For example, DEFINE, SET PROMPT, SHOW TIME, and WAIT are all executed merely by calling system services. But a few commands require an image because they are much more involved; this is indicated by the right-hand path. File commands like DIRECTORY and DELETE, compilers, editors, LINK, some SET and SHOW commands, RUN, and command procedures follow the right-hand path. Notice that the term "image" is not synonymous with "process"; refer back to Figure 2.1.

A close look at the right-hand path shows that whenever an image is to be executed, the previous one must be removed first if there is one left active. Then the image, stored in an .EXE file, can be activated. When the image completes, as indicated by the RET (return from subroutine) instruction, DCL regains control of the process: the image is rundown, open files

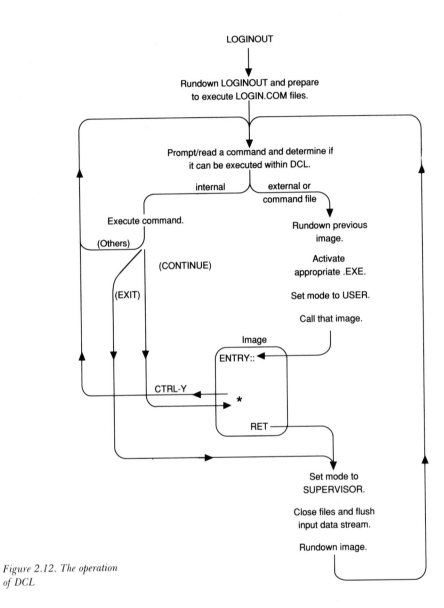

Figure 2.12. The operation of DCL

are closed, the keyboard type-ahead buffer is cleared, and the image is removed from memory.

An interesting feature of DCL is what happens when an image is interrupted: once the image is activated, it can be interrupted with the CTRL-Y key, as indicated by the asterisk. When CTRL-Y is struck, the DCL cycle is again entered at the top. If only internal commands are entered, the image remains intact and can be restarted with the CONTINUE command. For instance, a user can strike CTRL-Y, enter SHOW TIME, and then CONTINUE execution of the image. Errors caused by the image or encountered by DCL command interpretation merely return control to the DCL cycle and do not destroy the process. Errors in an image, depending on their severity, may cause the image to be rundown—one instance might be a Pascal subscript out of range causes the image to be terminated unless DEBUG is in control.

Thus, we see that the process provides an environment for image execution that is supported by DCL. DCL is a command interface between the user and the operating system, and it controls the process until an image is executed either directly with the RUN command or indirectly using a DCL command. Images are activated and rundown, but the process remains intact throughout the terminal session. The interactive process is destroyed only when the user executes the LOGOUT or the STOP command.

2.6. Image Creation

The concept of image is unique to the VMS operating system. Other operating systems do not separate the image from the process. To distinguish between these two concepts, this section elaborates on the image and the various stages it goes through. To begin, recall the steps performed when preparing a program for execution, shown in Figure 2.13. The compiler, in this case Pascal, reads the source file, which has a file name extension of .PAS, and creates an *object file*, which has a file name extension of .OBJ. The object file contains machine instructions plus additional information required to create the image.

All compilers generate code that calls subroutines to perform various services for the user, such as computation of a square root or conversion of a real number to ASCII for display. These are in addition to the system

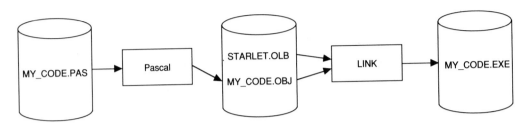

Figure 2.13. Steps in image creation

service and Run-Time Library routines provided by the VMS operating system. There are a number of reasons for this subroutine philosophy, but the most obvious is to spare the programmer the task of reinventing the wheel—for instance, the square root algorithm. Another reason for substituting a subroutine for in-line code is to keep the .OBJ file smaller.

In addition to these implicit subroutine calls, the programmer may make specific requests, such as a random number generator or certain mathematical functions, from a system utilities library. VMS provides an extensive library called the Run-Time Library (RTL). Type the DCL command HELP RTL to examine the breadth of utilities that are available. The point is that the object file of a single Pascal program is not the whole image because it does not yet include all the code necessary.

LINK

To complete the image, the Pascal object file must be concatenated and *linked* with these subroutines. The concatenation process is depicted in Figure 2.14. LINK examines the Pascal object file to find out which additional subroutines are required. Then it searches the library and extracts and combines, by concatenation, the object files that the user specifies with other object files from system libraries, such as SYS$LIBRARY:STARLET.OLB. The extension, OLB, refers to an object library.

The next step in the linking phase is not as apparent. Concatenating the object files causes the starting location of the subroutines to be changed. Recall that when a program is compiled, the first instruction is always assigned location 0, the second instruction is assigned to the next available location (not necessarily 1), and so forth. Figure 2.14 shows that MY_CODE

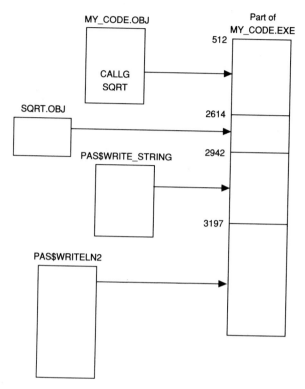

Figure 2.14. Concatenation of OBJ files

begins at location 512, followed by SQRT, which begins at location 2614, PAS$WRITE_STRING, which begins at location 2942, and PAS$WRITE-LN2, which begins at location 3197. Somewhere inside MY_CODE is a utility call to SQRT. The Pascal compiler has no idea what address to assign to the CALLG SQRT instruction. Instead, it marks the SQRT call so that LINK will supply the address. After the object files are concatenated, LINK locates all the references to SQRT in MY_CODE and supplies the correct address in the CALLG instruction. Similarly, it links all the subroutines by changing their code. The formal term used for this linking task is *binding*.

This discussion glossed over one point. Address 512 has special significance to the VMS system and the VAX; it marks the beginning of the second *page* of the image. As a debugging tool, addressing the first page is normally considered illegal. This helps the assembly language programmer find errors faster. Many algorithms tend to use small integer constants. This means that instructions like:

```
ADDL #5, COUNTER
```

meaning "add the value 5 to COUNTER," are often found in most assembly language programs. However, suppose that the "#" is mistakenly left off. Then the instruction means "add the contents of location 5 to COUNTER." But if location 5 is an illegal address, execution will be stopped immediately before the consequences of this error are propagated. Starting the image at 512 instead of 0 makes location 5 illegal, which protects the programmer from using small integers as addresses. Another common assembly language programmer's error is terminating a loop incorrectly. For instance, when clearing an array, if the loop termination condition is wrong, the clearing operation may extend into this illegal region. The resulting illegal memory reference that occurs helps the programmer find looping errors more quickly. These two types of errors are uncommon in Pascal code, but other compilers do not protect the user as well as Pascal does—FORTRAN is one example.

In summary, LINK performs the following functions to create the .EXE file:

- Searching the specified files for library subroutines
- Locating those subroutines and concatenating them with the user's specified OBJ files
- Relocating references across subroutines
- Relocating the subroutines

The output of LINK is called the image or executable file and is named with the .EXE extension. Figure 2.15 shows that the image file is divided into four parts. First, the *image header* contains summary information about the image, primarily the image's memory requirements and the disk location of the code. With these characteristics in one place, the entire file does not have to be read when the image is being set up for execution. The length of the image header is determined by the length of the image. The other three parts are the *image body*, which contains the actual VAX instructions; the *fixup information*, which locates the instructions in the image body that must be changed to complete the binding when the image is activated; and the *symbol tables*, which contain the names and locations of program variables used by DEBUG.

It should be pointed out that system routines such as Pascal and LINK

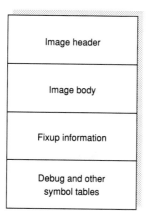

Figure 2.15. Image file format

are themselves images. They reside on the disk in a directory called SYS$SYSTEM, which can be easily verified with the DIRECTORY SYS$SYSTEM command. Software engineers at Digital linked Pascal to produce PASCAL.EXE, and an interesting question to ponder is how LINK was linked the first time. LINK also produces images for the entire operating system, which makes it a very powerful tool—a much more powerful tool than the average user will ever need.

2.7. Image Activation

Refer back to Figure 2.1 for the image activation, execution, and rundown cycle. This section describes activation, and the next section describes rundown. Every operating system must deal with the problem of starting an image, although the terms might vary. In VMS, the most common method of activating an image, from the user's standpoint, is with the DCL command RUN.

The user enters a RUN command to start an image. When DCL interprets that command, it calls on the VMS system service, $IMGACT, to perform image activation. This system service is not available to user programs. $IMGACT will be referred to here as the "image activator." The first step in activation is to examine the directory entry corresponding to the file name supplied with the RUN command. Without reading the file, its privileges are compared to the user's privileges to determine if execution is permitted. If the user is not permitted to execute the file, then an error message is displayed. But if execution privilege has been granted, the next step in image activation is to read the file and confirm the presence of an image header.

The image activator's primary task is to compute the image's memory requirements and store that information in the PHD, the process header. This computation is based on the memory information stored in the image header on disk. The image body is not loaded into memory when it is activated; rather, it is loaded as needed. The activator only prepares the process database so that the image body can be loaded into memory when required. Notice that the activator makes no judgment about the availability of memory. At this point, whether or not there is room in memory makes no difference in the activation algorithm; the memory availability decision is put off until the image begins execution.

In addition to determining how much memory the instructions require, the image activator computes the memory requirements of the *stack*. As you learned in an assembly language course, the stack is an essential part of any program and is used for calling subroutines and for data storage. Perhaps you noticed through the use of DEBUG that the stack pointer is automatically allocated prior to execution; no provision for it is made explicitly in the user's code.

Next, the image activator computes the privilege of the process that will be in effect while the image is executing. As described in the next section, VMS includes a mechanism to temporarily grant privileges to unprivileged processes.

After computing privilege, the image activator makes the final bindings, specifically to DEBUG (if specified by the user) and TRACEBACK (if not suppressed by the user). These two diagnostic routines are shared by all users. Finally, the image is activated either via DEBUG or at the user-supplied starting address called the *entry* (refer again to Figure 2.12, the DCL cycle). The image is now ready for execution.

The image activator must have all privileges, since it is designed to tamper with the very heart of VMS: the process database. Furthermore, it is running on the user's behalf as a part of his or her unprivileged process. Since a user cannot write code that will modify system data, how is this to be done at activation time? The process privilege must be raised temporarily.

To summarize, the following steps comprise image activation:

• Verifying file accessibility and type
• Computing the memory requirements of code and data and storing that information in the PHD
• Determining privileges of process

2.8. Image Rundown

After the image has executed, or when it encounters an unrecoverable error, it exits and returns to DCL. However, exiting is not simply a matter of executing an RET (Return from Subroutine) instruction. All evidence of it must be erased so that the next image to execute does not inherit any old data. For instance, occupied memory must be released and image-specific system services like outstanding I/O requests must be canceled. Notice by examining the DCL cycle in Figure 2.12 that rundown may not occur immediately because CTRL-Y exits permit internal commands to be performed. When the image does rundown, all of the activation logic is reversed, memory for the program and stack space is released, and privileges are restored to the process default value.

To elaborate on privilege manipulations performed at activation and rundown time, consider Figure 2.16. The default, or *authorized* privilege, is stored in the SYSUAF.DAT file and copied by LOGINOUT into the PHD when the process is created; it cannot be changed. During image execution, the *working* privilege is determined one of two ways. First, the normal user-created image executes with the authorized privilege. Second, many DCL commands require elevated privileges to perform their tasks. For instance, many of the SHOW command variations cause the image in a file called SHOW.EXE to be activated. In this case, process privileges are extracted from the KFE (Known File Entry) data structure and logically ORed with the authorized privilege to determine the working privilege. Notice that when the working privilege is computed, no privilege tests are made. Testing the working privilege is done as various system services are requested by the image. If the required privilege is not enabled, the service does not operate and returns an error flag, which in turn results in image termination.

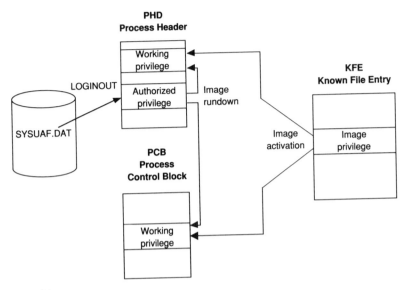

Figure 2.16. Process and image privileges

Image activation changes the working privilege, and image rundown resets it to the authorized value. For instance, the SHOW image privilege replaces a process's privilege in the PHD and PCB as part of the activation operation, thus raising the process privilege so it can show information about all processes on the system. Then, at image rundown, the authorized privilege reinitializes the PHD and PCB working privileges, thus lowering the process's privilege. Privilege inheritance takes place every time an image is activated; however, if the image is one the user created, there is no change to the process's privilege. This is a very important mechanism, and Chapter 7 will explain it in depth.

2.9. Subprocess Creation

Process creation is not limited to login. The user may also create processes in any of three ways: using the SPAWN command, in a program with the library routine LIB$SPAWN, or through the system service $CREPRC. The

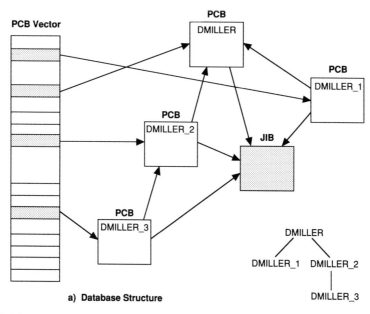

a) Database Structure

Figure 2.17. The job structure

b) Logical Structure

unprivileged user can only create what is termed a *subprocess*, which shares resources with the *parent* process. This design approach is a consequence of the subprocess implementation. Subprocesses use the same terminal the parent process uses, so sharing related resources, like I/O quotas, is a consistent and reasonable practice.

In VMS terms, the aggregate of the parent process and its subprocesses is called a *job*. Subprocesses are a resource and as such are controlled by the VMS operating system. As shown in the SHOW PROCESS display in Figure 2.11, the entry near the center on the right, labeled "Subprocess quota," shows the maximum number of subprocesses permitted. DMILLER is allowed 5. Just below the subprocess quota is an entry labeled "Max active jobs," which shows a value of 4. This means that DMILLER can log onto 4 terminals. By combining active jobs with subprocess quota, DMILLER can have 5 subprocesses active on each of the four terminals—4 processes and 20 subprocesses.

The data structures VMS uses to keep track of the processes in a job are illustrated in Figure 2.17. In part b of the figure, we see that the process

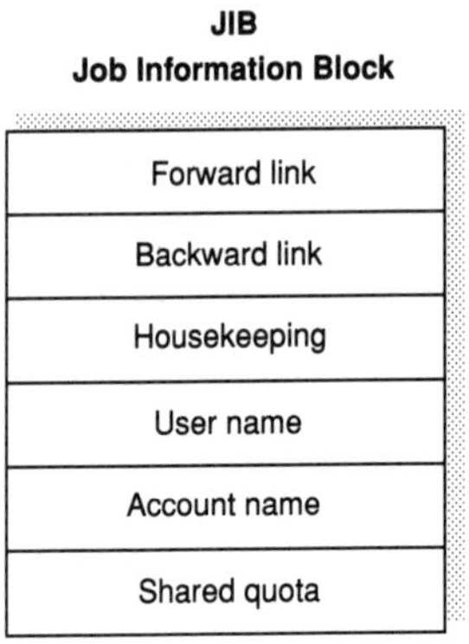

JIB
Job Information Block

Forward link
Backward link
Housekeeping
User name
Account name
Shared quota

Figure 2.18. Overview of the
JIB structure

DMILLER SPAWNed DMILLER_1 and DMILLER_2 because subprocesses point to their parent. Then, because subprocesses can SPAWN too, DMILLER_2 SPAWNed DMILLER_3. At the same time, note that each subprocess of the family tree is treated as an individual in the PCB vector in part a, and therefore they are scheduled and compete equally with one another for resources. Since they each have a PCB, they will have separate priorities, execution states, and so forth. All of the DMILLER family point to the same job information block (JIB), which contains the pooled quotas, including the active subprocess count. The JIB is detailed in Figure 2.18. The first three fields are the same as in the PCB, and the remaining fields contain information common to the family, like the user name, account name, and family quotas.

THE SPAWN COMMAND

SPAWN permits creation of a subprocess with the same privileges as the parent, so that a user may, for instance, compile a program and at the same time edit another program or send MAIL or execute PHONE. The general form of the SPAWN command is:

```
$SPAWN/qualifiers command
```

There are many qualifiers (or switches) on the SPAWN command, and this section illustrates just a few examples. Some qualifiers are illustrated below.

The command parameter is any DCL command, not including the "$" prompt. Both the qualifiers and the command are optional.

The first example shows how a user SPAWNs a subprocess to compile a very long program. To continue doing other things, like editing, while that program is running, the user can start the compilation with the command:

```
$ SPAWN/NOWAIT/NOTIFY PASCAL HMWK_DUE_10-2
```

which will:

- Create a subprocess, start PASCAL, and immediately return (the /NOWAIT qualifier) control to the parent.
- Execute the PASCAL image using HMWK_DUE_10-2 as input.
- When finished, display a message on the terminal (the /NOTIFY qualifier).
- Delete the subprocess.

The /NOWAIT qualifier tells DCL to continue execution of the parent process in parallel with the subprocess running Pascal. The subprocess is automatically named by suffixing a digit onto the process's name, such as DMILLER_1, as shown in Figure 2.17. However, the user has the option to name it. Once the SPAWN command has completed, and the subprocess has been created but not necessarily finished, the parent's "$" prompt will be displayed to indicate that any other command can be entered, say, another SPAWN command. Any DCL command may be entered in place of the PASCAL command in the example above, including RUN.

Errors associated with the previous PASCAL example will be displayed on the terminal, potentially disrupting any user activity such as an edit session. However, this default condition can be redirected through the use of the /OUTPUT qualifier on the SPAWN command. For example, if the user enters the command

```
$ SPAWN/NOWAIT/OUTPUT=SU.LIS SHOW USER
```

then all output from that command (the list of users logged in) will be stored in the newly created file SU.LIS.

Another example shows how to use SPAWN to create another command interpreter. That is, no command is specified, so DCL prompts for it. This is a neat trick but may be not too useful. The command looks like this:

```
$ SPAWN/NOWAIT/PROMPT="> "
```

This command changes the prompt character in this case to distinguish between the parent's prompt and the child's prompt. Sometimes, the user will receive a "$" prompt on the terminal and sometimes a ">" prompt; generally, they alternate. In this case, the subprocess is deleted when the LOGOUT command is entered in response to the ">" prompt. Only the parent process will be left running.

SPAWN is supported automatically in MAIL and some other Digital products, which is handy if the user has forgotten a user name or a file name in the middle of a MAIL session. The command:

```
MAIL> SPAWN
```

can be entered to create a subprocess. The MAIL prompt will disappear and the user will receive the "$" prompt instead. Then the commands TYPE or SEARCH can be used to locate the missing data. Finally, the LOGOUT command will return the user to MAIL.

2.10. Terminal LOGOUT

Process deletion is signaled when the user enters the LOGOUT command. At LOGIN, the system created the JIB (Job Information Block), PCB (Process Control Block), and PHD (Process Header). Now, these blocks must be unlinked—the JIB and PCB are returned to the VMS data block pool, and the PHD is freed for other processes. In unlinking and releasing these blocks, however, there is a difficulty: when the blocks disappear, the process logically disappears from the scheduler database. That is, the process must be executing to release its own blocks, but in releasing its blocks, it ceases to be a process and is therefore unable to execute. For example, the PCB is the scheduling entity, and without it, the process will never be considered for execution. So some care must be given to process destruction or else the database may not be wholly rid of the process.

As shown in Figure 2.19, when the user enters the LOGOUT command and DCL recognizes it, DCL calls a system service, $DELPRC (Delete Process; circle 1). The deletion algorithm is the inverse of the creation algorithm. This service first runs down the image left by DCL and then runs down (that is, removes) DCL by restoring any memory it occupied to the free memory pool. Notice that the process DMILLER is competing for the CPU resources up to this point without any difficulties; in other words,

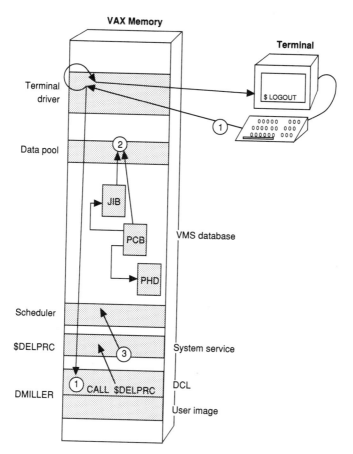

Figure 2.19. A process is deleted

$DELPRC is a subroutine running within the process. But, in order to release the database (circle 2), $DELPRC prohibits other processes from being scheduled; by doing so, it eliminates the possibility that the scheduler will encounter an inconsistent and incomplete database. Thus, higher-priority processes are temporarily usurped by the LOGOUT command. $CREPRC must resort to this trick too, for the same reason. Once these three data structures are annihilated, the process no longer exists. This means that when $DELPRC is finished, it cannot return to its calling point in DCL. So it calls the scheduler (circle 3), which causes the highest-priority computable process to execute.

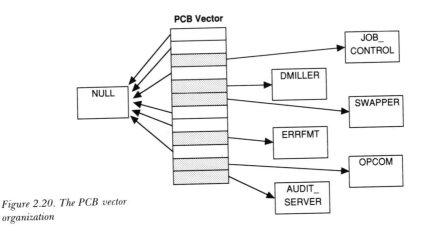

Figure 2.20. The PCB vector
organization

2.11. The Multi-User Database

Up to this point, only a single computer user has been considered. To complete the picture, we now consider what the process database looks like when there are multiple interactive users. The primary structure in the database is the PCB vector, each entry of which points to a PCB, which in turn points to additional information about the process.

Consider the PCB vector again and refer to Figure 2.20. Each entry of the PCB vector points to a process, a subprocess, or the NULL process. The NULL process is a historical artifact; earlier versions of the VMS operating system contained a priority zero process, called NULL, that looped indefinitely. The NULL process no longer is executed, and that pointer now serves to indicate that the PCB vector slot is empty. Unlike much of the rest of the process database, this vector is fixed; that is, its length is determined when the system is started and cannot be changed after the system is initialized. There is thus a limit on the number of processes supported by the system. Recall from Figure 2.17 that a subprocess takes a slot in the PCB vector. This means that all slots in the PCB vector can be full because of subprocess creation, not terminal logins.

Even without showing the JIB, PHD, and other blocks for each PCB specifically shown in Figure 2.20, it should be apparent that there are many separate blocks involved in the process database, each of which carries more information than can be dealt with here. This chapter presented a skeleton of the database; its fleshed-out version is much more complex. A more detailed but still incomplete picture of the database is found at the end of Chapter 4.

Certainly, the designers considered combining all of the database information into a single block. For instance, the JIB information could have all been contained in the primary PCB, and then the subprocess's PCB could have been a smaller version of the main PCB. The PHD seems to duplicate PCB information as well, so why not have combined the two? The justification for the complex structure chosen is difficult to explain, but the basic VMS design philosophy is to create data blocks only when necessary, giving the executing processes as much memory as possible.

Other reasons for the structure relate to performance issues that are beyond the scope of this book, but here are some heuristic observations. Data structures should have a fixed length whenever possible, because when fixed, the operating system code can access data within it by indexing alone. This is impossible if a particular data item is not in the same location in every copy of the block. To access variable-length structures, the code must be more complex; this increases operating system execution time—which equates to process overhead time. On the other hand, some variable-length structures are unavoidable. The image header, in particular, must have a variable portion because the image itself is variable. Variable-length structures conserve space within the system because they only use what they need. But if all system structures must be sized to accommodate the largest possible data item, then most of the time they will be partially empty because the maximum case is rarely encountered. The operating system designers must weigh these factors carefully before deciding on a particular database structure.

2.12. VMS Overview

The VMS operating system and the VAX architecture were designed at the same time, and the primary Digital design team kept both hardware and software issues in mind as they designed the two systems. The design of VMS cannot be easily separated from the VAX hardware features, and the unique VAX architecture can be traced to specific usages in the operating system.

One particular design feature we should introduce here is the four modes of protection enforced by the hardware. These four modes—kernel,

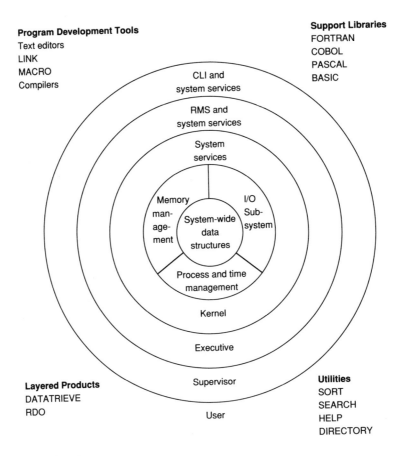

Program Development Tools
Text editors
LINK
MACRO
Compilers

Support Libraries
FORTRAN
COBOL
PASCAL
BASIC

Layered Products
DATATRIEVE
RDO

Utilities
SORT
SEARCH
HELP
DIRECTORY

Figure 2.21. Layered design of the VAX/VMS operating system

executive, supervisor, and user—are shown in Figure 2.21. Keep in mind that they are logical distinctions, not physical locations in memory. Kernel, the innermost (or most privileged) mode, is where the central functions of VMS execute. The full instruction set of the VAX is available to programs executing in kernel mode, and those instructions can access any portion of memory. The entire VMS database (scheduler, I/O, and memory databases) is accessible only in kernel mode, which means that if, for instance, a user-mode program attempted to access the VMS database, the hardware would abort the instruction and, hence, the program. Most of the system services operate in the kernel mode because they operate on the VMS database.

The executive mode is reserved for RMS, the record management services. This collection of services manages all the files on disk. VMS system services, like $QIOW, are called to do the actual disk I/O because programs operating at the executive level cannot access all the necessary memory locations or use certain instructions. Similarly, the CLI executes in supervisor mode, calling both RMS services and VMS system services to perform its functions. The least privileged and by far the greatest number of programs (i.e., user-written programs) execute in user mode, as do the utilities, compilers, editors, and certain Digital products.

The reason for layering the functions of the operating system is twofold. First and most obvious is the security; second, not so obvious but equally important, is maintaining system reliability. Programming errors can cause problems, and the operating system is prone to errors just as any program is. Although a bug in a program prohibiting further execution may be a nuisance to users, a bug in the operating system, which affects all users, can be a disaster. System programmers make a serious attempt to detect and correct operating system bugs prior to each release by systematically performing a series of routine in-house tests (alpha testing) and by permitting selected users (beta testing) to try out the new operating system for a time. But these testing techniques do not guarantee success, and eventually the operating system must be released to the general customer. Since it is never possible to remove all the bugs from a program, their influence must be minimized. If the system is layered, a bug at one level is less likely to cause an avalanche of errors resulting in a system crash. Layering does not eliminate errors, but it does isolate them.

MONITORING SYSTEM PERFORMANCE

Any user may observe various aspects of the operation of the system with the MONITOR command, and this text will show how to interpret the information this command provides. In particular, the MONITOR MODE command shows the percentage of the time the VAX is operating in the various protection modes. Figure 2.22 contains a typical display. In addition to the four modes mentioned, there are four other categories listed on the figure. At the top is Interrupt Stack, which shows I/O activity, and under it is the MP Synchronization line, which has to do with connecting several VAX computers together (MP means Multi-Processor, a topic not covered in this book). Further down is Compatibility Mode, which allows the VAX to emulate

```
                                    VAX/VMS Monitor Utility
              +-----+               TIME IN PROCESSOR MODES
              : CUR :                    on node BSU::
              +-----+               17-OCT-1990 20:22:26

                                   0       25      50      75      100
                                   + - - - + - - - + - - - + - - - -+
Interrupt Stack                16 :******
                                   :       :       :       :       :
MP Synchronization                 :
                                   :       :       :       :       :
Kernel Mode                    21 :*********
                                   :       :       :       :       :
Executive Mode                  7 :**
                                   :       :       :       :       :
Supervisor Mode                    :
                                   :       :       :       :       :
User Mode                      56 :*************************
                                   :       :       :       :       :
Compatibility Mode                 :
                                   :       :       :       :       :
Idle Time                          :
                                   + - - - + - - - + - - - + - - - -+
```

Figure 2.22. Typical display of
$ MONITOR MODE command

the PDP-11. This feature was available on early VAX models to encourage PDP-11 users to migrate to the VAX without changing their software. Idle Time is at the bottom. This is a condition that the operating system finds itself in when it has nothing to do, but it is not a separate VAX state.

2.13. Related Issues

Although this chapter's examples relate to interactive processes, a process does not necessarily have to be connected to a terminal. SWAPPER, ERRFMT, and JOB_CONTROL are VMS examples of *detached* processes. The unprivileged user cannot create detached processes because they are uncontrolled. That is, since they are not under control of a keyboard, their input and output are undefined.

There are certainly more ways than one to structure the process database. And all of them involve trade-offs. For instance, instead of being created on demand, the database could already exist in some limbo state to be filled in when a user logs in. The advantage to this method is that it takes less time to start a process, but it requires that unusable memory space be dedicated to all of the unused processes, thus limiting resources.

A more "open" operating system structure may not set a quota on resources, and if subprocess creation is unlimited, keeping track of subprocesses becomes easier for the operating system. But this ease comes at the risk of possible user abuse through accident, neglect, or mischief. Any user on such a system could create subprocesses infinitely, potentially locking out other users. Finally, an operating system may have exactly the same subprocess quota for all users, so that the quota maintenance algorithm is identical in all cases. The price paid for this design is that the maximum needs of one user determines the quota for all of them, again leading to the possibility of abuse.

All time-sharing operating systems allow processes to be given a variety of privileges because users have a variety of needs, knowledge, and skills. In a multi-user system, for instance, not every user should be allowed to modify the global user authorization data, but should have control over his or her privacy. And in the name of privacy, not every user needs to know what other users are doing on the system. On the other hand, the accounting system must know about all processes on the system, and the system manager should be able to monitor any user. The issue of privacy is still developing on some operating systems, especially in local area networks (LANs) of personal computers.

The distinction between the operating system and the command language varies broadly across the industry; for instance, UNIX (the operating system) permits the user to create shells (the command language) in much the same way that VMS does. Other operating systems are very restricted; IBM's JCL (Job Control Language) is embedded in the operating system, and the user has no way of modifying it.

Finally, the concept of the image as distinct from the process is unique to VMS. Most operating systems make no distinction between the two. The VMS design combines the command language interpreter and the command's image into a single process in order to reduce the overhead of creating a process every time a command must be executed. Again, this is a design issue related to system performance; creating and destroying a process are expensive in any operating system. The opposite view is that when another image is required, it is started as another process, which can also be expensive.

In studying VMS, one must keep in mind that it was designed for the VAX. It is unlike UNIX, which has become a generic, portable operating system.[2] An operating system that is optimized for the computer hardware, like VMS, requires less overhead, but is difficult to transfer to another architecture. On the other hand, a generic operating system, like UNIX, that is implemented on a particular hardware configuration may not be efficient but transferring it between machines is relatively simple. For instance, the layered design of the VMS system is uniquely suited to the VAX and would be very difficult to transfer to another architecture.

2.14. Summary

The process concept is pivotal in understanding an operating system, but when the concept is translated into code, there exists a very involved database that must be manipulated. It is a credit to operating system developers that this important concept appears trivial in today's operating systems. As with many great discoveries, this simplistic appearance bears witness to the elegance of the present solution. The process concept has been refined to the point it is at today only through thousands of man-hours of thought and development over many years.

This chapter described the creation and deletion of a VMS process and distinguished it from the activation and rundown of an image. We have also made a distinction between the operating system, VMS, and the command language interpreter, DCL—the principal user interface to the system. Some time was spent describing the DCL cycle to see how commands were executed in relation to images.

This chapter examined a portion of the VMS process database—the PCB vector, the PCB, the JIB, and the PHD blocks—and showed how these link together. It also indicated how multiple processes and subprocesses and their related structures were represented in the database. In addition to the blocks just mentioned, there are others in the database that become attached to the PCB as needed.

In describing these VMS entities, we have demonstrated the use of several common DCL commands. SHOW SYSTEM presented parts of the entire process database from the multi-user perspective. SHOW PROCESS showed detailed information concerning a single process. And SPAWN

---

2. UNIX was not originally intended to be portable, but its powerful design and compactness made it easy to become so.

illustrated how the user may create additional processes without logging into another terminal.

Having seen the examples and specifics of the VMS operating system, the reader is left with an impression of the importance and centrality of the process concept. Understanding comes through firsthand knowledge, not definitions.

ACRONYMS

$CREPRC	Create Process system service
$DELPRC	Delete Process system service
$GETJPI	Get Job/Process Information and wait system service
$HIBER	Hibernate system service
$IMGACT	Image Activator system service
$QIOW	Queue I/O and Wait system service
ACB	AST Control Block
ASCII	American Standard Code for Information Interchange
AST	Asynchronous System Trap
CALLG	Assembly instruction for subroutine call
CLI	Command Language Interpreter
COM	Computable process state
COMO	Computable Outswapped process state
CPU	Central Processing Unit
DCL	Digital Command Language
DOS	Disk Operating System
HIB	Hibernating process state
JCL	Job Control Language
JIB	Job Information Block
LEF	Local Event Flag wait process state
LOGIN.COM	User LOGIN file
PCB	Process Control Block
PHD	Process Header
PID	Process Identification
RET	Assembly instruction to return from subroutine
RMS	Record Management Services
RTL	Run-Time Library
SYSUAF.DAT	System User Authorization File

SHORT ANSWER EXERCISES

Note: Depending on the defaults your system manager has chosen, your account may have to be modified to do some of these exercises. For instance, you may not be permitted to SPAWN subprocesses.

1. Systematically determine which keys will start the login procedure.
2. If you add up the time column in Figure 2.5, it does not equal the "Uptime" value. Why is that?
3. Devise a method to determine how long a SPAWN command takes in the subprocess. It should take less time than a LOGIN does because the SYSUAF.DAT does not need to be consulted nor does the DCL image need to be started because it is already running.
4. Through the use of the SHOW SYSTEM command, devise a method to determine how much CPU time is required by JOB_CONTROL to create a process.
5. Through the use of the SHOW SYSTEM command, devise a method to determine how much CPU time is required by SWAPPER in the creation of a process.
6. Through the use of the SHOW SYSTEM command, devise a method to determine how much CPU time is consumed getting the process started at login time.
7. Devise a method to determine how long LOGOUT of a process takes.
8. When a RUN command is entered, the file's privileges are verified. If accessible, the file contents are checked next. What error message is produced when an attempt to RUN a nonexecutable file is made? Does RUN check the file extension?
9. Does the SHOW PROCESS/QUOTA show the dynamic value of subprocesses and jobs, or are they the static, UAF-specified value? Presumably, both the static and dynamic values are stored someplace. Dynamic subprocess quota means the static value minus the number of current subprocesses. Dynamic max active jobs is similarly defined.
10. What is the meaning of the (*) symbol in the SHOW PROCESS/SUBPROCESS display?

PAPERS

1. Discover SPAWN limitations, e.g., maximum number of children, condition of child when parent stops, the behavior of CTRL-Y, and other interesting facts. Organize this information into an informal report.

2. Research the history of the word "process." When was it introduced and by whom? Did it mean the same thing in that original usage as it means today? A good way to approach this question is to examine older operating systems textbooks.

Scheduling and Context Switching

3

It is convenient to describe a process as reading data, processing data, writing data, and then looping back to read more data. This single-user model is shown in operation over time (although without any particular time scale) in Figure 3.1. Chapter 1 indicated that the input/output (I/O) operations can easily dominate the execution time. Such a process is termed *I/O-bound* or *terminal-bound*. On the other hand, if the process requires only a little I/O, and does a lot of computations between I/O operations, it is called *compute-bound* or *CPU-bound*. In any case, when the process is performing I/O, the processor is idle.

What is wrong with the picture in Figure 3.1? It is an economic problem: three equally expensive resources of the computer—the memory, the processor, and the I/O devices—should be fully utilized to achieve the best return on investment. However, the figure shows that much of the time, two of them, the processor and the I/O devices, are idle. And because it is not full, memory is sometimes underutilized too. This peculiar behavior was first noticed in the 1950s, and the obvious solution then was to have more than one process share the three resources. But a process must reside in

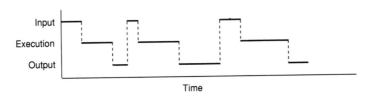

Figure 3.1. Execution of a typical process

memory (or in *core*, as memory was called then) in order to execute. Memory was expensive and therefore limited, so sharing was not very practical until the mid-1960s, when the price of memory began to drop dramatically. Soon, it became clear that several processes, not just two or three, could share the computer resources. Processes sharing memory are said to be *multiprogrammed.*

But "fitting" several processes together in a temporal sense is an impossible jigsaw puzzle. No combination of two or more processes will be so "complementary" that they mesh both I/O and processor time exactly. Look at part a of Figure 3.2, which was derived from Figure 3.1, except that the Input and Output lines were combined for simplicity. Next, in part b, a second process, Process B, is shown executing by itself. Then, in part c, the two processes are meshed to share the I/O and CPU resources. To see how part c is derived, look at the execution line only, and notice that the processor starts executing Process B (circle 1) and then switches to Process A (circle 2) when Process B performs I/O. As Process B finishes its I/O, an attempt to fit its next execution segment·fails because the processor is still busy with Process A, so Process B is delayed (circle 3), pushing subsequent Process B activities forward in time. This delay is indicated by the diagonal dotted lines for Process B only. Process A experiences no delays in this example. Because they access independent terminals, multiple I/O operations (circle 4) typically can be performed simultaneously; there is thus no waiting on the I/O line. Observe that there are still gaps in the diagram—for instance, the CPU is not 100 percent utilized, which means that a third process could be added to fill in the gaps more completely.

There are three points to be made about Figure 3.2. First, process waiting is necessary to make it work. Second, even though there are two processes in memory, there are still "empty" time slots in the input/output and execution portions of the scenario, so the computer system is not completely busy. And third, the total execution time of the two processes running

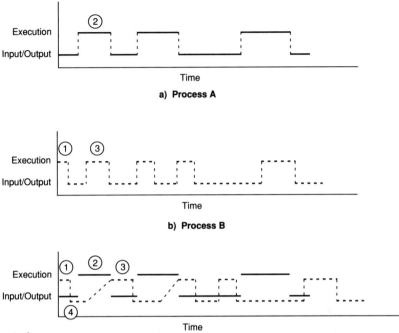

Figure 3.2. The composite execution of two processes

together is greater than if either had exclusive use of the machine. But if the two processes ran in serial, that is, if Process A executed first by itself, followed by B alone, the total execution time would be longer.

Elaborating on the topic of process waiting, another view of what happens to processes in an operating system is shown in the state diagram in Figure 3.3. A process entering the system (at system login, for instance) does not automatically begin executing, but is queued for execution like other processes in the system already. The *scheduler* selects which of the processes in the ready state should become the executing process. The one chosen may voluntarily give up the processor at a later time by exiting the system (at system logout), or it may perform an I/O operation and therefore wait until the operation is complete as illustrated in Figure 3.2. The I/O operation blocks the process from further activity, forcing it to wait in this state until the I/O has finished. Then the I/O completion logic changes the process's state from blocked to ready.

Controlling the execution switches between processes is the respon-

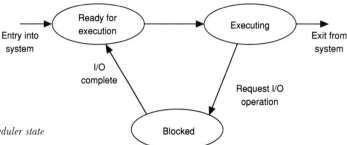

Figure 3.3. A scheduler state diagram

sibility of the process scheduler. It may seem from our example that the scheduler is rather trivial, its only job is to choose between processes, but actually it is quite complex. This chapter develops a simplified version of the scheduler for illustration.

The operating system scheduler is usually defined as the program that assigns the processor *resource* to an executable process. However, processor scheduling is not the only scheduling that an operating system must do. Scheduling is also necessary for terminals: the system must decide which terminal to service first if two users strike a key simultaneously, and in this case, the hardware interrupt scheme usually dictates the service order as first come, first served. Line printers also need scheduling. One user's listing cannot be interrupted by another listing request, but suppose a second and then a third listing request is sent to the printer program. Should these requests be scheduled first come, first served? Still another scheduling task for the system is for the disk resource. When a process requests files from the disk, chances are there are other requests outstanding too.

The operating system is responsible for scheduling many resources in a multi-user environment, and for this reason, it is often referred to as a *multi-resource manager*. This chapter only describes the problem of scheduling the processor.

3.1. Scheduling Terms

To describe the scheduler fully requires defining several terms. To begin, there are three distinct scheduling algorithms: batch, interactive, and real-time. From the user's standpoint, the scheduler algorithm establishes the nature of the operating system. For instance, one may say that VMS is a time-sharing operating system. However, the operating system is more than a scheduler, as shown in Chapter 2. Indeed, the VMS scheduler is less than 100 lines of code, yet all of VMS contains more than two million lines.

BATCH SYSTEMS

A *batch* system collects a sequence of requests, a job, from a user—for example, a compile, followed by a link, and then an execute—and runs them at a time it determines is optimal. That is, the request may be delayed for a time. Designed for a static production situation like payroll or monthly invoicing, a batch system can either execute jobs in serial (one at a time) or in parallel (multiprogram), as depicted in Figure 3.2. This latter method is predominant today.

INTERACTIVE SYSTEMS

An *interactive* system (also called *terminal, conversational, time-sharing*, and occasionally *time-slicing*) is one in which the user directs each step of the request and the system responds to it immediately. The interactive system is user-adaptive and geared to problem solving. It is well suited to the research environment, where the requests are apt to change frequently.

In an interactive system, when two processes are ready to be executed, instead of one waiting for the other to complete, as in Figure 3.2, the two share the processor. Figure 3.4 is adapted from the example in Figure 3.2. Notice in the figure that two processes, KALHONE (the solid line) and STINGRAY (the shaded line), seem to be executing simultaneously. But this cannot happen because the CPU can only execute one instruction at a time. The enlarged area shows what is actually taking place. The rectangles represent CPU time the process is in the execution state. The spaces between the rectangles represent the time that the process is waiting in the ready-for-execution state. The figure implies that one process executes for a small amount of time, called a *quantum*, and then the other executes, with the result that neither process is delayed in entering the execution phase. However, the time a particular process takes to complete execution is certain to be longer in interactive systems even though the execution time, or the number of instructions the process executes, is the same as in the batch case.

There is one fundamental difference between batch and interactive systems. In an interactive system, no single process is allowed to control the

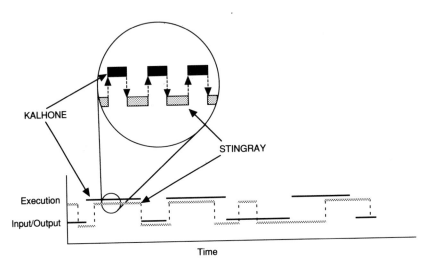

KALHONE

STINGRAY

Execution

Input/Output

Time

Figure 3.4. Time-sharing the
processes in Figure 3-2

CPU for more than a few tenths of a second, or else the other users on the system will experience a longer than acceptable *response-time*. In a batch system, no such constraint is required (although there may be other constraints). Therefore, the scheduler in an interactive operating system must intervene to reassign the executing process more often than a batch system scheduler does.

The batch scheduler is needed only occasionally—when a process relinquishes the processor voluntarily. But the interactive operating system scheduler executes more often, so less processor time is available for the users than in a batch system. In other words, scheduler *overhead* is higher in interactive systems than in batch systems, and interactive users pay a premium for the *on-line* convenience.

However, the high overhead is worth the expense. Studies in the late 1960s indicated that interactive programmers are not as likely to spend as much time looking for errors as batch programmers are, so they tend to use more of the computer resource. But the interactive user finishes the task sooner and so is more productive than the batch user. There is a trade-off to consider: the batch user takes longer, but spends less money in computer time; whereas the interactive user is faster, but requires more computer time. The conclusion is that both economics and schedule must be considered when selecting batch or interactive development systems.

Lately, *transaction* systems have been replacing traditional batch applications. These are systems that support ATMs (Automatic Teller Machines), for example. This type of operating system can be described roughly as an interactive batch system, which means that when the transaction is presented to the computer system, it is processed in its entirety as quickly as possible.

REAL-TIME SYSTEMS

The third type of operating system, called *real-time,* controls such systems as automobile carburation and ignition, airborne weapons, and oil refineries. Real-time operating systems must accept data from many transducers or sensors (temperature, radar returns, flow rates, velocity, and so forth), then make computations and decisions based on that data, and finally transmit control signals to other components (such as heaters, valves, nozzles, actuators, and flaps). That is, as quickly as the transducer data is available, computations must be made and the control signals generated. A real-time system must be able to accept input, process it, produce output, and then be ready to accept more input with minimal delay, and it must be able to keep up with the input data with little or no queuing. A jet fighter, for example, flies 1,000 feet per second, so the operating system-application combination must react within milliseconds to be effective.

NONPREEMPTIVE AND PREEMPTIVE SCHEDULING

There is an attribute, or characteristic, associated with these three operating systems: preemptive or nonpreemptive.

Early operating systems were designed to be *nonpreemptive* (at least, that is what they are called now). This means that a process controls the processor until it voluntarily gives it up, either by completing execution or by making a system request, such as a read or write operation, requiring that the process wait. That is, when the process requests certain system services and it can no longer run, it gives up the processor. This results in scheduler activation to locate and start another process. Figure 3.2 shows a nonpreemptive system.

In nonpreemptive scheduling, when the system completes a request,

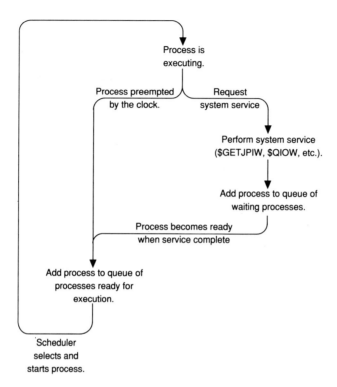

Figure 3.5. Preemptive
scheduling

such as I/O, for a process, that process will have to wait until some other process relinquishes control of the processor before the original process can continue. The result is that one process cannot take control of the processor from another unless the latter willingly relinquishes it.

On the other hand, a *preemptive* system, represented by Figure 3.4, permits one process to take the processor away from another. In a time-sharing system, whenever a process is selected for execution, the scheduler sets a countdown timer. Then, if that process does not give up the CPU before the timer expires, the operating system regains control via an interrupt and reactivates the scheduler. The scheduler then removes the running process from execution and selects another to run. This algorithm was outlined in Figure 2.2 and is presented again in Figure 3.5 with a system service emphasis added. Notice that a preemptive system includes nonpreemptive logic too, in that a process may voluntarily give up processor through a specific system service request such as $GETJPIW or $QIOW.

PRIORITY

Finally, each process has a *priority*. Priority and preemption are closely related, but priority can be applied to schedulers on all three types of operating systems. In batch systems, a priority can be given to the job. When one job is complete, the scheduler scans all the remaining jobs and selects the highest-priority one to execute next. In time-sharing and real-time systems, each process is assigned a priority by the system, the user, the designer, or the system manager, and a higher priority implies more immediate service from the processor. When a system is designed with a priority scheme, then preemption may also come into play in the following manner: if Process A becomes ready while Process B is executing, the scheduler is called to determine if B should continue running or if A should preempt it. The higher-priority process will be chosen. On the other hand, as shown in Figure 2.2, interrupts cause temporary process discontinuation in order to respond to a hardware request. I/O interrupts are not considered to be preemptive. I/O interrupt processing is required in all systems for maintaining active use of the I/O devices.

COMPARISON OF INTERACTIVE AND REAL-TIME SYSTEMS

Both interactive and real-time systems must respond to external stimuli: the interactive system reacts to user-created terminal requests, and the real-time system reacts to transducer reports. One difference between the two is that all interactive terminals are treated equally, and time quantum preemption is required to implement equality, but real-time interrupts are prioritized by the designers. When a real-time process is activated by a sensor interrupt, the ISR (interrupt service routine) controls the processor until it completes unless a higher-priority sensor interrupts and needs service; there is no quantum preemption. Another difference is that an interactive system is generalized and operates over a wide range of demands and user loads; occasionally, large demands degrade its response time. But a real-time system is designed for a specific environment and contains a limited, known set of well-characterized processes. The system is "tuned" to its environment and is designed to operate at peak efficiency under all known load conditions.

System type	Characteristic		
	Time-shared	Preemptive	Priority
Batch	no	no	optional
Interactive	yes	yes	optional
Real-time	no	yes	yes

Figure 3.6. Summary of scheduling characteristics

Figure 3.6 summarizes the six terms and how they relate to each other. In its pure form, a batch system is neither time-shared nor preemptive, but it may contain a priority scheme. Interactive systems time-share the processor, and they use preemption to implement time-sharing. These two characteristics result in more operating system overhead than batch systems do. Interactive systems usually include a priority scheme, although it is not required. Real-time systems do not time-share and are preemptive according to a priority assigned by the designers. The highest-priority process always executes first, and processes with equal priority are commonly scheduled on a first-in-first-out (FIFO) basis.

To clarify the difference between an interrupt and a preemption, remember than an interrupt is caused by a hardware event. Literally, the executing process is interrupted (and stopped) and an interrupt service routine begins execution in order to act on the hardware event. When the interrupt processing is complete, either the interrupted process can be resumed or it can be preempted by a higher-priority process. Figure 2.2 depicted this duality.

3.2. The Scheduling Problem and Goals

This section examines the problem facing the CPU scheduler and describes several algorithms to be used in resolving it. This is what the scheduler must do: from among the processes that *are able* to execute, it must decide which one *will* execute. There are many ways to do this depending on the goals or policies of the designers. This section outlines several algorithms, no one of which can fulfill the desired goals perfectly. In fact, useful schedulers are composites of these algorithms. After the general techniques are described, a working scheduler is illustrated by examining VMS in detail to show how the various methods can be combined.

The discussion of scheduling techniques begins with a look at possible goals the scheduler can use to decide which of several processes should be executed. To put this another way, what is it that the scheduler is attempting to accomplish? Does it merely need to keep the processor busy or does it have other objectives? It turns out that there are many conflicting objectives presented to the scheduling algorithm.

Here are several realistic goals the scheduler may attempt to achieve in the three operating system environments: batch, interactive, and real-time.

First In, First Out (FIFO). This goal applies only to batch systems. The first job presented to the scheduler is executed to completion and then returned to the user, and then the next one is executed. Jobs are processed one at a time, in a serial fashion, which is fair because no one user has an advantage over any other user. If the operating system is extended to service multiple users in batch mode, FIFO is impractical and undesirable because the execution times of the jobs vary. A scheme involving priority must be included.

Maximize Throughput. This goal, which applies only to batch systems, forces as many jobs through the CPU resource per unit time as possible. This scheme is different from FIFO. The arrival order is not considered, but, instead, the shortest job is selected to run first. Selecting the short job first means that more jobs will be processed in a unit of time. A single long job may take a very long time to be completely executed because smaller jobs will step ahead of it to attain the throughput goal. This goal can be applied to either a single user or a multiprogrammed batch system.

Minimize Turnaround. This goal also applies only to batch systems. The idea is to complete an "average" job as soon as possible so as to minimize the amount of wall-clock time an average user must wait for completion. This measure applies to individual jobs, not the aggregate. By minimizing the amount of time the average user must wait, the system can satisfy the majority of the user community. The scheduler operates from information provided by the user, normally an estimate of execution time. To determine the average execution time of jobs in the queue, the scheduler examines all of them. But this implementation has several difficulties. Nonaverage users are entitled to a reasonable turnaround too; they cannot be forced to wait for several hours if their estimate is merely 50 percent higher than the average. If they are forced to wait too long or too often, they may deliberately misrepresent information in order to be treated as average. This behavior must be discouraged so that all estimates will be accurate. The most common approach of enforcing this is to discontinue execution when the estimate is exceeded.

In a comparison of these three goals, it becomes clear that a scheduler cannot achieve all of them. To maximize throughput, the scheduler must concentrate on the shortest jobs first, and to minimize turnaround, it must concentrate on the average job. Moreover, the FIFO goal does not allow the scheduler to pick either of the other methods as goals.

Maximize Consistency. For maximum consistency in batch systems, a job should run for the same amount of wall-clock time every time it executes, day in and day out. For maximum consistency in interactive systems, the job should expend the same amount of CPU time every time it executes. The latter is a difficult goal to attain in a time-sharing system because multiple users' demands vary with the time of day. Consistency is important in an operational environment. For instance, it is important to know how long it will take to generate payroll checks so that the task can be completed before it is time for the checks to be handed out.

Minimize Turnaround to the Most Important Customer. This goal applies to either batch or interactive systems. The user community is pyramid-like: a few users are at the apex, while the majority lie at the base or in between. All users are not equal in a system with this goal. There are many (non-technical) reasons for this type of scheduling; for example, some users are willing to pay more for faster service, and some jobs are simply deemed more important. A priority-like characteristic must be attached to each job so that the scheduler can recognize its importance.

Minimize Keyboard Response Time. Applied only to interactive systems, the goal is to make a single user think he or she is the only one using the system. Every interactive system must take a certain amount of time to react. The user normally equates keyboard echo time to response time. For a user to believe the system is fast, the response time must be short, but "fast" is a subjective measure and varies according to the particular task at hand. When editing, a user is normally satisfied if each keystroke is echoed in less than about half a second, but finds an echo longer than two to three seconds very annoying. On the other hand, a user must be willing to wait much longer for a Pascal compilation because more computation is involved.

Maximize Utilization of Expensive Components. The various components of the computer (memory, processor, disks, printers, etc.) can be compared by their cost per unit of time, as in dollars per second. From an accountant's standpoint, it makes sense to get the maximum use out of the more expensive components, even at the risk of underutilizing those that are less expensive. For example, since the disk drive is more expensive than a printer, an effort should be made to execute processes that use the disk a lot, whether or not they use the printer. A process that uses both the disk and the printer is the most welcome process in this system, but one that uses more disk than printer is the next choice.

For a real-time system to react quickly to stimuli external to the computer, the goal of its design should be to deliver an interrupt to a process as quickly as possible. That is, the measurement tranducers are attached to the computer in such a way as to generate an interrupt whenever any external stimuli are available. The problem these systems must address is that the measurement device takes a finite time to collect data and transform it into a digital format. Usually, it does some sort of averaging as well. The data are not simply streaming into the computer continuously, but arrive discretely, from time to time. This permits the processor to accept data from several sources, do the necessary computations, and generate output control signals. Normally, real-time systems process data from several sources— human as well as mechanical. So, in a sense, real-time operating systems multiprogram the processes to accommodate multiple sensors. The process for which the sensor data is intended must operate on the data and voluntarily yield the CPU before the next data packet arrival. However, not all interrupts are equal in importance, and a real-time system designer needs to define a hierarchy of interrupt priorities. The goal of a real-time system is to minimize operating system overhead while maximizing the application's CPU utilization.

Minimize Interrupt Delivery Time to a Process. This goal applies only to real-time systems, which are so named because they respond to actual, real-world events as fast as necessary. When data collected by external sensors is available, the host computer is signaled by an interrupt. The host reads the data and delivers it to a process. The object is to minimize the delay caused by the operating system and deliver the data as quickly as possible to the processing program.

This section described a number of goals a scheduler can attain. Since many of these goals conflict, the scheduler cannot attain them all, so a conscious decision must be made by the designers (and, perhaps, the sales manager) to design the scheduler to appeal to a certain marketplace. Usually an operating system can support only one scheduling technique, batch, time-sharing, or real-time, although a few support batch and time-sharing simultaneously. The VMS operating system is unusual in that it combines all three. The scheduler is constructed in such a way that it can achieve multiple goals.

3.3. General Scheduling Solutions

This section discusses algorithms the scheduler can employ to support the previously defined goals. Even though some goals suggest a solution, for example FIFO, others, like minimize keyboard time, do not. In every case, it is presumed that the scheduler has access to a queue of processes that are eligible for execution, and it must select one of them according to one of the following techniques.

Round Robin or FIFO. Round robin is FIFO applied in either a batch or time-sharing environment. Where FIFO selects the first process on the list and permits it to execute until it is done, round robin achieves a fair distribution of the processor among several eligible time-share processes. These eligible processes are arranged in a queue; the process at the front of the queue is the next to run. In time-sharing systems, when quantum expires, the process is stopped and moved to the end of the queue and the next process on the queue is run. The amount of time in a quantum ranges from 0.01 to 0.1 seconds. In a batch system, when a process relinquishes the processor to perform a system service, the scheduler selects the next available process. In either system, an unblocked process is added to the end of the ready queue.

Shortest Job First (SJF). This algorithm is applied to batch systems that need to maximize throughput. The scheduler selects the shortest job from the ready queue. To do this, it must have some information about each job's estimated execution time which, in a batch system, is normally provided by the user. However, SJF can apply to other scheduling systems within the operating system. In particular, the VMS operating system applies this algorithm to its print queues, and in this case, the execution time is not explicit but derived; it is directly proportional to the length of the file to be printed.

Shortest Remaining Time (SRT). This batch scheduling algorithm is a variation on the "shortest job first" algorithm. When the process gives up the processor, its remaining execution time is computed by subtracting the actual execution time from the estimated execution time. Then the scheduler executes the "shortest job" remaining in the ready queue. The distinction between the SJF and the SRT algorithms is that the estimated execution time is decremented as execution progresses in the SRT algorithm; this allows the scheduler to reevaluate the execution order periodically. The SJF algorithm does not include a reevaluation step; the shortest job in the queue has priority over all others.

Priority. Processes are ordered according to a priority scheme. Only when the highest-priority process voluntarily relinquishes the processor will another process be selected to execute. If a high-priority process becomes able to execute, it will preempt the executing process with a lower priority. The preempted process must wait to continue until no higher-priority process is ready.

If the system permits more than one process at each priority level, multiple processes can be eligible for execution at a given priority level. In this case, some method to break the tie must be devised, and the easiest solution is to apply round robin within each priority level, thus combining these two scheduling algorithms. The combination creates the data structure depicted in Figure 3.7. This data structure contains all processes eligible for execution, with processes at various levels linked together in a queue. The scheduler will select the first process in the highest-priority queue, AWCS in the example. Newly unblocked processes will be added to the end of the queue corresponding to their priority. When AWCS exhausts its quantum, it is placed at the end of the queue, and process SILK is selected for execution. When there are no processes left at level k, the first process at level k-1 (MOOSE in the figure) is selected. If a priority k process (call it SPEEDBALL) becomes unblocked while MOOSE is executing, it is preempted—that is, MOOSE is stopped and SPEEDBALL is started. This hybrid of priority and round robin is similar to the VMS scheduling algorithm.

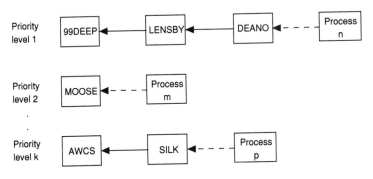

*Figure 3.7. Priority/round robin
data structure*

Aging. An aging technique, generally used in conjunction with priority, is exploited by both batch and time-sharing systems. In a batch system that guarantees turnaround time, the priority is aged, or raised, to ensure that a process approaching its deadline will finish in time.

In a time-sharing system, the process priority is dynamically modified to match its activity. For example, in VMS, priority is raised on I/O-bound processes and lowered on CPU-bound ones.

Feedback. The feedback technique is another term for the aging algorithm when applied to interactive systems, in which the criteria is not age but process response time. A process doing a lot of terminal I/O (thus using the processor very little) is aged to a higher priority. Increasing the priority of I/O-bound processes minimizes the response time at very little expense in terms of processor utilization. A time-shared process that uses the processor a lot is no longer interactive[1] and should not be allowed to compete with processes that are still interactive. A CPU-bound process has its priority decreased so it no longer competes with I/O-bound processes. For example, an editor process's priority is raised because it is highly interactive, and a Pascal compilation lowers the priority because it requires no user intervention. The user editing on the system thinks it is very fast, while the user waiting for the compilation to finish is given no cues at all about the system's response time.

---

1. Not interactive in this instance means that the user is not entering data, the process is not displaying data, and the processor is being used much of the time.

System type	Algorithm				
	Round robin	Shortest job first	Shortest remaining time	Priority	Aging or feedback
Batch	yes	yes	yes	optional	optional
Interactive	yes	no	no	usually	usually
Real-time	yes	no	no	yes	no

Figure 3.8. Summary of scheduling algorithms

Figure 3.8 summarizes the processor scheduling algorithm's usage in the three system types. A "yes" means that an algorithm may be found in a given operating system, depending on the designers' decision. As the figure shows, round robin can be found in all types of operating systems, whereas SJF and SRT can be found only in batch systems. Priority can be found in batch, is normally found in time-share systems, and will always be found in real-time systems. And aging or feedback algorithm can be found, if priority is included, in batch or time-sharing systems, but never in real-time systems.

3.4. An Example Program: Hibernate

The example program in this section causes a process to go through several state changes, which can be monitored using tools supplied by VMS. Figure 3.9 contains an example Pascal program showing, first, how a process advances through scheduling states under programmer control and, second, how to use and call several common system services from a Pascal program.

The program itself is straightforward: it asks the system for the time of day (line 29) and displays it (line 30). Then it behaves like an alarm clock; it schedules a wake-up call 30 seconds from now and puts itself into a state called *hibernate* (lines 31 and 32). This is a form of blocked state with particular characteristics. Finally, when the system wakes up the process, the program again requests the time and displays it (lines 33 and 34).

The following is a line-by-line explanation of the code. This is necessary because several nonstandard Pascal statements are employed in the code and the calls to system services may be new to many readers.

```
 1        {===================================================}
 2        {                                                   }
 3        {                    TIMER.PAS                      }
 4        {                                                   }
 5        {===================================================}
 6                     { get the required info for system_services }
 7 [INHERIT ( 'SYS$LIBRARY:STARLET' ) ]
 8
 9        {===================================================}
10        {        This program will display the time and   }
11        {        date, hibernate for 30 seconds.          }
12        {===================================================}
13
14 PROGRAM TIMER (INPUT, OUTPUT);
15
16 TYPE
17     $QUAD = RECORD              { define a quadword for the time }
18       i : UNSIGNED;
         j : INTEGER;
19     END;
20
21 VAR                                        { time sent to $BINTIM }
22     ascii_time : PACKED ARRAY [1..20] OF CHAR;
23     binary_time : $QUAD;            { time returned from $BINTIM }
                                       { time and date variable }
24     now_time : PACKED ARRAY [1..23] OF CHAR;
25
26 BEGIN
27     ascii_time := '0 0:0:30';                { 30 second delta time }
                                        { convert 30 secs to binary form }
28     $BINTIM ( ascii_time, binary_time );
29     $ASCTIM (TIMBUF := now_time);        { get the current time }
30     WRITELN (now_time);                      { and print it out }
31     IF odd ( $SCHDWK ( DAYTIM := binary_time ) ) THEN
                                        { if no error on the wake-up }
                                                  { then hibernate }
32        $HIBER;
33     $ASCTIM (TIMBUF := now_time);        { get the current time }
34     WRITELN (now_time);                      { and print it out }
35 END.
```

Figure 3.9. A Pascal program
that hibernates

Line 7. Pascal requires that all variables and subprograms be defined before they are referenced. To save the Pascal programmer the task of coding the system service declarations, Digital has included a family of files called STARLET. The most efficient way to use these definitions is with the INHERIT directive, which causes SYS$LIBRARY:STARLET.PEN to be accessed by the Pascal compiler. (The .PEN file is not printable, but there is a printable version in the same directory called STARLET.PAS; it is very lengthy—well over 100 pages—so it is not wise to print it. If you are curious, use one of the editors to examine how the various system services are defined.) When the program is linked, STARLET.OLB, the object library of system services, is automatically accessed by LINK. STARLET.MLB is a Macro library and contains the same information as STARLET.PAS. It is intended for use by Macro assembly language programmers.

Lines 17–19. One of the system services this program calls, $BINTIM, requires a quadword. *Quadword* is a nonstandard Pascal TYPE and must be defined. A quadword is eight bytes long, so the closest convenient definition is two INTEGERs. The least significant half, i, is declared UNSIGNED while the most significant half, j, is a signed INTEGER. Although correctly defined, the program does no arithmetic with $QUAD variables. The Digital convention for naming nonstandard TYPEs includes a leading "$", as in $QUAD.

Line 23. The newly defined TYPE $QUAD is used to define the variable "binary_time."

Lines 27–28. The internal format of time maintained by VMS seems very strange indeed. It is referenced to midnight, November 17, 1858—the base time for The Smithsonian Institution's astronomical calendar—and the units are hundreds of nanoseconds, which means the number gets to be quite large. The exact form is not important, however, because VMS provides a system service to convert from an ASCII character sequence to the internal form; this is $BINTIM. The ASCII string is passed into $BINTIM in the form 0 days, 0 hours, 0 minutes, and 30 seconds, and $BINTIM returns with the equivalent internal form in "binary_time." As indicated in the comment, the ASCII input form is called "delta" time, which means "the time from now." The value returned in binary_time will be used in line 31. A second form of time also recognized by $BINTIM is called "absolute" time. The syntax of absolute time is dd-mmm-yyyy:hh:mm:ss. The "-" and ":" are required punctuation; "dd" is the day; "mmm" is a three-letter month;

"yyyy" is the year; and "hh," "mm," and "ss" are hours, minutes, and seconds, respectively.

$BINTIM is actually a FUNCTION, but VAX Pascal permits calling any FUNCTION as if it were a PROCEDURE. If $BINTIM is used as a FUNCTION, the INTEGER value returned indicates success or failure status of the conversion. All system services are functions and report to the calling routine in the same way. $BINTIM cannot fail because it is converting a valid time string. If there is any question as to the validity of the time string, the $BINTIM status should be checked. Line 31 shows a method of examining the system service call return status.

Lines 29–30. $ASCTIM is called to ask the VMS system for the current time; it is returned in the argument in ASCII format and then displayed by the WRITELN call. The $ASCTIM call is a nonstandard Pascal usage. It has four arguments that the user can verify by typing HELP SYSTEM_ SERVICES $ASCTIM or by looking at STARLET.PAS with an editor. But the particular form of the call on line 29, that is, the "tell-me-what-time-it-is" request requires only one argument, and the other three default properly. For reference, the HELP display indicates which arguments are required and which are optional. In this particular case, to supply this single argument, the formal parameter, TIMBUF, is named on the left side of the assignment operator (: =), and the actual parameter, "now_time," is named on the right side. In VAX Pascal, any FUNCTION or PROCEDURE can be called this way; this form of the argument list does not require the arguments to be in any order, nor do all the arguments have to be present. Calling $ASCTIM in this mode cannot result in an error.

Lines 31–32. The $SCHDWK (Schedule Wake-up) call requires one argument—namely, the time to wake up. It sets a process alarm clock to go off in 30 seconds, which is the value derived from the $BINTIM call. If setting the alarm is successful, the $HIBER (Hibernate) call puts the process to "sleep" by putting it in a blocked state called HIB. This system service changes the state of the process from CUR to HIB, and thus the process becomes ineligible for execution. When the alarm trips, the VMS operating system will change the process state back to COM (computable), and thus it becomes eligible to run again.

If the returned value of a VMS system service is ODD, the routine was successful; an even value indicates an error. The actual value returned shows what kind of error was encountered, and the meanings of these values

```
$ RUN TIMER

   3-DEC-1990 11:15:13.56
   3-DEC-1990 11:15:43.80
```

Figure 3.10. Output of hiber-
nating Pascal program

are found in the VMS documentation. Notice that the program checks the return status of the $SCHDWK call. If $SCHDWK returns an ODD value (no error), then the $HIBER call occurs. If $SCHDWK returns an even value (error), the program does not hibernate.

Lines 33–35. Once again, $ASCTIM is called to get the current time, the time is displayed, and the program exits.

Figure 3.10 contains actual output produced by the execution of this program. In response to executing, two lines display the time. A most interesting observation should be made however: the difference between the two times is 30.24 seconds, even though TIMER requested a 30-second hibernation; almost a quarter second is unaccounted for. You might suspect that the WRITELN explains this discrepancy, but examination of the program reveals that the code between the two $ASCTIM calls contains only one WRITELN. The terminal that executed this TIMER example runs at 1,200 baud, so the approximately 25 characters account for only 0.208 seconds (25 characters × 10 bits/character/1,200 bits/second). The 0.03-second remainder can be attributed to $SCHDWK and $HIBER, which means a system service costs 10 milliseconds. However, usually 1 millisecond (0.001 seconds) is estimated for a system service call. The remaining time must be explained by the fact that TIMER was executing on a time-sharing system; 0.03 seconds were used by some other process that was running after TIMER came out of hibernation. In other words, this process did not preempt the running process.

It might be interesting to execute TIMER several times to see what the average discrepancy is. This experiment should be performed both on a busy system and on an idle one to prove that other processes delayed the execution of TIMER when it finished hibernating. If the system is idle, the time difference should get very close to 30.21, never less. On a busy system, that difference can be larger because more processes are in the COM queue when TIMER is added; hence, it must wait for all the others.

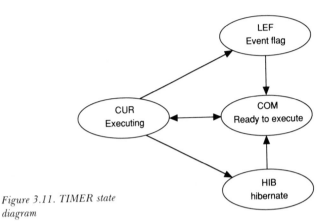

Figure 3.11. TIMER state diagram

3.5. An Elaboration of the Example

The user's view of the hibernating process has been presented. This section now examines the operating system's view. Before the execution of the Pascal program TIMER, the process has already been created because the terminal is logged on and DCL is executing. It is the RUN command that causes the image TIMER to begin executing within the process, in place of DCL. When the TIMER image is executing, it controls the process until TIMER exits back to DCL.

When TIMER executes, it will force the process into a variety of execution state changes, which are depicted in Figure 3.11. Briefly, when executing (in the CUR state), TIMER can voluntarily change to one of two blocked states: LEF (Wait for a Local Event Flag) during a WRITELN service request, or HIB (Hibernate) because of the $HIBER service request. Movement from the two blocked states, LEF and HIB, is permitted only into COM, never into the CUR state directly. The scheduler changes the state from COM to CUR. Thus, the user program has some control over the state of the process, but other state changes take place because of the VMS scheduler.

Figure 3.12 presents a time-ordered version of these state changes. A more detailed, system-oriented explanation of TIMER follows here. The figure is not correctly scaled in the time direction, but is intended to show the sequence of state changes. Each plateau shown represents a state. In addition to the state changes depicted in Figure 3.12, the process may also

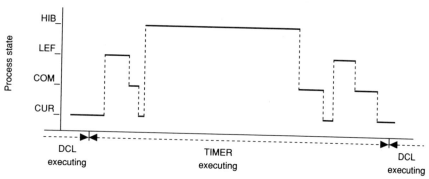

Figure 3.12. TIMER state transitions over time

be preempted by other processes and its state changed from CUR to COM numerous times, but those changes are not indicated in the figure.

While looking at Figure 3.12 more closely, also refer to the program listing in Figure 3.9 as the description proceeds. The RUN command requests DCL to start the TIMER image. Of course, the process must be currently running (CUR) for image activation to begin. Once TIMER commences execution, it makes two system service calls ($BINTIM and $ASC-TIM), which do not cause state changes, and then does the first WRITELN (line 30) to display the current time. As discussed in Chapter 1, the WRITELN causes a third system service call, $QIOW. So the process waits in state LEF while the data is being transmitted to the terminal.

When the data transmission is complete, the process becomes computable (COM) once again, but may have to wait in the queue until the CPU is free to execute it. Since there are other users on the system, it is likely that another process will be executing when TIMER becomes ready to execute again. TIMER will execute eventually, and when it does, it calls two more system services: to schedule its wake-up call (line 31) and then to hibernate (line 32). Hibernation causes the state of the process to become HIB, which is another form of a wait state. (For its own convenience, the VMS operating system distinguishes the various wait states.) In the HIB state, TIMER is no longer considered for execution, but a 30-second countdown timer has been activated for it within the operating system. Incidentally, this countdown timer can be used for quantum too. A clock is essential

```
$ SPAWN/NOWAIT RUN TIMER
%DCL-S-SPAWNED, Process DMILLER_1 spawned
 3-DEC-1990 11:16:13.56

$ SHOW PROCESS/CONTINUOUS DMILLER_1
```

Figure 3.13. Commands to pro-
duce Figure 3.14

for the implementation of any time-sharing operating system, and one more time request, for quantum management, is quite easily implemented.

When 30 seconds have expired, the clock interrupts the processor. The clock interrupt handler causes TIMER' state to be changed back to COM. When TIMER is selected to run, $ASCTIM is called again (line 33), and the time is displayed on the screen via the WRITELN. This causes the process to be put into the LEF state again. When the data transmission to the terminal is complete, the state is changed to COM and, when scheduled, the process becomes current again. Finally, TIMER exits back to DCL, which will rundown the TIMER image and prompt the user for another command.

SHOW PROCESS/CONTINUOUS

Performance tools are not unique to the VMS operating system; other operating systems also offer them. Such tools provide information that aids programmers in debugging, testing, and optimizing program behavior. The tool described here is not the only way to present this information either: Digital and third-party vendors offer other approaches for VMS installations.

The only way to watch a process executing is with another process. DCL provides a command that allows the observation of an image execution over time, called SHOW PROCESS/CONTINUOUS. To examine the operation of TIMER, we create a subprocess for it and then watch it using SHOW PROCESS/CONTINUOUS in the parent process. Figure 3.13 contains the commands used to produce a snapshot of the display, and Figure 3.14 is the snapshot, which is updated once a second.

We look first at the commands in Figure 3.13. The goal is to execute TIMER and, at the same time, have the system show what is happening to the image. To do this we use the SPAWN command, which was introduced in the previous chapter, and SPAWN a subprocess that executes the RUN TIMER command. The "Process DMILLER_1 Spawned" message indicates that the subprocess has started. (DMILLER_1 is the name the system

	Process	DMILLER_1	11:16:16
State	HIB	Working set	241
Cur/base priority	9/4	Virtual pages	1835
Current PC	7FFEDF8A	CPU time	00:00:00.72
Current PSL	03C00000	Direct I/O	1
Current user SP	7FF45910	Buffered I/O	111
PID	000003CD	Page faults	256
UIC	[FACULTY,DMILLER]	Event flags	E0000001 00000000

DUA1:[FACULTY.DMILLER.CS410]TIMER.EXE;4

Figure 3.14. TIMER execution shown with $ SHOW PROCESS/CONTINUOUS

automatically bestows on the subprocess.) The current time is then output by TIMER. Next, the parent process (DMILLER) prompts for another command. The second command entered is the SHOW command, which displays the activity of the subprocess. Since two processes are attached to a single terminal, it might be an awkward situation. If both processes require input from the keyboard, it can be difficult for the user to distinguish which process is prompting and which process is requesting data. But in this case, TIMER requires no input and produces only two lines of output, so there is little difficulty.

The SHOW command is keyed as soon as possible and generates a display like the one in Figure 3.14. The primary field of interest is the "State" field at the top of the left column. Notice that TIMER is hibernating. When it comes out of hibernation, the "State" field will change, as depicted in Figures 3.11 and 3.12. The state changes happen very quickly, so it may be necessary to perform this experiment several times to see all of the states TIMER reaches after HIB. SHOW does not execute soon enough to display any states prior to HIB, and the LEF state may be impossible to see because the terminal is being used by TIMER instead of SHOW. Another way to perform this experiment is to log on to two adjacent terminals, entering SHOW command first on one terminal and then RUN TIMER on the other one.

There are several other fields of interest in the SHOW PROCESS/ CONTINUOUS display. The top line names the process and displays the time of day. The bottom line shows the complete name of the image file executing. The "CPU time" displayed in the right column on the fourth line is the actual number of CPU seconds used by the subprocess since it was created. In this example, it is the amount of time to execute lines 26–32 in Figure 3.9, which makes two system service calls, performs the first WRITELN, and then hibernates. During hibernation, no CPU time is expended.

Time-sharing operating systems assign a priority to each process. VMS priorities range from 0 (the least important) to 31, with interactive processes falling between 4 and 9, as indicated in Figure 3.14. The terminal process's priority is higher while it is idle and lower while it uses the processor. This statement can be verified by the figure: the current priority is 9 and varies throughout execution.

Other entries recognizable to assembly language programmers in Figure 3.14 are the values of the PC, PSL, and SP. Most of the remaining fields will be explained in the discussion of paging in the next chapter.

3.6. The Clock

This section will take a break from scheduler topics to consider another related software-hardware subject, the clock. To understand the operating system, it is necessary to have some familiarity with the computer hardware's components. The clock is one of these components. It is often taken for granted in the operating system and is not well understood by most programmers. The two functions required of a clock on a time-sharing system are maintaining the *time-of-day* and acting as a *countdown, watchdog,* or *interval* timer. These two functions are commonly performed with one clock.

The hardware clock can be implemented most easily by providing a capability to interrupt the CPU periodically, say, every few milliseconds. When the interrupt occurs, the ISR will update a time-of-day counter. To compute the date and time, the counter is used to determine the number of interrupts that occurred since the time of system startup. For example, assume that the clock interrupts every 10 milliseconds and the system was started at 12:03 by the operator. When the counter value is 1,000, it represents 10,000 milliseconds or 10 seconds; hence, the time is 12:03:10.

In addition, the clock acts as an interval timer, which is needed for applications such as the TIMER program and for quantum management. Used as an interval timer, the clock works like this: when the system service receives the $SCHDWK request, it assumes that the units are correct. For instance, a 30-second request is 30,000 milliseconds, and this value is stored in a second location in memory called the interval counter. Then, whenever the clock interrupt routine updates the time-of-day counter, it must also reduce the interval counter. When the interval counter becomes 0, 30 seconds have elapsed, and the requesting process must be informed.

A second implementation of the clock is to put both the time-of-day and interval counting logic into hardware. The time-of-day function might be performed entirely by an I/O-like device. Then, whenever the operating system has to know what time it is, for instance, to calculate charges incurred by the process, it interrogates the clock for the current time. Exactly how the interval timer is implemented varies. A common hardware implementation is to provide a register which is loaded with the negative of the desired time and have the hardware increment the register until overflow occurs. Overflow is easier to detect than zero because only one bit is involved.

Independent of its hardware implementation, the clock is also used in a time-shared environment as a watchdog timer. This is an involved requirement because several different processes may have different countdown requirements, and the system must keep track of them all, whether or not the process is active and without regard to the order of the requests. It does this by keeping a chronological queue of timer requests, as depicted in Figure 3.15. Generally, each request in the queue must be adjusted to start up after the request that preceded it. The figure represents a snapshot of the queue two seconds after DEER_HUNTER made a 10-second request; hence, the time remaining is now 8 seconds. A microsecond before the figure was produced, CRAWDAD made a 45-second request. Obviously CRAWDAD's request cannot be honored until DEER_HUNTER's request is completed, so it is linked following DEER_HUNTER's. When DEER_HUNTER's request has been satisfied (in 8 seconds), there will only be 37 (45 − 8) seconds remaining until CRAWDAD's request needs to be serviced. Thus, CRAWDAD's queue entry contains a difference value, not the requested value.[2] The way this data structure is defined, only DEER_HUNTER's internal counter is decremented as the clock interrupts. Thus the length of

---

2. A timer queue entry could contain both values. The subroutine responsible for making a queue entry could also be assigned to check the consistency of these two values on entries already in the queue. An inconsistent value would imply that either a system software error or a hardware memory error occurred.

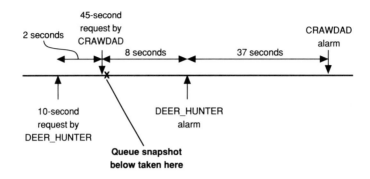

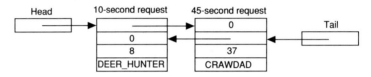

Figure 3.15. A typical timer queue

the timer queue does not create a performance issue in implementing this timer.

Figure 3.16 shows the timer queue after process FIZGIG makes a 15-second request, 6 seconds after process DEER_HUNTER's request, that is, 4 seconds after Figure 3.15. DEER_HUNTER's request has been reduced to 4 seconds at this time, which causes FIZGIG's request to be inserted into the queue because the queue is ordered by time. The 15-second request is changed to 11 (15 − 4) seconds relative to the end of DEER_HUNTER's request. This forces an 11-second reduction in the rest of the requests in the queue. CRAWDAD's was originally scheduled for 37 seconds after DEER HUNTER; now it is reduced by 11 seconds to 26 seconds, which represents the time after FIZGIG's request is honored that CRAWDAD's request will be honored.

Even with two clocks, one used for time-of-day and one used as an interval timer, the timer queue entries are time-ordered, and the first becomes an interval counter. The remaining entries are represented as a delta time from the previous entry. If a new timer request is made, its entry is inserted chronologically into the queue, thus changing all entries to the right of the insertion.

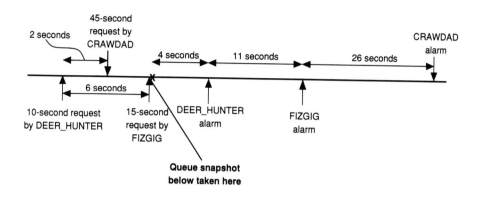

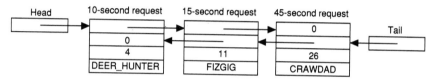

Figure 3.16. Timer queue after
a request is inserted

3.7. VMS Scheduler Database

Proper understanding of the VMS scheduling algorithm presented in the next section requires an introduction to the scheduler's data structures. This material further details the PCB (Process Control Block) structure outlined in Chapter 2; and, it points out that the PCB is linked into several data structures.

The scheduler keeps track of all the processes in the system by assigning the PCBs to a queue corresponding to the process's state. Processes that are able to execute are in the COM state and are further arranged by priority. As indicated in Figure 3.17, there is a separate queue for each priority level: BLUEADEPT and GLAMDRING are at priority 10 and TROOPER is at priority 4. A flag longword indicates which priorities have empty queues; a bit position set to 1 indicates that the corresponding queue contains at least one PCB, and 0 means the PCB queue is empty. The flag longword allows the scheduler to quickly identify the highest-priority process. A VAX instruction, called FFS (Find First bit Set to one), is used to test each bit of the flag longword.

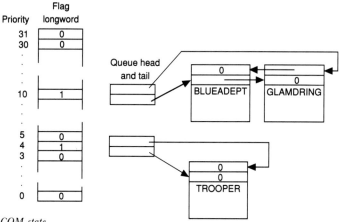

*Figure 3.17. The COM state
database*

That there is a queue maintained at every priority level is significant
because the VMS system will apply the round robin algorithm to the PCBs
at a given level. The process that had been executing is inserted at the end
of the appropriate priority queue with a single VAX instruction designed
for this purpose, INSQUE (Insert Entry in Queue). Likewise, the new process selected comes from the head of a queue and is removed with a single
VAX instruction, REMQUE (Remove Entry from Queue). These two instructions are designed for double-linked lists and perform all the pointer
manipulation necessary to ensure the consistency of the queue.

The data structure for all other process states, shown in Figure 3.18,
is not as complicated as the COM state is because priority does not affect
queuing. Processes are entered in the appropriate state queues, and there
is one queue per state, as the figure indicates. Depicted in the figure are
two processes in the LEF state, ODIE and MUNSKI, and one in the HIB
state, WHAMO. The order of the processes in a queue is not significant
because they are not serviced in any particular order. However, the INSQUE
and REMQUE instructions are the most convenient and fastest means of
manipulating the PCBs. Every PCB in the system has a state associated with
it, and so it must be on one (but only one) of the two structures described
in Figures 3.17 and 3.18.[3] Processes that are not in the COM state are blocked

3. Chapter 5 will introduce one other structure. The CEF (Common Event Flag) state
does not conform to either structure described.

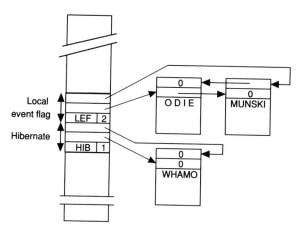

Figure 3.18. Scheduler database
for all states except COM

for some reason. When a process is unblocked, the PCB is returned to the COM queue corresponding to its priority.

Figure 3.19 presents a display produced by the VMS Monitor utility showing process states. This display is produced by the command MONITOR STATES, and in it, all possible process states are shown. Associated with each state is the count of processes, represented in histogram form. As with all the Monitor displays, this one is updated periodically, in this case, every three seconds. The values shown are derived from averaging the actual queue lengths over a three-second period.

3.8. VMS Scheduler Algorithm

The VMS scheduler is one of the most versatile available in any operating system. It can accommodate batch, interactive, and real-time processes. Every process on the system has a priority associated with it, ranging from 0 (the least important) to 31. Within this range, priorities numbered 16 and above are considered real-time. A process running in real-time is not time-shared, nor is its priority changed. Batch jobs are typically assigned a base priority of 3. Interactive users create batch processes with the SUBMIT command, which creates and adds a process to a special-purpose queue called

```
                                        VAX/VMS Monitor Utility
                      +------+             PROCESS STATES
                      : CUR :              on node BSU::
                      +-----+            3-MAR-1990 14:09:04

                                  0        10        20        30        40
                                  + - - - + - - - - + - - - - + - - - - +
     Collided Page Wait          :
     Mutex @ Misc Resource Wait   :
     Common Event Flag Wait     11 :***********
     Page Fault Wait              :
     Local Event Flag Wait      10 :**********
     Local Evt Flg (Outswapped)  1 :*
                                  :        :         :         :         :
     Hibernate                   2 :**
     Hibernate (Outswapped)      3 :***
     Suspended                    :
     Suspended (Outswapped)       :
     Free Page Wait               :
     Compute                     1 :*
     Compute (Outswapped)         :
     Current Process             1 :*
                                  + - - - + - - - - + - - - - + - - - - +
```

*Figure 3.19. Typical output of
the $ MONITOR STATES
command*

SYS$BATCH. The VMS system permits multiple batch queues, and proc-
esses within each queue compete with one another; that is, batch processes
will be time-shared when there are multiple queues. Interactive processes
usually have higher priority than batch processes, so if an interactive process
is computable, it, not the batch process, is run first. Interactive processes
typically range in priority from a lower limit of 4 to a maximum of 9. The
remaining priorities, 0, 1, and 2, and 10 to 15, are assigned at the system
manager's discretion.

In this particular priority assignment scheme, real-time processes
preempt time-shared ones. Very little code in the scheduler is real-time-
specific. In other words, as designed, the scheduler accommodates real-time
processes without making them special cases. Likewise, because of their low
priority, batch processes are run when nothing else is able to execute on the
system. The scheduler is designed to specifically accommodate interactive
users. Its underlying design goal is to provide terminal users fast response
to a keystroke. How does the VMS system balance the process load comprising CPU-bound and other noninteractive applications with the processes
that expect instant response to keystrokes? Through an algorithm that favors

the user entering data from the keyboard and producing displays on the terminal over other interactive users.

Figures 1.15 and 2.4 presented VMS models, the second more detailed than the first. A third model, shown in Figure 3.20, adds detail that indicates where the scheduler fits in the VMS system.

In the figure, the scheduler is identified in the left-hand path. System services are requested by the executing process, and interrupts are the result of some activity outside of the current process. Whether a process is interrupted or requests a service, the current process continues execution or the scheduler is called to switch processes. This design philosophy is based on reducing the system overhead. For instance, $ASCTIM (right branch of Figure 3.20) can be done so quickly and efficiently that rescheduling because of it is useless. That is, since nothing happens to change the priority configuration of the eligible processes, the process requesting the $ASCTIM will be chosen again, since the current process was initially selected because it had the highest priority, and the $ASCTIM request does not change that. Likewise, in certain cases, interrupts do not cause preemption because no higher-priority process becomes computable as a result of the interrupt. But the completion of an I/O operation (left branch) means that a process has changed from a blocked state to a ready state. Since a process has become eligible to execute, the scheduler should reevaluate the priority situation and perhaps allow that unblocked process to run.

When the scheduler is called, it has three specific tasks to perform. First, the current context, the environment of the executing process, must be saved so it can be restarted at a later time. Next, a new process must be chosen to execute. Finally, the new process's context must be fetched, loaded into the processor, and then started. In the VMS system, because of its specifically tailored instruction set, the scheduler is less than a page of assembly code.

The three steps on the left side of Figure 3.20 are just a part of the overall scheduling algorithm. Figure 3.21 expands that logic.

There are three reasons for starting the scheduler, and it has two entry points. First, note in the upper right-hand corner of Figure 3.21 quantum expiration, which means that the currently executing process has exhausted its quantum. In the VMS system, a quantum counter is kept in each PHD; there is no watchdog timer entry for this purpose as previously described. This counter is reduced at every clock "tick" or interrupt by the clock interrupt handler. When the value becomes 0, the executing process

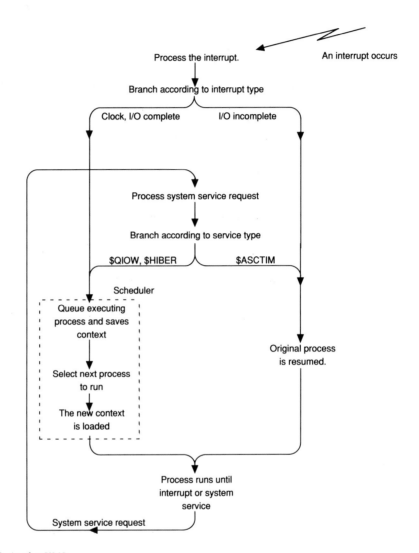

Figure 3.20. Another VMS model

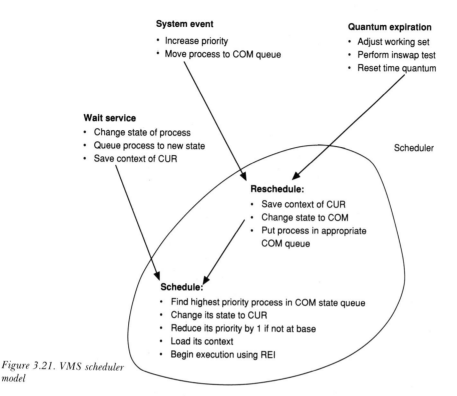

System event

- Increase priority
- Move process to COM queue

Quantum expiration

- Adjust working set
- Perform inswap test
- Reset time quantum

Wait service

- Change state of process
- Queue process to new state
- Save context of CUR

Scheduler

Reschedule:

- Save context of CUR
- Change state to COM
- Put process in appropriate COM queue

Schedule:

- Find highest priority process in COM state queue
- Change its state to CUR
- Reduce its priority by 1 if not at base
- Load its context
- Begin execution using REI

Figure 3.21. VMS scheduler model

must give up the CPU. In this case, two memory-resource-related tasks are carried out: adjusting the working set and performing swapping tests. These are listed in the diagram and are discussed in detail in Chapter 4. Even though the process is not going to continue executing immediately, the quantum must be reset.

The second reason for starting the scheduler is shown in the upper left-hand corner of Figure 3.21. System events are not connected with the currently running process and instead result from interrupts. These interrupts include completion of some process's I/O request and a $SCHDWK timer expiration, and these events return a process to COM state. Associated with each of these events is a priority boost to be added to that process's current priority. Figure 3.22 lists typical priority boosts; a process's priority cannot be boosted above a maximum value. The priority of real-time processes is never changed, since it is the priority boost that makes interactive programs responsive. However, because interactive I/O is rewarded, the priority of interactive processes is raised above that of CPU-bound processes,

Event	Boost
Disk I/O complete	2
$SCHDWK wakeup	3
Terminal output complete	4
Terminal input complete	6
Process created	6

Figure 3.22. Typical priority boosts

whose priority is lowered. This is so users with interactive processes will have satisfactory response time.

After its priority is increased, the targeted process is moved from its wait queue to the COM queue. Moving the process to the COM queue means the process's PCB is linked to the priority queue of the newly computed priority. Refer to Figure 3.17 for the COM state data structure.

System events and quantum expiration will cause "reschedule," which is the first entry to the scheduler. This means that the context of the currently executing process must be saved and its PCB linked in at the end of the COM queue that corresponds to its priority. Linking the PCB to the end implements round robin scheduling at a given priority level.

The third reason for starting the scheduler, the wait service, is caused by the currently executing process—for instance, $QIOW and $HIBER requests are wait services. The process's state is changed according to the service requested, LEF in the case of a $QIOW, and the PCB is linked into the queue corresponding to the state. This data structure was shown in Figure 3.18. The priority in the wait queue makes no difference because the wait states are insensitive to priority. The process will return to the COM state when the specified system event occurs and be queued by priority at that time. When the PCB becomes ready to move back to the COM queue, it can be anywhere in its wait queue. Finally, the context of the process is saved, and the wait service enters the second scheduler entry point.

At "schedule" entry, the scheduler finds the highest-priority COM process, removes it from the queue, and changes its state to CUR. Its priority is reduced by 1 if it is not already at its base priority, in anticipation of the next trip through the scheduler. Real-time processes are always at their base; hence, their priorities are never reduced. A CPU-bound process will reenter the figure from the upper right corner when its quantum expires and return to the COM queue at the lower priority. An I/O-bound process will eventually get rescheduled because of a system event and have its priority boosted. The schedule path concludes by loading the context of the newly selected process and starting the new process using an REI (Return from Exception or Interrupt) instruction. Chapter 8 will expand upon the use of this instruction.

The VMS scheduler maintains several separate blocked states, not just one, as indicated in Figure 3.3. The reason for this separation is to speed up the unblocking operation. For instance, when an I/O operation is complete, the scheduler must search the LEF list for the corresponding PCB so that the process can be added to the COM queue. Keeping all the processes blocked for I/O on one list makes the search faster. This may seem like a subtle refinement, but the majority of the processes are waiting most of the time. This can be quickly confirmed by examining a MONITOR STATES display, as in Figure 3.19.

3.9. Context Switching

Context switching occurs when one process temporarily discontinues execution and another process resumes execution in its place. Context switching is performed by the scheduler.

To better understand the meaning of a process's context, consider an example: suppose a process is using register R5 to store the result of a computation, as shown in Figure 3.23, in the process MAGNUM on the left, and then the system changes context to process TBART, as indicated. Notice that TBART also needs R5. To permit both processes to use R5, the context switch includes saving MAGNUM's R5 in memory to preserve it and restoring TBART's R5 from a different part of memory. Then TBART can continue executing at its SUBL instruction. Each process has its private save area—the hardware PCB (stored in the PHD). Notice that the instructions themselves are not considered part of the context because they are already in memory. One process's instructions are inaccessible to the other process; they are not shared. Only the registers require special treatment because

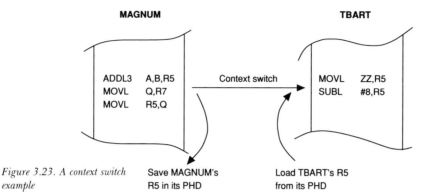

Figure 3.23. A context switch example

they must be shared by all processes. There is only one set of registers on a VAX.

Later, in the switch back from TBART, MAGNUM'S R5 is restored from its hardware PCB before MAGNUM restarts. There is no reason to demand that the switch be from TBART to MAGNUM; it can be from any process. Furthermore, there is no way for MAGNUM to detect that there was a context switch because it is restarted in exactly the same condition as when the previous switch took place.

The context of a process includes the high-speed registers, the condition codes, and information concerning the memory locations of the process. When the context is saved, information is extracted from the various hardware registers and stored in memory. When the context is restored, the information is moved from memory to the registers. On most computers, this requires several instructions. For instance, one register at a time must be copied to memory, and the condition code bits may have to be treated separately too. The memory utilization information is quite extensive as well, although that varies widely across the various machines.

Once the VMS scheduler has determined which process is to be started, the LDPCTX (Load Process Context) instruction becomes central in starting the new process. LDPCTX is an example of how the VAX hardware has been tailored to meet the needs of the operating system. It has no operands, and it expects the operating system to initialize the PCBB (Process Control Block Base) register prior to its execution. The PCBB is an internal processor register (IPR) that points to the hardware PCB contained in the PHD (Process Header). A pointer in the software PCB is used to locate the hardware PCB. This is the process context, and it includes:

- Kernel, executive, supervisor, and user stack pointers. Each execution mode has its own stack to enhance performance and to establish system security.
- Fourteen general registers. These are R0 through R11, AP, and FP.
- The program counter (PC) and processor status longword (PSL). The PC points to the next instruction to be executed. The PSL includes the condition code and the execution mode.
- Page base registers (for P0 and P1) and the length of each page table. This information is used to locate the program in memory.
- Asynchronous system trap (AST) level. The hardware supports a technique for notifying a process of asynchronous events with the least possible delay. The AST level shows how to locate a waiting AST. Chapter 8 discusses ASTs in greater detail.
- Performance monitor enable bit. This bit is used to signal external hardware to collect execution data related to a specific process without interfering with the operating system. If a process's execution is to be followed through a multiprocessing environment, this is an essential signal.

Figure 3.24 contains the complete hardware PCB description. There are two PCBs for each process, one for hardware and one for software. The hardware PCB contains everything that is needed to restart the process at the point it was stopped.

The LDPCTX has a companion instruction, called SVPCTX (Save Process Context), to save the context in the hardware PCB. Since these two instructions are intended for use only by the operating system, the unprivileged user cannot use them in any programs.

3.10. VMS Organization

The key to any software design is to separate the problem into easily identifiable, independent functions, each with a simple interface that is easy to understand and use. The internal data structure of a given function must be hidden from other functions, and the calling sequences must be short, easy to understand, and unambiguous. Only by careful isolation of its functions can a system be built that will evolve for years or even decades. This design policy applies to operating systems and applications alike.

Kernel stack pointer	
Executive stack pointer	
Supervisor stack pointer	
User stack pointer	
R0 register	
R1 register	
R2 register	
R3 register	
R4 register	
R5 register	
R6 register	
R7 register	
R8 register	
R9 register	
R10 register	
R11 register	
Argument pointer register	
Frame pointer register	
Program counter	
Processor status longword	
P0 base register	
AST Level	P0 Length
P1 base register	
	P1 Length

Figure 3.24. The hardware
PCB or context

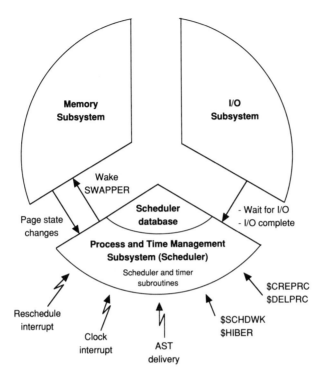

*Figure 3.25. The scheduler sub-
system of the VMS kernel*

The nucleus of the VMS operating system has been defined in a way that minimizes functional interfaces. This kernel, as it is called, is divided into three subsystems, presented in Figure 3.25, called the memory subsystem, the I/O subsystem, and the scheduler subsystem. Each subsystem is divided into its database and the subroutines that operate on the data. Notice that there are interfaces between the scheduler and both the I/O and memory subsystems, but they are simple. The two I/O interfaces should be familiar. Both the "wait for I/O" and "I/O complete" signals cause a state change to the process.

Figure 3.25 also shows typical external interfaces, including hardware interrupt paths and system services. The clock interrupt and system services such as $CREPRC and $SCHDWK have been introduced; the reschedule interrupt and AST deliveries will be discussed later in the book.

The MONITOR SYSTEM display parallels the VMS kernel. Note in

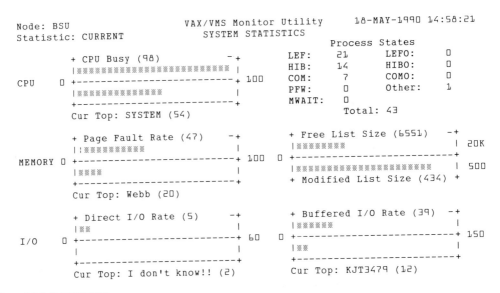

```
Node: BSU                    VAX/VMS Monitor Utility    18-MAY-1990 14:58:21
Statistic: CURRENT               SYSTEM STATISTICS
                                                     Process States
        + CPU Busy (98)          -+    LEF:    21    LEFO:    0
        |▨▨▨▨▨▨▨▨▨▨▨▨▨▨▨▨▨▨▨▨ |    HIB:    14    HIBO:    0
CPU   0 +--------------------------+ 100  COM:     7    COMO:    0
        |▨▨▨▨▨▨▨▨▨▨▨▨ |               PFW:     0    Other:   1
        +--------------------------+       MWAIT:   0
        Cur Top: SYSTEM (54)                    Total: 43

        + Page Fault Rate (47)    -+    + Free List Size (6551)  -+
        |:▨▨▨▨▨▨▨▨▨ |               |▨▨▨▨▨▨ |          | 20K
MEMORY 0 +-------------------------+ 100 0 +-------------------------+
        |▨▨▨▨ |                       |▨▨▨▨▨▨▨▨▨▨▨▨▨▨ | 500
        +-------------------------+       + Modified List Size (434) +
        Cur Top: Webb (20)

        + Direct I/O Rate (5)     -+    + Buffered I/O Rate (39)  -+
        |▨▨ |                       |▨▨▨▨▨ |
I/O    0 +-------------------------+ 60  0 +-------------------------+ 150
        |                          |       |▨▨ |
        +-------------------------+       +-------------------------+
        Cur Top: I don't know!! (2)    Cur Top: KJT3479 (12)
```

*Figure 3.26. $ MONITOR
SYSTEM showing state
summary*

Figure 3.26, the top two sections labeled "CPU" and "Process States" concern the scheduler subsystem; the center of the display, labeled "MEMORY," is information about the memory management subsystem; and the lower two displays, labeled I/O, show the I/O subsystem performance. In the upper right-hand corner, the states of all the processes in the system are presented in summary form. Only a few of the common states are detailed; the remaining are lumped into the "Other" category. In the upper left-hand corner, the processor utilization is displayed.

In this example, the CPU is busy 98 percent of the time, and the SYSTEM process is the highest user with 54 percent. Chapter 4 describes the meaning of the memory statistics, and Chapter 8 describes the I/O displays.

3.11. Related Issues

The exact nature of the scheduler and its database obviously varies with each operating system. The VMS scheduler, a large and involved implementation, is at one end of the complexity spectrum; at the other end is a scheduler for a single-user system like MS-DOS. Is the intricacy of the VMS scheduler necessary? The answer depends on the intended customer. The VMS operating system is considered to be orders of magnitude too complex for a stand-alone PC system, but it solves the problem of supporting a large number of users, providing fair time-sharing and a high degree of privacy.

The VAX/VMS system is an approach to computation that minimizes cost and maximizes performance through the sharing of minicomputer resources. Another approach that includes shared resources is currently under development—a LAN (local area network) of microcomputers. It is too early to tell if this is a better, more cost-effective way to host multiple users who need to share data and other resources occasionally. LANs still suffer from privacy and protection issues as well as response time lags when they access a common database or peripheral.

This examination of implementation issues pointed out several VAX instructions that primarily support the operating system. In particular, the save and load context scheme is an essential element of time-sharing and any other type of preemptive operating system. If the hardware does not support complex instructions, the operating system must perform the equivalent functions itself using simple instructions. Normally, it is faster to perform the context switching functions in hardware. One example: Digital's PDP 11/45 did not have save/load context instructions, and the equivalent functions took roughly 20 instructions to load and 20 more to save.[4] This shows that it is false economy not to include a pair of context maintenance instructions and other special instructions in the instruction set.

As we have stated, the operation of the scheduler is tightly linked to the type of operating system: batch, interactive, or real-time. Once the type is defined, the scheduler can be designed according to combinations of several techniques. Often, these techniques are embellished and recombined for various reasons. The VMS operating system is the dominant example of combined techniques. Over its 10-plus-year history, the VMS scheduler algorithm has gone through various changes as its designers have learned more about its practical operation and have discovered situations that did not fit the textbook scheduler algorithms. Textbook solutions are only an initial approach to a very complex problem. It is extremely difficult to investigate a scheduler through simulations because the hardware and software system behavior is so difficult to model.

---

4. The 11/45 has 8 general registers and 8 more for memory management. There were some miscellaneous bits that had to be saved and loaded in addition to these 16 registers.

When an operating system is executing, it is doing so in response to a process's direct or indirect request. For instance, to perform a $QIOW, the operating system must perform numerous subtasks that consume the processor and other resources rather than permit the user's process to execute.

3.12. Summary

In this chapter, we first examined the purpose of an interactive system—it is primarily for sharing expensive computer hardware among several users, none of whom require dedicated usage. Time-sharing was especially important in the 1960s when only a single class of computers—mainframes—was available. Next, we described the scheduler including its possible goals and the possible range of solutions. There are three classes of operating systems: batch, interactive, and real-time. In the design of an operating system, certain goals are set on the basis of its projected utilization and they must be kept in mind throughout the life of the product.

In looking at the scheduler, we saw that it models the processes in its database. Processes move from state to state under their own control, because of the other processes's activities in the system, and because of interrupt activity. A Pascal program demonstrated several state changes and its code was described. The SHOW PROCESS command demonstrated how to examine those state changes; and the progression of state changes was illustrated with several diagrams.

Since the Pascal example is related to the computer clock, we sidestepped the scheduler issue to elaborate on how the clock hardware is utilized and how the operating system makes use of the clock.

We examined the VMS scheduler algorithm and its database in some detail to see how it was designed to favor the interactive user while still supporting batch and real-time users. It does so using a dynamic priority scheme to control its interactive users. In this presentation, the scheduler was put in the context of the whole VMS operating system structure.

The essence of a multiprogrammed operating system is a process's context. We explained how two processes could share the registers and then described the load and save context operations. The process context supported by the VAX was detailed, and the two instructions developed specifically for switching contexts were described.

The scheduler's place in the VMS kernel was illustrated along with typical interfaces. The purpose of creating an operating system kernel was briefly discussed.

ACRONYMS

$ASCTIM	ASCII Time conversion system service
$BINTIM	Binary Time conversion system service
$HIBER	Hibernate system service
$QIOW	Queue I/O and Wait system service
$SCHDWK	Schedule Wakeup system service
AP	Argument Pointer register
ASCII	American Standard Code for Information Interchange
AST	Asynchronous System Trap
ATM	Automatic Teller Machine
COM	Computable process state
CPU	Central Processing Unit
CUR	Currently executing process state
DCL	Digital Command Language
FFS	Assembly instruction to Find First Set bit in a longword
FP	Frame Pointer register
HIB	Hibernating process state
INSQUE	Assembly instruction to insert a queue entry
IPR	Internal Processor Register
KESU	Kernel, Executive, Supervisor, User
LAN	Local Area Network
LDPCTX	Assembly instruction to load process context
LEF	Wait for Local Event Flag process state
PC	Program Counter
PCB	Process Control Block
PCBB	PCB Base register
PSL	Processor Status Longword
REI	Return from Exception or Interrupt instruction
REMQUE	Assembly instruction to remove a queue entry
SP	Stack Pointer
SVPCTX	Assembly instruction to save process context

SHORT ANSWER EXERCISES

1. Using HELP, look at SYSTEM_SERVICE $BINTIM and compare the definition there to the one used in Figure 3.9.

2. Using EDT/READ_ONLY SYS$SYSTEM:STARLET.PAS, compare the definition of $BINTIM to the one used in Figure 3.9.

3. Using HELP SYSTEM_SERVICE, try to find the system service routine that translates internal binary time to an ASCII string; that is, what system service performs the opposite function of $BINTIM?

4. Maybe it has occurred to you that the difference between two delta times, or between two dates, can be easily calculated using two calls on $BINTIM and subtracting the resulting binary times. Unfortunately, $QUAD arithmetic is not part of Pascal. You might think that a system as powerful as the VMS operating system would provide a way to do $QUAD arithmetic. Using HELP, see if you can locate some possible $QUAD arithmetic routines. For those of you thinking of an assembly language solution, I would like to point out that there is no SUBQ operation. (Hint: RTL is the Digital acronym for run-time library; there are several RTL subdivisions.)

5. Code, compile, and execute the TIMER program in the text.

6. If you are familiar with writing DCL programs (see Anagnostopoulos, *Writing Real Programs in DCL*), write an equivalent to TIMER and see if it executes in the same manner—that is, does it use $HIBER too?

7. Show where each of the Pascal statements in Figure 3.9 is executed in Figure 3.12.

8. What is the purpose of including interactive and real-time scheduling on the same machine? Why should a scheduler have to support these two options?

9. What is the effect of increasing the time quantum?

PROJECTS

1. Using HELP, look at the various formats of "delta time" under SPECIFY DATE_TIME DELTA and compare them to the $BINTIM definitions. The formats defined are more general than stated in the text. For instance, there are other ways of specifying 30 seconds. Using the error detecting logic of $BINTIM, write a Pascal routine that accepts

keyboard delta time, passes it to $BINTIM, and checks the returned error flag. Then try various delta-time formats to see which are really valid.

2. Design, code, and test a program that prompts for a time (rather than using the built-in 30-second constant). Of course, the user may make a mistake, and the program should recover from user errors.

3. As suggested in the text, execute TIMER several times to see what the average discrepancy is on your system. Average the time differences you observe. This experiment should be performed on both a busy system and an idle one to see if the process load makes any difference. Write a short paper describing your experiment and the results. Include an unscaled timing diagram that includes all of the events between (and including) the two $ASCTIM calls.

4. Design, code, and test a program that computes the difference between two date-time specifications. I suggest using $BINTIM to convert each time to binary and then use a run-time library to subtract the two and, finally, $ASCTIM to convert the result.

PAPERS

1. Historically, it has been difficult to define real-time systems. Even the name has changed. Over the years, these systems have been called "near real-time," "sub-second," and "instantaneous." Review the literature to record how many terms and definitions you are able to find, and be certain to include your references. What is the earliest reference to this class of system that you can find?

Paging and Memory Management

GOALS

Multiprogramming

How paged programs behave

Working sets and locality

Paging metrics

Hardware required to support paging

4

Previous chapters briefly mentioned processes co-residing in memory or multiprogramming. This chapter will describe how this is done. Chapter 1 showed that the delay caused by character transmission was significant in an interactive system. A rule of thumb is that a time-sharing user consumes only one second of CPU time for every minute he or she is connected to the computer—in other words, one user uses one-sixtieth of the computer's resource. In Chapter 3 we justified sharing CPU by showing that a single process does not use all parts of the computer system all the time. Sharing computer resources is an economic necessity. Therefore, to optimize the total resource, the time-sharing operating system must switch from one process to another, executing a portion of each process at every switch. However, the process switching time must be fast so that the overhead incurred does not outweigh the sharing benefit. In the early 1960s, system designers realized that to minimize this context switch time, the set of executing processes must be resident in memory, which implies that the processes must co-reside in some fashion.

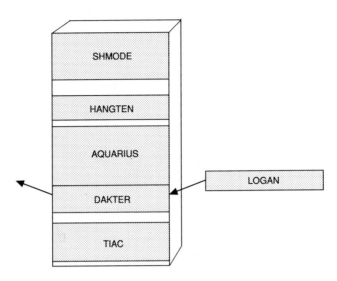

Figure 4.1. Processes stacked in memory

MULTIPROGRAMMING

The most obvious approach to multiprogramming is simply to assign physical memory to each process as it logs in; this is called *contiguous allocation*. But this solution has many drawbacks. The first drawback is determining the size of the allocation because the amount of memory space a process might need cannot be determined at login. One solution is to equate a process to an image. For example, in VMS terms, Pascal, LINK, and RUN could be considered separate processes and allocated contiguous memory long enough to execute. When they complete, memory could be deallocated. In effect, this allocation scheme defines a process. It implies that the entire process must fit into memory with room to spare for other user's processes as well.

Another drawback to contiguous allocation is *fragmentation*. To understand this term, assume each process has a different memory requirement; memory might look like Figure 4.1 at some point. Now assume that one of the processes, DAKTER, for instance, finishes and a smaller process, LOGAN, is started and put into the hole left by DAKTER. This leaves some unused space, termed a *fragment,* and, over time, many such fragments are created.

There are three well-known algorithms for allocating memory: *first-*

fit, best-fit, and *worst-fit.* First-fit scans the spaces and assigns the new process to the first space that is large enough. The advantage of this algorithm is its speed: all free spaces do not have to be searched. The best-fit algorithm scans all the unused spaces and then selects the one that creates the smallest fragment. This scheme is intuitively appealing because it keeps the fragments small. However, the small fragments result eventually in a condition where no large spaces remain. The worst-fit algorithm is the opposite of best-fit; it looks for a space that will cause the largest fragment to be created. As with best-fit, all unused space must be tested. Although this may at first seem counter-intuitive, its advantage is that when it breaks up large spaces, the fragments will still be usable.

These three algorithms have been investigated through simulation, but there is no clear-cut best solution. In every case, the long-term difficulty is that some of the fragments will be too small to use, and eventually these small spaces will become scattered throughout memory. There are several variations on first-fit, best-fit, and worst-fit that attempt to compensate for their difficulties, but none is very satisfying.

All three algorithms share a common problem: how to return allocated space to the free space pool. And this problem is complicated because space is not returned to the pool in the same order it was removed. The general approach to pool management is to maintain a list of all free memory spaces in a way that permits coalescense of two adjacent spaces into one. There are several algorithms for this free space manager; this form of memory management is presented in most data structures texts.

OVERLAYS

A third and more serious drawback to contiguous allocation is that the process must be smaller than physical memory. A technique called *overlays* is a solution to this problem and has been employed for many years. It is required by many MS-DOS applications today. Figure 4.2 illustrates overlays. In the top part of the figure, the process is subdivided by the programmer into three major pieces: the MAIN program, Function A, and Function B, just as, for example, a word processor might be divided into the main program, a data entry routine, and a spell checker. The lower part of the figure shows that the total process is larger than physical memory, but large enough to hold either branch: the MAIN and A or the MAIN and B. The MAIN and one function are loaded initially into memory until the second function

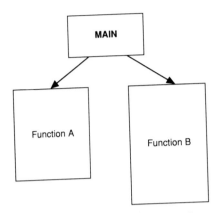

a) A Logical Division of the Application

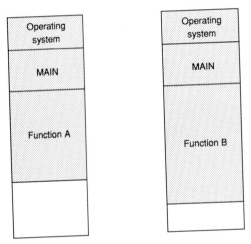

b) Two Overlay Configurations

Figure 4.2. An overlay example

is required. Then the second part is read and overlays the first. MAIN remains resident because it contains data required by both overlays. The number of branches is arbitrary, and the branches may be further subdivided. Although overlay techniques solve the size problem, reading the overlay from disk is time-consuming and so the subdivision of the process is crucial. We once reduced the run time of a program from four hours to ten minutes just by changing the overlay structure.

Multiprogramming was implemented in the mid 1960s, even with their attendant problems, primarily on the IBM 360 batch systems. The IBM 360 approach divided memory into *fixed-size partitions*, which permitted variable size processes, but which, once initialized, could not be changed. This approach is called "multiprogramming with a fixed number of tasks" (MFT). The system selected which task or process was to occupy each partition. Memory fragmentation was guaranteed because no process exactly filled a partition, but the management of the processes in memory was much easier. Overlays were used if the partition was too small for the process.

A variation of MFT divided memory into *variable-sized partitions*. That is, partitions were allocated dynamically as the processes appeared. This is called "multiprogramming with a variable number of tasks" (MVT).

DYNAMIC LOADING

It is not necessary for the entire process to be resident before execution is started. Some parts of the process will not be executed until the very end, and others may not be executed at all. For instance, unless the user makes a specific error, certain error messages will never be displayed. To take advantage of this property, the operating system loads only a part of the process. But, in loading only a part, the operating system is also assuming the responsibility of loading other parts as they are required. Implicit in this *dynamic* loading action is the fact that the operating system must also unload (or release) sections of memory as they are no longer needed, freeing physical memory to receive other parts of the process.

Consequently, what appears to the user as a whole process is, during execution, imaginary, or *virtual*, because the operating system does not treat it as a whole. Instead, it is arbitrarily segregated into parts for the convenience of the operating system, and the user is unaware of this activity and has little control over it.

Since the amount of *physical* memory is limited, interactive operating systems load parts of several users' processes into different sections of memory.

When switching from one user to another, the system wastes no time waiting for the second process to be loaded. But, when process loading is required, other resident processes are available for execution. This results in *overlapped* execution and I/O activity and, therefore, improved overall utilization of the computer system.

This dynamic loading solution permitted multiple processes to reside simultaneously in memory and was proposed around the same time partitioning was implemented. This solution, now called *memory mapping*, is dominant in the industry today.

The size of the process pieces and whether or not they are uniform are still debated topics. If the pieces are uniform, they are called *pages*. If not, they are called *segments*. (Think of a segment as a variable-length page.) Both paging and segmenting offer a solution to the problem of using the limited physical memory. Since the process is divided into small pieces, only the piece that is currently executing must reside in memory, and the rest can remain on disk until needed. And because only a portion of a process is memory-resident at a given time, either paging or segmentation permits the process to be larger than physical memory. This means that the number of multiprogrammed processes is variable and limited by policy rather than technology.

Segmentation, which was pioneered by IBM on the 360 model 67 in the mid 1960s, permits the process structure to define the segment boundaries. Depending on implementation specifics, a segment can be as small as a subroutine or as large as an entire process. Of course, segment sizes are limited by the physical memory size, but they are normally larger than pages. In any case, the operating system must deal with the difficult problem of fitting various-sized segments into a memory configuration that contains miscellaneous-sized spaces. It is possible to imagine a condition in which a segment cannot fit into physical memory because the available spaces are too small. Furthermore, space coalescing is required whenever a segment is freed. These are the same problems that confronted contiguous allocation designs.

The advantage of paging over segmentation is that all the holes in memory are the same size and coalescing is unnecessary, so the *memory manager* is considerably less complex. But page boundaries are arbitrarily distributed throughout the process without regard to process structure, and this results in other problems. The Atlas computer (1961) was the first that supported paging. Paging is implemented in some form on many of Digital's computers, the IBM 370 series, and on most microcomputers.

4.1. Paging Introduction

This chapter investigates paging thoroughly. In particular, it will show how VMS and VAX work together to solve paging problems. In addition to showing how the operating system implements paging, the chapter will make observations about process performance in a paged, multiprogramming environment.

Paging is one of the most clever advances in the history of computer hardware and software. It is an artifact supported by hardware made expressly for the benefit of software, in particular, for time-sharing systems. Unlike many other hardware advances, which are made simply because the technology improved, paging directly benefits software applications. It adds a level of complexity to the hardware that would never be allowed if hardware designers had their way.

Consider the following example of paging. A VMS user has logged on; hence, a process has been created. The user enters a RUN command to activate an image. (Refer to Figure 2.12 for the DCL command cycle.) As discussed in Chapter 2, image activation consists of reading the specified .EXE file from disk into memory in order to execute it. But, and this is very important to understand, the entire file is not read into memory at the time the RUN command is entered. In fact, the file is read in page-by-page, as it is required. The entire file may never need to be moved into memory. Say the user's program contains an error that terminates the image immediately, then moving the entire program into memory would be a waste of I/O resources and memory.

The image that resides on disk is artificially divided into pages. Typically, pages are at least 512 bytes long, as in the VAX, although they can be larger in other machines. On *demand*, a page of the image is copied from disk into a *frame* of memory. Memory is divided into frames; each is the same size as a page. (Other terms for a frame are *physical page* or *page frame*. The image page is sometimes called *virtual page*. For the rest of this chapter, a virtual page will be referred to as a page.)

The program itself demands the pages as it executes. This point is developed in Figure 4.3. The page of an image contains a collection of machine instructions and data. The figure assumes that the shaded page was read into memory, and, normally, instructions on that page are executed consecutively; the first instruction is executed, then the second, and so forth. Certainly, there will be branch instructions that will disrupt this sequential execution, but that makes no difference in this explanation. Eventually, the

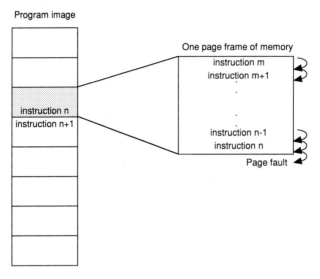

*Figure 4.3. Sequential instruc-
tion execution leads to a page
fault*

instructions will run off the end of the page, and in the virtual image, they
continue onto the adjacent page. The illustration assumes that the new page
is not in memory; it is still on disk. When an attempt is made to execute an
instruction beyond the current page, or, more precisely, when the program
counter (PC) is advanced beyond the end of the frame, an *exception*[1] is generated. This particular exception is called a *page fault* or a *translation not valid*
exception, and as with all other interrupts and exceptions, the operating
system is called to service it. In this case, the operating system reads the
required page from the image file into a frame of memory. When the read
is completed, the image can continue execution on that new page. To test
your understanding, suppose that there is a branch instruction on this second
page that changes the PC back to the first page; is a page fault generated?
No, because the first page is in memory already.

A fault is a software-caused interrupt that occurs when the process
attempts to access a nonresident page. The operating system responds to a

---

1. Digital makes a distinction between an interrupt, which is generated asynchronously,
and an exception, which is generated by a process.

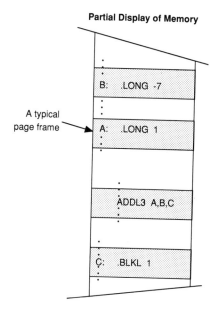

Figure 4.4. Partial layout of an image with an ADDL3 instruction

fault by faulting (or *paging* or *page fault handling*). That is, it copies the faulted (or *demanded*) page from disk to memory. *Demand paging* is the term used for this mechanism (involving faulting and paging) by which a process moves, page by page, from disk to physical memory in response to interrupts.

A page fault can be generated at any step in the instruction cycle—for instance, during an attempt to fetch an operand for an instruction—because, on the VAX, the instruction can cross a page boundary. In Figure 4.4, two variables, A and B, are added together, and the result is stored in C. The instruction is on one page, one operand is on a second page, the other operand is on a third page, and the result is to be stored on a fourth page. In this example, a single instruction causes three page faults, one for each operand, if those pages are not already resident in memory. There is no reason for separating the instruction and operands and doing so can cause page faults. On the other hand, it is certainly possible for all the operands to be on the same page as the instruction. In another example, if indirect addressing is involved, even more page faults can be generated by a single instruction.

4.2. Paging Behavior

The *principle of locality* means that execution tends to dwell in one region of the process for some time and then passes into another region; only small subsections of a process are active at a time. Another way to state this principle is to say that memory locations that have been recently referenced are likely to be referenced again in the near future. For example, any program is likely to contain several subprograms (Pascal PROCEDUREs and FUNC-TIONs or FORTRAN SUBROUTINEs and FUNCTIONs, etc.), and within each are looping structures that clear arrays, read data, make computations, and so forth. The process will spend a certain amount of time first looping in one region, then in another. Such behavior is characterized graphically in Figure 4.5a. It shows the value of the program counter (PC) over a given range of time, say 10 milliseconds. The solid ramps represent sequentially executing statements; the dashed discontinuities are caused by subroutine calls, gotos, if-then-else, and case statements. The branch at the bottom of the loop is shown as a dashed line too. Repetitive patterns are caused by loops of one kind or another.

Horizontal lines represent page boundaries in this model, and the first time a solid path crosses a horizontal line, a page fault occurs. The horizontal scales of the two graphs in Figure 4.5 are identical, so the intersection point is dropped down to the lower graph (part b). This graph indicates when page faults occur over time. No faulting may happen for periods of time because all the executing code is already resident. Then an execution pattern change may occur; for instance, a subroutine might be called that is outside the *active* frames. This will cause one or more page faults until the subroutine code is faulted into memory. Notice that the pages are not faulted sequentially. The structure of the program and the values of the data determine the page fault order, and there is no way to anticipate it.

In actual practice, it is difficult to collect data like that presented in Figure 4.5 without special hardware instrumentation. For a real program, which may run for only a few seconds, such graphs would be lengthy and probably contain too much data to interpret intelligently. To make the data more usable, we compress the time scale; for instance, the unit of time could be compressed to 100 milliseconds, 1 second, or even several seconds. If the graph in Figure 4.5b is compressed to 1-second increments, it might be presented like the histogram in Figure 4.6, which depicts the entire life cycle of an image. It should not be too surprising that the figure shows an initial flurry of page fault activity that gradually tapers off to zero. The reason for

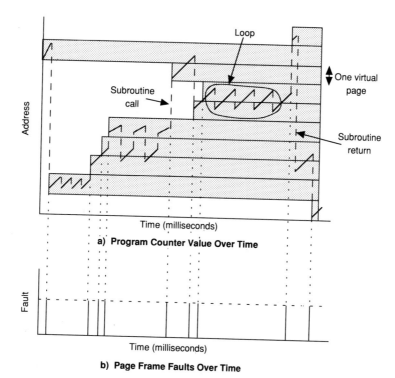

a) **Program Counter Value Over Time**

b) **Page Frame Faults Over Time**

Figure 4.5. Instantaneous behavior of a hypothetical program

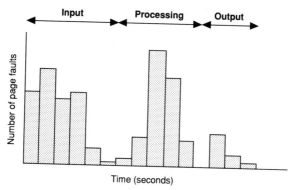

Figure 4.6. A process page fault histogram

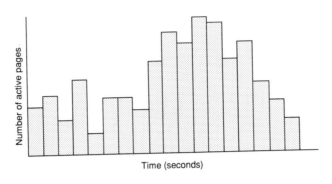

Figure 4.7. An active page histogram

this is that once a page is in memory, further access to it will not cause a page fault. Once all pages have been faulted into memory, no further paging takes place. Then, when the process enters its computation stage, which likely involves new pages of code, additional paging is required. Finally, some exit processing must be performed—for instance, printing the results and closing files. This processing is typically performed on pages that were never previously accessed, so there may be an increase in faulting activity just before program termination.

As explained in the introduction, there may not be enough physical memory for all processes to be simultaneously resident. Furthermore, the point of a time-sharing system is to share resources, one of which is memory. If a process attempts to claim all the memory resource, other processes are penalized. A possible solution is to not retain a page in memory if it will never be accessed again and to simply reuse that frame by putting an active page in the place of the inactive one. However, this turns out to be a very difficult algorithm to implement because the operating system cannot determine which pages will never be accessed again.

WORKING SET

A concept closely related to locality is that of the *working set*. This is the collection of *active* pages in memory at a given time. As shown in Figure 4.7, a program's behavior is characterized by the number of active pages, rather than the number of page faults, in a given unit of time. For example, in the figure each bar of the histogram represents the number of pages in the working set during a time period. Notice that unlike Figure 4.6, there is no period that zero pages are needed; that would mean that no pages are being used in a unit of time, which is nonsense. The goal of the operating system is to allocate frames of memory to contain the working set—no more and no less. If a process has too many pages, the memory resource is being wasted because it contains inactive pages. If there are too few pages available to the process, the working set is too small and page faults occur more often than necessary. This behavior is called *thrashing*, and it is undesirable because each page fault requires operating system overhead to process.

4.3. Page Management Algorithms

The memory management subsystem is the second part of the VMS operating system kernel. It is composed of the page fault handler, page management, the SWAPPER, and a memory status database.

To control the working set size for each process, the memory management subsystem determines which pages in the current working set have become inactive so that, when a demand for a new page is made, it replaces the old, inactive page with the newly faulted one. Put another way, the system must determine which page of the working set to remove to make room for a new one because the maximum working set size is limited.

There are several page replacement algorithms, and this section introduces two of the most common ones; the others are variations of these two. The simplest algorithm is a FIFO scheme. A list is maintained to record the order that frames were added to the working set, and a maximum list size is defined for the process. Then, when the list is full, the first frame is released and the newest one takes its place. This scheme appears to work because, on the basis of the principle of locality, the older the frame is, the less likely it is to be used again.

Extending the philosophy of FIFO page replacement is an algorithm called LRU (Least Recently Used). Intuitively, LRU selects a replacement page that has not been used in a long time; this is not necessarily the page least recently faulted. A page is used or *referenced* whenever an instruction is read from it or data is read from or written onto it. Although appealing, LRU is a difficult and expensive algorithm to implement. Ideally, the hardware should time-stamp each page as it is used. This is a burden on the hardware, but that isn't the operating system's problem. As in the FIFO algorithm, a list of the process's frames is maintained. The problem the operating system faces with time-stamping is locating the "oldest" page in the list. Since the list is in no particular order, every entry in it must be examined, and the search must be performed every time a page fault occurs. This amounts to a processing overhead the user must pay for in lost CPU cycles. A further problem with time-stamping is that, to be unambiguous, it must consist of several bits, which equates to memory overhead. The number of bits depends on the run-time of the longest process expressed in the smallest granularity the clock permits. For instance, to maintain 10-millisecond granularity for 24 hours (86,400 seconds) requires 24 bits.

A more realistic implementation of LRU page replacement is to associate a single bit, called a reference bit, with each page. Each time the page is referenced, the bit is set by the hardware. Then, when a page needs to be removed from the working set, any page with a reference bit of zero is assumed to be inactive and available for replacement. The software periodically clears all the bits—for instance, at each clock interrupt. A variation of the reference bit is to associate a reference counter with each page, which is incremented each time the page is referenced. However, like the reference bits, the counters must be cleared periodically. And, like the time-stamp method, this scheme requires a search of the page's counter values to determine the least recently referenced page.

The penalty of choosing the wrong page to replace is that it will have to be faulted back into memory once again at a later time. Moving a page from disk to memory is time-consuming. Of course, other processes will have an opportunity to execute while the page is being read, so the CPU is kept busy. However, the faulting process is occupying memory while waiting for the page, and memory is a resource other processes could be using. From the users' viewpoint, unnecessary page replacement is wasteful.

VMS MEMORY MANAGEMENT

As an introduction to the VMS memory management or paging algorithm, consider the initial configuration of the system with no users on it. Physical memory is either occupied by VMS *resident* routines or by its data. The remainder of frames in memory are linked together to form a *free list*. Figure 4.8 shows that when a process is created, frames are removed from the free list and put in the process's working set list. As the process executes, if the working set becomes too big, frames are removed from it and placed on either the free list or the *modified list*. And if a frame is erroneously removed

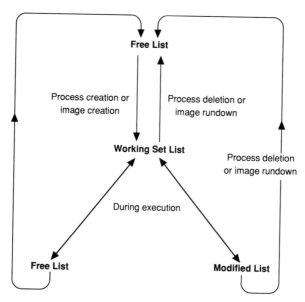

Figure 4.8. VMS memory management algorithm overview

from the working set list, it is restored from the modified or free lists. When
the process is deleted, all its frames in the working set and the modified list
are added to the free list.

In general, when a page fault is generated, it is serviced by the page
fault handler, which moves the requested page into the working set. At the
same time, the handler must respect the other processes and fairly allocate
physical memory among them all. The primary responsibility of the page
fault handler is controlling the process's working set list. One approach is
to permit any working set to become as large as necessary, but this could
restrict other processes from expanding their working sets. An alternative
approach is to limit each process's working set, realizing that a process may
thrash as a result. This has the advantage that every process can get at least
a minimum number of frames into its working set. The VMS operating
system implements this latter approach. The thrashing process is handled
as a special case with a working set determination algorithm.

Figure 4.9 presents a more detailed version of this paging algorithm.
Starting at the top of the figure, a process requires that a new page be added
to its working set. So, the first step in the algorithm is to determine if the

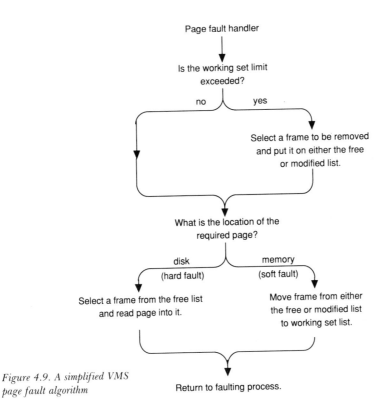

Page fault handler

Is the working set limit
exceeded?

no   yes

Select a frame to be removed
and put it on either the free
or modified list.

What is the location of the
required page?

disk   memory
(hard fault)   (soft fault)

Select a frame from the free list
and read page into it.

Move frame from either
the free or modified list
to working set list.

*Figure 4.9. A simplified VMS
page fault algorithm*

Return to faulting process.

faulting process has reached its maximum working set size. If it has, it must give up one of its frames in order to make room for the newly faulted one. It picks the oldest frame owned by the process under the assumption that an old frame is most likely to be inactive. The age of a frame can be easily identified from a FIFO list of frames in the working set. The oldest frame on the list is moved from the working set list to the end of one of two other lists: the free list or the modified list. The free list is used if no changes have been made on the page—for instance, if it contains only instructions. The modified list is used if changes have been made—for instance, if data has been stored on the page. The handler knows the difference because the memory management hardware maintains this information in a 32-bit long-word associated with each page, called the *page table entry* (PTE), which describes the condition of a page. The hardware sets the M-bit (M stands for modified) of the PTE whenever any data is written to the page (see Figure 4.17). The M-bit is cleared by the VMS system when the frame is first allocated to the working set and set by the hardware whenever any bit on the page is changed.

The second step of the algorithm in Figure 4.9 is to locate the requested page; it could be on disk or in memory already. This information is kept in the PTE also. Initially, the PTEs are created by the image activator, and each PTE points to its corresponding page in the .EXE file. The .EXE file has an image header, which, among other things, contains Image Section Descriptors (ISDs). Created by LINK, an ISD describes the memory requirement of an image section. The image activator uses information in the ISDs to create PTEs.

If the PTE indicates the desired page is on disk, the page fault is called a *hard fault* and a disk read is necessary. However, the required page may be in memory already, in either the free list or the modified list. The reason it may appear in one of these lists is that sometime earlier it was removed from the working set because it was the oldest entry. This is called a *soft fault*, and this logic accounts for prematurely removing a page from the working set. This unnecessary removal is easily corrected with little overhead because the page is not actually transferred in memory; instead it merely changes list membership. On the other hand, if the algorithm properly removed the page and it is truly inactive, the frame it occupies is available to be reused by another process.

A hard fault takes much longer to satisfy than a soft fault because the page must be read from disk. Servicing a hard fault requires that a frame must be removed from the free list and added to the process's working set list. This frame is used to receive the page read from disk. By making the free list FIFO, frames coming from a process's working set are added to the back of the lists, and when a frame is needed by a process, it is removed from the front. This means a process's oldest page is retained in memory as long as possible, which increases the likelihood of a soft fault.

The paging algorithm applies to both process creation and deletion and to image activation and rundown. Thus, when an image is activated, it faults pages into memory. And when an image is rundown, its frames must be returned to the free list. At image rundown, the working set list is reduced to a minimum size, but it still maintains frames belonging to the rudimentary process, such as DCL code. Similarly, frames that were moved to the modified list in the course of execution are also moved to the free list.

Another aspect of the paging algorithm is the maintenance of the working set size. Instead of simply assigning a fixed maximum number of frames to a process's working set list, the VMS operating system attempts

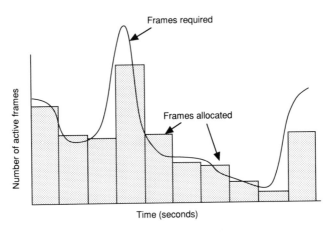

Figure 4.10. VMS working set behavior

to determine the required working set maximum dynamically. The VMS paging algorithm recognizes that the working set maximum is not a static, constant value, so it increases and decreases the number of frames allocated to a process depending on its behavior during execution. When the program requires more frames, memory management assigns them if they are available; when the process seems to have too many, memory management takes some away. Figure 4.10 illustrates this activity. The solid line shows the number of frames required in the working set. The actual number of frames allocated by the VMS system is represented by the histogram. That is, the VMS paging algorithm adjusts the working set size periodically but inexactly. The algorithm allocation lags and averages the required curve. This should be expected since the program is not able to anticipate page requirements, and, instead, responds to the page fault rate generated by the process. Intuitively, the VMS system increases the working set list size when the page fault rate increases dramatically and reduces it when little or no page faulting occurs. This is an extreme statement and is better made in terms of lower and upper page faulting rate thresholds.

To maintain the behavior illustrated in Figure 4.10, the paging algorithm computes a page fault rate (in faults per second) throughout the process's lifetime. If the fault rate exceeds an upper threshold, the paging algorithm responds by increasing the working set size. But if the fault rate decreases below a minimum threshold, the working set size is reduced, which causes it to release its frames. A low fault rate implies that the total working set is resident, and it is likely that too many frames are allocated to the process. Any fault rate between these two thresholds is considered acceptable, so the paging algorithm takes no action. In the figure, the open area between the solid line and the histogram implies that the process is generating an excessive number of page faults; this condition is called *thrashing*.

4.4. VMS Swapping Algorithm

The reduction or lack of free physical memory does not limit the number of processes. When the active processes fill all of physical memory—that is, when the number of entries in the free list becomes small—a possible response is to inhibit further process creation and image activation. But the VMS operating system does not do this. Instead, it establishes more room in physical memory with three additional strategies: management of the modified list, reduction of all working sets, and removal of inactive processes from memory. Modified list management is called *paging*, and removing inactive processes is called *outswapping*. Conversely, *inswapping* operations restore processes to memory.

While the paging algorithm is responsible for adjusting the working set limit, it is the SWAPPER process that is responsible for these three, more massive memory management activities. The SWAPPER is unusual within the VMS operating system in that it is a process and most of the rest of the VMS elements are procedures. Because it is a process, its time of execution is under the control of the scheduler. In a SHOW SYSTEM or MONITOR PROCESS display, SWAPPER is always found in the HIB state executing at priority 16, as if it were a real-time process. This elevated priority is necessary to ensure that SWAPPER runs before any time-shared process. Periodic (once-per-second) execution of a VMS procedure within the scheduler, called SCH$SWPWAKE (SWAPPER Wakeup), determines whether or not SWAPPER should be scheduled for execution. SCH$SWPWAKE makes a cursory assessment of physical memory utilization—for instance, it determines if the modified list becomes too large, the free list becomes too small, or an outswapped process becomes computable. SCH$SWPWAKE, rather than SWAPPER, makes this determination to save two context switches, to and from SWAPPER, every second. If SCH$SWPWAKE determines that SWAPPER is required, it changes SWAPPER's state to COM, thus forcing it into execution prior to the next time-shared process.

When SWAPPER executes, it can create more free pages in a number of ways. SWAPPER tests both the modified list and the free list length. Regardless of the free list size, if the modified list becomes too large, it is reduced by being copied into the *paging file* on disk. The modified list is then attached to the free list, thus increasing available memory. At a later time it may be necessary to move some of these frames back into memory. This is another form of a hard fault, except that the page resides in the paging file instead of in the image file. Reading this file is accomplished in the following manner: The page fault handler prepares a QIO request for the faulted page and all pages adjacent to it in the paging file. This collection of pages is called a *cluster*. The page frames required to receive the cluster are removed from the free page list. All the pages read are flagged to be in the process' working set. This algorithm reduces the paging file I/O activity and is valid because, according to the locality principle, if one modified page of a process is required, probably others will be needed too.

If free space becomes too small, the second strategy is applied; reduction of all working sets. SWAPPER increases free memory by uniformly shrinking all processes in the hope that the adaptive working set model[2] is not up to date. It does this by moving a portion of the working set of all processes to either the free list or the modified list. This reduction will probably cause some thrashing initially, as a few of the processes restore their working sets.

The SWAPPER includes a third strategy for controlling memory free space, which, because it is much more expensive than the two other mechanisms, is applied only as a last resort. If the amount of free memory falls below a certain threshold, something must be done to allow those processes in memory to continue to execute without thrashing if their working sets cannot be expanded. SWAPPER's solution is to eliminate inactive processes from memory in stages. A second file, called the *swapping file,* is used to store whole processes. Notice that the paging file was used to store the modified page list and therefore contains parts of several processes, but the swapping file contains some processes' entire working set. Normally, a low-priority process in one of the wait states is removed first, but the actual algorithm is much more complex. Processes subjected to this outswapping activity are considered to be in an outswapped substate—for instance, hibernate outswapped (HIBO). The complete list of outswapped states is displayed by the command MONITOR STATE. Copying a process to the

---

2. The working set adaptation logic discussed in the previous section is not part of SWAPPER; it is part of the page management software.

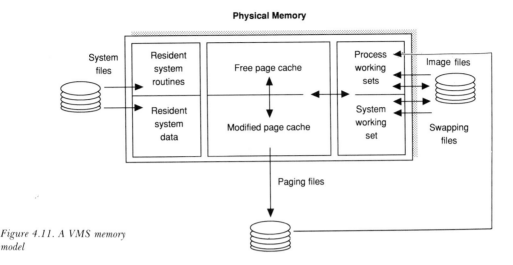

Figure 4.11. A VMS memory model

swapping file is done in two stages: first, the pages in the working set are moved, freeing those frames, and second, if necessary, the process's paging tables are also moved. The page tables must first be updated to reflect the fact that the process has been written to the swapping file; then the process's page tables are written to the swapping file. If the process has pages on the modified list, they are handled by the second strategy: they will be written to the paging file. When the process is returned to memory, its entire swapped working set is returned. In other words, a swapped process is returned to memory in its entirety from the swapped file rather than faulted back page by page.

Thus, memory can be modeled as in Figure 4.11, segregated into three partitions. Part of the VMS system resides permanently in memory, part of memory belongs to the working sets of the processes, and paged VMS and part of memory is cache to be assigned as needed. As shown in this model, on the left of the figure, the resident portion of the operating system is read into memory at system startup and resides there permanently. As shown in the center of the figure, when the modified list cache becomes too full, it is written to the paging file to free memory. Later, if a page in the paging file is faulted, it is first moved back into the modified list cache and then to the working set. Although high-speed memory cache is normally associated with hardware, in this case, it is a software-supported, easily accessed repository of reusable memory frames. On the right of the figure, image files enter memory as part of the working set, but when the free page list cache becomes

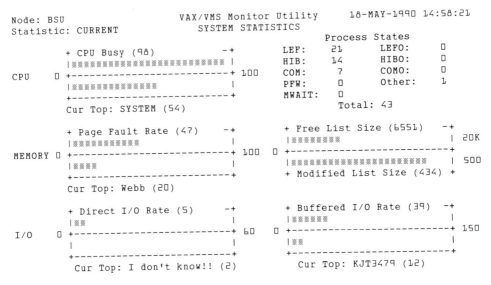

```
Node: BSU                    VAX/VMS Monitor Utility     18-MAY-1990 14:58:21
Statistic: CURRENT               SYSTEM STATISTICS
                                                     Process States
         + CPU Busy (98)        -+      LEF:    21    LEFO:       0
         |*********************** |     HIB:    14    HIBO:       0
CPU    0 +----------------------+ 100   COM:     7    COMO:       0
         |*************          |      PFW:     0    Other:      1
         +----------------------+       MWAIT:   0
         Cur Top: SYSTEM (54)                         Total: 43

         + Page Fault Rate (47)  -+      + Free List Size (6551)    -+
         |**********             |       |********                  | 20K
MEMORY 0 +----------------------+ 100  0 +------------------------+
         |****                   |       |********************** | 500
         +----------------------+        + Modified List Size (434) +
         Cur Top: Webb (20)

         + Direct I/O Rate (5)   -+      + Buffered I/O Rate (39)   -+
         |**                     |       |******                    |
I/O    0 +----------------------+ 60   0 +------------------------+ 150
         |                       |       |**                        |
         +----------------------+        +------------------------+
         Cur Top: I don't know!! (2)     Cur Top: KJT3479 (12)
```

*Figure 4.12. $ MONITOR
SYSTEM of $RUN*

too small, the working set portion of a process is swapped from memory, which frees some of the memory resource. Both user processes, and some parts of the system, are eligible for swapping. Later, when a swapped process can execute again, and if there is enough free page list cache, the working set is swapped back into memory. In the figure, the working set is connected to both free and modified cache, and frames move back and forth as required.

4.5. Paging Metrics

This section describes the paging-related measurement tools available in the VMS operating system. The examples provide a more intuitive feeling for what the memory management subsystem is doing. Figure 4.12 reproduces the output display for the command MONITOR SYSTEM, which is updated every six seconds. Memory management statistics are found in the middle of the display. In the center left-hand box labeled MEMORY, the top half of the box represents the average number of page faults per second. Our example shows that there was an average of 47 page faults per second in the most recent six-second interval—that is, 282 faults altogether. It also shows both soft and hard faults, separated by the vertical bar (hard faults are on the left of the bar). As this example shows, all of the 47 faults are soft, but no numeric value is displayed to indicate the precise hard and soft breakdown. The lower half of the MEMORY box shows which process produced the most page faults during those six seconds. There is no way to distinguish hard faults from soft faults at the process level. Our example shows that Process Webb faulted the most at 20 faults per second. Notice that the process's name, not the image name, is displayed. An unprivileged user cannot find out the name of another user's executing image.

The center right-hand box of the figure shows the sizes of the free and modified frame lists. In this case, there are 6,551 free frames, and maximum free space cache is 20,000 frames. There are 434 modified frames on a list designed to hold 500. When this limit is reached, SWAPPER must move modified frames to disk, as described in the previous section.

EXPERIMENTING WITH MONITOR

To see how paging activity is reflected in this display, perform a simple experiment. As previously described, faulting occurs when an image is activated. It occurs in other situations also, but the activation condition is easy to create. Log in on two adjacent terminals to perform this experiment. Enter the command MONITOR SYSTEM on the first terminal and then, once it has been initialized, RUN any image on the second terminal. After the RUN command is entered, you will notice a sudden increase in the number of page faults in the top half of the left-hand MEMORY box. You may also notice that your process is briefly the "Cur Top" in the lower half. Try executing other images such as SEARCH and PASCAL to see that different page fault rates are observed. When you LOGOUT of that second terminal, you will probably see a change in the free list and modified list sizes in the right side of the MONITOR display.

There are three other MONITOR options that display the page fault information: MONITOR IO, MONITOR PAGE (which displays additional details about memory management paging like I/O rates), and MONITOR PROCESS/TOPFAULT (which displays the seven highest page faulting processes). However, there is no way to collect working set data with MONITOR, although the system maintains that information. In general, MONITOR collects system-wide information, whereas the SHOW PROCESS/ CONTINUOUS display presents process-specific information, as Figure 3.14 showed. In the upper right corner of Figure 3.14, the system displays the

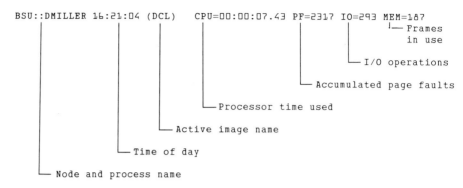

Figure 4.13. Status line pro-
duced by CTRL-T

current working set list size for the process and the number of pages in the image. The accumulated number of page faults (since process creation) is also displayed.

USING CTRL-T

Another tool provided by the system, CTRL-T, permits the user to measure several performance characteristics of a process. It is important for a software engineer to be able to ascertain a process's performance in its environment. Many performance difficulties are not the fault of any one algorithm in the application per se, but a combination of the operating system environment and the multitude of algorithms within the process. CTRL-T is normally active on a VMS system, but if it is not, it can be activated with the DCL command

```
$ SET CONTROL=T
```

which allows the user access to this tool. Depressing CTRL-T displays a one-line encapsulated status message, which is illustrated in Figure 4.13 along with the meanings of the various fields. CTRL-T can be used *anytime*; it is not simply another command. For instance, it can be used to see what time it is during an edit session. Also, during program execution, a software engineer can tell if the program is in a computational loop by looking at successive CPU times. The I/O field can show whether the program is caught in a disk read or write loop.

The MEM and PF fields are the reason for mentioning CTRL-T now.

The MEM field shows exactly how many pages are allocated to the process at that instant; it is the working set size. The PF field shows how many page faults have occurred since the process (not the image) was started. To determine the number of page faults an image generated, depress CTRL-T before the RUN and again after the image is finished and compute the PF difference.

This section demonstrated two memory management measurement tools, Monitor and CTRL-T. These are not the only performance tools available, but others provided by Digital are not included in the off-the-shelf system. Third-party tools are also available, and it is imperative for software engineers to understand these tools for two reasons. First, application designers need all of the debugging tools available to be effective, and second, as professionals, software engineers are expected to understand how the system and application interact and interfere with one another. They must understand both the VMS operating system and the application when designing, and they must be aware of how to use the system optimally. They should also be able to tell if they are needlessly reducing the effectivity of the system, although this is much more difficult to detect.

4.6. Thrashing

When the working set is too small, page faults will occur more often than necessary. This phenomenon is called *thrashing*. Allocating too many frames to the working set of a process wastes the memory resource, depriving other processes of physical memory. Allocating too few frames forces the image to page fault unnecessarily. If the number of frames a process is allowed to use is restricted, whenever a new frame is faulted, memory management will have to remove a page from the working set to make room for the new one. But if the removed page is actually part of the working set, another page fault will occur when that page is referenced again, driving still another page of the working set out. In this situation, the page fault rate causes unnecessary system overhead, and system performance will suffer.

A THRASHING EXAMPLE

Figure 4.14 illustrates a two-dimensional array that exactly fills two pages; the first row is stored in one page, and the second row is stored in the other.

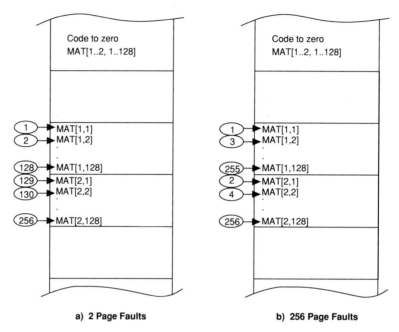

a) **2 Page Faults**   b) **256 Page Faults**

Figure 4.14. A thrashing example

The program merely clears every element of the array. For simplicity, assume that the code is entirely contained on a third page. There are two ways to write this program. In Figure 4.14a, all the columns in the first row can be zeroed and then all the columns in the second row can be zeroed too. This solution has two pages in its working set. (A typical working set size is much larger than two pages. This working set is two for illustration purposes.) Alternatively, in Figure 4.14b, the program can zero both rows in the first column, then zero both rows in the second, then the third, and so forth. This is a three-page working set solution. The circled numbers in the figure show the order in which the data are accessed in each method. The only code-level difference in the two techniques is the order of the nested FOR loops. A coder would not give a second thought to these two techniques, since they appear to be identical.

To show thrashing in operation, assign two pages to the working set. One page contains the code and the other the data. Assume that the instruction page has already been faulted into memory and stays there through the entire example. When the program zeroes MAT[1,1], a page fault occurs to bring that page into memory. If the program continues zeroing the array in row order, as in Figure 4.14a, the next cell to be zeroed will be MAT[1,2], and no fault will occur because it is on the same page. Continuing with MAT[1,3] and so forth, the only other fault that will occur is when the program zeroes MAT[2,1]. Half of the matrix is cleared before that second fault occurs. Presume that the first data page is selected for replacement, not the code page, and the other half of the matrix in read into memory. The second half of the matrix is then cleared. Only three faults occur: one for the code, one for the first half of the matrix, and one for the second half.

In Figure 4.14b, on the other hand, if the program clears the array by zeroing both rows in column 1 first, then both rows in column 2, the second element to be zeroed will be MAT[2,1]. But a reference to MAT[2,1] causes a page fault and the frame occupied by MAT[1,1] is replaced. This means that the MAT[1,1] frame must be linked to the modified list (it was changed) and the new frame copied from disk image. The third element to be zeroed is MAT[1,2], but that page is not in the working set any more, so a page fault occurs again, the two data pages are exchanged, and so forth. In the final analysis, a page fault occurs for every element zeroed, and so the computer spends most of its time exchanging pages and little time executing the user program. An inconsequential implementation like this can cause serious performance degradation on the entire system, not just the single process, because every page fault uses system resources like the CPU, thus depriving others of that resource. The process performing the implementation represented by Figure 4.14b is thrashing. Of course, if the working set were assigned to be three, then the code page and the two data pages could reside in memory simultaneously.

The VMS operating system has specific mechanisms that keep the thrashing process from degrading the system too badly. The VMS scheduler and memory manager work together to minimize the global effect of a thrashing process. There is nothing that can be done to eliminate thrashing, but other users can be isolated from its effects.

First, a compute-bound process such as the one above tends to remain at or near its base property as a function of the scheduling algorithm. This means that it will run only when no other interactive users are running. In addition, considerable disk activity may be caused by thrashing, which, depending on how other processes's files are distributed on the disks, might disrupt interactive users because of the disk demands.

Second, the memory manager measures the page fault rate and permits the working set to grow, within bounds, whenever it detects a high fault rate. There are three working set thresholds partially under control of the user. The VMS terms are *limit, quota,* and *extent,* and they are used in the following manner. When an image is rundown, the working set size is reduced to its limit. The quota is the nominal maximum a process is permitted. If a process is thrashing when the working set size is set to its quota, and if there is a sufficient number of free frames in memory, the working set can be expanded to the extent value temporarily. However, this value is never guaranteed, and the working set can be reduced at any time by the SWAPPER, so the frames allocated above the quota are considered to be "on loan" to the process and are reclaimed as soon as possible.

This example demonstrated how the code of an inconsequential problem effects the working set size without the designer's knowledge. This demonstration can be easily applied to more involved designs. There is no practical way for a designer to determine an application's working set size until it can be measured. Digital documentation indicates that 200 faults per second is reasonable, but that figure depends on many factors, primarily CPU's power. In the VMS operating system, correcting a thrashing condition can be as simple as increasing the working set quota with the DCL command SET WORKING_SET. When this is not possible, because physical memory is limited, a detailed analysis of the dynamic paging requirements of the process will identify the algorithm and data structures that contribute to the problem. The software engineer should expect to redesign the process when the analysis is complete.

4.7. Virtual-to-Physical Address Translation

An important detail avoided so far is the translation of a virtual address in the process to a physical address in memory. As previously explained, only a few pages, not the entire process, reside in memory at any one time. This section describes the algorithm used to locate the pages in memory in two ways: first, by partially tracing execution of a simple instruction, and second, by looking at the functions of the supporting hardware.

Tracing an instruction's execution requires assembly language experience. Examine a single instruction, INCL A, located in the middle of a virtual page in Figure 4.15. This instruction increments the variable "A," a

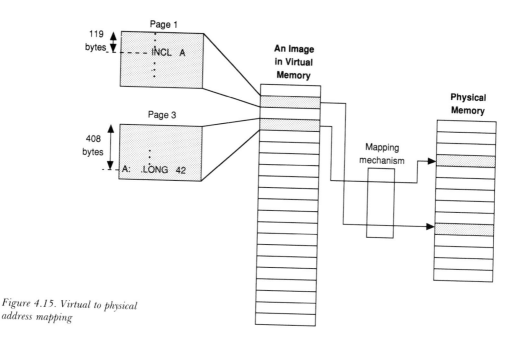

Figure 4.15. Virtual to physical address mapping

32-bit quantity. For this discussion, the instruction is on page 1 and the variable is on page 3. In the figure, the instruction begins 119 bytes into page 1 and the variable is located 408 bytes into page 3. In the center of the illustration, the image is contiguous in virtual address space; page boundaries are invisible and unimportant. The physical view of memory is shown on the right of the figure; two of the image's pages are scattered in memory because the image is neither contiguous nor totally resident. Scattering pages in memory is a major advantage of paging systems. To support this feature, some mechanism must *translate* or *map* the virtual addresses into physical addresses. In other words, the system must keep a record of where the pages have been placed in physical memory so they can be located when needed. This mapping mechanism is modeled to the right of the middle of the figure and is a combination of hardware and software.

The 32-bit address VAX architecture is subdivided into three fields, shown in Figure 4.16, called *region*, *page*, and *offset*. The region field can take on four values: 0 is called process 0 or the P0 region, 1 is called the process 1 or P1 region, and 2 is called the SYSTEM or S0 region. Region 3 is not used by the hardware and is illegal in current VAX architecture. The 21-bit page field contains the page number, which ranges from 0 to

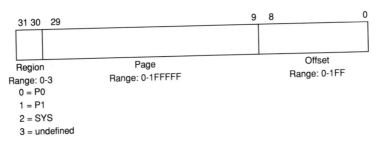

Figure 4.16. VAX virtual address format

2,097,151 (or 2 mega-pages). Thus, a 6-mega-page process can be constructed, theoretically, with two mega-pages in each of the three regions. However, this turns out to be practically impossible the way VMS is designed. P0 contains the majority of the user's instruction image, and the user's data resides in P1 space. The offset field is 9 bits long, meaning that the maximum offset is 511. Thus, there are 512 bytes on a page. This number may be familiar in another context; it is the size of a *block* on disk, which is not a coincidence but part of the VAX design.

To see how the addressing fields are applied, return to the example in Figure 4.15. The instruction is at offset 119 (77 hexadecimal), page 1, and region 0. To compute the virtual address, the page number is shifted 9 bits or multiplied by 200 (hexadecimal) and the offset is added; in P0 space, the upper two bits of the 8-"digit" number have no effect. Thus, the virtual address becomes 00,000,277 (hexadecimal). By a similar computation, the virtual data address of variable A is 00,000,798. The 9-bit offset field makes this algorithm somewhat awkward to do mentally; an alternative is to change the hexadecimal numbers to binary, concatenate the binary values, and then change the binary back to hexadecimal.

The PTE (page table entry), introduced earlier, relates the virtual page number to its physical frame number. In the VMS system, there are two page tables for every process: one for the P0 region and one for the P1 region. There is also a SYS region page table that all processes share. Each page in the image has a corresponding PTE. Figure 4.17 shows the format of one such entry. Concentrate on only three fields: *valid* or the V-bit, *modify* or the M-bit, and *frame number*. If the V-bit is 1, the page is in memory at the specified frame number. When the V-bit is 0, the page is not in the process's working set, and bits 26 and 22 indicate where it is. When the

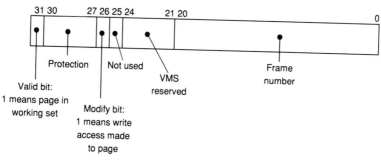

Figure 4.17. VMS page table entry (PTE) format

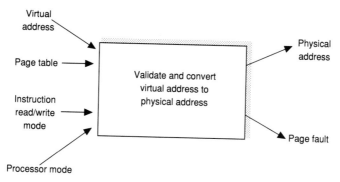

Figure 4.18. A functional model of the VAX address translation hardware

V-bit is 0, a page fault will be generated if the program attempts to access the corresponding page. If the page is resident in memory and the M-bit is 1, a modification has taken place somewhere in the page; that is, the page has been changed because some data on the page was changed.

Figure 4.18 illustrates the hardware *translation* model. This corresponds to the box labeled "Mapping mechanism" in Figure 4.15. In order for the hardware to perform the required virtual-to-physical address conversion, it must have four items of information. Two of the required items are the virtual address and the process's paging table. The other two, which it needs to perform the security functions, are the processor mode (kernel, executive, supervisor, or user) and whether the address is to be used to read

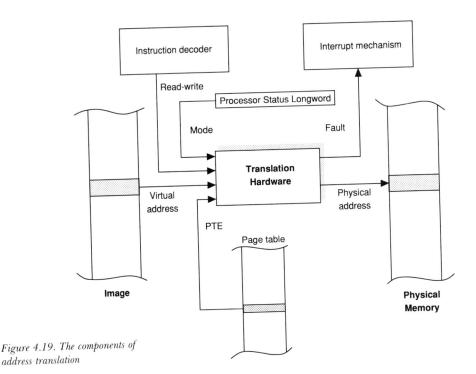

Figure 4.19. The components of address translation

data from or write data into memory (read-write mode). The output of the hardware is either a physical address or one of two faults. In this latter case, the fault could either be a legitimate "page not present" fault caused by a 0 V-bit, or it could represent an error like "address invalid" or "access not permitted."

We have now introduced all the components and can complete the translation model. Figure 4.19 brings the virtual image, the translation hardware, the page table, the processor mode contained in the processor status longword (PSL), the read-write indicator from the instruction decoder, and physical memory into a single picture. However, since it is customary to ignore the hardware interfaces in order to make the diagram easier to understand, the virtual-to-physical mapping is represented with only the page table in Figure 4.20, which also shows page and frame numbers so that the mapping algorithm can be illustrated more fully.

To trace the translation steps in Figure 4.20, begin at the top of the instruction cycle in Figure 1.13, where an instruction is read from memory into the instruction register for decoding. The program counter (PC) points

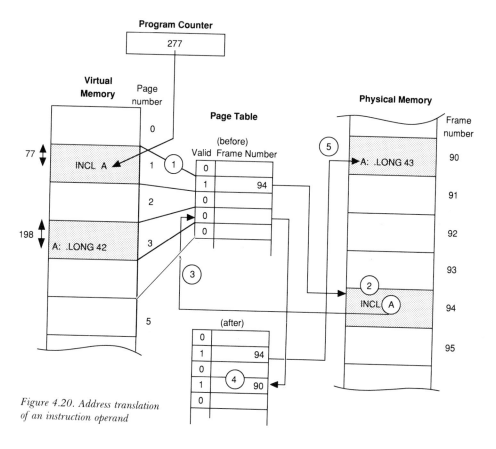

*Figure 4.20. Address translation
of an instruction operand*

to the instruction in the virtual image, not physical memory. It is page 1, offset 77 (hexadecimal) or 277. To locate the instruction in physical memory, start with the page number part of the virtual address (circle 1) and use it as an index into the page table to locate the page's PTE. The V-bit of that PTE is examined to see if the page is in memory yet. In this case, assume that it is, so the frame number is extracted from the PTE. The frame number, 94 (hexadecimal), is combined with the virtual address offset, 77, to form the physical address, 00,012,877, thus locating the instruction (circle 2). Notice that the page offset in the virtual image must be the same as the frame offset in physical memory; there is no hardware provision to do otherwise. The physical address is no longer 32 bits long; rather, it has become 30 bits, but there is no way to express this with an 8-digit number. Physical addresses are always 30-bit quantities on the VAX. The amount of physical memory installed in the computer is determined by the system manager, and the maximum memory varies from model to model. For instance, the smallest physical memory limit is found on the 3100 microVAX, 32 megabytes; the VAX 6000 maximum is 512 megabytes.

Once the physical address has been computed, the instruction is fetched and decoded. At this point in the instruction cycle, the operand, "A," must be read from memory (circle 3). As Figure 4.15 indicated, it lies offset 198 (hexadecimal) bytes from the beginning of page 3; thus, its virtual address is 00,000,798. The virtual address translation algorithm is repeated and the PTE for virtual page 3 is examined. This time the V-bit is 0 and causes the translation hardware to generate a page fault. This page fault exception handler examines PTE bits 22 and 26 to determine the location of the virtual page. This example assumes the page is on disk. The page fault handler selects memory frame 90 to receive the page. It reads the page and sets the PTE V-bit and frame number (circle 4) before returning to the process. The example shows the updated page table as changed by the fault handler. This algorithm is outlined in Figure 4.9.

While the required page is being read from disk, other processes may execute. The process in our example is placed in page fault wait state (PFW) during the page read, since it cannot continue execution until the read is complete. Like any other I/O operation, a PFW gives other processes the opportunity to execute, and it is another example of how the resources are shared among the processes.

When the page read is complete and the page fault handler has updated the page table, the process is returned to the COM state and, eventually, will be selected to execute. When that happens, the VAX hardware begins the instruction cycle by fetching the INCL instruction again. However, when the operand address is translated this time, page table entry 3 is complete so that the operand physical address can be computed and the instruction can be executed entirely (circle 5). Finally, notice that the value of A changes in physical memory, not in the image; the image is never changed. Upon completion of this instruction, the M-bit on page 3 is set to 1, although this is not shown in the figure.

Security or protection information is maintained on a page-by-page basis too and is stored in the page table—bits 27–30 of Figure 4.17. Each page is marked with a 4-bit code indicating the mode of the processor (kernel, executive, supervisor, or user) and accessibility permitted (none, read-only, or read-write). For instance, a code of 0 means that the page is inaccessible to all processor modes. A code of 2 (0010) means that only kernel programs can read or write on the page. A code of 4 (0100) means that every mode has read-write access to the page. And a protection code of 12 (1100) means that user mode can read the page but not write on it, while all other modes of the processor have both read and write access.

This section closes with an anecdote. In Figure 4.20, the instruction in memory is on page 1, which is in frame 94. As explained, since the operand is on another page, a fault will occur. Now, suppose that the memory manager decides to reuse frame 94 for page 3, instead of frame 90 as in the example. Of course, this means current frame 94 will no longer be available. So after page 3 is read into frame 94, the instruction is restarted and, of course, another page fault occurs because page 1 is no longer in memory. Page 1 will have to be retrieved from the image file. But since the algorithm failed once, it will probably fail again and choose frame 94 to receive page 1. This is credible, since an LRU algorithm may choose frame 94 since it is as yet unused. This case represents a very special error called a *page fault loop,* in which the same frame is used to receive both pages. This error has occurred on at least one time-sharing operating system: SUMMIT on the CDC 3800.

4.8. Multi-User Paging

Up to this point, we have looked at the effect of paging on a single process and on the global paging characteristics. This section expands the picture by examining how paging operates in an environment of multiple users. Each process has its own pair of page tables for P0 and P1. Figure 4.21 shows two processes, and for simplicity's sake, each process is shown with a single P0 page table. Some of the pages are valid and in memory, and are shaded in the figure. Some pages are not valid. Remember that there must be one PTE for every page in the image even if that page is not currently in memory. As mentioned, there is no reason the process's pages residing in physical memory should be assigned with any pattern, so the frames are shown scattered in memory.

A fortunate side effect of paging is that the two processes cannot possibly interfere with one another. This means that there is no possibility for COSMOS to accidentally or deliberately access the frames used by REGI because the two virtual processes are kept physically separated in memory by their page tables. To see why, examine Figure 4.21 again. Notice what happens when Process REGI runs off the end of page 3 in memory. Does

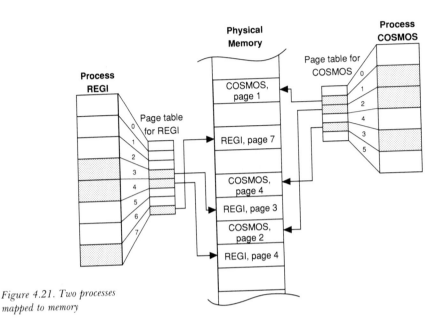

Figure 4.21. Two processes mapped to memory

it start executing instructions in the frame owned by Process COSMOS? At first glance, it might seem so because the two frames are adjacent in memory. But the continuity of a process is governed by the page table order, that is, its virtual memory order, and not by the physical memory order. So when REGI runs off page 3, it continues executing on its own page 4, which is two frames away in physical memory. If a process was able to change its page table, it could modify PTEs to read or write data of any process in memory. Clearly, this must be prohibited for the sake of privacy, so the process header (PHD), the host data structure of the PTEs, is inaccessible, even to its owner.

MEMORY SHARING

However, it is reasonable to want to share memory with another process for two reasons. Memory sharing allows processes to share data and thus communicate and to share instructions, thus reducing the number of copies of an image in memory. Figure 4.22 shows how two processes can share memory. The same two processes share a frame of memory: virtual page 2 in Process COSMOS and virtual page 7 in Process REGI. They can do this

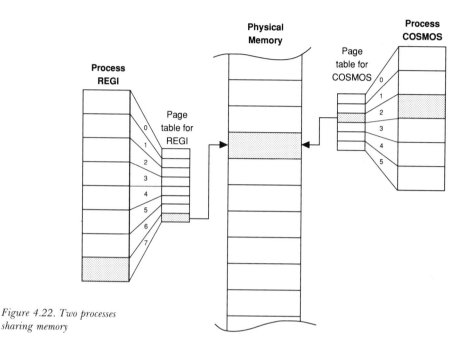

Figure 4.22. Two processes
sharing memory

because both page tables are built to point to the same frame of memory.
VMS permits processes to share memory in two ways: by a privileged use
of LINK and through system services.

To return to the motivation behind shared memory, the most typical
example is two processes using the same editor, that is, sharing the editor
instructions. Editors are the most popular images on a general-purpose
system, and it does not make sense to load a separate image each time it is
needed by a user. The instructions are never changed, so only a single copy
is required. Also, faulting the image into memory for each process is a waste
of disk time. The immediate reaction to sharing the editor might be that
the processes will somehow get mixed up with one another. But remember
that what makes one edit session different from another is the data, not the
edit program code itself. There is no difficulty in one process accessing one
part of a program and another process accessing a different part. Actually,
the two processes can access the same instruction because they are merely
reading it, and only one process is executing at a time. So when one process
is preempted, its PC is saved. The second process then continues where it

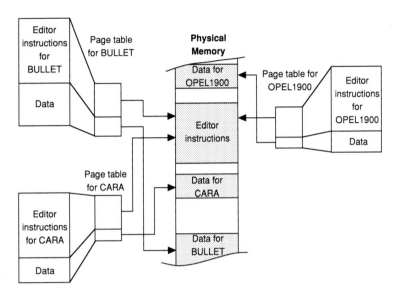

Figure 4.23. Three processes sharing an editor

left off previously by restoring its context. Remember that each process has a private PC, which is part of its context. Thus, there is no limit to the number of processes that may share the editor code.

But—and this is the essential point—the data for each process must be unique and separated. Figure 4.23 conceptualizes this idea in a schematic fashion, leaving out the page and frame details to show the larger picture. It also shows process frames arranged contiguously in memory, which is not accurate but is convenient to draw. Each process appears to have a private copy of the editor in virtual space, but there is only one copy in physical memory. In the figure, the three processes have different amounts of data. Thus, it is possible for one process to be operating in an entirely different part of the editor from that occupied by another process.

Sharing the editor saves the system time, since the image does not have to be transferred from disk as often and thus the disk is freed for other purposes. Also, because duplicate pages from the shared images are not maintained in memory, memory space is available for other users. By extending image sharing to all system utilities, the overall result is better system performance.

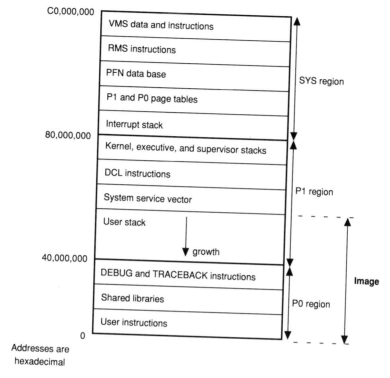

Figure 4.24. Process virtual space

PROCESS ORGANIZATION

It is exactly this sharing mechanism that permits processes to share the operating system code. First, look at the relationship between a user image, DCL, and the VMS operating system and how they communicate with one another in virtual memory. To start with, there are the three page tables associated with each process: P0—for the user's image, P1—used by DCL and the process specific data, and SYS—used by VMS. At the time a user image is executing, virtual memory space is divided into three distinct areas, as shown in Figure 4.24, each 1 gigabyte, or 40,000,000 (hexadecimal) bytes, long. The figure shows an example of what occupies each region. P0 space contains the user image, including shared run-time library (RTL) routines and DEBUG if requested. P1 space contains the data stacks for all execution

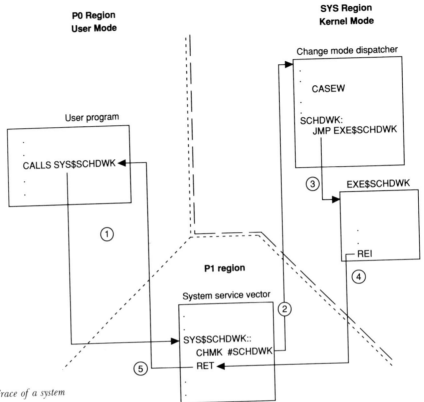

Figure 4.25. Trace of a system service call

modes (kernel, executive, supervisor, and user). The user stack is "un-bounded," and it grows downward toward the P0 region; the other three stacks are limited. When the image is rundown, the user stack is annihilated along with all traces of P0 region. In other words, P0 space and the user stack constitute the image. The SYS region is where the operating system and its data reside; in particular, the page tables for all three regions are in SYS space. When the operating system is executing, it usually uses the kernel stack located in P1 space. RMS, the record management system, uses the executive stack. DCL and DEBUG use the supervisor stack. Each process has its own P0 and P1 page tables; there is only one SYS page table, and all processes share it.

The VMS system is part of the virtual address space of the process, as indicated in Figure 4.24. To show what this means, Figure 4.25 traces a user process as it makes a system service request, a call to $SCHDWK. The compiler creates a CALLS instruction to SYS$SCHDWK[3]; this instruction is in the user image. When executed, the CALLS causes the specified arguments to be stored on the user stack, then it causes control to be transferred to the system service vector in P1 space (circle 1). The system service vector is a series of short subroutines required to call system services.

THE CHANGE MODE INSTRUCTION

The vector may seem like an unnecessary intermediate step, since the compiler-generated code could enter the operating system directly. However, the vector serves an important purpose: if the system service routine interface changes, only the vector must be changed, not the compiler. Because of the large number of compilers Digital maintains, the vector is a much easier and more accurate instrument for controlling entry to the operating system. The important feature of the system service vector is the inclusion of the CHMK instruction, (circle 2), which does a number of things:

- Changes the execution mode of the VAX from user to kernel, thus gaining privileges.
- Switches from the user stack to the kernel stack.
- Causes an exception directed to the change mode dispatcher within the VMS operating system.

The CHMK instruction contains one operand, #SCHDWK, which is used in a CASE instruction in the dispatcher to select the requested system service. The particular CASE entry simply branches to the appropriate system service (circle 3), EXE$SCHDWK.[4] The system service has complete access to all parts of the process, since it is kernel-privileged. (All system services have access to the entire process addressing space because they are executing in kernel mode.) In particular, access includes the arguments on the user stack and related data in the image. To perform its function, the system service may need temporary variables or may need to call other subroutines within itself, and it can use the kernel stack for these operations. By using the kernel stack, the system service leaves the user stack, which

3. $SCHDWK is a synonym for SYS$SCHDWK, and the programmer may use either spelling. This relationship is expressed in STARLET.PAS.
4. EXE$SCHDWK is the VMS entry point for the code that performs the SYS$SCHDWK system service. The user's process calls $SCHDWK, but the VMS internal name of the routine is EXE$SCHDWK. This naming convention is used for all VMS system services.

contains user data, undisturbed and thus more easily accessed by the VMS system. Notice that to service the request, there has been no context switch, only the mode of execution has changed from user to kernel to permit the operating system a higher level of privileges than the user is entitled to. This is where the protection bits of the PTE become important. A page that is inaccessible to the user has now become accessible to the operating system because the execution mode has been changed. This is necessary because the operating system must access its own data structures as well as the user's in order to complete the request. On the other hand, the user is unable to access operating system data structures because they are shared by all users. Access to common data structures must be carefully controlled. Only the operating system can be trusted to change its data properly.

If the process is preempted while in the operating system—for instance, if its time quantum is exceeded during this part of execution—the context of the process is saved, including all the stack pointers and the PC. Then another process can execute without affecting this one because the stacks remain undisturbed. Even if the second process does a $SCHDWK and executes exactly the same operating system instructions, the service is using a different user and kernel stack to read and store its data so there is no interference between the two requests. Eventually, the first process will execute again, its context will be restored, and it will continue where it left off.

To continue with the example in Figure 4.25, EXE$SCHDWK finishes by executing an REI (Return from Exception or Interrupt) instruction (circle 4), which causes the process to return to P1 space. At the same time, the REI instruction switches back to the user stack and lowers the VAX execution mode from kernel to user. So the REI instruction performs the opposite functions to those performed by the CHMK instruction. The system service vector simply returns to the user program (circle 5) using the RET instruction, and the user image continues execution.

4.9. Paging the Page Tables

Paging the page tables was observed as a desirable feature in the SWAPPER discussion earlier in the chapter. This fact is justified in this section. Consider how big the page tables are for a 4,087-page image. Not really very large, this image is approximately the default limit of a typical unprivileged user's image. It requires 4,087 PTEs, and each entry is 4 bytes long, totaling 16,348 bytes. There are 512 bytes to a page, and so to contain the page table of this relatively small image, 32 pages (about 1 percent) are required. However, the last page is not completely filled. As discussed in the chapter's introductory remarks, paging does not eliminate fragments, but it does minimize them. The case when unusable memory is within the image is called *internal fragmentation.*

Now, assume that there are 40 processes on the system, each with an average of 4,000 pages in its virtual image; that means 160,000 pages are required for these images. The operating system must accommodate over 1,200 pages that contain nothing but page tables. To appreciate this number, a megabyte of memory contains 2,048 pages, so 1,200 pages amounts to more than half a megabyte. On a 10-megabyte system, 5 percent of memory is consumed by page tables if they must be resident in memory. To reduce this overhead, the operating system pages the page tables in the same way it pages the process.

There is nothing special the system must do to page the page tables; they are loaded into memory on demand just like the rest of the user's process. It is unlikely that an entire 4,087-page image is in the working set; maximum working set sizes tend to be less than 1,000 pages on small applications. If a certain group of pages is in the working set, then so must the corresponding PTEs because every reference to memory requires access to the corresponding page table entry. Figure 4.26 illustrates this concept, showing that the P0 and P1 PTEs in the PHD (process header) point to the image. The SYS page tables point to the PHD; that is, the upper two bits of the PHD virtual address are 2. The SYS page tables have PTEs for the SYS page table also; they point to themselves. Unlike user page tables, the SYS page tables are permanently resident in memory. Figure 4.26 is similar to Figure 4.20, except it shows that the page tables are located in virtual memory just as the program is.

4.10. VAX Address Translation

To this point, the paging logic has been simplified so that several other vital points might be presented. This section examines the VAX hardware address translation algorithm in detail. To support translation, six registers of the internal processor register (IPR) set are used to locate page tables—a pair

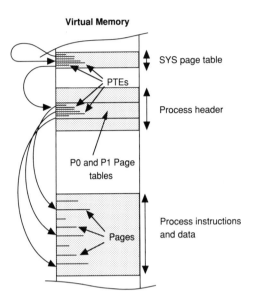

Figure 4.26. Page tables are used to reference the entire process

for each of the regions, P0, P1, and SYS. One register of the pair contains the address of the appropriate page table; the other register contains its length. The P0 and P1 pairs are part of the process's context; hence, they are saved in and restored from the hardware PCB at every context switch. This is how the process maintains its own private page tables. The SYS page table is shared because VMS is shared and implicitly part of every process.

Two figures are used in this description; all numbers on them are hexadecimal. Refer to Figure 4.27 first. The program counter (PC) contains the virtual address (VA), which needs to be converted to a physical address (PA). The upper two bits of the virtual address determine which of the three page tables are to be used. In this example, the PC value of 42,90A refers to the P0 region because the two high-order bits are zero. Circle 1 suggests that the page number (214) is extracted from the PC and checked against the P0 length register (P0LR) to ensure that the PC address is in the paging table at all. If it is beyond the virtual image range, a length violation exception occurs and the process must be stopped. This means the user has addressed beyond the limits of the image.

If the length test succeeds, translation continues with the PTE being

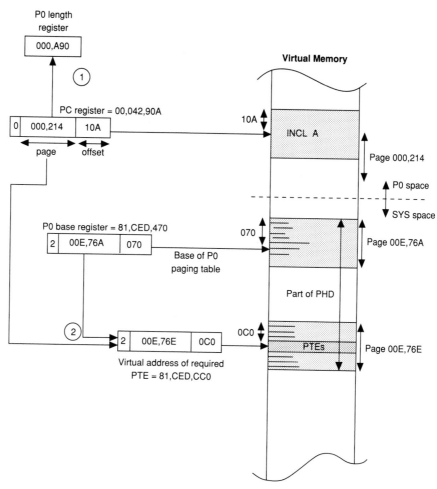

Figure 4.27. Creating a virtual
address of the PTE for the PC

located in the PHD. Notice on the right that the virtual space is divided into P0 and SYS space and that P1 space is ignored by this example. Circle 2 shows the page number multiplied by 4 (yielding 850) and added to the P0 page table base register (P0BR) to form the virtual address of the PTE needed to do the translation (81,CED,CC0). The multiplication is required because each PTE is 4 bytes long. The address of the PTE is needed because the PTE is the goal of this algorithm. But the address of the PTE is virtual too, so it also must be translated. This is a key point in understanding the algorithm. To say it another way, we now have a second virtual address (VA), the PTE location, that needs to be converted to a physical address. The VA of the PTE is always in the SYS region shown by the 2 in the region field. The VA location is guaranteed by the hardware; whenever changed, the P0BR must be set to a value greater than or equal to 80,000,000 or an exception will occur.

Figure 4.28 continues the translation algorithm. Physical memory is now on the right, and the PC and the VA of the PTE have been copied from Figure 4.27. At circle 3, the page number of the PTE is extracted and verified to be within the SYS page table by comparison with the SYS length register (SLR). If this comparison fails, the PTE address is out of range and, as with the previous check, a length exception is generated and the process must be aborted. This error is more serious than the previous one because it implies that the VMS operating system, not the user, has made an error—VMS has loaded a bad address into the P0 base register.

If the length comparison is successful, the page number is multiplied by 4, yielding 39,DB8, and added to the SYS page table base register (SBR), as shown at circle 4. This value is a physical, not a virtual, address because the SYS base register always contains a physical address. The SBR is initialized at system start-up and is never changed. This computed value is the physical address of the PTE (circle 5) that holds the frame number (4,AF0) of the PTE needed to translate the PC. The frame number and offset are combined to form a physical address, 95E,0C0 (circle 6). The figure indicates that the PTE V-bit is set, which means that the PTE is valid; that is, a frame has been allocated to the page.

At circle 6, the second PTE is read and the low-order 21 bits (43) are extracted. The offset of the PC address is combined with this frame number to produce the physical address of the INCL A instruction, 8,70A (circle 7).

To summarize this algorithm, the PC address needs to be converted from virtual to physical. What is new in this description is that the address of the page table needed for translation is also virtual and needs to be

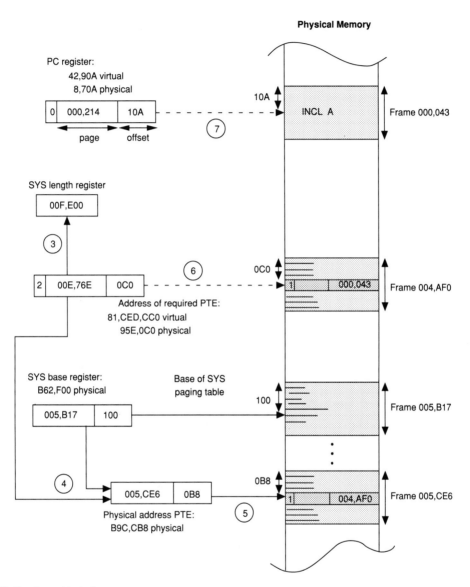

Figure 4.28. Creating a physical
address of the PTE and the PC

converted to a physical address too. This is true for all P0 and P1 addresses, but when addressing into the SYS region takes place, physical, not virtual, addresses are created from the page table. Therefore, both P0 and P1 address conversions require two memory reads to locate the two PTEs prior to accessing memory.

These two additional memory accesses may seem like a severe penalty to pay for a paging system, but they are the result of a series of trade-offs. For instance, if the P0 page tables were designed to yield frame numbers, only one extra memory access would be necessary, but the page tables would have to be contiguous in physical memory and unpageable. Our previous discussion showed why it is desirable to make process page tables pageable. Additionally, if physical addresses were contained in the user page table, these two requirements, continuity and pageability, would make the page tables difficult for the software to manage. Since page tables are allocated dynamically, finding a physical space large enough to hold a process's page table is exactly the kind of problem that the paging concept solves. The virtual page table solution presented still requires that the SYS page tables be contiguous, but there is only a single copy of them, and, even so, the tables are relatively small, static, and unpaged.

ACCELERATING ADDRESS TRANSLATION

To minimize the additional memory accesses requires a hardware solution. The VAX includes two caches for this purpose; one for PTEs and one for memory. The first cache is designed to minimize PTE fetches and is incorporated into the address translation hardware. The most recently used PTEs are kept in a high-speed associative *cache* memory called the *translation buffer*. The cache is much smaller than primary memory but 3 to 10 times faster. The size and speed parameters can be manipulated by the hardware designers to reduce the cost of this additional hardware. When a process repeatedly accesses the same page, no memory read or translation need take place; the cache provides the PTE instead. As long as the process executes within a few pages, no translation is performed, which saves memory accesses and thus decreases instruction execution time. However, this cache must be flushed with each context switch; this is done automatically with the load context (LDPCTX) instruction.

The underlying principle that makes translation buffer cache work is the same one that underlies the working set concept: the principle of locality. This states that programs repeatedly access the same range of locations. But

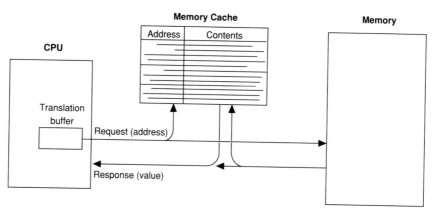

Figure 4.29. Read operation using cache memory

there is a question of the optimum size of cache, for if it is too small, the locality accommodated must likewise be small and cache will satisfy the CPU only a small percentage of the time. To say this another way, the larger cache is, the bigger the program loop it can accommodate. But making it too large results in a more expensive computer.

A second cache, *memory cache*, is located between the memory and CPU so that recently accessed memory locations are fetched from cache instead of memory. Since cache is much faster than memory, the timing expense of memory accesses is reduced under locality conditions. A typical memory cache is between 32K and 256K bytes and is two to four times faster than main memory. No flushing of this cache is required at context switch time; it flushes itself through the action of the executing process.

Figure 4.29 illustrates this cache model. The memory translation logic within the CPU contains the translation buffer. The memory cache is located between the CPU and primary memory. To understand how cache works, consider the following example. When the CPU requests data from memory, the request is sent to both cache and memory. If cache can fulfill the request, it cancels the memory request and satisfies the CPU sooner than main memory could have. If cache does not contain the requested data, memory delivers the data to both it and the CPU. Now initialized, cache can satisfy subsequent requests for that location. The problem of when to replace a cache entry and which one should be replaced is very much like the page replacement algorithm, except it has now been moved into hardware, which is likely to be controlled by a microprocessor.

This very brief description of cache operation will leave many questions unanswered; however, a more detailed study is not within the scope of this book. Suffice it to say that most computers incorporate one or more caches in their design, and one thing is clear—advancing technologies will change cache implementations drastically.

The key issue of the virtual-to-physical address translation algorithm is that two translations must be made, one to locate the page table entry and one to locate the target address. These two translations are necessary to permit page table paging, which is required to alleviate the problems caused by page tables that are contiguous or too large. Double translation is expensive in time, so the hardware is designed to minimize this drawback. The translation buffer maintains PTEs, making the two translations necessary only the first time the page is referenced. Even so, since the translation buffer is related to a process's virtual structure, it must be reset every time the context is switched. Thus, a process will encounter a certain set-up cost each time it is restarted.

Memory caching has nothing to do with the translation problem, but it does speed up the memory access time in general. It is not necessarily process-related, so no special care must be taken when changing contexts—unreferenced entries in memory cache will eventually migrate out of it.

4.11. Page Database

The major part of the design of an operating system is spent on its data structures rather than its algorithms. The majority of the required algorithms have been well researched and documented by this time, and their implementation accounts for the success of the operating system. The operating system's performance can also be dramatically affected by its data structures. This section will bring the two major data structures together and examine how the operating system exploits them.

THE PROCESS HEADER

The PHD is illustrated in detail in Figure 4.30. It is divided into two parts—fixed and variable. The fixed part contains indexes to locate information in

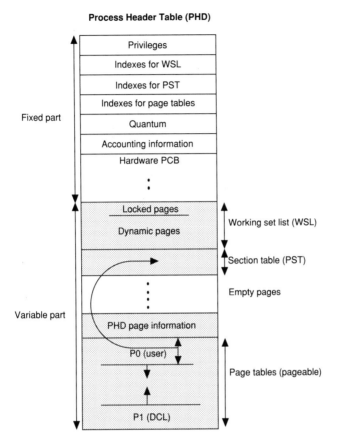

Figure 4.30. Overview of the process header (PHD) structure

the variable section, and it also contains the hardware PCB, privilege information, and some accounting data. The variable part is further subdivided into the WSL (Working Set List), the PST (Process Section Table), PHD paging information, and the PTEs. Of these four, only the page tables are permitted to page.

The process headers for all active processes are stored in the SYS region, in a structure called the *balance slots*. Also stored there is a structure called the PHD index base (PIXBAS), which is used to link balance slots to the rest of the process's data structure. These two structures interact as pictured in Figure 4.31. The Qth entry of the PIXBAS corresponds to the

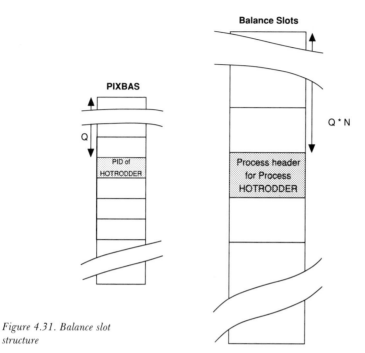

Figure 4.31. Balance slot structure

Q^{th} entry of the balance slots. Each balance slot has a fixed length, N in the example, so multiplication is required to locate the specific PHD. If the value of an entry in the PIXBAS is zero, the corresponding balance slot is not in use. A nonzero value is a process identifier (PID), which acts as the link to the process control block (PCB), the pivotal data structure in the system.

All balance slots are the same size, so linked lists are not involved in the overall structure. Because the slots are the same size, they must be sized for the largest process in the system, which in a university environment, is often smaller than many system images like LINK and Pascal. Therefore, the PHD structure often contains unusable space.

PAGE FRAME NUMBER DATABASE

The second major data structure in the memory management subsystem is the page frame number (PFN) database. The PFN contains information about all processes; it maintains a global picture of memory utilization. Figure 4.32 contains a portion of the page frame number database. Beginning

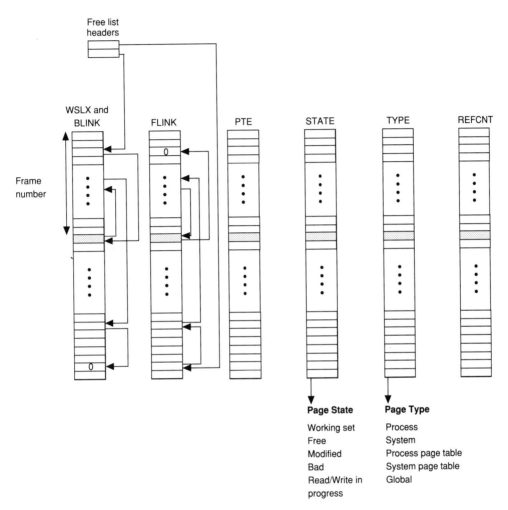

Figure 4.32. A portion of the page frame number (PFN) database

at memory frame 0, there is an entry associated with every pageable frame of memory, although frame 0 is not used. Nonpageable VMS resides in the highest part of physical memory, and the PFN database does not extend that far. Since the resident portion of the VMS operating system is never moved, reduction of the PFN database gives the user processes as much room as possible. The PFN requires 18 bytes per frame if the installed physical memory system is less than 32 megabytes, and 22 bytes per frame for larger memories. For example, 1 megabyte of memory, 2,048 frames, requires 45,056 bytes or 88 frames of PFN data, almost 5 percent. This database is not pageable and is addressed in the SYS region only.

Figure 4.32 shows only six of the eight arrays in the PFN database, all of which are accessed the same way, by using frame number as an index. At the right of the figure, the REFCNT array counts the reasons a frame cannot be moved to the free or modified list. For instance, if the frame is in a working set, the REFCNT is set to 1. The TYPE array indicates what kind of data is contained in the frame. The STATE array indicates the status of that frame, for example, in the working set, in the free list, etc., and also indicates if the frame is in transit between disk and memory. Note that a page can be flagged as bad, which is detected when data is read from disk into the frame.

The PTE array links the frame to the process; it contains an address of the PTE referencing the frame. Frames on the free, modified, or bad list use the BLINK or FLINK structures as the backward and forward links. Figure 4.32 indicates a free list thread. If the frame is in the working set list (WSL), BLINK takes on another role, and WSLX is used to locate the page in the working set list. In addition to the structures shown in Figure 4.32, other arrays are included in the PFN database to record shared page use and to support the SWAPPER.

Finally, Figure 4.33 brings the scheduler database and page database together in an overview diagram. This makes it easier to visualize the whole picture than when looking at only one structure at a time.

The most interesting link shown in Figure 4.33 is from the frame back to the owner of that frame recorded in the PCB. This is not an easy route and requires an explanation. Within the PFN database, the PTE array contains the address of the page table entry that resides in the balance slot. All balance slots are the same size, so computing the difference of the PTE address and the balance slot base, then dividing by the slot size, results in a slot index. Using that index on the PIXBAS yields the process identification

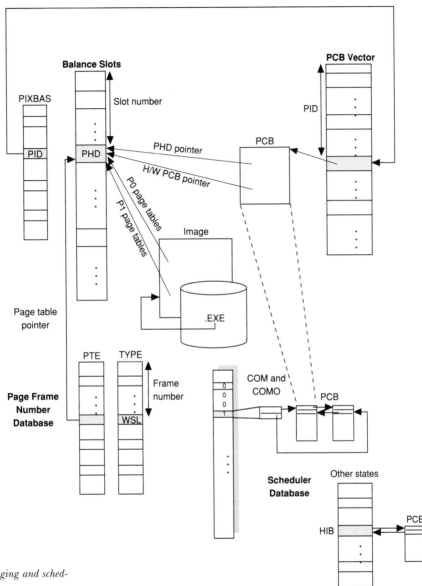

Figure 4.33. Paging and scheduling database

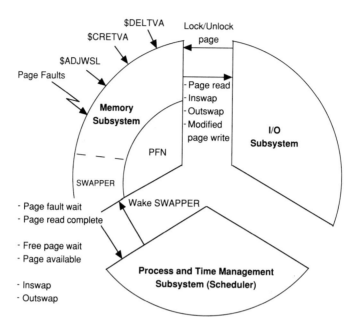

Figure 4.34. The memory man-
agement subsystem of the VMS
kernel

(PID), which, as mentioned, is an index into the PCB vector. Each PCB
vector entry points to a PCB, which is the required information.

The PCB does not "float" in the data structure picture, but is a member
of one of the lists in the scheduler database in the lower right of the diagram.
The PCB points to the PHD directly as well as to the hardware PCB within
the PHD. The PHD is initialized from disk when the process is created and
modified each time an image, the .EXE file, is activated.

4.12. VMS Memory Management Organization

Chapter 3 illustrated the scheduler subsystem of the VMS kernel. Figure
4.34 presents the detail for the second third of the VMS kernel, the memory
management subsystem. The database portion is the PFN database; however,
the process header (PHD) is also part of this database. The subroutines

consist of the page fault interrupt handler, page manager, and the SWAP-PER process, and the system services supported by this subsystem that create and delete virtual memory. $CRETVA (Create Virtual Address Space) is used during image activation, $DELTVA (Delete Virtual Address Space) is used during image rundowns, and $ADJWSL (Adjust Working Set Limits) is used by the SET WORKING_SET command to change the working set size in response to memory demands.

The memory management part of the kernel requests page I/O from the I/O subsystem via special calls designed to reduce the I/O overhead. The I/O subsystem responds with a request to lock the page frame into the working set list. Frames must be locked whenever I/O is taking place on them to prohibit the memory manager from reallocating them. In particular, a page that is waiting for an I/O operation may appear to be inactive and hence eligible to be removed from the working set, but this cannot be allowed because once the page is put into the free list, it can be assigned to another process. To prevent removal from the working set list, the REFCNT in the PFN database is incremented. When the I/O is complete, the REFCNT is decremented again to unlock the frame.

Memory management may cause the process execution state to change because of a process faulting pages or because memory has insufficient page frames. There are three possibilities (page fault wait, free page wait, and inswapping) and corresponding responses (page read complete, page available, and outswapping) listed in the figure.

4.13. Related Issues

It is possible to design a system in which the operating system does not execute in the context of the process. This allows the user more virtual space but makes operating system communication more difficult because of the inherent separation of virtual space—the operating system has no convenient way of reading and writing data in the user's process. One solution is to provide a pair of special instructions to move the data. These instructions are special because they permit the operating system to reference both page tables. The PDP 11/45, for example, has one instruction to move data from the operating system to the process and another to reverse the direction. But the data to be transferred has to reside on the process's stack.

A second difficulty encountered when the operating system is not part of the process virtual space is that overall system operation changes significantly too. In particular, a context switch can only take place when the process is executing and not when the operating system is executing. This results in serious performance considerations. For instance, when the time quantum expires, the process cannot be preempted until the process code is executing again, because if the operating system is executing, it must finish the service request because there is no way to associate the operating system's context with the process that made the request. Thus there is a delay in responding to the quantum expiration and this may affect the response time.

An alternative to maintaining working sets for each process is using a more global algorithm. A process is given a page frame whenever it demands one, provided there are any free frames. If there are none available, the oldest or least recently used frame is taken from whatever process is using it and reassigned to the current process. Frames are reassigned without regard to ownership and without limits, and when a process is deleted, all of its frames become free. This scheme is not fair because a heavily faulting process will be given as many frames as it needs, and a process that exhibits very localized behavior will be given only a few. When the localized process wants more, they may not be available because the heavy faulter has them already. On the other hand, the heavy faulter is more likely to lose a frame when a demand is made.

Another paging solution is to *prepage* a process. That is, when a page fault occurs, a memory frame is allocated to that page and a few following it. This algorithm is based on the locality principle in this way: if one page is needed, probably several virtual pages following it will also be required.

It is not necessary that the page tables be pageable, but without this feature, the memory overhead may be more than users are willing to tolerate. This is a design trade-off issue: hardware design complexity versus user flexibility. Whether or not the page tables are pageable, a page translation cache is required to achieve good performance.

When a page fault is satisfied, the instruction is restarted. This is a design solution and depends on the computer's instruction set. For instance, on the VAX, an auto-increment operand cannot be permitted to increment again and again each time the instruction is restarted. Other more complex instructions, such as the MOVC (Move Character), may fault partway through the move because either the source or the destination string is not resident in memory. When the required page is available, the MOVC must continue from that fault point. Therefore, the hardware must have some provision for recording these partially executed instructions so that they can be continued after the fault. This is the reason the MOVC uses registers in the course of execution.

Historically, page tables were kept in registers, to reduce translation time and make the translation buffer unnecessary. However, these registers become part of the context and therefore need to be reloaded (but not saved) at each context switch. For example, the PDP-11/45 had 16 registers, which resulted in very large pages, but permitted virtual addressing.

4.14. Summary

A multiprogrammed system must have a provision for permitting several users' processes to co-reside in physical memory; more than one process must have the capability to occupy memory at a time. Historically, the motivation for this was economic. Even today, when a computer is purchased to serve several users, it should be as well utilized as possible at all times to make it the most cost-effective. A single process is unlikely to use a processor 100 percent of the time because an average process, especially an interactive one, performs many time-consuming I/O operations.

A second motivation for co-resident processes is to enhance response time. If the process is in memory, ready to be executed, the interactive user will not experience unacceptable delays to keyboard-entered commands.

This chapter dealt with how multiple processes are able to co-reside in memory. We first introduced the multiprogram concept by considering its historical alternatives. Initially, because of the small address space of early computers, processes were either very small or were subdivided into overlays by the programmer. Today, many of the applications for microcomputers, such as word processors and spread sheet programs, are still implemented with overlays.

In today's time-sharing operating systems, processes are arbitrarily subdivided into pages. We explained how a process faults its pages into memory and how it behaves in a paged environment. Dominant in this discussion was the concept of a working set and the principle of locality. The page fault handler administers physical memory, determining and maintaining a working set for each process.

We interpreted the VMS Monitor display in order to offer an intuitive picture as well as a method to observe system metrics of the global aspects of the page fault handler.

The paging and swapping algorithms supported by the VMS operating system were examined; they showed that VMS moves pages from the working set to a memory cache in an effort to minimize the impact of erroneously selecting an active page for removal. The cache contains the free page list and the modified page list. The free list contains unchanged pages, whereas the modified list contains pages that have been changed during execution. When a page is missing from the working set, a page fault occurs. The VMS operating system defines two classes of page faults, hard and soft. Soft faults are satisfied from the memory cache, but a hard fault requires a disk access. No matter how intuitively appealing, this caching model leads to additional complexity, because the modified list cannot be allowed to grow indefinitely.

Beyond working set management, VMS supports another mechanism for freeing memory, called swapping. If the software free page cache becomes too small, inactive processes are swapped in their entirety to a special file on disk, the swap file. Swapped processes are returned to memory only when they become active again, so certain processes that are hibernating for relatively long periods, like JOB_CONTROL, are often moved to the swapping file when memory shortages occur.

A process that is assigned an inadequate number of frames to contain its working set will thrash. Page management algorithms must permit thrashing for short periods because they cannot anticipate the future demands of a process. In fact, thrashing is apparently a common VMS phenomenon. In one instance, a dedicated application on a MicroVAX II was observed in which almost half of the 20 executing processes were thrashing. The system designers and programmers were entirely unaware of the situation; all they had noticed was that their system had poor response time. Thrashing was examined in some detail, and an example demonstrated how easily a programmer can create this condition unknowingly.

The VAX paging hardware was examined to demonstrate that a powerful concept like paging requires a significant level of support from the hardware. Remember that the user's page tables are themselves paged. The reason for doing this is to reduce the amount of memory space needed by a process—if a certain part of a process is inactive, neither those pages nor the corresponding pages tables need to reside in memory. System page tables are part of memory-resident VMS and are never moved. We briefly examined how hardware caching supports both the translation mechanism and memory accesses in general.

Finally, the page database that supports the memory management subsystem was described. This database has two components: The PFN database, which describes the status of physical memory, and the PHD, which describes the virtual status of the process. These two databases are connected through the PFN database and consume a considerable amount of physical memory.

ACRONYMS

$ADJWSL	Adjust Working Set Limits system service
$CRETVA	Create Virtual Address Space system service
$DELTVA	Delete Virtual Address Space system service
$SCHDWK	Schedule Wakeup system service
BLINK	Backward Link in PFN database
CALLS	Assembly instruction for subroutine call
CHMK	Assembly instruction to Change Mode to Kernel
COM	Computable process state
CPU	Central Processing Unit
DCL	Digital Command Language
FIFO	First In, First Out
FLINK	Forward Link in PFN database
HIB	Hibernate process state
HIBO	Hibernate Outswapped process state
INCL	Assembly instruction to increment a value by one
IPR	Internal Processor Registers
KESU	Kernel, Executive, Supervisor, User
LRU	Least Recently Used
M-bit	Modify bit
MFT	Multiprogramming with a Fixed number of Tasks
MVT	Multiprogramming with a Variable number of Tasks
P0LR	P0 Length Register
P0	Region 0 of virtual memory
P1LR	P1 Length Register
P1	Region 1 of virtual memory
PA	Physical Address

PC	Program Counter
PFN	Page Frame Number
PF	Page Fault
PFW	Page Fault Wait process state
PHD	Process Header
PIXBAS	PHD Index Base
PSL	Processor Status Longword
PTE	Page Table Entry, array in PFN database
REFCNT	Reference Count array in PFN database
REI	Assembly instruction to Return from Exception or Interrupt
RET	Assembly instruction to return from subroutine
RMS	Record Management System
RTL	Run-Time Library
SBR	SYS Base Register
SLR	SYS Length Register
SYS	System region of virtual memory
V-bit	Valid bit
VA	Virtual address
WSLX	Working Set Link index

SHORT ANSWER EXERCISES

1. Convert each of the VAX virtual hexadecimal addresses to hexadecimal region, page, and offset.
   a. B5,A34,B02
   b. 00,E00,1FF
   c. 55,003,AA9
   d. EA,449,BB2
   e. 92,802,ED3

2. Trace the steps that take place when an image in P0 space attempts to address beyond its virtual limit and causes a page length violation fault.

3. In the style of Figure 4.5, part a, draw the instantaneous behavior of a segment of code containing:

```
REPEAT
  IF  . . . THEN
       . . .
  ELSE
       . . .
UNTIL . . .
```

4. In the style of Figure 4.5, part a, draw the instantaneous behavior of a segment of code containing:

```
WHILE . . . DO BEGIN
  IF  . . . THEN
       . . .
  ELSE
       . . . (call a subroutine)
END
```

Assume that part of the time, the THEN branch is taken, and part of the time the ELSE branch is taken.

5. In implementing the LRU algorithm using the reference bit, what difficulties may be encountered?

6. Why is the user page table pageable on the VAX?

7. Refer to Figure 4.28. Show how the PC physical address is computed once the frame number is known.

8. How many bytes does the SYS page table occupy in the examples in Figures 4.27 and 4.28?

9. Consider Figure 4.5. Why do all the solid lines have positive slopes? Is it possible to have a compiler instruction that creates a line with a negative slope? What is it?

10. Draw a picture like Figure 4.4 to illustrate how the following instruction can generate two page faults when fetching its operand.

```
INCL @PTR_COUNT
```

11. Exactly how many bytes are there in two megabytes?

12. Twenty-one bits in the page number field of the address represent two mega-pages, Figure 4.16. Figure 4.24 shows that each region is a gigabyte long. Show that two mega-pages are equivalent to a gigabyte.

PROJECTS

1. This exercise deals with the design and code of a program. Write a program that will display a temporal page fault histogram like the one in Figure 4.6. Use the $GETJPI system service to acquire the fault data for your process and display it in real time. To work, this program will have to execute as a subprocess because, due to restricted privileges, only processes in your group can be accessed by $GETJPI. A sample $GETJPI call from Pascal is found in Figure 5.4.

2. In the previous project, a second method is a major, more general programming task. Research the Monitor documentation to find out how the fault data is recorded. Then design a program that can read the recorded data and display the histogram for any single process, as specified by the user.

3. The balance slot size is fixed at the time the system is started. Determine the size of the biggest possible process your system will permit. The easiest approach to this problem is to create a program with a very large array in it. Keep increasing the size of the array until Pascal, LINK, or RUN indicates that the image is too large. What part of the system notices that your process is too large? How do you determine exactly what the page limit is?

4. The purpose of this project is to observe, gather data, and report the characteristics of two similar programs. Here is the theory behind this project: any program will thrash in the wrong environment. The wrong environment occurs in either of the following cases:

    a. The page frame resource for the process is sufficiently restricted.
    b. The program is too big for the environment that has been allocated.

    Therefore, the following is true in all programs: page faults will be constant over a range of page frame resources, but the faults will increase dramatically when the number of frames is reduced to a certain value. This is graphically illustrated in Figure 4.35; the knee of the curve defines the point at which the program's behavior can be characterized as "thrashing."

    I suggest you follow the procedure below to conduct your investigation.
    a. The array is defined like this:

    ```
    HOG: ARRAY [1..128, 1..500] OF INTEGER;
    ```

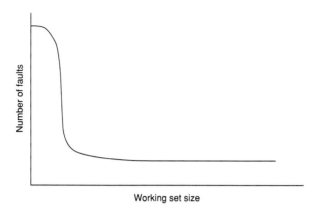

Figure 4.35. Behavior of a
thrashing program

Write two programs (and compile and link them), one to initialize
an array like this:

```
FOR I:=1 TO 128 DO
    FOR J:=1 TO 500 DO
        HOG [I,J] := 0;
```

and another to initialize the array like this:

```
FOR J:=1 to 500 DO
    FOR I:=1 TO 128 DO
        HOG [I,J] := 0;
```

b. Execute the two programs on one terminal while observing the Page
management statistics portion of the MONITOR SYSTEM display
on the other terminal. This can be done with two adjacent terminals.
The reason for watching the display is merely to observe the system,
not to gather data.

c. Use CTRL-T on the terminal running the program to determine
the number of page faults and CPU utilization for each program;
then neatly record this data. You should probably execute several
times at each working set value to determine an average number
of faults.

d. Reduce the size of your working set using the command:

```
$ SET WORKING_SET/EXTENT=xxx
```

e. Loop to step c. until you have collected enough data to create a curve for each program that illustrates its thrashing characteristic. Make two graphs: one for faults and one for CPU time. Plot both curves together on the same axes to compare them.

5. When a process is thrashing, does it affect overall VMS performance? Observe the effect on VMS subjectively and report your findings.

6. Write a program that causes a page length violation. Note how VMS responds to this error. Is the image run down or does it remain in the process? How do you know?

PAPERS

1. Research the issues involving cache memories. There are so many questions that you should concentrate on just one—for instance:
   a. What are the most common physical properties of cache at this time? Look at size, speed, and technology used for several machines including Digital, IBM, Motorola, and National Semiconductor.
   b. How does one manufacturer (Digital, for instance) handle modified memory locations? Are they sent to main memory and invalidated in cache? Are they changed in both places?
   c. How does cache behave if a DMA transfer into one of its locations takes place? For that matter, how does it even know such a thing took place?
   d. What algorithm does a particular cache use to determine what memory location is to be replaced by a newly demanded location? Limit yourself to discussing only one cache system rather than attempting to survey the entire industry.
   e. We suggested that memory and cache are in communication so that cache cancels a memory fetch. Is this really the way it works? Look to see how this problem has been solved on one cache system. Of course, the reason to cancel the fetch is to allow a DMA to take place, but do the designers care about that problem?

2. What is the point of the swapping file? Why not use the image file to store the outswapped image? In fact, why outswap at all? Simply use the image file when a new copy is needed.

3. Digital claims that paging rates of 300–400 frames per second are acceptable. I've found that the Pascal compiler operates at about ten

times that rate in the "as-delivered" system. Investigate the paging rate of Pascal on your system and write a report that includes the method used to collect the data, the actual data collected, and your conclusions.

4. The SET WORKING_SET command is not well-documented. Write an explanation of this command that can be understood by VMS novices. Beyond the use illustrated in project 4, what is the use of this command?

5. The CTRL-T feature can be turned on or off by the user. If you were to design the CTRL-T feature, in which existing VMS data structure would you store its status? Describe your solution and reasoning. You may want to sit at a terminal to see how it really works; for instance, if you are logged in on two terminals, will a SET NOCONTROL=T on one terminal disable the CTRL-T key on the other one as well? What about subprocesses? What do you conclude? Is CTRL-T associated with the account, the job, or the process?

6. The following paper explores three aspects of VAX page implementation that were discussed briefly in the book.

   a. Page tables must be contiguous in whatever space they are used, virtual or physical. Why? What part of the page translation algorithm depends on continuity?

   b. If user processes did not have virtual page tables, the VMS operating system would have an added burden of managing memory. Illustrate and explain this additional effort.

   c. The SYS tables are not virtual and yield physical, not virtual, addresses. This seems to contradict b above. Yet SYS page tables cause no trouble within VMS. Why? What is special about the SYS page tables that makes them exempt from the difficulties noted in b?

Process
Synchronization

5

Chapter 4 showed how the paging hardware keeps processes from interfering with one another. The very feature that empowers a multiprogramming system also protects a process from accidental interference by other processes and ensures privacy as a result. However, this advantage also poses a problem: how do processes communicate? Communication is a necessary and reasonable thing to want to do, but achieving it shouldn't mean the advantages of paging must be given up.

The topic of *process communication* is broken into two parts, synchronization and data sharing. The first is covered in this chapter, the second in Chapter 6. Normally, to synchronize means to coordinate the actions of several independent units, such as synchronized swimmers or watches. The implication is that these units do exactly the same thing at exactly the same time—there is spatial and temporal duplication. But when applied to software, *synchronize* means the operation of one process affects or controls the operation of another.

There are a number of synchronization methods available to the application designer, and the specific method chosen depends on trade-offs.

Method	Speed	Data volume	Use	Processes
Hibernate-Wake	Fast	One bit	Risky	Two
Event flag	Fast	One bit	Risky	Multiple
Mailbox	Moderate	Small-moderate	Safe	Two

Figure 5.1. A synopsis of syn-chronization techniques

Figure 5.1 presents a synopsis of three methods commonly implemented on operating systems.

The first method of process synchronization, called *hibernate-wake*, is implemented in the VMS operating system by two system services, $HIBER and $WAKE. $HIBER was introduced in conjunction with TIMER in Chapter 3. That example used $SCHDWK to set a timer, which created a "wakeup call," and then it executed $HIBER to block the process. Instead of using $SCHDWK, this chapter will show how a second process can unblock the hibernating process using $WAKE. $HIBER and $WAKE act as signals between processes, and they are fast. However, since only one signal is involved, one bit of information is passed between the processes. Using the hibernate-wake method requires caution because the execution order of the system services is essential. The VMS implementation of hibernate-wake is best suited to a pair of processes.

The second line of Figure 5.1 shows an *event flag*. This is a signal also; therefore, only one bit of data passes between processes. Event flags are a fast synchronization method and, like hibernate-wake, involve error-prone code sequences. As a result, this method also requires responsible implementation. Event flags have a broader application than hibernate-wake does and can be either assigned to specific processes or "broadcast" to several processes.

On the last line of Figure 5.1 is *mailbox*, a special form of I/O that takes place between two processes, permitting them to send messages to each other. Normally, I/O occurs between a hardware device and a process, and mailboxes are a special case of that concept. Compared to the first two synchronization methods, a mailbox is slower, but it allows more data to be passed between processes. The message length ranges up to several hundred

Figure 5.2. Romeo and Juliet

bytes, depending on the operating system implementation. Mailbox synchronization is easier for the software engineer to implement and has little risk because a greater burden of the synchronization logic is performed by the operating system. Mailbox messages are exchanged by two processes and cannot be easily "broadcast."

To illustrate how an application can synchronize two processes, this chapter will first suggest an application and then implement it three different ways using VMS system services. The first example uses $HIBER-$WAKE, the second event flags, and the third a mailbox. After each of these solutions, we will examine how the VMS operating system implements the particular technique internally. The advantages and disadvantages of each technique are illustrated by example.

5.1. An Example

This example of process synchronization is easy to envision. Figure 5.2 shows two terminals sitting side by side, called ROMEO and JULIET, that will be programmed to perform the familiar balcony scene. We enter RUN ROMEO on one terminal and RUN JULIET on the other, but the difficulty becomes immediately apparent: the two processes must be cognizant of each other so that JULIET displays one line, then ROMEO his line, throughout the scene. The two processes must alternate execution of WRITELNs until the dialogue is complete, or else one process will display the entire dialogue without waiting for the other.

This example is not a typical application, but it is simple to describe and program, which is necessary in understanding the software tools to be demonstrated. Once understood, these tools can be applied to other synchronization applications that may not be so simple to describe. Besides, this example is amusing.

ROMEO and JULIET must each know when the other is done and therefore when to start their part of the dialogue. The two must synchronize their WRITELN operations. The basic algorithm is easily stated by looping through the following three pseudo-code lines:

- Wait for your cue.
- Say your part.
- Cue the other actor.

The programs will not loop, of course, but (in Pascal) each will be a series of WRITELN statements with the appropriate cue and wait instructions. There is a minor protocol problem in that one actor, JULIET, must start the dialogue unconditionally, but thereafter the two processes alternate.

$HIBER-$WAKE, event flags, and mailboxes will be applied to this example. The three solutions will be illustrated in three programs in VAX Pascal, but the implementation details in all three cases are presented as exercises at the end of the chapter. After each program, the VMS data structures and algorithms necessary to support the solution will be described. Detailing the design of the operating system that implements process synchronization is good preparation for the more complex issue, process communication, described in Chapter 6.

5.2. A Solution Using $HIBER-$WAKE

The first example is implemented using $HIBER and $WAKE because the concept of hibernating has already been introduced. $WAKE is new, but its action is straightforward. It is used to undo a $HIBER and so cannot be executed by the hibernating process but only by another process. A process cannot $WAKE itself if it is hibernating and has no need to $WAKE itself if it is already awake. $WAKE will cue the other process and $HIBER will wait for a cue.

An unprivileged user can $WAKE any process he or she started. Since

```
PROGRAM JULIET (INPUT, OUTPUT);          PROGRAM ROMEO (INPUT, OUTPUT);
        .                                        .
        .                                        .
        .                                        .
$SETPRN ('JULIET');                      $SETPRN ('ROMEO');
WRITELN ('Romeo, Romeo. etc.');          $HIBER;
$WAKE (prcnam:='ROMEO');  -------------->> WRITELN ('R: line 1.');
$HIBER;
WRITELN ('J: Line 2.');   <<------------- $WAKE (prcnam:='JULIET');
                                         $HIBER;
$WAKE (prcnam:='ROMEO');  -------------->> WRITELN ('R: line 2.');
$HIBER;
WRITELN ('J: Line 3.');   <<------------- $WAKE (prcnam:='JULIET');
                                         $HIBER;
$WAKE (prcnam:='ROMEO');  -------------->> WRITELN ('R: line 3.);
$HIBER;
             <<--------------------------- $WAKE (prcnam:='JULIET');
        .                                        .
        .                                        .
     etc.                                     etc.
```

Figure 5.3. ROMEO and
JULIET using $HIBER-
$WAKE

two processes are involved in this example, the user must also be permitted
to create two simultaneous jobs. The value in the "Max active jobs:" field,
output by the command:

```
$ SHOW PROCESS/QUOTA
```

which was displayed in Figure 2.11, will show how many terminals can be
used at one time. An alternative way of running two processes is using
SPAWN to run ROMEO and then executing JULIET with RUN on a single
terminal, but this produces a less interesting display.

Figure 5.3 contains portions of the programs laid side by side. We
have already shown how to use system services in Chapter 3 and have omitted
the Pascal declarations to shorten the example. The two listings are connected with arrows to show the order the statements execute in concert.
Both ROMEO and JULIET begin by naming their respective processes with
the $SETPRN (Set Process Name) system service, since the $WAKE system
service needs either a process identifier (PID) or process name to work. The
process identifier is an arbitrary number assigned when the process is created
and is difficult to obtain. On the other hand, the process name can be
changed by the user at any time, either with the DCL command:

```
$ SET PROCESS/NAME='JULIET'
```

or with the $SETPRN system service. The process name is case-sensitive in the VMS operating system; 'juliet' and 'JULIET' are considered different. DCL is usually not case-sensitive. Furthermore, many other text strings in system services are case-sensitive, too. The inclusion of the $SETPRN call causes the two processes to be deterministic; we might forget to enter the SET PROCESS command, so using the system service ensures that the process name is correct. *Deterministic* means that the phenomenon will be repeatable every time it is done. In particular, the program will always yield the same output for a given input. A program which produces various output for the same input is called *nondeterministic*.

Refer again to Figure 5.3. JULIET begins with her opening line while ROMEO initially hibernates. When JULIET is done with her line, she $WAKEs ROMEO and then hibernates herself. ROMEO executes while JULIET is hibernating and displays his first line, then he $WAKES JULIET and $HIBERs again. This pattern continues until both players finish. Note that the $HIBER system service has no arguments; it only applies to the process that requests it and cannot be directed at another process.

The $WAKE-$HIBER order is essential; reversing the two at any point will put both players into a *deadlock,* or *deadly embrace,* forever in the hibernation state. This is not such a bad idea for lovers, but it is an unfortunate situation for synchronized processes, and difficult to diagnose. SHOW SYSTEM will prove that both processes are in the HIB state, but it will not show which of the two is at fault. In this example, however, the terminal dialogue will suggest the source of the error directly.

When we coded and ran the complete program in Figure 5.3, it seemed to run too fast. There is a simple way to slow it down—direct the process to wait a short time before each WRITELN. The TIMER program illustration of Chapter 3 is provided in the VMS run-time library. It is called LIB$WAIT and has a single argument—the number of seconds, expressed as a real number, that the user wishes to delay. Like system services, run-time library routines must be inherited into the Pascal program; thus, the INHERIT line must be expanded like this:

```
[INHERIT ( 'SYS$LIBRARY:STARLET',
           'SYS$LIBRARY:PASCAL$LIB_ROUTINES' ) ]
```

To use LIB$WAIT to delay, to $HIBER for one and a half seconds, the following call is made:

```
LIB$WAIT (1.5);
```

```
FUNCTION YOU_ARE_THERE: BOOLEAN;

VAR
  ERR: INTEGER;
  ITEMS: ARRAY[1..3] OF INTEGER;

BEGIN
  ITEMS[1] := 0;
  ITEMS[2] := 0;
  ITEMS[3] := 0;
  ERR := $GETJPIW (prcnam := 'ROMEO', itmlst := ITEMS);
  IF ( ERR = SS$_NORMAL ) THEN YOU_ARE_THERE := TRUE
  ELSE YOU_ARE_THERE := FALSE
END;
```

Figure 5.4. A simple GETJPIW procedure

STARTING THE PROCESSES

At this point, it appears that the two programs will behave correctly. However, suppose JULIET attempts to $WAKE ROMEO before the process has been properly named or before it is even started. This will result in $WAKE returning an error because JULIET is not permitted to wake a nonexistent process. The program in Figure 5.3 does not allow for this case. Before JULIET can be allowed to execute, ROMEO must already be executing. If that condition cannot be guaranteed, JULIET should wait until ROMEO is executing before issuing the first $WAKE; additional code must be added to JULIET to implement this. In theatrical terms, ROMEO must be on stage before JULIET starts her first line.

An analysis including alternative start-up conditions must be done whenever processes are to be synchronized; the programmer should attempt to anticipate possible initialization problems such as what if ROMEO starts before JULIET? What if JULIET starts before ROMEO? Or what if JULIET reaches the $WAKE before ROMEO executes the $HIBER? The start-up problem is examined in more detail later.

$GETJPIW (Get Job and Process Information and Wait) is the system service that determines the status of a process. A $GETJPIW sample is coded in Figure 5.4, merely asking if the process named ROMEO exists. $GETJPIW will request specified information about a job and wait, rather like a $QIOW, until all the information has been assembled before it returns to the calling program. In this case, since the process name is stored in the PCB (process control block) and that information is immediately available, the wait is not actually necessary, but is included as good coding practice.

In the $GETJPIW call, the ITEMS ARRAY normally contains a list of attributes that the user wishes to know about the process. Since this is a variable-length list, the final entry is filled with zeros to indicate the end of the list. In this example, no attributes are required, so the ITEMS list contains only one entry, which indicates it is empty. $GETJPIW will return the value SS$_NORMAL if ROMEO is a valid process name and something else if it is not. So, suppose that there is no process named ROMEO. Should JULIET do the following?

```
REPEAT
UNTIL (YOU_ARE_THERE);
```

This code loops until ROMEO finally shows up "on stage." This is termed *busy wait* and is not a recommended solution in a time-sharing environment because it runs "continuously." How will ROMEO ever get started if JULIET is using all of the CPU cycles? In practice JULIET will eventually end her quantum and be replaced by the next processes in the COM queue, so ROMEO will execute. Of course, JULIET will stay on the queue too, perhaps consuming her next quantum looping as well; she will appear to be CPU-bound. Why should JULIET execute so often? When she finds that ROMEO is not ready, she should wait a little longer. This results in much better utilization of the CPU from a global viewpoint. So, a preferable solution may look like this:

```
WHILE NOT YOU_ARE_THERE DO
LIB$WAIT (2);
```

This code tests if ROMEO is available and, if not, waits two seconds before testing again. JULIET does not use the CPU for her entire quantum; only a little bit of it is needed to test and then hibernate for several quanta. This waiting technique is known as *polling* and is found in a variety of applications.

IDENTIFYING SYSTEM SERVICE ERRORS

There is one final pragmatic issue that must be discussed. Whenever system services are used, the programmer should include error-checking code that ensures that the system service operated correctly. All system services are functions,[1] and the value of the function indicates the success or failure of

---

1. VAX Pascal permits a FUNCTION to be called as if it were declared as a PROCEDURE. But when it is used this way, the value returned by the FUNCTION is lost.

the system service. SS$_NORMAL is the returned value that indicates success, and its value is 1. Other odd values are considered successes also, but convey other information depending on the system service. An even value returned by the system service indicates an error and is normally displayed so that the reason for the failure can be investigated. Therefore, a system service call should resemble the following, for example:

```
ERR := $WAKE (prcnam:='ROMEO');
IF ( ERR <> SS$_NORMAL ) THEN
BEGIN
    WRITELN ('WAKE error:');
    $EXIT (ERR)
END;
```

The code above will identify an error condition, if one happens, and discontinue program execution. The WRITELN statement is added to aid in debugging and to help locate the particular system service call. Program execution stops when the $EXIT system service call displays a phrase identifying the error, as shown below:

```
WAKE error:
Nonexistent process
```

The phrase, "Nonexistent process," refers to the error encountered by the $WAKE system service; it is the English phrase corresponding to the integer stored in ERR as translated by $EXIT. If the error phrase does not help in pinpointing the error, the user's next step in locating the problem is to read the detailed Digital documentation for the appropriate system service.

5.3. A VMS Description of $HIBER-$WAKE

There are no special data structures associated with the $HIBER and $WAKE system services; Chapter 3 described the process states and how they are changed. Specifically, that chapter examined how a process can change its own state using $HIBER. That one process can affect the state of another one is a new concept shown in this example.

The $WAKE service must first locate the named process. The process name is stored in the PCB, and since the PCBs are all in the system's database, a simple sequential search of the names of all PCBs must be performed. The PCB vector is used to locate all the processes known to the system (refer to Figure 2.20), and if the PCB cannot be found, an error is returned to the requesting process. However, if the designated PCB is found, the special bit in it dedicated to the $WAKE service is set to indicate that a $WAKE has been ordered.

Next, the state field in the PCB is examined. If the targeted process is in the HIB state, it is forced into the computable state and the wake bit is cleared, but if it is not in the HIB state, the $WAKE service returns to the process that requested the $WAKE without performing any further action and without reporting an error—in effect queuing the $WAKE request. Notice that the wake request has not been lost because the wake bit in the target PCB has been set. If that process ever attempts to perform a $HIBER service, the service tests to see if the wake bit is already set. If it is, it is cleared and the hibernate request is not honored; the process will continue execution. This activity ensures that a $WAKE issued too early will be honored.

Below are the steps the $WAKE and $HIBER system services must perform to accomplish their functions.

$WAKE Algorithm
- Locate the PCB corresponding to the target process named in the argument.
- If the PCB is not found, return to the caller with an error condition; otherwise continue.
- Set (to 1) the wake bit in the PCB.
- If the PCB of the targeted process indicates it is in HIB state, change it to COM state and clear (to 0) the wake bit.
- If the PCB is in any other state, do nothing further.
- Return to calling image.

$HIBER Algorithm
- Examine the caller's PCB. If the wake bit is set (1), clear it (to 0), ignore the request, and return to calling image.
- If the wake bit is clear (0), change state to HIB.
- Call the scheduler.

5.4. A Solution With Event Flags

The use of event flags eliminates the start-up problems in the $HIBER-$WAKE solution. With event flags, either ROMEO or JULIET may be started first and no special code (like YOU_ARE_THERE) need be inserted to account for special cases. Instead, the two processes will share 2 bits from a 32-bit *common event flag cluster*. Three operations can be performed on these event flags: they may be set (to 1) with $SETEF (Set Event Flag), they may be cleared (to 0) with $CLREF (Clear Event Flag), or a process may block itself until a specified bit is set using $WAITFR (Wait for event flag set). The $WAITFR service will put the process in a blocked state if the event flag bit is clear. Then, when the bit is set, the process state is changed to COM. The blocked state is either common event flag (CEF) or local event flag (LEF) depending on the event flag number. Analogous to the wake bit in the PCB, if the event flag is already set, $WAITFR will not block the process.

The three event flag system services mentioned above perform the following functions:

$SETEF Algorithm
- Locate and set (to 1) the specified event flag.
- Locate all processes waiting (CEF or LEF state) for that event flag and change their states to COM.
- Call the scheduler.

$CLREF Algorithm
- Locate and clear (to 0) the specified event flag.
- Return to the calling image.

$WAITFR Algorithm
- If the specified event flag is set, return immediately.
- If the specified event flag is clear, change the calling process's state to either LEF or CEF (depending on the event flag number) and queue the PCB appropriately.
- Call the scheduler.

Common event flag clusters are designed to be shared by two or more processes; there are two common event flag clusters available to every process. The first cluster contains 32 event flags numbered 64 through 95, the second contains event flags 96 through 127. There are also event flags

```
    PROGRAM JULIET (INPUT, OUTPUT);          PROGRAM ROMEO (INPUT, OUTPUT);
        .                                        .
        .                                        .
        .                                        .

    $ASCEFC (64, 'CUE');                     $ASCEFC (65, 'CUE');
    WRITELN ('Romeo, Romeo. etc.');          $WAITFR (65);
    $SETEF (65); ----------------------->>   $CLREF (65);
    $WAITFR (64);                            WRITELN ('R: Line 1.');
    $CLREF (64); <<----------------------    $SETEF (64);
    WRITELN ('J: Line 2.');                  $WAITFR (65);
    $SETEF (65); ----------------------->>   $CLREF (65);
    $WAITFR (64);                            WRITELN ('R: Line 2.');
    $CLREF (64); <<----------------------    $SETEF (64);
    WRITELN ('J: Line 3.');                  $WAITFR (65);
    $SETEF (65); ----------------------->>   $CLREF (65);
    $WAITFR (64);                            WRITELN ('R: Line 3.');
               <<----------------------      $SETEF (64);
        .                                        .
        .                                        .
      etc.                                     etc.
```

Figure 5.5. ROMEO and
JULIET using event flags

numbered 0 through 63, but these are called local event flags and are not available outside of the owner's process. The common event flag cluster is named by the user at the time it is created or when it is first associated to the process; cluster names are case-sensitive and limited to 15 ASCII characters.

The functional operation of ROMEO and JULIET remains the same, but different system services are used. That is, in the programs in Figure 5.5, only the synchronizing calls between the WRITELNs have been changed. A comparison of this new program to Figure 5.3 shows that $SETPRN has been replaced by $ASCEFC (Associate to Common Event Flag Cluster), $WAKE has been replaced by $SETEF, and $HIBER has been replaced by $WAITFR. The basic logic used is:

- WRITELN my part.
- Set the other actor's event flag to wake it up ($SETEF).
- Stop; wait for my event flag to be set ($WAITFR).
- When I wake up, clear my own event flag—($CLREF).
- WRITELN my next part and so forth.

Figure 5.5 introduces a new step not needed in $HIBER-$WAKE: clear the event flag in preparation for the next cue. In $HIBER-$WAKE, the VMS system automatically cleared the wake bit. But when using event flags, it is necessary for the process to clear its event flag after it wakes; otherwise, the next wait operation will find that the event flag is still set and so will not wait. The $SETEF-$WAITFR-$CLREF progression is compulsory just as $WAKE must precede $HIBER. Any modification to the order may result in a deadlock.

The example outlined in Figure 5.5 uses two event flags in the first cluster; we named it CUE. The $ASCEFC system service performs the following functions.

$ASCEFC Algorithm
- Search for the specified common event flag cluster.
- If not found, create and initialize all 32 event flags in the cluster to zero.
- Connect the cluster to the PCB of the requesting process.
- Return to the calling image.

$ASCEFC has two arguments, a flag number and the cluster's name. We have arbitrarily chosen 64 for JULIET and 65 for ROMEO. A process may associate to either event flag cluster using the $ASCEFC call; however a process is not allowed to associate to more than two. The $ASCEFC call's first argument can be any event flag in a cluster. In other words, any value from 64 to 95 will indicate that the process wants to associate to the first event flag cluster.

The cluster is referenced by a user-specified name instead of the process name.[2] It is created when the first process associates to it, and all the event flags (64–95) are cleared at that time. When subsequent processes associate to the existing cluster, no change is made to the event flag settings, so it does not matter whether ROMEO or JULIET is started first. If ROMEO starts first, it waits because its event flag (65) is clear. If JULIET starts first, it executes its first line and then sets ROMEO's flag. Furthermore, there is no problem if ROMEO has not started when JULIET sets event flag 65; ROMEO's event flag will be set without ROMEO executing, so when ROMEO associates to that cluster, flag 65 is already set. Thus, ROMEO will start executing right away.

---

2. The process name does not matter in this application; it is never used.

STARTING THE PROCESSES

We present three start-up scenarios to ensure that there is no possibility of creating a situation that causes either deadlock or unintended operations:

1. *Initial Condition:* JULIET associates to the cluster, executes her first WRITELN, and sets ROMEO's event flag. Then ROMEO starts, and associates to the cluster.

   Analysis: Either process can continue execution. If JULIET executes next, she executes the $WAITFR, leaving only ROMEO to execute. If ROMEO executes next, cluster association does not change any of the event flags, so ROMEO continues through its first WRITELN.

2. *Initial Condition:* JULIET associates to the cluster, executes her first WRITELN, sets the ROMEO event flag, and waits. Then ROMEO starts, and associates to the cluster.

   Analysis: Since JULIET has already set ROMEO's event flag and is waiting, only ROMEO can execute. ROMEO's $WAITFR is ignored, and he executes his first WRITELN.

3. *Initial Condition:* ROMEO associates to the cluster, then JULIET is started.

   Analysis: Either can execute. If ROMEO executes first, he will wait because all of the event flags in the cluster are initially clear. After that, only JULIET can execute. But, if JULIET executes first, she associates and executes her WRITELN. ROMEO cannot execute beyond his wait until JULIET sets ROMEO's event flag.

In all cases, we want the same thing to occur—namely that JULIET WRITELN her part first and ROMEO wait for his event flag to be set.

5.5. A VMS Description of Event Flags

Common event flags are kept in a structure called the common event flag block (CEB), shown in Figure 5.6. A single CEB is created for each cluster, containing the 32 event flags and the name of the cluster. As with all dynamic structures in the VMS operating system, the first three longwords contain links and identification information. Whenever the $ASCEFC system service is executed, the list of CEB structures is searched linearly for the specified name. If a cluster of the same name does not exist, a CEB is created and

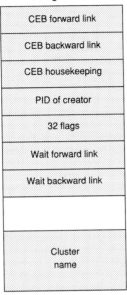

*Figure 5.6. Common event flag
block essentials*

linked into the existing list and to the requesting process. When the CEB is
created, the PID (Process ID) is stored in it to aid VMS debugging.

A double-linked list is maintained for all common event flag clusters
created in the system. Figure 5.7 shows how the CEBs are linked together
and how a process is linked to the cluster. Two processes, ROBBOB and
TACONUTS, share Cluster P and are also associated to other clusters independently; presumably Cluster M and Cluster N are to be shared with
other processes. Recall that every process control block (PCB) must be a
member of one of the state queues in the system. For instance, suppose that
ROBBOB is in the computable queue (COM) and TACONUTS is currently
executing (CUR). If TACONUTS executes a $SETEF or a $CLREF service,
the appropriate event flag cluster is not located by the cluster name; instead,
the system service locates the CEB using the flag number and cluster pointer
in the PCB. The PCB has only two slots reserved for CEB pointers, one for
event flags 64–95 and the other for 96–127. Therefore, a process may only

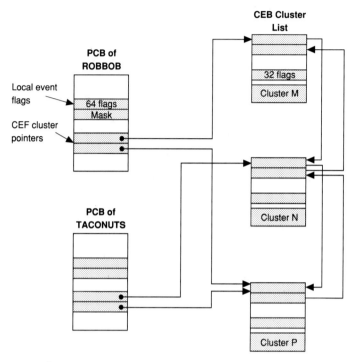

Figure 5.7. Two processes sharing event flag clusters

have two clusters associated to it at any one time. Once the CEB is located, the specific event flag modification can be made. The time-consuming operation (searching) is the association of the cluster, not the manipulation of the event flags.

The companion to $ASCEFC is called $DACEFC (Disassociate Common Event Flag Cluster). Figure 5.5 does not call this system service because it is performed automatically as part of the image rundown logic. When the last image has disassociated, the cluster is removed from the cluster list.

If a process is blocked, waiting for a common event flag to be set, the execution state is common event flag wait (CEF) and the process's PCB becomes a member of the cluster's wait queue, depicted in Figure 5.8. This figure shows that there are no processes waiting for any event flags in Cluster N, and process KQ108 is waiting for an event flag in Cluster M. Two processes, ROBBOB and TACONUTS, are waiting for one or more event flags

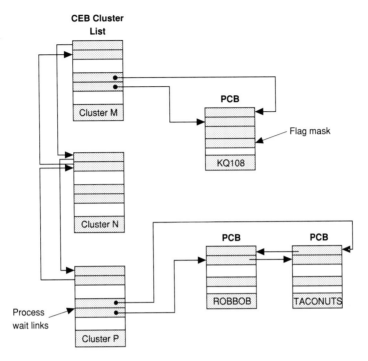

Figure 5.8. Processes waiting for common event flags

in Cluster P. The number of the event flag that the process is waiting for is stored in a PCB field called the *flag mask*. This design permits ROBBOB and TACONUTS to wait for different flags within the same cluster.

These queues of waiting processes are not stored like the wait queues described in Figure 3.18. This exception is a result of the event flags service's design—it permits faster access to waiting PCBs. Specifically, every time an event flag is set, a search of waiting processes must be performed. The way these queues are structured in Figure 5.8 limits the length of the search to only PCBs waiting for a given cluster. If the alternative design shown in Figure 3.18 was used, a single queue of all processes waiting for event flags would require longer searches, hence higher operating system overhead.

Whenever an event flag is set using $SETEF, the corresponding bit is set in the CEB. Then, all processes in that cluster's wait queue are tested against the resulting configuration of event flags. If a given process is waiting for that specified event flag to be set, the process becomes computable once again and is removed from the CEB's wait list and placed on the appropriate COM queue according to its priority. All waiting processes are tested, so several processes may become computable simultaneously because one bit was set.

LOCAL EVENT FLAGS

LEFs (local event flags) do not require this elaborate structure or treatment. As indicated in Figure 5.7, the 64-bit local flag and mask structure is contained in the PCB itself. When an event flag is set or tested by the process, the PCB is accessed directly on the LEF queue and no searching is required, and therefore no sharing of LEFs between processes is possible. This is also the reason that LEF wait queues are treated as described in Figure 3.18.

GENERALIZING EVENT FLAG SYNCHRONIZATION

Synchronizing more than two processes using event flags is a trivial extension of this two-process example. An event flag must be assigned to each process; the controlling process merely selects which of the other processes to execute next by setting the event flag corresponding to that process.

5.6. A Solution With a Mailbox

Our final example of synchronizing two processes uses a mechanism called a mailbox. One process sends mail to cue the other, and the receipt of the message is the cue for the second to begin execution. The first process then waits for the arrival of mail, which signals that the first process can continue execution.

In VMS, the mailbox mechanism is implemented using $QIOW. Instead of using the Pascal WRITELN instruction, the example program will call $QIOW directly. As in the previous two examples, the fundamental structure of ROMEO and JULIET changes very little; only the names of the system service calls change. Figure 5.9 contains the two programs.

First, the example must create a mailbox, just as an event flag cluster was created. An unprivileged user is permitted to create a temporary mailbox, which means that it is destroyed at image rundown time. The system

```
PROGRAM JULIET (INPUT, OUTPUT);            PROGRAM ROMEO (INPUT, OUTPUT);
TYPE                                       TYPE
  $WORD = [WORD] 0..65535;                   $WORD = [WORD] 0..65535;
VAR                                        VAR
  CHAN: $WORD                                CHAN: $WORD;
       .                                          .
       .                                          .
       .                                          .

$CREMBX (chan:=CHAN,                       $CREMBX (chan:=CHAN,
       lognam:='CUE');                            lognam:='CUE');
WRITELN ('Romeo, Romeo. etc.');
WRITE_MAIL (CHAN);   ----------------->>   READ_MAIL (CHAN);
                                           WRITELN ('R: line 1.');
READ_MAIL (CHAN);    <<-----------------   WRITE_MAIL (CHAN);
WRITELN ('J: Line 2.');
WRITE_MAIL (CHAN);   ----------------->>   READ_MAIL (CHAN);
                                           WRITELN ('R: line 2.');
READ_MAIL (CHAN);    <<-----------------   WRITE_MAIL (CHAN);
WRITELN ('J: Line 3.');
WRITE_MAIL (CHAN);   ----------------->>   READ_MAIL (CHAN);
                                           WRITELN ('R: line 3.);
                     <<-----------------   WRITE_MAIL (CHAN);
       .                                          .
       .                                          .
     etc.                                       etc.
```

Figure 5.9. ROMEO and
JULIET using a mailbox

service $CREMBX (create mailbox) creates the mailbox.[3] It requires a mailbox name as input and returns a channel number to be used by the $QIOW system service. This channel number is selected by the system and must be used as input to $QIOW. The actual value and meaning of the channel number are unimportant.

Consider this model: the $CREMBX system service causes the system to create a virtual input/output tube. Unlike a normal hardware device, data pushed into one end of this tube via a write operation is extracted from the other end using a read operation. This tube only exists as long as the images using it exist; when the images disappear, so does the tube. Data is written to and read from the tube in the same way that all input and output is handled, using $QIOW. As a reminder, this system service queues the input or output operation and waits for its completion, and in the case of a mailbox write, completion can have two definitions:

3. VMS permits the creation of permanent mailboxes as well, but the unprivileged user is permitted to create only temporary mailboxes.

1. The message has been pushed into one end of the tube.
2. The message has been received at the other end of the tube.

Completion can also have two definitions in the case of a mailbox read:

1. The process is ready to receive a message, but there is no message.
2. The process has received a message.

In some applications, these distinctions are important, but this example does not take advantage of the difference. In fact, ROMEO and JULIET will wait until the message is received in both the read and write operations because that is the default meaning of the $QIOW.

Figure 5.9 has laid the two programs side by side and shows arrows between them to indicate their interaction. It is important to see that all three synchronization techniques exhibit the same structure, but use different system services. This high-level program is simpler than the two previous examples shown in Figures 5.3 and 5.5. The WRITE_MAIL feeds directly to the corresponding READ_MAIL statement, and then waits until a message arrives from the other actor. MONITOR PROCESS or SHOW SYSTEM shows that the state of the process waiting at the READ_MAIL statement is LEF (wait for local event flag), which is used by the system for all input/ output services. There is one nonstandard Pascal statement in Figure 5.9 that needs explanation. The VMS system requires that the channel number be a (16-bit) word in every context; since Pascal integers are 32 bits long, a special, nonstandard declaration must be made to accommodate VMS system services. The TYPE declaration at the top of the program creates a 16-bit integer.

The two low-level procedures READ_MAIL and WRITE_MAIL have been presented separately, in Figure 5.10, to avoid cluttering Figure 5.9. Superficially, they appear to be identical, except for a single difference: the "func : =" line. They will not compile in the form presented because MBX CHAN must be a 16-bit word, not an INTEGER. As with the previous two examples, the complete solution is left to the reader and is presented as an exercise at the end of the chapter.

$QIOW USAGE

$QIOW is a complicated call, so, its four arguments should be described. The first argument (chan) must be the channel number created by the

```
PROCEDURE READ_MAIL (MBX_CHAN: INTEGER);

VAR
  BUFFER: CHAR;

BEGIN
  $QIOW ( chan := MBX_CHAN,
          func := IO$_READVBLK,
            p1 := BUFFER,
            p2 := 1 );
END;




PROCEDURE WRITE_MAIL (MBX_CHAN: INTEGER);

VAR
  BUFFER: CHAR;

BEGIN
  $QIOW ( chan := MBX_CHAN,
          func := IO$_WRITEVBLK,
            p1 := BUFFER,
            p2 := 1 );
END;
```

Figure 5.10. A listing of
WRITE_MAIL and
READ_MAIL

$CREMBX system service. It is an input argument and used to connect the
mailbox to the I/O call. The second argument (func) indicates the function
to be performed by the $QIOW; in one case, it indicates a read, in the other,
a write. The two constants, IO$_READVBLK and IO$_WRITEVBLK, are
defined in STARLET.PAS. They request virtual block (VBLK) transfers.
The third (p1) and fourth (p2) arguments name the buffer to use in the
I/O operation and its length, respectively. The buffer either contains the
message to be sent (in the case of write operations) or is intended to receive
the message (in the case of read operations), and in this example, the actual
data sent and received is unimportant. There are additional arguments in
the $QIOW call, but these four are sufficient for this example.

The two mailbox routines perform a simple task: informing the calling
routine that a mailbox operation has taken place. There is only one byte of
data exchanged, and that byte is meaningless; the fact that it has been
transferred is the only information the mailbox delivers.

GENERALIZING MAILBOX USAGE

If there are more than two processes to be synchronized, these two mailbox routines must be expanded. Unlike $HIBER-$WAKE and event flags, mailboxes are not directed at a particular process. $HIBER-$WAKE requires process names to function; event flags require specific event flag assignments for each process. When using a mailbox, the writing process merely sends mail to the mailbox without an address attached to it; likewise, the receiver has no idea who the sender is unless that information is included in the message itself. In the case of two processes, this lack of identification is no problem, but a difficulty arises when three or more processes are connected with a mailbox. Only one process can be the reader; there is no way to broadcast a mail message. And only one of the processes will receive the message even though there may be two attempting to read it. The system will select which of the two will be the recipient.

One approach to synchronizing more than two processes is to set up multiple mailboxes—for instance, one mailbox for Processes A and B, another for A and C, and a third for B and C. This approach ensures that no ambiguity will ensue, but several mailboxes are required. Another solution is to encode more information into the message. For instance, if A wants to send a message to B, it prefixes "B" to the message. In the read routine, B examines the message, and, if it does not see the "B," sends it out again. Thus, the message is passed around until the proper recipient finally reads it.

5.7. A VMS Description of Mailbox

As indicated, mailboxes behave like standard I/O devices except that only processes communicate with them, whereas standard I/O devices consist of processes communicating with physical devices. To keep the mailbox interface consistent with physical I/O operations, Digital software engineers modified the existing $QIOW mechanism to accommodate mailboxes. Within the I/O subsystem, however, the mailbox is a very different device indeed, primarily in that its queue of messages is maintained within the I/O database.

All mailbox names are prefixed with "MBA" and then appended with a *unit number* not longer than four digits. MBA0, MBA1, and MBA2 are reserved for use by the system. A search of the logical tables using the command below will reveal the names of the active mailbox "devices" that are defined.

```
$ SHOW LOGICAL /ALL
```

When the mailbox is created, it is assigned a logical name, like "CUE" in our programming example in Figure 5.9. Since the system assigns the unit number, it is difficult to refer to the mailbox by its physical name.

Each time the $CREMBX service is called to create a mailbox, it first searches for the logical name supplied by the user in a logical name table [4] to determine if the specified device already exists. If there is no match, a mailbox device is created. $CREMBX does this by combining the characters "MBA" and a VMS-generated unit number and then searching the existing mailbox device names to make sure this new device does not duplicate any of them. If there is a duplication, another unit number is created and the search is repeated. When a mailbox device is created, an entry is added to the logical name table as well as to the mailbox device list. But if the logical name supplied is found, $CREMBX recognizes that the device has been created already. This algorithm is analogous to the $ASCEFC operation discussed earlier.

$CREMBX Algorithm
- Search the logical name table for the name specified in the system service argument.
- If there is no match, add that logical name to the table, and create the corresponding mailbox device and link the two together.
- Create a channel control block (CCB) and link it to the mailbox device.
- Return the channel number to the calling image.

Whether or not a mailbox existed previously, a channel control block is created in user space and linked to the mailbox. The channel number, not the logical name, is used when processes are reading and writing mail messages using $QIOW; this speeds up the operations.

MAILBOX OPERATIONS

Both read-write cases are outlined in a general algorithm presented in Figure 5.11. They are:

- Write followed by a read
- Read followed by a write

---

4. The VMS operating system contains several tables for storing of logical names.

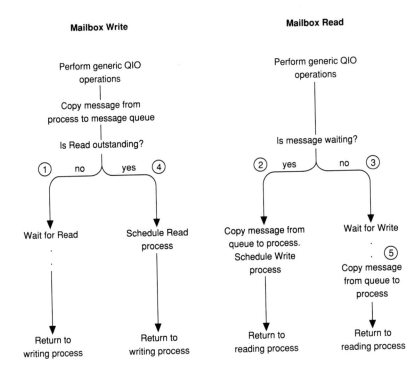

Figure 5.11. Mailbox algorithm overview

In the figure, both operations begin with generic $QIO operations, including checking for correct arguments and creating and initializing the required data structures.

In the first case, write followed by a read, the message is copied from the writing process and queued into a VMS data region to make it accessible to the reader. Then, if there is no outstanding read request (circle 1), the writing process is blocked. Later, when a mailbox read is requested (circle 2), the message is copied from the queue to the reading process. At the same time, the writing process is unblocked and executes again as soon as it is scheduled. The reading process is not blocked in this case.

In the second case, read followed by a write, if the reading process discovers that the mailbox is empty (circle 3), it is blocked until the writing process delivers a message. When the write takes place (circle 4), the reading process is unblocked and the writing process continues execution because the message is delivered immediately. At a later time, when the reading process is scheduled, the message is copied from the queue (circle 5) and the reading process continues execution.

The algorithm also works if there is more than one reader or writer, or more than one of both, on a single mailbox. For instance, consider three processes: two writers and one reader. If one process writes to the mailbox, it is blocked. When the second process writes, it too is blocked, but the queue is properly ordered. That is, the reading process extracts the first message on the first read operation, and thus the corresponding writer is unblocked and the second writer continues waiting.

5.8. Related Issues

The UNIX operating system provides a number of the process synchronization mechanisms mentioned in this chapter, but the nomenclature is different. The *fork, exit,* and *wait* services provide a way to spawn subprocesses and synchronize them. The wait service can also be paired with a *signal* service for synchronizing. A *pipe* behaves like a mailbox for passing data between processes.

The OS/2 operating system also provides many of these services under the same names and offers the user a pipe and a *queue* (mailbox), although the queue is much more powerful than VMS's mailbox. OS/2 also provides a signal system service, which is a limited form of event flags. Process state changing services are also available, such as *sleep* and other timed services.

5.9. Summary

Process synchronization was illustrated by the example of ROMEO and JULIET, which looked at three different implementations of synchronizing:

1. $HIBER-$WAKE
2. Event flags
3. Mailboxes

After each Pascal solution was outlined, the VMS data structures needed to support each technique were defined. $HIBER-$WAKE involves only a single bit in the PCB, and event flags introduce the CEB list with links to the PCB and lists of waiting processes. Mailboxes are actually implemented in the I/O subsystem itself and for that reason are very complex.

Under closer examination, these data structures exhibit advantages and disadvantages that the designer must balance when making use of them. For instance, mailboxes are less prone to creating a deadlock, since only one system service ($QIOW) is involved, but mailbox overhead is much higher than that of the other two structures because a mailbox provides a general communication capability that was not shown here; these examples used only a small subset of mailbox capabilities.

Although this chapter concentrated on a two-process synchronization example, it is important to understand that this is an unusually easy implementation because the two processes always alternate. When more than two processes are involved, the implementation is more difficult because the processes cannot rely on this symmetry. For instance, if three actors were to play a scene, actor 1 would not unconditionally wait for actor 2, but instead would have to wait for a specific cue; sometimes from actor 2 and at other times from actor 3. The synchronization techniques discussed do not easily lend themselves to this more general case. In particular, mailbox synchronization must be more elaborate.

The discussion of these examples dealt with many pragmatic issues in VAX Pascal coding and in using system services correctly. In particular, we emphasized the system service return status and how to interpret the meaning of this value. We also returned to some of the system service argument types; we looked at $QUAD in Chapter 3 and had to use $WORD in this chapter.

ACRONYMS

$ASCEFC	Associate to Common Event Flag Cluster system service
$CLREF	Clear Event Flag system service
$CREMBX	Create Mailbox system service
$DACEFC	Disassociate Common Event Flag Cluster system service
$EXIT	Terminate image system service

$GETJPIW	Get Job and Process Information and Wait system service
$HIBER	Hibernate system service
$QIOW	Queue I/O and Wait system service
$SETEF	Set Event Flag system service
$SETPRN	Set Process Name system service
$WAITFR	Wait for Event Flag system service
$WAKE	Wakeup system service
ASCII	American Standard Code for Information Interchange
CCB	Channel Control Block
CEB	Common Event flag Block
CEF	Common Event Flag wait process state
CUR	Currently executing process state
DCL	Digital Command Language
LEF	Local Event Flag wait process state
LIB$SIGNAL	An RTL routine to terminate an image
LIB$WAIT	An RTL routine to hibernate a specified time
PCB	Process Control Block
PHD	Process Header
PID	Process Identifier
RTL	Run-Time Library
SS$_NORMAL	A system service return code

SHORT ANSWER EXERCISES

1. Describe a real-world application involving the use of synchronized processes. Do not limit your thinking necessarily to two processes.

2. Describe why the progression $SETEF(65)–$CLREF(64)–$WAITFR(64) will not work reliably. It is only necessary to prove it does not work with one example. *Hint:* remember that a process may be preempted at any point in its execution stream.

3. How many mailboxes are required for a system of five processes arranged in a star? That is, assume that every process communicates with all the others. Further assume that a mailbox is set up for each pair of processes, for instance, 1 to 2, 1 to 3, 1 to 4, 1 to 5, and so forth.

4. Why is the VMS operating system designed to make *all* processes waiting for a given event flag computable? Why not just stop searching the list and queue the first process found?

5. When a mailbox is created by the system, why does the VMS system have to make sure that the MBAx device name is unique? After all, it increments "x" each time a new mailbox is declared.

6. Consider the mailbox solution to the ROMEO and JULIET example. Why does this example work at all? In particular, what prohibits the sender from receiving its own message?

7. Refer to the $HIBER-$WAKE algorithm. According to that description, is it possible to queue several $WAKE requests to a single process?

8. Sketch a state transition diagram like Figure 3.12 for the common event flag solution of the ROMEO and JULIET problem.

PROJECTS

1. Complete a version of ROMEO and JULIET. Go to the library and find the passage in Shakespeare's play required to complete the dialogue. Then select one of the synchronization methods suggested. Solve the start-up and process name difficulties, if necessary. The mailbox solution requires special privilege (see project 8 below); otherwise, one of the processes must be run as a subprocess.

2. Complete the ROMEO and JULIET example with $SUSPND-$RESUME. This is a fourth synchronization method that was not mentioned because it is similar to $HIBER-$WAKE. The major problem presented in this project is finding the correct calling sequence for these services in the VMS documentation.

3. Repeat the ROMEO and JULIET $HIBER-$WAKE example using a single terminal and LIB$SPAWN within JULIET to start ROMEO. The start-up problem disappears.

4. Apply the synchronization solution to a system of three processes. Pick any of the three methods. Invent some clever application like Curly, Moe, and Larry, or use another play involving three characters.

5. Repeat the above with three processes using the mailbox method. There are two approaches to try:

   a. Pass a token around until it reaches the right process.

   b. Set up multiple mailboxes.

Running the mailbox on three terminals requires special privilege (see project 8 below).

6. Instead of ROMEO and JULIET, write two programs called ABBOTT and COSTELLO and simulate part of the "Who's on First" routine.

7. The $HIBER-$WAKE solution is still incomplete because it is not sufficient to know the process name; instead the name of the executing image must be known. $GETJPIW can be used in this case, but the code is much more involved. You will need the VMS documentation of $GETJPIW to get a solution running. This new and improved $GETJPIW call replaces the call in ARE_YOU_THERE in Figure 5.4.

8. This project involves creating two processes that share a mailbox; one process reads a line from the terminal and mails that line to the other. The second process displays the line and then reads a new line. That line is mailed back to the first process, where it is displayed. The two processes should be running on adjacent terminals.

   GRPNAM privilege is required for this project because unprivileged processes are not permitted to share logical name tables. In order to have $CREMBX use the *group* logical name table (instead of the *job* logical name table), perform the following command prior to execution of the image (we suggest you add it to your LOGIN.COM file):

```
DEF/TABLE=LNM$PROCESS_DIRECTORY LNM$TEMPORARY_MAILBOX LNM$GROUP
```

   Note: This project is a simplified version of PHONE. To implement PHONE, a program must mail a single character at a time. PHONE is considerably more involved than necessary for this project.

9. Refer to the $HIBER-$WAKE Pascal code. Code JULIET to determine the decimal value returned by $WAKE when the referenced process does not exist.

10. Surprisingly, VMS supplies no utility to show the status of event flag clusters, and DEBUG does not support any such facility either. Even so, when dealing with event flags, such a tool is very handy. Design, code, and test a program that periodically displays all 32 event flags in a specified cluster. The display should number the flags as well as display the hexadecimal value.

11. Extending the previous project, add the capability to change a specified flag from the program. The purpose of such a tool is to run it on a terminal while a certain application is being debugged on other

terminals. If the system gets into a deadlock condition, this tool can be used to detect the situation and change a flag to break the deadlock.

PAPERS

1. Discuss synchronizing n processes with these three techniques:
   • $HIBER-$WAKE
   • Event flags
   • Mailboxes
   That is, develop an algorithm for each technique involving n processes. What limitations are there in each of the techniques?

2. With respect to paper 1 above, which is the best method when n = 10? Defend your choice. What criteria did you use to determine "best"? Why?

3. Design an experiment to determine which is the fastest of the three process synchronizing methods.

4. Research synchronization implementations on other operating systems, e.g., UNIX, OS/2, Windows, and VM.

Process Data Sharing
and Critical Regions

GOALS

Understanding concurrence

Readers and writers

Critical sections

Locking mechanisms in VMS

Shared memory in VMS

6

In the examples in Chapter 5, there were no data shared between processes. This chapter will look at how processes cooperate to share data between them.

The data sharing algorithm is stated like this: one process creates the data; then, it signals another process (or processes) that the data are available for further manipulation. Another way to state it is this: one process prohibits all access to shared data while modifying it, and, when not modifying it, permits other processes to access it. In either case, the assumption is that the data are stored in a location that is accessible to all the processes involved. Four methods of data sharing are illustrated in Figure 6.1.

The first line of Figure 6.1 identifies files as a method of process data sharing; most readers are probably familiar with this. Files are used, for example, when a compiler needs to transfer data to the linker. It does so by creating a file that the linker receives as input. There is very little difficulty designing this interface because the two processes do not run at the same time.

But more complex data sharing is commonly done. To illustrate,

Method	Speed	Data Volume	Use	Processes
Files	Slow	Unlimited	Safe	Multiple
Shared memory	Fast	Moderate	Risky	Multiple
Mailbox	Moderate	Small-moderate	Safe	Two
Logical name	Moderate	Small	Risky	Multiple

*Figure 6.1. A synopsis of data
sharing techniques*

imagine the following interface between the compiler and the linker: suppose that as the compiler finishes each statement, the resulting code is passed to the linker, so that the compiler and linker operate together on a program. Although the file scheme still works, additional process synchronization is incorporated into the compiler and linker code. As the compiler finishes each statement and stores data in the file, the linker is informed. Likewise, the linker informs the compiler that the data in the file had been processed and the file is available for further additions. Although common and easily done, data sharing with files is the slowest method available. On the positive side, the amount of data that can be transferred with files is virtually unlimited; the process's disk quota is the only limitation.

On the second line of Figure 6.1, shared memory is shown to be the fastest method available for data sharing, but the amount of data to be shared is more limited than with files. The typical application that employs this method involves two or more processes executing simultaneously, which is termed *concurrent* or *parallel* processing. Shared memory involves careful and deliberate coordination between the processes so that they do not attempt to write into the same location of shared memory at the same time. Software engineers must design such interfaces with care because diagnosing and locating errors in this case is extremely difficult.

The third line of Figure 6.1 compares mailboxes to other data sharing techniques. This method is moderately fast but the amount of data that can be passed at any one time is much less than with shared memory. Mailboxes are used by only two processes, unlike files and shared memory, which allow unlimited process involvement. Mailboxes cannot broadcast messages; rather, the messages are directed implicitly at another cooperating process. On the other hand, mailboxes, unlike other techniques, do not require elaborate coordination schemes, making them easier to use. Since mailboxes were covered in the Chapter 5, they will not be discussed further.

On the last line of Figure 6.1 is *logical name,* originally a VMS term meaning a user-specified name for any portion of a file specification. The VMS operating system provides logical names to allow user applications to be independent of physical devices. For example, consider an application that refers to the logical name "DISK" for its files. At the time the application is developed, "DUA0" is the physical name of the disk to be accessed. Later, the desired disk becomes "DUA1." If this occurs, instead of changing the application source code statements that refer to "DISK" (there may be many source files within the application), a single DCL command, DEFINE, is used to reassign the logical name "DISK" to point to "DUA1" instead of "DUA0."

The VMS system designers realized over time that the logical name concept could be expanded to facilitate other, similar character substitution applications. Presently, a user may either enter DCL commands from the keyboard or enter commands from programs, through system service routines that manipulate the definition and translation of logical names. A logical name can be associated with any arbitrary ASCII message. However, logical names and their equivalents are limited to 255 bytes, and cooperating processes must still signal one another when data is available. This makes the technique as complicated as sharing memory. Using logical names to implement data sharing will not be discussed further.

Chapter 5 dealt with processes executing a known progression of actions: Process A knew that it must call Process B, B then knew that Process A was next, and so forth. This knowledge was built into each program. This chapter investigates process communication in a different setting. It will address multiple, cooperating processes again, but this time the process execution order is unknown and irrelevant. Instead, under certain circumstances that will be stated later, two or more cooperating processes will prohibit one another from executing certain portions of code. This is similar to the synchronized processes shown in Chapter 5, but not identical to them.

Exchanging data occurs when two processes want to share a resource. Formerly, a *resource* was considered to be a physical part of the computer system, like an I/O device or the CPU; the issue of sharing those resources was resolved by the operating system. Now, the concept of resource is extended to include data variables shared between processes, and the processes themselves must assume responsibility for sharing. The need for variable

```
PROGRAM SHARE (INPUT, OUTPUT);

VAR
COUNT: INTEGER;

PROCEDURE COMPUTATION;
BEGIN

  COUNT := COUNT + 2;

END;

BEGIN { main program }

  COUNT := 5;
  COMPUTATION;
  COUNT := COUNT + 1;
  WRITELN (COUNT);

END.
```

Figure 6.2. Accessing a global variable in Pascal

```
PROGRAM FIRST (INPUT, OUTPUT);

VAR
 [GLOBAL] COUNT: INTEGER;

BEGIN
  COUNT := 5;
  COUNT := COUNT + 1;
  WRITELN (COUNT);
END.
```

```
PROGRAM SECOND (INPUT, OUTPUT);

VAR
  COUNT: INTEGER; EXTERNAL;

BEGIN
  COUNT := COUNT + 2;
END.
```

Figure 6.3. Two images sharing COUNT

sharing is a natural consequence of our training; the concept is much the same as sharing variables between a main program and procedures within an image. In the case of a program, resource sharing is done in serial; that is, first one part of the program accesses the variable and then another. Consider the program in Figure 6.2. The variable called COUNT is initialized in the main program, incremented in the procedure COMPUTATION, and modified again in the main program. This is nothing new, and we expect the result displayed to be 8. This is called *serial* access to the variable COUNT.

Figure 6.3 introduces the idea of parallel access to a variable. It repeats the above example using two processes instead of a main program and a

```
(SECOND)   COUNT := COUNT + 2;        (FIRST)    COUNT := 5;
(FIRST)    COUNT := 5;                (FIRST)    COUNT := COUNT + 1;
(FIRST)    COUNT := COUNT + 1;        (FIRST)    WRITELN (COUNT);
(FIRST)    WRITELN (COUNT);           (SECOND)   COUNT := COUNT + 2;

              (a)                                    (b)
```

Figure 6.4. Two possible
execution threads for
Figure 6.3

subprogram. For this illustration we have resorted to a contrived Pascal syntax, and the code will not execute. The example in Figure 6.3 implies that COUNT resides in the program FIRST as a global variable and that it can be shared across process boundaries. The program SECOND indicates that COUNT is external to it, by implication, in FIRST. This syntax resembles the mechanism used to share subprograms within Pascal MODULES; however, it is pure fabrication for the purpose of this introduction. These Pascal-like programs were selected to make the following assumption: FIRST runs as the primary process on a terminal and SECOND runs as a subprocess. This can be done with the two commands:

```
$ SPAWN/NOWAIT RUN SECOND
$ RUN FIRST
```

Now, due to preemption, there is no way of telling in what order the two processes will be executed. That is, there is no way to know what the combined instruction execution order of the two processes will be because, for instance, the time quantum for one of the processes may run out before it is finished. Any preemption will allow the other to execute for a while, which means many instruction execution sequences are possible.

For example, two possible execution sequences, or *threads,* are suggested in Figure 6.4, labeled a and b. The program name in parentheses indicates which program the code line came from. In thread a, SECOND was the first to run, and in thread b, it ran after FIRST completed. Neither of these two threads will produce the desired results, but there are several other threads that will work correctly.

This example presents a new problem to many readers; two processes executing concurrently produce a variety of results. What makes the problem new is that there is now a possibility of many execution threads, which results in an unpredictable value of COUNT. Such *nondeterministic* behavior occurs when two processes share a variable without synchronization. Nondeterministic means that the process' answer (COUNT in this example) may be different from time to time since the execution threads differ.

The point of this introduction is to raise the nondeterministic problem, not to solve it. This chapter will first investigate the conditions under which shared variables become a problem; specifically: are there uses of shared variables that do not cause difficulties? Next, some conditions that are required to guarantee a specific thread of execution will be investigated. Finally, the chapter will show various VMS mechanisms that are designed to solve the problem. In the discussion, we will generalize application categories in which this problem occurs so that the programmer will become alert to this design consideration.

6.1. Concurrent Readers and Writers

Now, consider a more precise description of the problem of concurrent or parallel processing involving shared variables, one that describes the problem as *contention* for a variable. At a given time, a process is either a *reader* or a *writer*. An example of this, in very modest form, is illustrated by the following Pascal statement:

```
A := X + 1;
```

The constant 1 and the variable X are being read, and the variable A is being written. In another example, the following Pascal statement shows that X is both read and written at different times, whereas the constant 1 is only being read.

```
X := X + 1;
```

The variables of concern can be in any programming context. The following example illustrates that a READLN statement is a write operation for WEIGHT because the value of WEIGHT changes as a result of executing the statement.

```
READLN ( WEIGHT );
```

More precisely, a read operation examines the value of the variable, but does not change it. A write operation does change the value of a variable. Remember that this chapter is not referring to a file when speaking of reading and writing in this context, but rather to memory-resident variables.

```
TempA <- X              TempB <- X
TempA <- TempA + 1      TempB <- TempB + 1
X <- TempA              X <- TempB

Process A               Process B
```

Figure 6.5. Multiple readers and writers of X

MULTIPLE READERS AND WRITERS

Now, apply this definition of readers and writers to multiple processes rather than a single line of code in one process. The first example is presented in the segments of two processes represented in Figure 6.5. This example illustrates the point that a single compiler line often creates several machine instructions which are invisible to the software engineer. To analyze this problem, consider what is happening at the machine instruction level, not at the compiler level. An *atomic* instruction is one that cannot be interrupted; once begun, it will not be preempted for any reason. The figure shows two processes, each with an atomic sequence of read and write instructions created by the statement:

```
X := X + 1;
```

Naturally, the code generated is dependent on the computer's instruction set and compiler used.

The example implies that only X is shared by the two processes.[1] TempA and TempB are variables local to each process; they are not shared. The process segments are identical except for the local variable names. The figure shows that X is read by both processes in the first line, incremented (by way of a temporary variable) in the middle line, and written by both processes in the last line.

As in Figure 6.3, the order of execution of the two processes cannot be predicted because of process preemption between each atomic statement. Either process may be interrupted between statements and control passed to the other process. This results in many possible execution threads of the two processes, which may cause different final values of X. Figure 6.6 lists

1. We will illustrate how shared variables are declared, in a user program later in the chapter.

```
(A) TempA <- X                    (B) TempB <- X
(A) TempA <- TempA + 1            (B) TempB <- TempB + 1
(A) X <- TempA                    (A) TempA <- X
(B) TempB <- X                    (A) TempA <- TempA + 1
(B) TempB <- TempB + 1            (A) X <- TempA
(B) X <- TempB                    (B) X <- TempB


        Answer: X is 2               Answer: X is 1
```

*Figure 6.6. Two possible
execution sequences for
Figure 6.5*

```
TempA <- X                   TempB <- X
TempA <- TempA + 1           TempB <- TempB + 1

Process A                    Process B
```

*Figure 6.7. Multiple readers
of X*

two conceivable threads. Assume that X is initially zero. Note that the thread on the left results in X having a final value of 2 and the thread on the right results in X having a final value of 1.

The differing results seen in Figure 6.6 result from trying to share a variable across processes. The value of X computed by one process is replaced or overlaid by the computation made by the other process; the final value of X cannot be determined from one execution to the next. The conclusion to be drawn from the example in Figure 6.6 is that if multiple processes both read and write a shared variable, this sharing may result in the variable's showing inconsistent and undesired values.

MULTIPLE READERS

Figure 6.7 illustrates the second example. In contrast to the multiple readers and writers illustration in Figure 6.5, here, X is only read by both processes and never written at all. Of course, there are multiple execution threads as in the previous examples, but all the threads produce the same result because X is never changed.

```
TempA <- X               TempB <- X
TempA <- TempA + 1       TempB <- TempB + 1
X <- TempA

Process A                Process B
```

Figure 6.8. Multiple readers and a single writer of X

MULTIPLE READERS, SINGLE WRITER

The final example in this section, illustrated in Figure 6.8, contains multiple readers and a single writer. Again, multiple threads are possible, but according to our model, there is no difficulty because write contention does not take place; only one process is doing the writing. If A is executed first, B will operate on the incremented value of X, but if B executes before A writes the updated value to X, then B will operate on the old value of X, even though it does not write X. It could be that subsequent code in B depends on A updating X prior to B's execution, or it may not matter. Only the designer can decide if this is an unpredictable situation. Normally, this configuration of multiple readers and one writer causes no problem.

In summary, this section illustrated only the problem and not the solution and presented three examples in which two processes share a variable. These examples point up the importance of the way a shared variable is accessed, whether by reading or by writing. The first example showed that multiple writers sharing a variable present a special case in which non-deterministic results may be observed. But the second example showed that when only multiple readers share a variable, no special measures must be taken. Finally, the third example showed that when two processes share a variable but only one process writes to that variable, there are usually no difficulties.

The trouble noted is that the system of processes may not run predictably every time because the execution thread, i.e., the composite instruction sequence of the processes involved, is unpredictable. This is a problem that must be corrected.

The problem is not limited to two processes. It also exists when more than two processes are involved, and the same conclusions can be drawn—multiple writers create a nondeterministic situation.

6.2. Introduction to Classical Solutions

Processes can execute in parallel with no difficulties until they reach that portion of code that accesses a shared variable. When two or more processes write a shared variable, something special must be done to guarantee that a specific instruction thread is always executed. Insisting on a specific thread solves the problem of unpredictable results. Doing so allows the processes to execute in parallel except in certain regions of their code. In those regions, the processes must run one at a time—that is, in serial, in an analogous way that ROMEO and JULIET executed.

Processes that are sharing data need a means to ensure that each one's *critical region* of code is entered only by one process at a time. The critical region is defined by the software engineer to be the portion of code that modifies a shared variable. Processes may execute without restriction until one of them reaches the first statement of its critical region. If another process happens to reach its critical region at the same time, it must be prohibited from entering it until the first process exits its region, because only one process at a time is allowed to execute statements that modify a shared variable. Therefore, a global (or universal) protocol of signals must be established that controls entry to and exit from a critical region.

This model can be viewed another way. Mutual modifications, by two or more processes, to a shared variable are not permitted, so a method for *mutual exclusion* must be instituted. In other words, processes must access a shared variable in a *serial* manner (as opposed to parallel execution). To do this, they must be synchronized in manners similar to those shown in Chapter 5. Using the exact techniques described in Chapter 5 is somewhat awkward in this case, and there is a more efficient method.

Figure 6.9 presents two processes using the contrived protocol mechanisms LOCK and UNLOCK, which surround the two critical regions shown in Figure 6.5. These two mechanisms are not automatically applied by the operating system; the software engineer must identify critical regions and deliberately insert LOCK and UNLOCK appropriately. During execution of these processes, one process will eventually reach and execute LOCK

```
LOCK (X_MUTEX)          LOCK (X_MUTEX)
TempA <- X              TempB <- X
TempA <- TempA + 1      TempB <- TempB + 1
X <- TempA              X <- TempB
UNLOCK (X_MUTEX)        UNLOCK (X_MUTEX)

Process A               Process B
```

Figure 6.9. Multiple readers and writers of X

prior to entering its critical region. LOCK gives that process exclusive access to the variable X. If, at the same time, the second process tries to execute its LOCK, that LOCK will not be granted; instead, the process will be put into a wait state. Later, when the first process exits its critical region, as indicated by execution of UNLOCK, the action of UNLOCK puts the second process back into an executable state.

The second process then finishes its LOCK operation, gaining exclusive access to the shared variable, and parallel execution of the two processes can continue. LOCK and UNLOCK ensure that the two processes, which are normally executing in parallel, execute in serial *if* they both reach their respective critical regions at the same time. Another way to say this is that the two processes are unsynchronized except during attempted mutual access to a shared variable.

The argument associated with LOCK and UNLOCK, called X_MUTEX in Figure 6.9, is another shared variable used to maintain the status of the critical region. "MUTEX" is an acronym of the term "mutual exclusion." LOCK and UNLOCK require this argument so that they can be used by the collection of cooperating processes for multiple critical regions associated with several shared variables. Without such an argument, only one critical region could be constructed.

Notice that LOCK and UNLOCK are subtly different than the simple synchronizing operations demonstrated in Chapter 5. When using LOCK, the second process is not blocked unless it attempts to enter its critical region. If it does not enter its critical region, the two processes operate in parallel. Another difference between LOCK and UNLOCK and synchronization is that the former do not determine the execution order in the same sense that event flags do; normally, UNLOCK is implemented to execute the outstanding LOCK requests in FIFO order.

The classical names for LOCK and UNLOCK are P and V, respectively. These terms were coined by E. Dijkstra when he wrote his operating system, T.H.E., in the 1960s. The meanings of P and V are apparently controversial, but we do know that they relate to the Dutch words for *wait* and *signal*. The variable, in our example, X_MUTEX, is called a *semaphore*.

There is nothing simple or automatic about LOCK and UNLOCK. The software engineer must be fully aware of the existence of critical regions and the proper use of the LOCK and UNLOCK services provided by the operating system. Improper use will result in a deadlock and/or nondeterministic behavior. The programmer must also take care to define the critical region. Establishing critical regions that extend over unnecessary programming statements may result in degradation of the application system performance. Consider the extreme case where the first statement of every process is LOCK and the last is UNLOCK. The entire collection of processes is forced to execute in serial—first one process LOCKs, executes, and UNLOCKs, then the next one does the same thing, and so forth. Therefore, whenever the critical region is long, it is more likely that one process will make another wait, thus causing serial execution of processes to take place more often than necessary. This results in overall degraded performance.

LOCK AND UNLOCK IMPLEMENTATION

LOCK and UNLOCK can be implemented two ways: as an application subroutine or as a system service. If the system engineer chooses to design and implement LOCK and UNLOCK, there are several elegant solutions presented in other texts. However, they all have the same shortcoming; some form of process blocking is required in LOCK and scheduling is required in UNLOCK. To expand on this argument, blocking has already been justified and if several processes are blocked, waiting for the critical region to become free, it is the UNLOCK algorithm that must include logic to select which process's LOCK to execute next. But, since both blocking and scheduling are already provided by the operating system, the software engineer is needlessly duplicating existing code and, in all likelihood, finding it difficult to match the refined design found in the operating system's scheduler.

Therefore, the more sensible course for the software engineer to follow is to rely on system services.

As privileged system services, LOCK and UNLOCK can be called from any process and so they are shared among the processes and subject to the same restrictions that apply to concurrent processes. In particular, LOCK and UNLOCK share data and therefore they contain critical regions themselves. Unfortunately, they cannot call LOCK and UNLOCK to control them; they must control the critical region in some other way, with an atomic pseudo-LOCK and pseudo_UNLOCK instruction.

Recall that preemption is the reason two processes cannot both write into the same variable. Thus, the easiest, most common way to create a pseudo-LOCK is by not allowing preemption. This is done with an instruction that disables interrupts, because without the possibility of interrupts, no preemption can take place and the critical region is protected and becomes atomic, no matter how many instructions are involved. For instance, if interrupts are disabled, the clock cannot interrupt a running process and force another process to be current. Furthermore, if interrupts are disabled, there is no need to queue pseudo-LOCK requests because they cannot occur since no other process is permitted to execute. The pseudo-UNLOCK instruction merely enables interrupts again and no scheduling is required.

Without interrupts, time-sharing also ceases. However, the expense caused by temporarily suspending all time-sharing operations can be controlled by careful design of LOCKing and UNLOCKing the critical regions. In fact, the operating system is strewn with shared data and, as a consequence, this same mutual exclusion problem comes up much more often than one might suspect.

6.3. A VMS Solution in
Multiple Reader-Writers

This section presents two VMS implementations: creating a sharable variable and using the primary LOCK and UNLOCK system service, $ENQW, provided by VMS. The program described in this section[2] completes the ideas

---

2. We are only considering a uniprocessor system in this discussion. The reasoning and mechanisms are more elaborate in a multiprocessor system. Nonetheless, VMS supports multiprocessors with the same mechanism, namely $ENQW.

introduced in Figure 6.9—incrementing X in three steps. The reason for this cumbersome example is to assure that the program will be nondeterministic.

Most software engineers will recognize that the Pascal statement,

```
X := X + 1;
```

will compile into the single instruction,

```
INCL X
```

and if this was permitted, the point of the example would be lost because this instruction is atomic.[3] This instruction, once the page for X is memory resident, is uninterruptable, so it is deterministic because it cannot be preempted. But with many instructions, if an interrupt occurs when an instruction is partway through execution, the hardware will either finish the instruction before granting the interrupt or restart the instruction after the interrupt has been serviced. Chapter 4 showed that instructions can be interrupted in the normal course of execution because of page faults fetching the operands. For instance:

```
ADDL3 #1,X,Y
```

may be interrupted for each operand depending on its location, and if the instruction can be interrupted, it can be preempted. The point is that the critical region must be reduced to behave like a single uninterruptable instruction.

The program used for the example in this section is found in Figure 6.10. It suggests that three processes are incrementing the shared variable X. All three programs are nearly identical, and what differences there are have been noted in the following detailed description. The LOCK and UN-LOCK services are performed by the VMS system service $ENQW (Enqueue lock request and Wait) with various arguments. Briefly, the first call to $ENQW (line 10) declares the X_MUTEX variable name. The only loop in the program (lines 14–22) is included to enter the critical region several

---

3. Actually, there are several conditions that accompany this statement. X must be long-word aligned, i.e., the two low-order bits of its address must be zero. Furthermore, no direct memory input to X can be taking place. Finally, this is only true in a uniprocessor environment. For the multiprocessor environment, there are only seven instructions on VAX machines that lock accessed memory locations.

```
[inherit ('SYS$LIBRARY:STARLET',
         'SYS$LIBRARY:PASCAL$LIBROUTINES')
                                         Requires PRMGBL privilege
1   PROGRAM SHARED_DATA (INPUT, OUTPUT);
    VAR
2     X: [VOLATILE, ALIGNED(9)] INTEGER;   { shared variable }
3     LKSB: ARRAY [0..3] OF INTEGER;       { lock status block }
4     IN_ADDR: ARRAY [1..2] OF INTEGER;    { save lower and upper bounds }
5     ERR, I, TEMP: INTEGER;
6   BEGIN
7     IN_ADDR[1] := IADDRESS (X);          { address of lower bound of area }
8     IN_ADDR[2] := IADDRESS (X)+3;        { upper bound of area }
9     err := $CRMPSC (                     { create global X }
                    inadr := IN_ADDR,      { input: bounds of area }
                    flags := SEC$M_GBL +   { Global }
                             SEC$M_WRT +   { Read-write }
                             SEC$M_PERM +  { permanent section }
                             SEC$M_DZRO +  { zeroed }
                             SEC$M_PAGFIL, { page-file }
                    gsdnam := 'SHARED_X',  { logical name of area }
                    pagcnt := 1);          { one page section }
10    err := $ENQW (                       { declare the semaphore }
                    lkmode:=LCK$K_NLMODE,  { null mode }
                     lksb:=LKSB,           { status block address }
                    resnam:='X_MUTEX');    { name of lock }
11    err := $ascefc (64, 'synch');        { synchronize three cooperating
                                                                  processes }
12    err := $setef (64);
13    err := $wfland (64, 7);              { 2=flag 65, 4=flag 66 }
14    FOR I := 1 TO 9 DO BEGIN             { increment X 9 times }
15      LIB$WAIT ( 0.3 );                  { delay 0.3 second }
16      err := $ENQW (                     { lock - critical region }
                    lkmode:=LCK$K_EXMODE,  { exclusive access mode }
                     lksb:=LKSB,           { status block address }
                    flags:=LCK$M_CONVERT,  { convert lock to exclusive }
                    resnam:='X_MUTEX');    { name of lock }
17      Temp := X;                         { X := X + 1 }
18      Temp := Temp + 1;
19      LIB$WAIT ( 0.05 );                 { delay for effect }
20      X := Temp;
21      WRITELN ( X );
22      err := $ENQW (                     { unlock - critical region }
                    lkmode:=LCK$K_NLMODE,  { null mode }
                     lksb:=LKSB,           { status block address }
                    flags:=LCK$M_CONVERT,  { convert lock to null }
                    resnam:='X_MUTEX');    { name of lock }
      END;

23 err := $DGBLSC (gsdnam := 'SHARED_X'); { delete shared memory }

    END.
```

Figure 6.10. Pascal program:
multiple readers and writers
of X

times, increasing the likelihood of nondeterministic behavior. Preemption is further encouraged by the insertion of two LIB$WAIT calls in the loop, further forcing the three processes to become nondeterministic. The reader is urged to copy the program in the figure without the $ENQW calls in the exercises and then run several copies of it in parallel (using SPAWN) on a busy system to see how it behaves.

A DETAILED DESCRIPTION

Line 2.

X is declared to be on a page boundary by the attribute "ALIGNED," which is required because shared data is assigned by pages. This restriction should be obvious from the discussion of sharing in Chapter 4.

Line 3.

The lock status block must be four longwords; this data structure is required for the $ENQW call, but the internal structure of this data area is never referenced.

Lines 7–9.

The system service call $CRMPSC (Create and Map a Section) names and reserves one page for the single variable X to be shared between processes. This is not very efficient memory utilization, but serves to illustrate the point. The PRMGBL privilege is required to create this sharable variable (or *global common section*, as it is called in VMS terms).

The first argument of the call describes the lower and upper address limits of the area to be created; this information is stored in the array IN_ADDR, which has been initialized with the address bounds of X. Only four bytes are needed to store X, since it is an integer.

The second argument declares that this is a shared area. (This system service can be used to create memory-resident files also.) Further, it declares that data is to be both read from and written to the area and that the area is permanent. If permanent, the area will not be automatically deleted when all images using it are rundown. Only permanent sections can be shared in this way. An explicit system service call, in line 23, must be made to delete the section. Finally, the second argument also specifies that the section must be cleared (zeroed) when it is created.

The third argument declares the logical name by which this section is to be known. This name acts the same as the $CREMBX (Create Mailbox) and $ASCEFC (Associate Common Event Flag Cluster) names did: it provides a hook by which the VMS operating system links other $CRMPSC requests to this one. This section is called SHARED_X.

The final argument declares that one page is required. $CRMPSC capabilities go far beyond those utilized in this example.

The $CRMPSC system service is only one of several methods offered by the VMS operating system for sharing memory. Some methods do not even need system services; they can be done at compile and link time instead.

The LOCK-UNLOCK mechanism is controlled by the $ENQW system calls in the program, which are described in Lines 10, 16, and 22.

Line 10.

The first $ENQW call declares the lock name (X_MUTEX). All processes must name the lock identically so that VMS can correlate the requests properly. This is analogous to declaring a common event flag cluster in Chapter 5 or to requesting a channel using $CREMBX. The results of the system service are stored in the lock status block (LKSB).

The locking and unlocking are performed by the other two $ENQW calls (lines 16 and 22), which contain the LCK$M_CONVERT argument. The LOCK-UNLOCK calls receive needed information from the LKSB, which is initialized by this $ENQW call. In other words, the "resnam" argument is not required (or used) in these latter two calls (lines 16 and 22), and it is included only as documentation to remind the programmer of which lock is being referenced. This documentation function could also be performed by properly naming the LKSB. For instance, if a second MUTEX, called Y_MUTEX, were required, it too would have to be declared with an $ENQW call, which would require another LKSB. In this case, the two LKSBs might be named X_LKSB and Y_LKSB to differentiate them.

Lines 11–13.

Event flags are used to ensure that the three cooperating processes start together. By convention, when the flag is set, the process is ready. In the other two processes, flag number 64 would be replaced by either 65 or 66.

Line 13.

The $WFLAND (Wait For Logical AND) system service call is new; it stops a process until several event flags are all set. The first argument specifies the cluster, and the second argument, called the mask, indicates which event flags to test. All the event flags must be in the same cluster, and each bit in the mask corresponds to an event flag. Thus, bit 0 is for event flag 64, bit 1 is for event flag 65, and bit 2 is for event flag 66. The Pascal programmer specifies the mask by adding powers of 2 together, as indicated in the comment. A mask value of 7 corresponds to the three event flags, 64, 65, and 66. This system service call ensures that all three event flags are set before any of the processes can proceed into the code that increments X in lines 17 through 20.

Line 14.

This line initializes a loop for nine iterations. It is not likely that an application will require such involuted code as that found in the body of the loop. This code is intended to show, by example, how it is possible for processes to share a variable without a complicated example. Essentially, the code does the following:

```
FOR I := 1 TO 9 DO BEGIN
        { lock critical region }
        X := X + 1;
        WRITELN ( X );
        { unlock critical region }
END;
```

The other lines are included to complicate and accentuate the sharing difficulties.

Lines 15 and 19.

The LIB$WAIT calls are included to encourage the system to preempt the process. A VMS quantum is normally set to 0.020 seconds, so this program has requested waits longer than a single quantum to ensure that all three processes get a chance to run.

Line 16.

The LOCK is indicated by the lkmode: = LCK$K_EXMODE argument. The acronym means "exclusive mode"; that is, the process is requesting exclusive ownership of the LOCK. VMS will not allow the process to continue until the request has been granted. Another process making the same request will be blocked until the lock is "converted" to null or UNLOCKed.

Lines 17, 18, 20, and 21.

These lines increment and print X. The purpose of this temporary variable is to make the program nondeterministic.

Line 22.

The UNLOCK is done with the lkmode: = LCK$K_NLMODE argument. The acronym here means "null mode."

Line 23.

This line deletes the shared memory page, which is not done automatically because the page was declared to be permanent in line 9. Permanent sections are the only form permitted for this purpose.

EXECUTING THE PROCESSES

It is possible to SPAWN as many copies of the SHARED_DATA program as the quota permits, but when executing multiple processes, it is easier to understand the process interaction if each one increments a different power of ten within X; one process increments by ones, the next by tens, the next by hundreds, and so forth.

```
err := $ENQW (lkmode:=LCK$K_EXMODE,      { lock   - HEIGHT region }
              lksb:=LKSB1,
              flags:=LCK$M_CONVERT,
              resnam:='HEIGHT_MUTEX');

err := $ENQW (lkmode:=LCK$K_EXMODE,      { lock   - WEIGHT region }
              lksb:=LKSB2,
              flags:=LCK$M_CONVERT,
              resnam:='WEIGHT_MUTEX');
TOTAL := HEIGHT * WEIGHT;

err := $ENQW (lkmode:=LCK$K_NLMODE,      { unlock - WEIGHT region }
              lksb:=LKSB2,
              flags:=LCK$M_CONVERT,
              resnam:='WEIGHT_MUTEX');

err := $ENQW (lkmode:=LCK$K_NLMODE,      { unlock - HEIGHT region }
              lksb:=LKSB1,
              flags:=LCK$M_CONVERT,
              resnam:='HEIGHT_MUTEX');
```

Figure 6.11. Using multiple
locks on a single critical region

MULTIPLE MUTEX VARIABLES

Like $CRMPSC, $ENQW has many more capabilities than described here. It is designed for the entire spectrum of single and multiple readers and writers in a dynamic way. However, the description of this powerful system service is beyond the scope of this discussion, and the interested user should refer to the Digital documentation for more information. It is also important to realize that this use of $ENQW can be generalized; that is, a program with multiple shared variables should declare a lock for each of them. The critical region for each has to be identified, and the LOCK and UNLOCK calls must be incorporated into the code. For instance, it is possible that a particular application requires two shared variables, HEIGHT and WEIGHT, to be read. A coded solution might look like Figure 6.11. The two locks are requested first, each with its own lock status block, the READLN is performed, and the variables are then unlocked in reverse order.

DEADLOCK

Now, suppose another process was coded as in Figure 6.12. Notice that the LOCK order has been reversed. Normally, a programmer may not think

```
err := $ENQW (lkmode:=LCK$K_EXMODE,      { lock   - WEIGHT region }
                 lksb:=LKSB2,
                 flags:=LCK$M_CONVERT,
                 resnam:='WEIGHT_MUTEX');

err := $ENQW (lkmode:=LCK$K_EXMODE,      { lock   - HEIGHT region }
                 lksb:=LKSB1,
                 flags:=LCK$M_CONVERT,
                 resnam:='HEIGHT_MUTEX');

TOTAL := HEIGHT * WEIGHT;

err := $ENQW (lkmode:=LCK$K_NLMODE,      { unlock - WEIGHT region }
                 lksb:=LKSB2,
                 flags:=LCK$M_CONVERT,
                 resnam:='WEIGHT_MUTEX');

err := $ENQW (lkmode:=LCK$K_NLMODE,      { unlock - HEIGHT region }
                 lksb:=LKSB1,
                 flags:=LCK$M_CONVERT,
                 resnam:='HEIGHT_MUTEX');
```

Figure 6.12. Another use of multiple locks on a single critical region

this order makes any difference, but as pointed out in Chapter 5, order is extremely important when dealing with cooperating processes. When the two hypothetical processes, one like in Figure 6.11 and the other like Figure 6.12 are executed, there is the possibility that one process will LOCK the first variable and then be preempted. If the other process then LOCKs its first variable and attempts to LOCK its second one, it is suspended because the second lock is already owned by the first process.

Notice that when the first process executes again, it too will be suspended because the second process has LOCKed the variable it needs. At this point, neither process can proceed until the other UNLOCKs its variable. And neither will UNLOCK its variable because it cannot proceed. This is another case of the deadlock or deadly embrace mentioned in Chapter 5. But unlike the cases there, which will never resolve themselves, VMS $ENQW logic will detect this condition and change the status of one of the locks to permit one process to continue. This is a unique feature of $ENQW and important to the programmer because, in the case of a complex set of resources, a deadlock can occur. However, since it takes some time for the VMS system to detect the deadlock, the application slows down noticeably.

Two concepts have been introduced. The creation of a shared variable

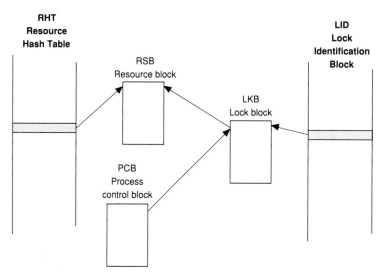

Figure 6.13. The lock resource structure

was accomplished through the use of the $CRMPSC system service. And the LOCK and UNLOCK primitives, which were used to enforce serial access of the shared variable, were implemented by the $ENQW system service.

6.4. $ENQW Data Structures

In this section, the term *resource* refers to the name given to the LOCK when it is created. In Figure 6.10, the resource is called X_MUTEX. This symbolic name is used by the system service to associate $ENQW system service requests made by several processes requesting the LOCK and UNLOCK operations. The resource name is used by the system service in the same way that the common event flag cluster name and mailbox are used in earlier examples.

A structural overview of the $ENQW system service is shown in Figure 6.13. Whenever a LOCK is declared via an $ENQW call, the resource name argument is hashed and the resource hash table (RHT) is searched.

The resource creation algorithm is different from the common cluster or mailbox logic because the VMS designers anticipated heavy usage of LOCK resources and decided that linear searching of an unordered list would not be as fast as a hashed search. If the resource name search reveals that the LOCK has not been declared yet, an entry is made in the RHT, and an RSB is created and linked into the RHT. If there is an RHT entry, the RSB has already been created. Whether or not an RHT entry is made, an LKB is built, and a LID entry is made. The LID is linked to the LKB, which is linked to the corresponding RSB. The LID is merely indexed by an arbitrary number assigned by the $ENQW system service.

The process control block (PCB) is also linked to the lock block. This connection is required to facilitate proper housekeeping of the lock structure if the image is rundown without explicit deletion of the image's LOCKs. Once this structure has been created, the LID number is returned to the calling process in the LKSB (Lock Status Block) argument of the $ENQW call. All subsequent $ENQW calls concerning a particular resource must be made with the LID number. Through use of the LID number, the system service directly accesses the LKB instead of using the hash table to find the RSB, thus making LOCK access as fast as possible. The following algorithm summarizes how the $ENQW system service declares the LOCK.

$ENQW (declaration) Algorithm
- Hash the resource name and search the RHT (Resource Hash Table).
- If the resource is not in the RHT, add it, create and initialize the RSB (Resource Block), and link the RHT to the RSB.
- Make an entry in the LID (Lock Identification Table), create and initialize the LKB (Lock Block), then link the LKB to the LID and the RSB.
- Link the PCB to the LKB.
- Store the LID index in the status block provided by the caller in the $ENQW request.
- Return to the calling image.

The system service builds an RHT entry and an RSB for each resource declared, and it builds a LID and an LKB for each process using that resource. This seems to be an unnecessarily complicated structure, but remember that it must permit multiple processes to use the resource and must easily adapt to several requests. Figure 6.14 shows how additional processes accessing the same resource are added into the LOCK structure. When

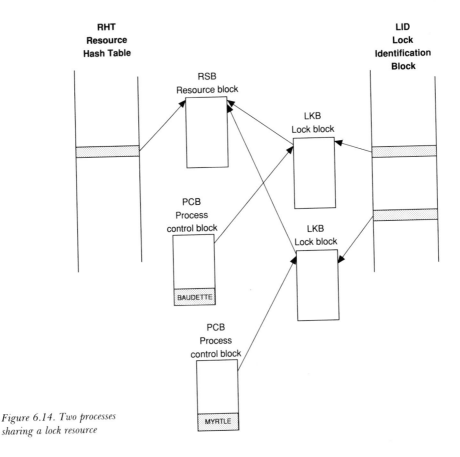

Figure 6.14. Two processes sharing a lock resource

another process declares the resource, the hash table is again used to locate the now existing RSB, and a new LKB is created and linked to the RSB. In this way, the additional processes will have a different LID number, yet still refer to the same resource.

$ENQW DYNAMIC ACTIVITY

The static structure of the LOCK resource has not been related to the dynamic activity that must be performed by the $ENQW system service. It is important to understand how this structure is used to grant a single process access and what happens to the remaining process, or processes, waiting or not using the LOCK. First the fundamental question to be asked is, "What state is the process in while waiting for a resource?" As with I/O operations, processes waiting for a lock are put into a blocked state, LEF (waiting for a local event flag).

Figure 6.15 reviews the RSB to itemize additional fields within it. The RSB contains the current status of the resource—in this example, either null or exclusive, and it contains the symbolic name assigned by the user, here "X_MUTEX". In addition, there are three pairs of queue head-tail pointers. One is used to link LKBs that have been "granted" the resource, another is for LKBs that are "waiting" for the resource, and the third links the LKBs that are waiting for a "conversion." This last queue head has to do with deadlock detection logic.

Figure 6.16 provides an example scenario to illustrate the $ENQW algorithm. It includes three processes modeled after the code in Figure 6.10. This example begins by assuming that all three processes, A, B, and C, declare the resource before any of them attempt to gain exclusive control. Thus, in line 1 of the figure, all processes are granted the resource, and its status is "null" because no process has it locked. The data structure is arranged so that the three LKBs are attached to the "granted" queue of the RSB.

Line 2 of the scenario assumes that Process B executes the $ENQW to gain exclusive control, which changes the resource status to "exclusive." This is so the algorithm can determine what to do with subsequent requests. All three processes remain on the granted queue, however, so that when Process C attempts to gain exclusive control of the resource in line 3, its LKB is moved to the wait queue because the resource is already in the exclusive status. Likewise, when Process A requests exclusive control (line 4), it too is added to the wait queue.

The wait queue is FIFO, so when B gives up "exclusive" rights to the resource, in line 5, the RSB status is momentarily changed to null. This permits Process C to be moved back to the granted queue and given exclusive control of the resource, changing the status back to exclusive again. Then, on line 6, when C gives up control, A is given the resource. When Process B attempts to regain control (line 7), its LKB is moved to the wait queue until Process A (line 8) gives up the resource. Finally, on line 9, Process B also gives up the resource, and the status in the RSB is changed to null and all processes are in the granted queue.

The following algorithm lists the steps the $ENQW system service takes to implement a LOCK or UNLOCK request.

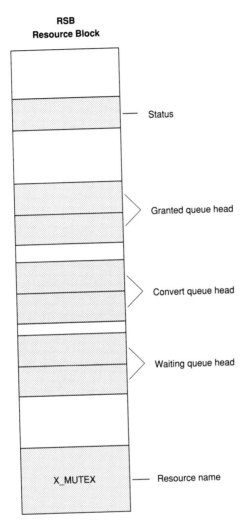

Figure 6.15. Resource block structure

Process activity	LKB queue membership			RSB — Resource	
	A	B	C	Status	Owner
1. All declare resource	Grant	Grant	Grant	Null	None
2. B converts to exclusive	Grant	Grant	Grant	Exclusive	B
3. C converts to exclusive	Grant	Grant	Wait	Exclusive	B
4. A converts to exclusive	Wait	Grant	Wait	Exclusive	B
5. B converts to null	Wait	Grant	Grant	Exclusive	C
6. C converts to null	Grant	Grant	Grant	Exclusive	A
7. B converts to exclusive	Grant	Wait	Grant	Exclusive	A
8. A converts to null	Grant	Grant	Grant	Exclusive	B
9. B converts to null	Grant	Grant	Grant	Null	None

Figure 6.16. A LOCK scenario
with three processes

$ENQW (LOCK-UNLOCK) Algorithm
• Using the LID index in the status block, locate the LKB.
• If it is a LOCK request, examine the RSB status and either grant the request or link the LKB on the appropriate queue and block the process.
• If it is an UNLOCK request, change the RSB status, and, if available, dequeue another process's LKB.
• Return to the calling image.

In looking at the finer detail of the LKB in Figure 6.17, we see the PCB links. Double links are required because the process may have declared more than one resource, and so the LKBs are threaded together as in Figure 6.18. The PID is carried in the LKB as redundant information to aid system debugging. The Status field contains the status that the process has requested the LOCK to be placed in (null or exclusive in our example). Naturally, the queue links are also found in the LKB along with the state name (waiting, conversion, or granted), which is used for debugging also.

Returning to the double linked thread of the PCB, the thread has to do with multiple resources declared by a single process. To understand this structure, think of a multilayered version of Figure 6.15, one with multiple RSBs assigned to a single process. Figure 6.18 shows a single process with three resources declared. The important part of this diagram is the PCB thread through the LKBs. Because the thread starts at the PCB, every lock

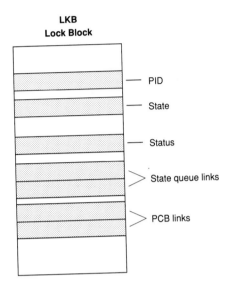

LKB
Lock Block

— PID

— State

— Status

State queue links

PCB links

Figure 6.17. Lock block
structure

the process owns can be located and identified if this thread is followed. If other processes used the same resources, everything except the RSBs would be duplicated, forming another layer on top of the existing diagram.

USING MONITOR

A typical MONITOR display is shown in Figure 6.19. The top line is a count of new LOCK requests, that is, any call to $ENQW. The next line shows the number of LOCKS that have been converted as illustrated in Figure 6.16. The third line is a count of $DEQ Dequeue Lock system service requests. There is no need in these examples to delete the LOCK structures created by $ENQW because image rundown will perform that operation.

"ENQs Forced to Wait Rate" is the count of LKBs queued onto an RSB. When using $ENQW, the user has the option of not waiting for the resource when it is busy. This is the meaning of the "ENQs Not Queued Rate." This option is not exercised in the examples.

On the deadlock lines, the VMS operating system counts the number of deadlock searches it performs (two on the figure) and the number of deadlocks it identifies (one). Notice that the specific deadlocked resource is

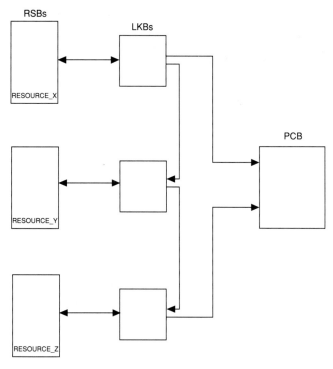

Figure 6.18. A process with
three lock resources

not named; the display only shows the fact that deadlocks are occurring and
are being resolved.

   At the bottom of the display, the total declared number of resources
(118 RSBs) and locks (122 LKBs) is presented. Throughout this display,
lines labeled "rate" indicate the average number over the measurement
interval, three seconds by default. The two total lines are not averages but
actual counts made sometime during the interval.

   This discussion has been merely an introduction to the LOCK mechanism supported by the VMS operating system, and has not shown it to its
fullest capabilities and complexities. For instance, because a deadlock situation is possible, the deadlock detection algorithm periodically examines all
LKBs on the wait queue to check for a possible deadlock, and if it finds one,
one of the entries on the queue is moved to the conversion queue to be
resolved.

```
                                      VAX/VMS Monitor Utility
                  +-----+             LOCK MANAGEMENT STATISTICS
                  : CUR :                  on node BSU
                  +-----+             4-JAN-1991 08:28:47

                                    0       5       10      15      20
                                    + - - - + - - - + - - - + - - - -+
    New ENQ Rate                  1 :**
    Converted ENQ Rate            3 :******
                                    :       :       :       :       :
    DEQ Rate                      2 :****
    Blocking AST Rate               :
                                    :       :       :       :       :
    ENQs Forced To Wait Rate        :
    ENQs Not Queued Rate            :
                                    :       :       :       :       :
    Deadlock Search Rate          2 :****
    Deadlock Find Rate            1 :**
                                    :       :       :       :       :
    Total Locks                 122 :**************************************
    Total Resources             118 :**************************************
                                    :       :       :       :       :
                                    + - - - + - - - + - - - + - - - -+
```

Figure 6.19. Typical output of the $ MONITOR LOCK command

6.5. Using Event Flags as Locks

The discussion of event flags in Chapter 5 might lead to the conclusion that event flags will also work as a LOCK. This is correct, but the implementation is somewhat difficult. Even so, event flags are probably faster than $ENQW and therefore worth mentioning. Only common event flags can be used for this application because they must be shared between several processes. Here is the crux of the difficulty with event flags: recall from Chapter 5 that *all* processes waiting for a particular event flag are returned to the COM state when the flag is set. In this way, the process execution order is deferred to the scheduler. Conversely, $ENQW is designed to service waiting processes on a FIFO basis. In summary, $ENQW ignores process priority and event flags honor it. This could be an important distinction in some applications.

To understand the use of event flags, assume that the event flag value

```
REPEAT                                ( Lock critical region )
  $WAITFR (flag_number);
  CONDITION := $CLREF (flag_number)
UNTIL CONDITION = SS$_WASSET;
  .
  .                     ( Critical region )
  .

$SETEF (flag_number);                 ( Unlock critical region )
```

Figure 6.20. Using event flags
as locks

has the following meaning: when the value is 1 (set), no process is in its critical region, and when it is 0 (clear), a process is in its critical region and all the rest of the processes must wait for the event flag to be set. The reverse of this proposal will not work because there is no system service that waits for an event flag to be cleared. (Physically documenting the usage of event flags in this way is always a good idea. Their meaning is often transposed by a programmer, perhaps because of their binary values.)

The event flag LOCK algorithm is coded in outline form in Figure 6.20. To LOCK a critical region, the process must first wait for the event flag to be set, indicating no other process is in its critical region. Then, after the process wakes up, it must clear the event flag and test to see if the clear was necessary—that is, it tests if the event flag was previously set. This test is the essential step. If the event flag was not previously set, that means some other process woke too, cleared the event flag, and is running in its critical region already. Hence, the process doing the test must wait again until the event flag is set. To do this, it loops back to the $WAITFR call. This loop is performed indefinitely until it finds that the event flag was set.

EVENT FLAG ANALYSIS

The significant code is in the REPEAT-UNTIL loop and will be analyzed in some detail to make certain that no deadlock situation can occur. Assume that two processes, A and B, are waiting to enter their respective critical regions because a third process, C, is already in its region. According to our definition, the event flag will be cleared in this case; thus, the two waiting processes, A and B, have executed the $WAITFR line and are currently in a CEF state.

Next, assume that Process C executes a $SETEF call as it leaves its critical region. This causes *both* waiting processes to become computable, but, of course, the scheduler must pick only one to run first, in this case, Process A. When Process A runs, the first thing it does is clear the event flag. $CLREF returns the event flag's value prior to clear operation,[4] SS$_WASSET. Now, assume that Process A is preempted at this point and Process B is started. It too executes the $CLREF statement, but this time, the previous value of the event flag will be clear (SS$_WASCLR) because Process A already cleared it. Hence, Process B must loop back to the $WAITFR to wait until Process A sets the flag again. When Process A is restarted, it will proceed into its critical region. Incidentally, this analysis assumes that the $CLREF system service call is atomic and cannot be preempted, which the VMS operating system will guarantee.

There is one more analysis to make. Suppose, after Process C leaves its critical region and sets the event flag, Process A starts, enters, and then exits its critical region before Process B is executed at all. That is, suppose that A is not preempted until after it leaves its critical region. Will B run? To be certain that no deadlock occurs in this case, begin with the same initial condition as in the previous analysis: the event flag is initially 0 and both Process A and Process B are in the CEF state because Process C is in its critical region. When C sets the event flag, both A and B become computable, as before, and A is chosen to run. This time, A clears the event flag, runs through its critical region, and sets the event flag again. Since no process is waiting for the event flag, nothing happens when it is set this second time; B is already computable, not waiting. When B finally executes, it clears the event flag successfully and enters its critical region without difficulty. Hence, there is no possibility of deadlock in this case either.

The algorithm to analyze possible deadlocks is the same one used in Figure 6.4 and Figure 6.5. That is, the programmer must look at all possible execution threads of the cooperating processes that may be caused by preemption and then, for each thread, must look at the results. If the logic is correct, and there is no deadlock for all of the sequences, then the proposed algorithm will work.

---

4. $CLREF returns one of two values, either SS$_WASCLR if flag was clear prior to system service request, or SS$_WASSET if the flag was set prior to system service request.

6.6. One Reader and One Writer

This section examines a special case of two processes sharing memory, one of which only writes, while the other only reads. The writer gathers or *produces* data, which is put into a shared memory area. The reader extracts or *consumes* data from shared memory. This application is quite common and therefore worthy of detailed discussion. It even has a special name in the literature—the *producer-consumer*. Perhaps its most obvious implementation in a VMS environment is through the use of mailboxes.

The special application of shared memory can be implemented without the benefit of any LOCK-UNLOCK mechanism; this method, called a *circular buffer,* is the subject of this section. In a circular buffer, the data structure consists of a shared array and two shared indexes into the array: one for the reader and one for the writer. The algorithm is powerful but, as usual, the programmer must be careful.

A condensed algorithm of each process follows:

- The writer process determines if an additional data entry will fit in the array and, if so, adds one entry and advances its index. If there is no room, it must wait.
- Asynchronously, the reader process makes sure there is data available in the array and, if so, removes one entry and advances its index. If there is no data, it must wait.

Therefore, both processes must keep track of the amount of data in the buffer, and, on the average, the reader must extract data from the buffer at least as fast as the writer puts it in, or else the buffer will overflow.

As with all code involving cooperating processes, the sequence of code to test and move data is paramount in this algorithm. In the following detailed description of the algorithm, the following definitions are used:

- The reader's index points to the first entry that contains data in the buffer.
- The writer's index points to the first empty entry after the last data in the buffer—the first available hole.
- The buffer is considered empty when the index values are identical, that is, when they point to the same entry.
- The buffer is considered full when there is only one empty entry in it.

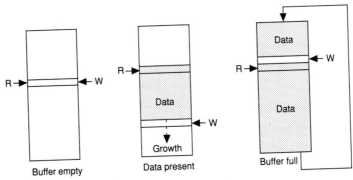

R points to the next entry to read
W points to the next entry to write

Figure 6.21. Definitions of a
circular buffer

Figure 6.21 illustrates these definitions. One characteristic of a circular buffer is that it can never be filled completely. Notice that in our definition, if we added one more entry to the "full" configuration, it would appear to be empty instead.

The full buffer in Figure 6.21 illustrates why this algorithm is called a circular buffer. When the writer fills the bottom entry in the array, the next entry to be used is at the top of the array. That is, the bottom is logically adjacent or contiguous to the top, so, essentially, this type of buffer has no beginning and no end.

Pascal is particularly well suited to implement this algorithm. The buffer should be declared as:

```
BUFFER: ARRAY [0..max_size] OF BUFFER_TYPE;
```

where the BUFFER_TYPE can be any arbitrary fixed-length data type. The lower limit of zero is important because the program will make use of the MOD function to maintain the circularity in the following way: whenever either process advances one of the indexes, it executes a statement like this:

```
INDEX := (INDEX + 1) MOD (max_size + 1)
```

which is effectively identical to the two statements below. However, the previous line, even though it appears shorter, probably takes longer to execute because of the division operation, MOD.

```
INDEX := INDEX + 1;
IF (INDEX > max_size) THEN INDEX := 0;
```

BUFFER EMPTY OR FULL

Before a version of the implementation of the two processes is presented, there is one additional issue that must be considered. What is to be done if the reader discovers the buffer is empty? Or, similarly, what if the writer discovers the buffer is full? This issue was addressed in Chapter 5 in some detail when starting JULIET; there are three generic solutions:

- Busy wait
- Poll
- Synchronize

OUTLINE OF THE PROGRAM

Figure 6.22 presents the essential consumer and producer code. For simplicity, the code contains a polling loop to take care of both the full and empty cases. The BUFFER declaration details are not included, nor does this program show how the BUFFER is shared by the two processes using $CRMPSC. Moreover, W_INDEX and R_INDEX, the array indexes, must be shared also, but the details are not given here. An overall processing loop is implied, and there is no indication where the producer is getting its data from or how the consumer is putting the data to use. In one situation, the producer could get the data from the terminal and the consumer could display that data. The skeleton code in Figure 6.22 also suggests that the code that produces data should be separated from the code that fills the buffer. Likewise, emptying the buffer and consuming the data are distinct operations in order that the data can be gotten in and out of the buffer as quickly as possible to avoid overflow problems in particular.

This producer-consumer solution works without any LOCK-UNLOCK logic because of the usage of the two indexes, not the buffer itself. Look at the producer—it reads and writes its index, W_INDEX, while the consumer only reads W_INDEX. Thus, W_INDEX is read and written by one process, but only read by the other; the same is true of R_INDEX. This is the third case discussed in the latter part of Section 6.1 and illustrated in Figure 6.8 (multiple readers, a single writer). It was shown to be safe as long as the importance of the updated variable was kept in mind.

```
PROGRAM PRODUCER (INPUT, OUTPUT);
. . .
BEGIN
. . .
            { produce data }
. . .                                       { loop while buffer is full }
WHILE ( W_INDEX + 1 ) MOD ( max_size + 1 ) = R_INDEX DO;
. . .
            { fill BUFFER [ W_INDEX ] }
. . .                                       { increment writer's index by 1 }
W_INDEX := ( W_INDEX + 1 ) MOD ( max_size + 1 );
. . .
END.
PROGRAM CONSUMER (INPUT, OUTPUT);
. . .
BEGIN
. . .
                                            { loop while buffer is empty }
WHILE ( W_INDEX = R_INDEX ) DO;
. . .
            { remove BUFFER [ R_INDEX ] }
. . .                                       { increment reader's index by 1 }
R_INDEX := ( R_INDEX + 1 ) MOD ( max_size + 1 );
. . .             { consume the data }
. . .
END.
```

Figure 6.22. Outline of
producer and consumer
programs

Consider the ambiguity question raised in Section 6.1 in light of the assembly language code in Figure 6.23. The two statements from the processes in Figure 6.22 involving W_INDEX have been extracted, and Figure 6.23 presents the essential assembly code that is produced. As pointed out, preemption takes place at the assembly level and, thus, can take place within any Pascal statement. So, to rigorously analyze the situation, every assembly level code thread should be considered. The particular phenomenon to be examined is the placement of the CMPL (Compare Longword) instruction in the execution thread; it is the only instruction that references W_INDEX in the consumer part of this example. The BEQL (Branch on Equal or Less

```
PRODUCER:
    W_INDEX := ( W_INDEX + 1 ) MOD ( max_size + 1 );

            ADDL3       #1,W_INDEX,R2       ; R2 <- W_INDEX + 1
            CLRL        R3                  ; make R2-R3 a quadword
            ADDL3       #1,max_size,R4      ; R4 <- max_size + 1
            EDIV        R4,R2,R5,W_INDEX    ; R5 <- (R3-R2) DIV R4
                                            ; W_INDEX <- remainder
CONSUMER:
    WHILE           ( W_INDEX = R_INDEX ) DO:

    WHILE_LOOP:
        CMPL        W_INDEX,R_INDEX         ; Compare W_INDEX:R_INDEX
        BEQL        WHILE_LOOP              ; Loop if equal
```

Figure 6.23. Assembly code from producer-consumer

than) execution location does not matter, since it makes no reference to W_INDEX. If the CMPL is executed before the producer's EDIV (Extended, 64 bit, Divide), the "old" value of W_INDEX is used in the comparison; if the CMPL executes after the EDIV, the "updated" value is used instead. It does not matter which value is used because the consumer will have to execute at most one additional poll loop if the "old" one is used instead of the "updated" one. And in either case, there is no chance of a deadlock, which is, after all, the main concern. Since the R_INDEX case is symmetric, a similar argument holds for it.

PITFALLS

This does not mean that there are no dangers inherent with circular buffers as a method of processes sharing data. As with all the previous examples involving communication processes, the order of the statements is essential and liable to be a source of errors that cause deadlock. For instance, if the consumer code is written as in Figure 6.24, there is a possibility that the producer will "overrun" the consumer because the R_INDEX is incremented too soon, before the data is actually removed from the array. The example in Figure 6.24 erroneously interchanges the increment and the removal

```
WHILE ( W_INDEX = R_INDEX ) DO;     { loop while buffer is empty }
R_INDEX := ( R_INDEX + 1 ) MOD ( max_size + 1 ); { increment }
. . .
      { consume BUFFER [ ( R_INDEX - 1 ) MOD ( max_size + 1 ) ] }
. . .
```

Figure 6.24. An illegal usage of
R_INDEX

```
WHILE ( W_INDEX = R_INDEX ) DO;     { loop while buffer is empty }
. . .
      { consume BUFFER [ R_INDEX ] without removing it }
. . .
R_INDEX :+ ( R_INDEX + 1 ) MOD ( max_size + 1 ); { increment }
```

Figure 6.25. A debatable usage
of R_INDEX

statements. Superficially, this looks like a reasonable improvement to the initial implementation because the removal and consumption operations are combined into a single statement; the data is consumned without moving it. But in an effort to improve the code, this violates the definitions by advancing R_INDEX before removing the data. This may cause the producer to reuse the entry before the data is removed.

A final point can be made before leaving this topic. Figure 6.25 presents a correct variation of the code in Figure 6.24. In it, the "removal" and "consumption" logic of the consumer process have been legally combined. However, there is one pragmatic difficulty with this solution: the producer is denied usage of the buffer for a longer amount of time because R_INDEX is not updated until the entry is entirely consumed. The time is longer because if the "consuming" functions are complex and execute directly on the data in the buffer, the producer may run out of buffer space before the consumer has released its entry. By removing the data from the buffer before operating on it, the consumer gives the producer one more entry in the buffer. But the only time the producer has to wait is when the buffer is within one entry of being full. When this producer-consumer system operates with a nearly full buffer, the buffer is probably too small anyhow and should be expanded. In other words, Figure 6.25 is quite unlikely to cause any difficulties.

In any producer-consumer situation, the underlying assumption is that the consumer can operate, on average, at least as fast as the producer. Hopefully, the consumer is faster than the producer; a margin of safety would be a good design consideration. However, if the producer is generating data in "bursts," average operation of the system may lead to erroneous conclusions; the buffer may have to be sized for the burst activity instead of the average. Incidentally, the design developed in this section has no provision for indicating that the producer has lost data or how much data has been lost.

6.7. Limitations of Shared Memory

Although a powerful tool, shared memory has one limitation that must be pointed out: memory addresses cannot be passed between processes. To show why this is so, this section recalls the discussion of virtual memory covered in Chapter 4, which showed that an address in the context of one process is meaningless in the context of another.

Consider a counter-example to illustrate this point. Refer to Figure 6.26 to see how one might store an address. In VAX Pascal, the function ADDRESS returns the address of the argument as a pointer (circle 1). Now, suppose that the processes ROBOMARGE and MICKIMOUSE wish to share both A_ADDR and A, as indicated in the figure. In ROBOMARGE, A_ADDR and A are on virtual pages 93 and 94 (hexadecimal) respectively; thus, the virtual address of A is page 93 plus some offset, so it has the hexadecimal form of 000126xx. In MICKIMOUSE, these two variables are on virtual pages 67 and 68; thus, the address of A is in the form 0000CExx. There is no reason to expect that the two processes will have the same address for A; remember that there is no connection between the two until they are executed. The compiler has no idea what is happening and neither does the linker; it is $CRMPSC that causes the two processes to share the same physical frame in memory.

It should be apparent that the address stored in A_ADDR is only valid in the context of ROBOMARGE and is meaningless in MICKIMOUSE because the virtual page numbers of the shared pages are different. Any reference in MICKIMOUSE (circle 2) that uses the address stored in A_ADDR will look at page 93 (in MICKIMOUSE) rather than page 67.

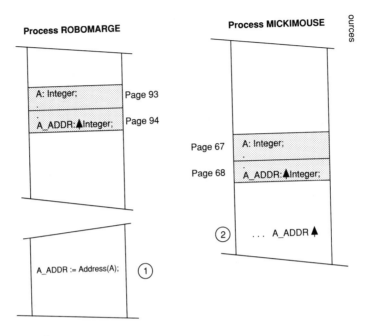

*Figure 6.26. Addresses in
shared memory*

To see the same point another way, again consider how memory is shared. In sharing, the page tables of both processes must contain the same physical frame number, as Figure 6.27 illustrates. There, both page tables containing the variable A point to frame 427 (circle 1), and its value is 7129. When ROBOMARGE references A, it thinks it is somewhere on page 93 (circle 2), and the hardware directs it to the proper frame. When MICKIMOUSE references A, it thinks it is on page 67 (circle 3), and again the hardware computes an address on frame 427; hence, both processes use the same frame and fetch the same value for A.

Examine what happens when using A_ADDR that contains an address rather than a data value. Its page has been assigned by the VMS system to frame 1023 (circle 4) in both processes. A_ADDR was initialized to virtual address (not a value) by ROBOMARGE, which is somewhere on ROBOMARGE's virtual page 93, as suggested in the previous figure. Then, if the code in ROBOMARGE uses A_ADDR as a pointer, it will access page 93 (in frame 427) successfully (circle 5). But if the code in MICKIMOUSE attempts to use A_ADDR as a pointer, it will also access virtual page 93 by

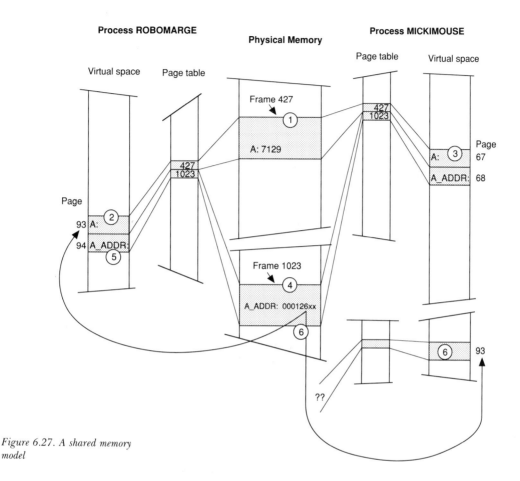

Figure 6.27. A shared memory model

decomposing the address 000126xx (circle 6), which is *not* frame 427 and may not be a valid address in the process context. MICKIMOUSE's page table does not show a PTE for page 93. In MICKIMOUSE's virtual space, the value stored in A_ADDR would have to be 0000CExx (page 67) to correctly address A.

Therefore, if only data is shared across processes, shared memory is a powerful tool. But addresses in memory cannot be passed between processes unless the virtual page numbers involved are identical, and this is difficult to arrange.

There is one final point to make regarding shared memory addresses. It has probably occurred to the reader already because it is so obvious, and it rounds out the discussion. Regardless of the kind of data that is being shared, shared memory assumes that the offset from the page boundary to the variable must be identical in all of the processes. The hardware has no way of compensating for varying offsets, and there is no way for the VMS operating system to determine if this restriction is being observed. This is the programmer's responsibility.

6.8. Related Issues

The literature is full of LOCK-UNLOCK solutions, but few, if any, are ever implemented in real operating systems. The literature is also replete with LOCK-UNLOCK solutions that do not depend on any operating system support or hardware. These solutions are dissatisfying to the application system designer who has tools available on the system, so we have demonstrated how the tools of the VMS operating system are used.

The most primitive and oldest semaphore mechanism employed by an operating system is disabling interrupts or elevating the interrupt level. Depending on the sophistication of the hardware, this mechanism provides a range of capabilities, from totally disabling all interrupts to selectively disabling them on a device-by-device level. Most operating systems make full use of this technique for short threads of code. Normally, interrupt controls are used to prohibit hardware from interfering with the operating system when hardware interfacing is required. For instance, when an interrupt is received from a keyboard device, the operating system disables interrupts on that device until it can fetch the required information from it. When the operating system has fetched the data, it again enables interrupts. This strategy is necessary because the device itself is unable to queue data; it depends on the operating system to receive the data before more arrives from the keyboard. However, as a safety measure, the hardware is probably equipped with an "overrun" flag. This flag is set if additional data arrives too soon so that the operating system at least knows it has fallen behind.

The operating system may also selectively disable interrupts in certain cases unrelated to I/O. Consider the paging algorithm once again; when the operating system is restructuring the paging database in response to a page fault, it cannot permit any other page faults to occur. In effect, this code is a critical region within the operating system. The following sequence of events shows how the operating system could get into trouble. Suppose it is processing a page fault for Process ONE when a keyboard interrupt for Process TWO arrives. That interrupt preempts the page fault logic temporarily. The device handler then determines if this interrupt has enough priority to restart Process TWO rather than Process ONE. Suppose Process TWO is started and another page fault occurs. Clearly, this cannot be allowed to happen; the paging database is not necessarily consistent because it was being modified in response to ONE's page fault and has not necessarily been restored to a consistent state yet. How does the operating system overcome this problem? One solution might be for it to totally disable all interrupts while in its critical region of the page fault logic.[5] Any operating system is full of such critical regions, and system programmers must carefully identify and protect them. The hardware is an essential aid to the functioning of the operating system.

6.9. Summary

This chapter is the companion to Chapter 5. It illustrated how processes synchronized or serialized their execution sequences and extended the process communication notion to examine how processes cooperate to share data. When sharing data, processes must be synchronized whenever they write common data, but otherwise they can run in parallel. We showed how uncontrolled threads of code in two processes lead to unpredictable results under some conditions; then we detailed the cases that caused problems by defining readers and writers and the read-write characteristics that led to the problem.

In looking at solutions, we first introduced the critical regions—those code sequences that are troublesome if multiple processes share them. The classical solutions involve some kind of signal-wait primitives, called P and V, surrounding this critical section. Then, we showed how they are applied by carefully examining the meaning and operation of LOCK and UNLOCK.

Next, we applied the LOCK-UNLOCK algorithm to a simple problem, with the VMS $ENQW system service, and we presented Pascal code and

---

5. The VMS operating system does not solve the problem this way, however, as explained in Chapter 8.

explained the implementation of the system service in the VMS operating system by looking at its data structures. The intricacy of the data structures demonstrated both the generality and the complexity of the system service.

To show that the synchronization tools can be used as a LOCK-UNLOCK operation, a program implemented the operators using event flags, which showed the benefit of a riskier but faster solution.

Finally, in presenting solutions to real problems, we looked at a special data sharing case called the producer-consumer to show that the LOCK-UNLOCK solution is not always required. In a two-process, data-sharing environment, if one process is a reader and one is a writer, certain liberties can be taken. This example was broken down to the assembly language level to show why it worked without critical regions.

In a related topic, we revisited briefly the shared memory discussion of Chapter 4. This form of process communication has its limitations also because addresses of data structures cannot be passed reliably this way without careful consideration.

ACRONYMS

$ASSIGN	Assign a channel system service
$CLREF	Clear Event Flag system service
$CRMPSC	Create and Map a Section system service
$ENQW	Enqueue lock request and Wait system service
$SETEF	Set Event Flag system service
$WAITFR	Wait for event flag set system service
CEF	Common Event Flag process state
CMPL	Assembly instruction to Compare Longwords
COM	Computable process state
EDIV	Assembly instruction to perform Extended integer Divide
FIFO	First In First Out
LIB$WAIT	An RTL routine to hibernate a specific time
LID	Lock Identification Table
LKB	Lock Block

MUTEX	Mutual Exclusion
PCB	Process Control Block
PID	Process Identification
PRMGBL	Permanent Global Privilege
PTE	Page Table Entry
RHT	Resource Hash Table
RSB	Resource Block
RTL	Run-Time Library

SHORT ANSWER EXERCISES

1. As suggested by Figure 6.4, list all of the possible execution sequences for Figure 6.3.

2. List all of the possible execution sequences for the following:

Process A

```
TempA := X;
TempA := TempA + 1;
X := TempA;
```

Process B

```
TempB := X;
TempB := TempB + 1;
X := TempB;
```

In this case, how many possible execution sequences are there? If you assume X := 0 initially, what are all the possible final values for X?

3. Extend the previous exercise to three processes, such that Process C contains the instructions:

```
TempC := X;
TempC := TempC + 1;
X := TempC;
```

How many execution sequences are possible when these three processes are running concurrently? How many values of X are possible? What are they?

4. Identify the critical sections in the following concurrent process code segments. Assume that "VARIB" is the shared variable.

a)

Process ONE   Process TWO

```
. . .                                  . . .
WRITELN ( 'First: ', VARIB: 0 );       WRITELN ( 'Second: ', VARIB: 0);
Q := VARIB;                            Q := VARIB;
LIB$WAIT ( 0.5 );                     LIB$WAIT ( 0.7 );
VARIB := Q + 1;                       VARIB := Q + 1;
WRITELN;                              WRITELN;
WRITELN ( 'First: ', VARIB: 0);       WRITELN ( 'Second: ', VARIB: 0);
```

b)

Process ONE   Process TWO

```
. . .                                  . . .
WRITELN ( 'First: ', VARIB: 0 );       WRITELN ( 'Second: ', VARIB: 0 );
VARIB := VARIB + 1;                   VARIB := VARIB + 1;
WRITELN;                              WRITELN;
WRITELN ( 'First: ', VARIB: 0 );       WRITELN ( 'Second: ', VARIB: 0 );
```

5. Analyze the following event flag code. It was derived from Figure 6.20, except the REPEAT loop logic was removed. List all possible execution sequences of the two processes. Then show one execution sequence that allows two processes in their critical regions at the same time. If you can find a case, this solution will lead to nondeterministic behavior.

```
$WAITFR (flag_number);        { Wait for region to be unused }

$CLREF (flag_number);         { Lock the region }
 .
 .                             { Critical region }
 .

$SETEF (flag_number);         { Unlock critical region }
```

6. Embellish Figure 6.14. Draw the RHT, RSBs, LKBs, LID, and PCBs and their links to one another given the following conditions:
   • Two processes are named ONE and TWO.
   • Each process has declared three resources: X, Y, and Z.
   • Currently ONE holds X exclusively, and TWO is waiting for it.

7. Design an event flag LOCK-UNLOCK solution using a WHILE loop instead of a REPEAT loop. The code for using event flags as locks is suggested in Figure 6.20.

8. In Chapter 5, $HIBER-WAKE was used to ensure that only one process at a time was executing. Why is this solution inappropriate for controlling a critical region?

9. The simple appearance of $ENQW, even in the proper place, does not ensure that the program is deterministic if the resource names are spelled incorrectly. Explain.

10. Derive an expression that computes the number of used buffer entries at a given time in the consumer producer model.

11. Add CEB, RSB, RHT, LID, and LKB structures to the Scheduler and Memory Database Overview, Figure 4.33.

PROJECTS

1. Copy Figure 6.10 and make two processes. Code one process to increment the units place and the other to increment the tens place in X. Error code 1561 returned by $CRMPSC is a success code meaning that the area did not previously exist and was created. PRMGBL privilege is required to create a shared region for X.

2. Copy Figure 6.10 and make three processes (see project 1). Do the processes simply take turns entering the critical area? Why or why not? Describe what is happening.

3. To appreciate the problem, remove the $ENQW logic from Figure 6.10 to see how two processes behave when sharing a variable in an uncontrolled manner.

4. This exercise involves creating two processes and a common buffer between them. One process reads a line, puts it in the buffer, and signals the other with an event flag. The second process displays the line from the buffer, then reads a new line, buffers it, and signals the first process. The first process displays the line and prompts for another line. This algorithm continues until the processes are stopped with CTRL-Y. The two processes should be running on adjacent terminals for the best effect. PRMGBL privilege is required for this exercise.

5. Common event flags can be used in the place of $ENQW with one limitation—there is no deadlock detection. The advantage is speed, of course. Devise and run a test that determines the cost of the two

schemes. The code for using event flags as locks is suggested in Figure 6.20.

6. Code Figure 6.10 using event flags instead of $ENQW, as suggested in project 5. Run three processes using the resulting code. Do the three merely take turns accessing X? Why or why not? Explain what is happening.

7. Develop a system of two processes and two shared variables using $ENQW. Deliberately create a deadlock situation as suggested by Figures 6.11 and 6.12, and report on how the VMS operating system detects and resolves the situation. Are the images aborted, do they wait forever, or is there a more graceful solution? The display produced by MONITOR LOCK will show if you have been successful in creating a deadlock.

8. Devise two programs, a producer and a consumer, that share three memory areas: a buffer, the write pointer, and the read pointer. Solve the buffer full and buffer empty cases more cleverly than indicated in the text (a busy wait is not very elegant).

9. Are LOCK names case-sensitive? You will have to code a pair of processes using $ENQWs with the resource name spelled in different cases to test this. Watch out, for the critical areas may never be accessed simultaneously; hence, even misspelled resource names (thus, unprotected critical areas) cause no apparent difficulties. In other words, you first have to prove there is a contention problem before you can claim to have solved it.

PAPERS

1. Research the controversy over the meaning behind the naming of P and V.

2. This chapter made the statement "The $CLREF system service call cannot be preempted, which the VMS operating system will guarantee." Analyze this statement; assume that $CLREF could be preempted in some state that might cause a deadlock to take place. At what point in the algorithm must the VMS system ensure that no preemption takes place?

3. Propose another definition for the two indexes used for the circular buffer application. Draw a picture of the three cases, empty, present, and full, as in Figure 6.21. Then, using your new definition, outline the producer and consumer code, using Figure 6.22 as a model.

Security, Protection, and Privacy

GOALS

Physical security

User privacy

Resource protection

VMS access controls

VAX-supported protection

7

The functions of security, protection, and privacy are in opposition to the purpose of the time-sharing system. That is, sharing and security are contradictory terms, and it is only with the advent of the "information age" that this dichotomy became apparent. Users cannot throw up their hands in disgust and simply ignore the situation either. Our global society depends on computers and the information that they process because national and international commerce depends on sharing information. No, the subject must be systematized, broken into smaller, manageable problems that can then be individually resolved. This chapter will define and discuss the major security issues and then illustrate solutions that are implemented by the VMS operating system. But this subject is by no means fully understood and will remain a rich area of research for years to come. It may not be as glamorous a study as some others, such as artificial intelligence, but it is at least as important.

Computer security has more than one definition. First, it is the protection of the physical machinery from theft, vandalism, and disasters like water, smoke, and fire. Second, it is protection from unauthorized access to computer resources, such as illegal logins either from remote locations or from a computer center. Third, it involves authorized users performing unauthorized tasks, say, a student with a course work account setting up a consulting business using the school's computer (this is more an *ethical* than a security situation). Fourth, it is related to the reliability of the system. If the operating system is prone to failure in an environment of programmers because of internal errors, the system is not very useful. Fifth, and last, it includes an authorized user attempting unauthorized access to other user or administration accounts. This final aspect of security is the primary subject of this chapter—security that is supported by the hardware and software. The other four definitions basically relate to the political and physical aspects of security and will be only briefly introduced.

Hardware and software security does not mean total and absolute privacy of all resources in the system, but selective privacy. Limited sharing is required on a time-sharing computing service, but in some cases, it becomes a political issue instead of a technical one.

A case in point: at one time, our system manager permitted all users read access to SYSUAF.DAT (the user authorization file). As described in Chapter 2, it contains account attributes such as user names and the corresponding true names; for example, it says that account DMILLER is owned by David Donald Miller. This policy was supposed to encourage open communication by making it easy for a user to locate a friend or classmate. But a few took advantage of this policy to create distribution lists for MAIL and send volumes of abusive junk mail. The system manager's response was to restrict access to SYSUAF.DAT to himself and the instructors. A related question is whether or not users, like BIGSTUD and CUDDLES,[1] want their true names to be public: is that decision better left to the individual?

Another important issue in a time-sharing environment is the right to know the names of files owned by any user: are these names private or public data? Our system manager has decided that, by default, file names are public but not their contents; but the user has control over this decision and can easily negate it.

How should the operating system be designed to accommodate varying policy decisions? The UNIX operating system permits all users access to any other user files in the default case, and, as in the VMS operating system,

---

1. Bemidji State University's policy is to permit students to select their own USERNAMEs, with certain restrictions. Limited censoring is necessary, just as states must censor personalized vehicle license plates.

this decision can be easily reversed by the user. Political policy issues are decided by people, but the operating system must have the technical capability to support the decisions.

In addition to implementing security on the basis of policies, the operating system must also protect its own integrity. This is a technical question, not a political one—a system that cannot operate reliably and deal with everyday programming accidents is not very useful. For instance, a program that totally clears memory because of an error in the computation of the termination limit of a loop cannot be tolerated in a time-sharing system because its action also erases the operating system's instructions as well as all other users' processes on the system. To maintain integrity and increase reliability, some technical means of prohibiting events like this must be included in the operating system design.

Finally, the system must protect itself against the deliberate attacks of knowledgeable, intelligent, and informed programmers, both unauthorized and authorized. The unauthorized user is normally discouraged by some sort of password system, but these are not impenetrable. An authorized user must have tools available to maintain his or her password, and the system should guarantee the privacy of user passwords. The authorized user must be limited to specific resources such as files and printers, and no others, and should not be permitted access to certain system resources or to other users' files unless specifically granted permission either by policy or by another user.

To recap, *security* is a broad term encompassing four areas:

- Physical protection of the computer and its peripherals, disks, and tapes
- Limited use of the computer facility
- Operating system reliability
- Data privacy

Section 7.1 discusses physical security of the computer facility and hardware. The remainder of the chapter addresses time-sharing security issues.

7.1. Physical Security

The protection of the physical computer is probably the best understood aspect of security, although many computers are not that well protected in this sense. Fire is a serious danger to a computer because its components are mostly plastic. Furthermore, once a fire starts, it spreads quickly; since a computer must be ventilated by cool air forced through its components, this air flow is an obvious detriment to fire containment. A computer that catches fire is often a total loss unless it is equipped with a very good fire extinguishing system, and even if the fire is stopped, the side effects of fighting it, such as water damage and rough handling, can be every bit as bad.

Most computer centers provide protection from accidental and malicious damage to the physical computer simply by locking the doors to the room that houses the mainframe. It is much more difficult to protect printers and other peripherals because they tend to be widely distributed and often are publicly available 24 hours a day. And it is nearly impossible to provide total security for tens or hundreds of terminals. Even a spilled cup of coffee can damage a keyboard, and there is no way to prevent this form of damage short of providing expensive terminals designed for harsh industrial or military environments.

If this form of trivial accident cannot be avoided, one can imagine how much more difficult malicious acts are to curtail. A single practical joker can easily damage a piece of equipment and thus reduce the ability of the system to serve many of its users. The computer center manager and its employees cannot be everywhere; it is up to the users themselves to be alert to mischief and misconduct and to act to stop it for their own good.

7.2. Limited Access

Granting an individual controlled use of a shared computer, or any shared resource such as a library or an automatic teller machine (ATM), requires three things:

- Something *possessed* uniquely by the user (e.g., ID card)
- Something *known* uniquely by the user (e.g., password)
- Something unique *about* the user (e.g., fingerprints)

For example, some campus computing centers require proof that the student is enrolled and has paid a fee for the privilege of using the computer facilities prior to entry. Usually this proof is in the form of an authenticated identification card. However, that proof only allows entrance into a room containing terminals and other computing equipment; the user still does not have access to the system unless he or she has a valid account on it. Most time-sharing systems require a user name and password to gain further access. In fact, the primary method the operating system has of protecting itself from unauthorized users is the password mechanism.

PASSWORDS

Using the password wisely is the user's responsibility. A trivial password such as a friend's name, a nearby street, or a favorite television show defeats its purpose, since anyone seriously attempting to break into an account will make these obvious guesses immediately. Thus, system managers should recommend the use of passwords that are not obviously connected to the user. This is good advice for any system that requires a password such as an ATM or safe combination.

After selecting a good password, the user should change it periodically. The VMS operating system keeps a history of the user's passwords, which prevents the selection of a password that has been used recently.

The VMS operating system furnishes several password-related mechanisms and even provides double password protection if the user so decides. Also, it can be programmed to enforce the changing of passwords on a regular basis, with the period of time between changes dictated by the system manager. The VMS operating system will aid in the selection of good passwords or, at the system manager's option, force the user to select a password from a randomly generated collection. The command:

```
$ SET PASSWORD/GENERATE
```

produces five possible passwords and presents them both spelled out and broken into syllables to aid the user in memorizing it.[2] The generate option requests the command to create nonsense passwords by combining random syllables, each one two or three syllables long—for example:

pixcoj	pix-coj
askiyaks	as-ki-yaks
akeyayb	a-ke-yayb
etmave	et-mave
sermmdem	sermm-dem

2. Passwords should never be written down.

The user can either enter one of the five selections or instruct the system to generate five more.

If the user decides to choose his or her own password, it will be screened against a file of commonly used passwords. If it matches any of them, it will be rejected. The system manager has control over this list so that locally known common passwords can be added to it.

The selected password is stored in the User Authorization File, SYS$SYSTEM:SYSUAF.DAT, for reference by the system when the user next attempts to logon. Clearly this file must be protected from accidental disclosure to unauthorized users. Digital handles this requirement in two ways, first, by encrypting each password before storing it, and, second, by deliberately failing to provide a decryption utility. The scrambled password cannot be unscrambled by anyone, not even the system manager, because there is no decryption algorithm; this is called one-way encryption. Even if the security of the SYSUAF.DAT is compromised in some way, a simple DUMP of its contents will not reveal the passwords in normal or "clear" spelling. If a user forgets his or her password, the only recourse the system manager has is to assign a new one.

No systems, except those requiring the highest security, require fingerprints, retina matching, finger length, or similar proofs of identity. The technology has not progressed enough to make such tests very convenient, although they are difficult to counterfeit and might be quite effective.

7.3. System Reliability

In the 1950s, one of the first lessons learned by the designers of early operating systems was that code sometimes goes awry in the midst of debugging, and when it does, it may destroy the operating system at the same time. For example, if an I/O address on a read request is wrong, the data may be read into the part of memory containing the operating system code. Since the hardware in the 1950s did not support any protection mechanism, protection was left entirely to software. One clever but simple software stratagem used to detect the destruction of any part of the operating system was to perform and save a checksum, which is computed by summing together each instruction in the operating system as if it were a number. Each time a program finished execution, the checksum was recomputed and verified. If it failed, the operating system was reloaded automatically, without op-

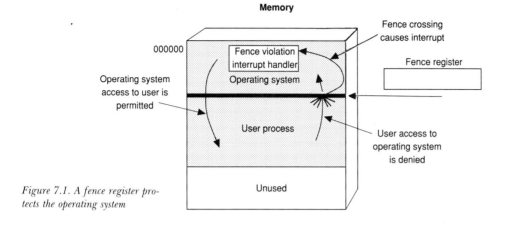

Figure 7.1. A fence register protects the operating system

erator intervention, prior to starting the next program. This checksum saved untold hours in lost computer time. It protected the innocent user but not the program that caused the problem in the first place. Without it the user with the problem might have left a time bomb in the operating system, triggered to explode later.

This early protection scheme was an attempt to guarantee system integrity and increase system *reliability*. The programmer could still read or change any location in the operating system, but if it was changed, it would be detected upon program termination. The question of intrauser protection was not an issue because these early operating systems were designed for batch operation and only one user at a time executed on the computer.

In the 1960s, while designers were still concerned with batch operating systems, a more elaborate, hardware-supported method of isolating the operating system from the user was implemented. A logical *fence* was erected between the two, which the system could cross, but not the user. This was implemented by a single register that contained an address. Every time a memory access was made, the fence register was interrogated by the hardware to make sure the fence was not being crossed. If it was, an interrupt was generated, and the operating system resolved the problem as illustrated in Figure 7.1. Normally, the operating system resided on the low-address side of the fence because interrupt vectors were defined by the hardware to begin at or near location 0.

As time-sharing systems were designed and put into operation, it became apparent that the hardware would have to continue to protect the operating system, and, since multiple users would be residing simultaneously in memory, user-to-user protection had to be considered as well. This was not a privacy issue at all, merely a pragmatic concern that a runaway program might destroy other innocent users' programs. The introduction of a computer capable of paging was not only an advance for time-sharing, it also provided a mechanism for protecting and isolating users, as Chapter 4 explained. But paging, by itself, does not necessarily protect the operating system from the user. The user process and the operating system must still work in concert; that is, if the user is unable to access the operating system, how will the user's process request its services? And if the operating system is unable to access the user's process, how will it send data to and receive it from the operating system?

There are two solutions to this sharing and protection dilemma. Chapter 4 explained the first solution: the operating system and process share virtual space and may address one another. This may appear to be an extreme solution because it seems (on the surface) to return to the systems of the 1950s; allowing a process unrestricted access may destroy the operating system. Obviously, this is not the case, and Section 7.4 will fully explore how the VAX is designed to protect the operating system.

The second solution truly separates the process address space from the operating system and makes the user's virtual space totally independent of the system's virtual space. This isolates the two, but makes communication difficult. The design can provide the operating system with two special instructions, one to read data from the user process space and another to write user data, or it can arrange for the two to share some small amount of common memory to be used strictly for communicating.

No matter how the operating system is protected, the process must be provided with a special instruction, a system service instruction, which the hardware treats as an internal interrupt to gain the operating system's attention and transfer execution from the process to the operating system—rather like an elaborate subroutine call. Conversely, the operating system must be provided with an instruction that returns to the process.

Designers also in the 1960s recognized that if the time-sharing operating system was to be totally in charge of the computing environment, certain instructions would have to be prohibited from general use, for instance, a HALT or any I/O instruction. As a result, computer designers developed a two-tiered instruction set: the operating system could use the full set; the user, only a subset. Of course, the hardware instruction decoders had to know when to restrict the instruction set, so the concept of execution mode was introduced. The operating system ran in "executive mode" and the user ran in "user mode." The system service instruction would trigger the hardware to the executive mode, and the operating system return instruction would return it to user mode.

7.4. VAX Hardware Protection Mechanisms

This section describes two VAX mechanisms that separate the user from the system and thereby protect the system. First, it will discuss how the operating system gains control of the full instruction set of the VAX; then, it will explain how memory is protected from unauthorized access.

The hardware that keeps the users and the operating system separate must be simple and fast because it is used so often. At the same time, it must be tamper proof against even the most persistent programmer. Switching between the two execution modes should be automatically performed by the hardware, not by an instruction.

CHMK INSTRUCTION

The VAX instruction used to enter the operating system is called change mode (CHMx) and is used to change privilege or execution levels as well as instruction sets, where "x" can be K, E, S, or U. The rationale behind four levels was introduced in Figure 2.21. CHMK changes the processor execution level so that full access to the instruction set is permitted. Changing levels is also related to memory protection, and the two are used in conjunction, as will be explained later in this section. The operating system returns to the user with an REI (Return from Exception or Interrupt). Figure 4.25 illustrated a CHMK-REI scenario.

The CHMK, detailed in Figure 7.2, is normally executed by DCL in the user's process to change to kernel mode. It has one argument, which specifies the system service requested. The figure shows the stack pointer register and the program counter, which are the most important registers in the system and are included in the 16 general processor registers. When executed, the first thing the CHMK instruction does is save the user stack pointer (SP) register in the hardware PCB (process control block) and then copy the kernel stack pointer from the PCB to the SP register (circle 1). This step preserves user data by switching stacks. Switching to the kernel stack gives the operating system a temporary data area independent of the

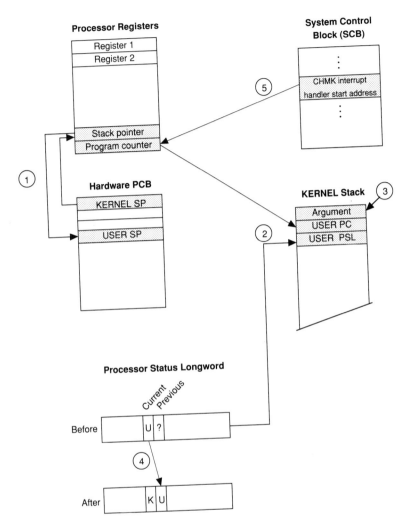

Figure 7.2. Operation of the
CHMK instruction

user's. Next, the program counter (PC) register and processor status long-word (PSL) are saved on the kernel stack (circle 2), recording the user return location and processor status. This is a very small context switch that differs from a full context switch operation in that only three items of the process context have been saved: the SP, PC, and PSL. At the end of the system service routine, when these three registers have been restored, the user context will again be complete. If the system service requires other general registers, it is responsible for saving (on the kernel stack) and restoring them again. The CHMK instruction argument is also stacked (circle 3).

The next step (circle 4) records the current processor mode (which is the privilege level) in a two-bit field of the PSL that only the hardware can change. In this step, the current execution mode is moved to a field called Previous Execution Mode and then the Current Execution Mode field is changed to indicate the new execution mode—kernel in this case. (The reason for Previous Execution Mode field is not apparent yet, but it has a practical purpose and will be explored later in the chapter.)

The last step in the operation of the CHMK instruction occurs when the PC is reassigned an address from the system control block (SCB) (circle 5). This address is the beginning of the CHMK dispatcher, which directs all system service calls to the appropriate routine. The dispatcher uses the CHMK parameter, saved on the kernel stack, to determine which system service was requested.

The kernel stack is in P1 memory; see Figure 4.24. Since the CHMK must store data into memory when stacking the argument, PC, and PSL, there is a possibility that a page fault will occur during its execution. If a page fault occurs, the instruction is interrupted and a new page frame must be assigned for the stack, and then the CHMK instruction is restarted at circle 1. This hardware design philosophy is consistent throughout the entire VAX design. If, instead, the VAX were designed to continue instruction execution after an interrupt, the context of the process would be more complicated because it would have to account for all possibilities of partially executed instructions. Therefore, the argument, PC, and PSL stacking is not actually done until three longwords are available on the kernel stack in physical memory.

REI INSTRUCTION

The CHMK instruction has a logical counterpart, an "unchange" mode instruction called REI, used to return from the system service to the user's

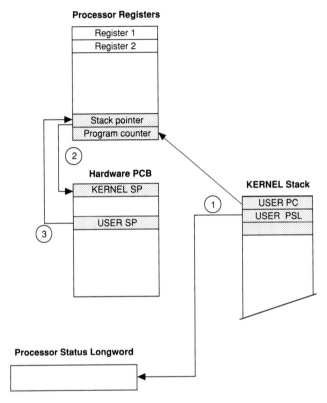

Figure 7.3. Operation of the REI instruction

image. All the information the REI needs is stored on the current stack, the kernel stack in this case, as shown in Figure 7.3. The PC and PSL are popped from the kernel stack (circle 1). (In general the REI pops from whatever stack is active.) Then the SP is saved in the kernel position of the hardware PCB (circle 2) and the user SP is restored from the PCB to the SP register (circle 3). Notice that the kernel's PC and PSL are not saved. This may appear to be an error, but it is unnecessary because the next time the user's program requests a system service, another CHMK instruction will be executed. Remember the models of the operating system earlier, like Figure 2.4? They treated the operating system as a collection of services and interrupt routines that run to completion before returning to the user. So every time the operating system is called to perform a service, the PC is initialized from the SCB and the PSL is modified appropriately. Therefore, the previous value of the operating system's PC is unimportant.

In executing the REI, the hardware performs one more vital check. The current mode of the restored PSL must not increase the privilege level of the process or else the REI becomes like the CHMK. In other words, if the processor is executing in user mode and an REI is executed, the current mode of the PSL on the stack is checked before it is moved to the PSL register. If the PSL on the stack indicates a switch to kernel mode, an error has occurred and a "reserved operand fault" is generated because a user to kernel change increases privileges. This important safeguard is provided to prevent a programmer from increasing privileges without entering the operating system. If a user were permitted to play this trick on the system, he or she would have access to the complete instruction set and control the computer.

LAYERED DESIGN OF VAX/VMS

The VAX designers have extended the two-layer scheme described earlier to four layers called kernel, executive, supervisor, and user. Kernel is the only mode with access to the full instruction set; the other three operate using the restricted subset of instructions. However, the operating system is actually spread across three levels, kernel, executive, and supervisor.

Figure 7.4 shows the kernel at the center of the VMS operating system. Typical system services are shown surrounding the three subsystems and placed to suggest which subsystem they are using—for instance, $WAKE is related to the Process and Time Management subsystem. At the executive level, the $GETTIM system service is placed to suggest that it too is related to Time Management. Executive mode contains the record management system (RMS), which is VMS's high-level file system. RMS uses $QIO to perform its tasks and thus has no need for the kernel privileges. The outer rings of the illustration are supervisor mode, which contains the CLI, and user mode, which holds the system utilities of all classes: compilers, libraries, and various application products. These support applications are not strictly part of the operating system, but they are provided by Digital.

Another reason for separating the VMS operating system into four components is its size and complexity. VMS is a large operating system, comprising over 2 million lines of code, developed by many software engineers working for more than 12 years. Furthermore, it must execute reliably 24 hours a day, year after year in a variety of applications at thousands

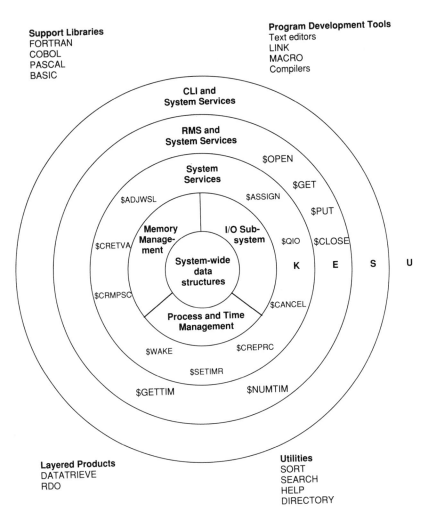

*Figure 7.4. Layered design of
the VAX/VMS operating system*

of sites throughout the world. No large system of software is totally error-free, and occasionally, a user may exercise a part of the operating system in a way that uncovers a latent error. For instance, if a user encounters an error in DCL that calls $QIO illegally under certain circumstances, this error is isolated from the kernel of the VMS system because DCL is less privileged. It does not cause the entire installation and all its users to stop, only a single user. The VMS kernel remains intact and running.

Entry to executive mode is gained via a CHME instruction that works like CHMK except that it uses the executive stack instead of the kernel stack and, instead of the CHMK dispatcher, there is a CHME dispatcher. In supervisor mode, the CLI is responsible for itself; it uses the CHMS instruction to change modes, dispatching certain run-time library routines to the appropriate system service. There is no obvious use for a CHMU instruction, although the hardware is designed for this option.

It is important to realize that the change mode instructions only permit inward movement to "higher" modes, whereas the REI only permits outward movement to "lower" modes. For example, kernel system services cannot execute a CHMU instruction to get to user mode; only an REI will permit this mode change. The reason is that the CHMx does not restore a context; it creates one. It is the REI that restores the context.

INTERRUPTS AND EXCEPTIONS

To show how each CHMx dispatcher is located by the hardware, it is necessary to present a more detailed discussion of the interrupt-exception structure on the VAX. In the VAX architecture, there is a special processor register called the system control block base (SCBB) register, which contains the starting address of a data structure called the system control block (SCB). The SCB is an array (also called a vector) with one entry for each possible interrupt or exception, and each entry in the array contains information necessary to locate the corresponding interrupt service routine. Figure 7.5 depicts this data structure. There are at least 128 entries in the SCB, and some VAX models have more. (These will be detailed in Figure 8.9.) Most other architectures fix the equivalent of the SCB at a certain location in memory, but by having a register point to the SCB, this vector can be moved anywhere by VMS. VAX designers have provided for more generality to permit the operating system less restricted memory use. There are no "off-limits" memory locations arbitrarily chosen by the hardware designers. This permits more flexibility in the operating system design, because the oper-

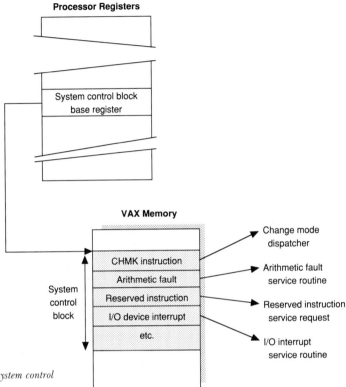

Figure 7.5. The system control block overview

ating system changes size from machine to machine permitting the SCB to "float" in memory, and it is easier to accommodate variations in hardware configurations.

The SCBB register is not one of the 16 registers found in assembly language. It is one of a group of registers called internal processor registers (IPRs) that are accessed by software with only two instructions, move from processor register (MFPR) and move to processor register (MTPR). The hardware also has access to these registers. A user program containing either of these two instructions will not execute; this is because the instructions are privileged and can only be executed in kernel mode.

Figure 7.6 illustrates a view of the interrupt logic of the VAX. Notice that some of the representative interrupt signal lines, like the *instruction decoder* and the *arithmetic logic unit* (ALU), are connected to components within the VAX, and others are connected to *I/O controllers,* which can be considered part of the peripheral devices.

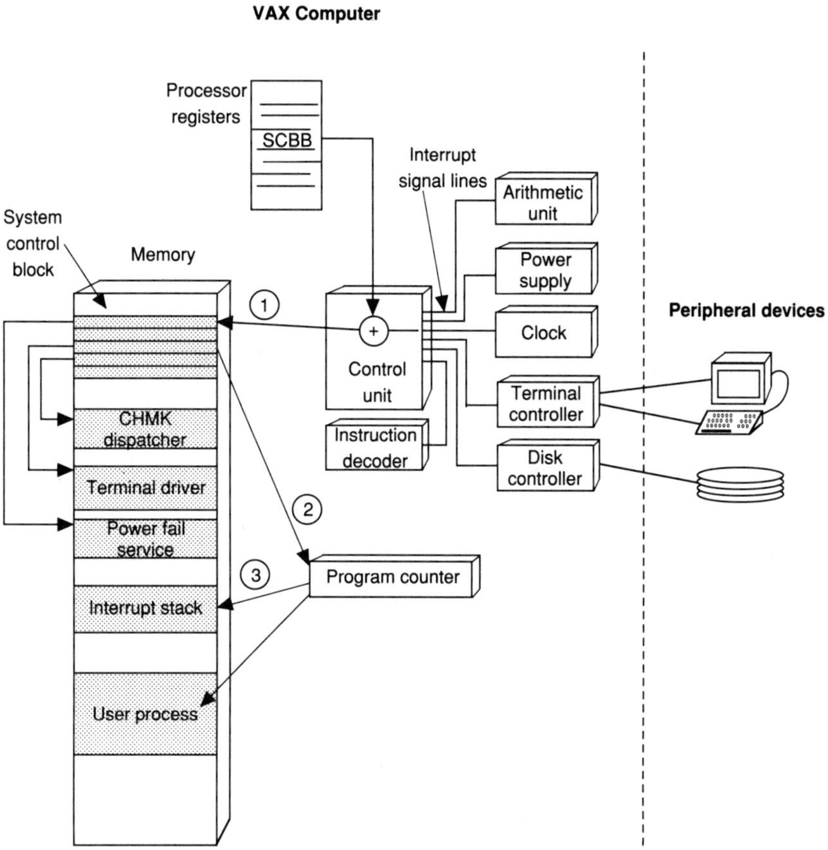

VAX Computer

Figure 7.6. An overview of the
VAX interrupt logic

INTERRUPT LOGIC

In Figure 7.6, when one of the 128 interrupts or exceptions occurs, the
control unit adds the interrupt line number to the address value in the SCBB
register. The resulting address is used to locate the appropriate SCB entry
(circle 1), and the corresponding entry becomes the new PC (circle 2). The
PC of the running program must be saved prior to being replaced by the
SCB entry so that the REI can restore the PC later. The PC is saved on
the kernel stack or the *interrupt stack* (circle 3); this is determined by a particular bit setting in the vector.

The PC replacement causes a context switch, resulting in the instructions in the interrupt service routine to be executed. Then, after the interrupt service routine has completed, it executes the REI, which causes the saved PC to be restored by popping it from the stack. This returns the CPU to the interrupted program. These steps are exactly the same as CHMx logic, except they are initiated by software, not hardware.

CONTROLLING MEMORY ACCESS

We have demonstrated how the process is interrupted and the processor changed to a privileged execution mode and then restored to the user mode. This protection mechanism is controlled by the hardware and closely associated with the interrupt and exception operations. Now, it is important to discuss the second hardware protection mechanism involving the addressing structure.

Chapter 4 explained how the paging hardware conveniently keeps processes from interfering with one another, but did not show how the image is kept from tampering with the operating system. It is essential to keep the operating system intact.

As shown in Figure 4.17, protection information is maintained in the page table entry (PTE) and applies to every page of the process, including the operating system. Each page is marked with a 4-bit code—bits 27 through 30 of the PTE—indicating the mode of the processor (kernel, executive, supervisor, or user) and permitted access (none, read-only, or read-write) on the page. For this scheme to be effective, the pages containing these PTEs must be marked to be inaccessible to all but the kernel mode. If not specifically prohibited in this way, a user could change the protection bits of all the pages in its page table and then read and or write anywhere in virtual memory.

There are two ways in which the protection bits are used. Chapter 4 described one way: the paging hardware validates accesses when it translates the address, as indicated in Figures 4.18 and 4.19.

PROBEx INSTRUCTIONS

The second way is with two special-purpose instructions, probe-read (PROBER) and probe-write (PROBEW). These instructions are used by all the system services to determine the validity of the arguments passed by the user before they are used. Suppose that the user requests a READ operation

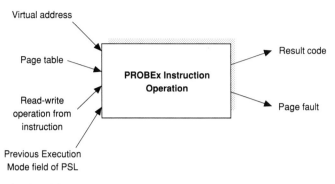

Figure 7.7. A functional model of the PROBEx instruction

illegally (either by accident or design) using an address that is actually located somewhere in the operating system rather than in the user's image. If this operation were allowed, it could destroy the operating system, so it must not be permitted. The PROBEx instructions depend on the Previous Mode field stored in the PSL (in fact, they are the only ones that use it); they are designed to be executed by the operating system in kernel mode to ask questions about the process's context. Continuing the READ example, the $QIO service uses the PROBEW instruction to test if the buffer supplied by the user is accessible for writing data. It is also used to make certain that the buffer is large enough to hold the data. This information is supplied in the p1 and p2 arguments of the $QIO, as illustrated in Chapter 5. The PROBEW must be used because the user is reading from a device and writing into memory.

Figure 7.7 illustrates the PROBEx instruction. Its arguments contain the addresses of the block to be checked. Its operation resembles the address translation figure in Chapter 4, and the two algorithms are similar, although the resulting output is slightly different. The PROBEx instruction does not return a physical address but a result code to indicate whether or not the virtual address is valid. Notice that a page fault may occur as a side effect of this instruction, so the instruction can also be used to fault a page into memory.

The first step in the PROBEx algorithm is to find the appropriate page table entry (PTE) corresponding to the virtual address in the input arguments. This is done by indexing into the process's page table. Once the PTE has been located, the algorithm next determines page accessibility using the protection field in the PTE and the Previous Execution Mode field (bits 22 and 23) of the PSL. If access is denied, the instruction is finished.[3] If access is permitted, the "valid" bit (bit 31) also is examined. If the page is not in the working set, a page fault is generated and the instruction is completed. The condition code is set to indicate whether the instruction succeeded or failed, and it is tested by the $QIO service. A detailed description of the other PSL fields can be found in Figure 8.2.

The hardware design of the VAX, specifically the processor mode and page access mechanisms, is the linchpin in operating system safety because the hardware protects the operating system from user accidents and abuses. However, neither of these mechanisms is completely automatic, and careful attention in the coding of the operating system is still required to ensure its proper operation. For instance, if a programmer coding a system service routine forgets to include a PROBEx instruction, the user who calls that system service with a bad argument may penetrate the system.

Realizing this possibility, the VMS designers loaded the system with defensive code that validates its data structures in order to maintain *fail-soft* operation and make errors easier to detect. This is true of various VMS data structures—for example, before the scheduler starts a new process, the PCB for that process is checked to make certain it really is a PCB. If it is not, the system is stopped immediately with a BUG instruction. This is yet another case in which the VAX design includes an instruction that specifically supports the operating system.

7.5. Logical Protection Mechanisms

Just as the hardware helps to provide increased system reliability, the operating system software algorithms also ensure protection, especially for user data files. The concepts presented here are not limited to data files and can be applied as a more general resource protection instrument.

ACCESS MATRIX

The commonly accepted model for resource protection is called an *access matrix*, in which the two axes are labeled domains and objects. The *domain*

---

3. The hardware translation version of this algorithm would generate an access violation exception at this point.

Domains	Objects						
	GRADES	LETR-1	ASMT_1	HMWK1	HMWK1	SYSUAF	NOTICES
DMILLER	CRWED		CRWED	RW	RW		R
INTRO_VAX			R				R
JOKER		CRWED		CRWED			R
NISSAN					CRWED		R
SYSTEM	CRWED	CRWED	CRWED	CRWED	CRWED	CRWED	CRWED

Figure 7.8. *An access matrix*

is the set of users or groups of users, and the *object* is the entity that needs protection. The objects in the access matrix can include every file in the system as well as other system resources such as terminals, disk drives, semaphores, and system images. The matrix is very large but quite sparse. Its contents are termed the *access rights*; they record the accessibility of the particular object by the specific domain. Figure 7.8 illustrates a simplified example of the access matrix.

As a means to more clearly define the access rights, that is, the values of the matrix entries, the following abbreviations are used: R for read, W for write, D for delete, E for execute, and C for control. A blank means that the domain has no rights to the object. Of this list, only C, control, needs elaboration. The other rights refer to the object rather than the access matrix, but with C, the rights themselves may be changed; that is, the domain with control rights can change the access matrix entry for that object. Other rights that could be considered are P for propagation of the rights to new versions of the file, H for hide or do not display the rights, and U for use the rights of the directory. The range of rights is not limited to the ones in this example.

Figure 7.8 shows four users in the domain: DMILLER, JOKER, NISSAN, and SYSTEM, and one group, INTRO_VAX, which includes JOKER and NISSAN. There is no way to discern the members of the group in this matrix because information regarding group membership is not carried there but in another structure to be discussed later. In the example matrix, DMILLER has access to five files, including all rights to GRADES and ASMT_1, read and write access to both HMWK1 objects, and read access to NOTICES. Ownership information is not necessarily carried in the matrix, but can be implied by the domain; users who have control have effective ownership because they can do anything, potentially, to the file and can grant themselves the rights they do not have. The two HMWK1 objects have different ownership, one is owned by JOKER and the other by NISSAN, as indicated by the control right. The figure suggests that an HMWK1 file has been created by both JOKER and NISSAN in response to the homework assignment, ASMT_1. The two have read access to ASMT_1 through the INTRO_VAX group and have given read and write access of their respective HMWK1 files to DMILLER, who can make changes to the files as necessary. JOKER also has a private file called LETR-1, and all users and groups have read access to NOTICES, which is a message from the system manager. Notice that SYSTEM, the system manager's account, has all rights to all files, which raises a question of policy: should SYSTEM automatically have all rights and therefore not even occupy an entry in the access matrix? Or, should the owner of the file have total control over rights to an object and be able to deny even SYSTEM rights? The answer to this question lies with the designers.

In order to save space, the matrix concept is not implemented directly because it is sparse. There are two ways to view efficient matrix implementation. First, by traveling down a column for a given object, we see that only a few domains have any access rights at all to a given object; for example, a particular file may be accessed by only a single domain, and other files may be read by several domains but written by only one. In the Digital literature, this vertical implementation is called a *capability-based system* or the *access control list*. Logically, this list is attached to the object for rapid reference.

The second way to view matrix implementation is horizontally. Traveling along a row we see a given domain has access to only a few objects, and most objects are inaccessible. For instance, INTRO_VAX can only read two objects in our example. The horizontal view is called an *authority-based system*. This data structure is attached to each domain.

Even though rights are most easily understood when they are directed at files, they can be generalized and object-sensitive. The definitions of the rights change depending on the nature of the object. For example, consider the VMS definitions for a file and for a directory in Figure 7.9, which introduces extensions to the execution and deletion rights. For example, execution of a file is well understood, but what does execution of a directory mean? In the VMS operating system, it means that wildcards on certain commands behave differently depending on the rights. In implementing access rights, the operating system must clearly state these definitions.

Other object classes besides files can be included in the access matrix, including volumes (disks, tapes, floppies), shared memory, devices (termi-

Right	Definition if file	Definition if directory
Read	Read, type print, or copy	Type, print all entries: wildcards honored
Write	Write or modify	Create new data files
Execute	Execute if program	Type, print specified entries: wildcards not honored
Delete	Delete	Delete if empty
Control	Change rights	Change rights

Figure 7.9. Object-sensitive rights definitions

nals, printers, mailboxes), and queues (batch, printer, card reader), and for each class, the rights must be defined. For instance, what does it mean to have rights to delete the card reader or to execute a mailbox? Figure 7.9 must be completed for all possible objects and rights.

The access matrix is a powerful means of controlling the rights of the system's users, but it is up to the system manager to develop a policy for granting those rights. Probably everyone should be allowed to add entries to the printer queue, but should everyone be allowed to display the printer queue's contents? This right permits anyone to see the names, and perhaps the lengths, of the files that other users are printing. Consider the following scenario in which the file names are available: a student may be printing out a homework assignment, but a classmate, noticing the file name, may run over to the printer ahead of the owner, tear off the listing, and use it to extract some valuable information. When the owner arrives at the printer to look for the listing, it is gone and there is no traceability. Sometime when the printer appears to have a large queue, for instance, on a night before homework is due, issue the following command to see how your system manager feels about this question:

```
$ SHOW QUEUE/FULL SYS$PRINT
```

Does this display show a lengthy list of print jobs or does it contain only entries for the listings that you have submitted? Are the user names and file names displayed too?

7.6. VMS Implementation of Object Protection

The VMS operating system supports the vertical view of the access matrix, the access control list. It also supports two other access control policies. To determine the rights a domain has to an object, VMS interrogates the following mechanisms in order:

1. Access control lists
2. User identification codes (UICs)
3. Privileges

If the access control list associated with the object shows the user has specific approval or denial, the search ends there; otherwise, the search continues into the UIC logic level. If the access question is still not settled at this level, the privilege logic is tested. These three mechanisms are discussed in detail in the following.

VMS ACL IMPLEMENTATION

As stated, the access matrix is sparse, and the reason for this is that most objects in the operating system are files. A modest operating system with 500 accounts and 10,000 files (which is only 20 files per user) requires 5 million entries in the access matrix. Even for a virtual system, this is an excessive use of memory. Typically, a vast majority of the files can be accessed only by the owner and the system manager. But if, on the average, a file can be accessed by 5 accounts, only 1 percent of the 5 million entries in the access matrix have any data in them.

One space-saving approach adopted by some operating systems that support the access matrix concept is an access control list (ACL), stored with the object, naming all users with any access rights to the object. This completely eliminates the need for an access matrix. However, although it is an excellent solution in terms of both time and space, the ACL omits a detail that VMS designers considered necessary: permitting users to be logically grouped, like INTRO_VAX in Figure 7.8. The reason for grouping users is that creating and managing a long list of users for a given file has three disadvantages. First, storing individual names takes more room and it is time consuming to search the list. Second, it must be reviewed and possibly modified whenever a user is added to or removed from the SYSUAF.DAT file. Finally, it is difficult to reliably enter names in the first place. The practical

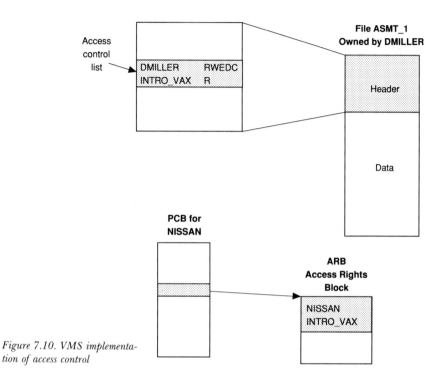

Figure 7.10. VMS implementation of access control

requirements of speed, size, and system management make grouping a desirable feature.

One application of this grouping feature is to gather all the user names in a particular class. Then the instructor declares a particular file to be read accessible by that group rather than by all the individual users. This idea is presented in Figure 7.10 and is an extension of the example in Figure 7.8. In the top right half of the figure, the file ASMT_1, owned by DMILLER, is logically broken into two parts, the header and the data. Part of the header contains the ACL, which records all domains (users and groups) that have access to the file along with the access rights (read, write, execute, and delete). The ACL is maintained by the user who has control rights—normally, the owner. The example shows that two users have access, DMILLER and INTRO_VAX.

In the lower half of Figure 7.10, the user, NISSAN, logs into the system. The SYSUAF.DAT contains a list of the names of all groups NISSAN belongs to, which is attached to the process control block (PCB) in a data structure called the access rights block (ARB). In this case, NISSAN's ARB contains the group INTRO_VAX. The system manager controls group membership as well as the rest of the user-related information in the SYSUAF.DAT.

When NISSAN attempts to access ASMT_1, the access algorithm used to determine rights simply scans the ACL (in the file) with each entry of the NISSAN's ARB to see if a match can be made. First, NISSAN is compared against the ACL entries, then INTRO_VAX is used to search the ACL.

Note that the order of the ACL is important. Suppose DMILLER wants NISSAN to have more rights than the rest of the group, perhaps because NISSAN is the grader and requires write access to ASMT_1. Then the ACL should be ordered like this: DMILLER, NISSAN, and INTRO_VAX. In this way, the search algorithm matches on NISSAN before matching on INTRO_VAX.

VMS UIC PROTECTION

The second method of protection supported by the VMS operating system is called UIC, *user identification code*, which was transported from Digital's PDP-11 operating system to the VMS system, although its form has been changed drastically. UIC control was the predecessor to ACL controls, and it is still useful. Where ACLs provide fine control at the individual user level, UICs provide coarse control over access privileges. In its original form on the PDP-11, the UIC divided the user community into four domains: System, Owner, Group, and World, and this was done with a pair of octal numbers. In the VMS operating system, UICs have been extended to alphanumeric strings.

Essentially, the UIC offers the same capabilities access control lists do, except that there are only four domains with no provisions for redefining them. As with ACLs, the types of objects are unlimited and there is no matrix; the access information for all four domains is carried by the object. When ACL control was added to the VMS system, it did not supersede UICs; UIC control is still valid and is widely used in computing centers when there is no reason to define the community with more granularity. It is fast, compact, convenient, and easy to manage.

This is how UIC control works. All users are assigned a unique UIC when they enter the SYSUAF.DAT. The most common syntax of the UIC is [group,member]. The *member* is called the *Owner* domain, and all members with the same *group* field are in the *Group* domain. There are multiple members in a group but a member cannot be in more than one group. The *System* domain is defined as a user with a special group name. The *World* domain is simply all accounts.

The access rights are: control, read, write, execute, and delete. The control right is implied in the UIC scheme, and it cannot be changed; System and Owner have control access, whereas Group may have it under certain conditions and World never has it at all. This means that the Owner of an object and the System group may unconditionally change the object's access rights, even if they have no other right. The four rights, read, write, execute, and delete, can be assigned to or deleted from any of the four domains. To determine an object's accessibility, the system checks the domains in the following order: Owner, World, Group, and System.

Specifically, object access rights are stated as a quadruple containing the four domains in the following order:

```
( System rights, Owner rights, Group rights, World rights )
```

and each access right is abbreviated: R for read, W for write, D for delete, and E for execute. For example, the following quadruple means that System has full access and Owner may not delete the object. The Group and World domains have no access rights at all to the object.

```
( RWED, RWE, , )
```

The UIC and ACL protection rights of a file can be easily determined with the following DIRECTORY command. This command displays both UIC and ACL protection settings:

```
$ DIR/SECURITY BTUS.PAS
```

Figure 7.11 contains sample output from this command. The top line names the directory. The second line shows the file name, its owner (in square brackets), and the UIC rights quadruple (in parentheses). The remaining lines show all the access control list entries, one per line. Each line shows the domain identifier, ODIE for instance, and the access rights granted to that domain.

When a file is created, it is assigned default access rights determined by the user. The default is initialized in the user authorization file; however, a user can change a file's protection at any time with the command:

```
Directory DUA1:[FACULTY.DMILLER]

BTUS.PAS;16            [FACULTY,DMILLER]      (RWED,RWED,,)
            (IDENTIFIER=[2118047A,ODIE],ACCESS=READ)
            (IDENTIFIER=[17B3879D,AZTECK],ACCESS=READ)

Total of 1 file.
```

Figure 7.11. Typcial output of the DIRECTORY/SECURITY command

```
$ SET PROTECTION=(SYSTEM:rewd, OWNER:rewd, GROUP:rewd, WORLD:rewd) file
```

To remove all access for a particular domain, the user specifies no rights for it. For instance, to remove world rights on a file, the command is:

```
$ SET PROTECTION=W file
```

In the case above, only one domain is changed; the other three remain unchanged.

Figure 7.12 illustrates a simplified UIC access algorithm that is supposed to answer the question, "Is the object accessible at level X by a given user with a specific UIC?" Upon entry, the system knows the object's name, the user's UIC, and the requested access right level (RWED). The object's owner UIC and the quadruple are associated with the object itself. At the top of the flowchart, first, the user UIC is compared to the owner UIC, and if they are the same, the access level requested by the user is compared to the level permitted in the object; then, the algorithm tests if the access type recorded in the Owner field of the quadruple is the same as the access type requested. If so the object is accessible, and access is granted.

If the Owner field and the access type are not the same, the World access level of the object's quadruple is tested. If it is the same as the desired access, then access is granted. Notice that even the object's owner can fail the first test and pass the second one. For instance, if the quadruple is

```
( REWD, D, , RE )
```

and the owner attempts read access, it will be granted on the basis of the World field because the Owner field denies read privilege.

If the World test fails, the Group UIC of the object and user UIC are compared. If they are the same, then the object's Group access in the quad-

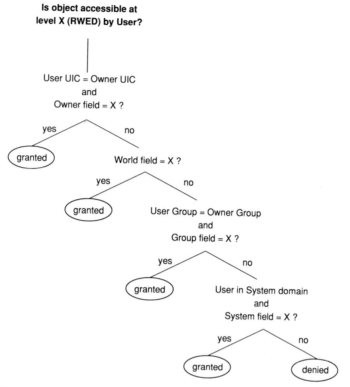

Figure 7.12. UIC access algorithm

ruple is compared to the desired access. If they are the same, the object is accessible.

If not, or if the groups are different, the user UIC is tested against the System domain according to the Group name. If the user is not in the System domain, then access is denied; otherwise, the object's access quadruple is again tested to finally determine accessibility.

VMS PRIVILEGE PROTECTION

VMS has a third method of object protection called *privilege,* which, like UIC, was carried into VMS from RSX-11. There are 64 bits reserved for the privilege scheme and, hence, the possibility of 64 privileges. Only four of those bits will be discussed here, since the rest are designed to protect system objects not covered by either the ACL or UIC mechanisms.

The primary reason for this third level of protection is that the system needs faster, finer granularity on object protection than the UIC gives. As with UICs, privileges are embedded in the SYSUAF.DAT and changeable only if the user has the specific privilege, SETPRV. Normally, the system manager assigns privileges when an account is opened. Process privileges can be determined with the command:

```
$ SHOW PROCESS/PRIV
```

The bottom of Figure 2.11 showed a typical display.

Four privileges also enter into the UIC protection algorithm: BYPASS, READALL, SYSPRV, and GRPPRV. Figure 7.13 presents an enhanced UIC algorithm, to which additional tests have been added. These four privileges are intended to override the UIC tests. The BYPASS privilege permits unconditional and unlimited access to an object; the READALL privilege permits read and control access; and SYSPRV causes the user to be treated as if he or she were in the system domain. These three privileges act without regard to the UIC. GRPPRV behaves like SYSPRV if the user's group and the owner's group are identical and, thus, acts somewhat like a group system manager. Notice that READALL, SYSPRV, and GRPPRV privileges are granted in addition to any rights the user is already entitled to, since the tests are made after the UIC tests are checked.

In addition to modifying the UIC algorithm for file access, privileges uniquely control certain system utilities. The ACL is capable of managing any kind of object, but, historically, privileges supersede ACLs. ACL logic was not added to the VMS operating system until it was a well-developed product.

Privileges are much faster to test than an ACL, speeding system performance when certain objects are referenced often. All system services call the same system service routine, $CHKPRO, to determine if a specific privilege is granted. This routine has to identify which of the 64 bits is under test, test it, and report the results. The bit test operation is very fast on the VAX.

Here is a description of a few of these additional privileges and an elaboration on how they are used showing the variety of objects they apply to. The ALTPRI privilege allows a user to increase the execution priority of any process in the system. Without it, the process priority may only be lowered. The GROUP privilege allows a user's process to affect and interrogate

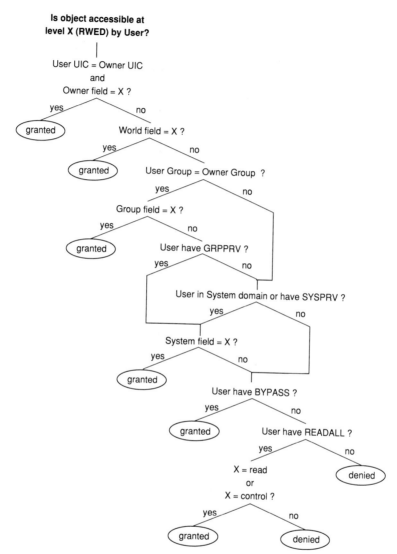

Figure 7.13. UIC and privilege access algorithm

other processes in the group through the use of several services that have been discussed, among them, $SUSPND, $RESUME, $WAKE, $SCHDWK, and $GETJPI. In other words, it permits creation of a wider arena of the synchronization system services, which is convenient in the building of application systems. The OPER privilege permits the OPCOM (Operator Communication Manager) process to be executed by the specified user. Obviously, the computer operator must be given elevated privileges to communicate with the users, to manage the terminals, and to start and stop spooling queues on printers, card readers, and tapes. Lastly, SETPRV controls the privilege list for a domain.

PRIVILEGED IMAGES

This chapter has so far merely alluded to the ability of unprivileged users to run privileged images. Now, there is sufficient background to explore this subject more fully. The 64-bit privilege quadword was introduced in Figure 2.16. Each bit of the quadword corresponds to one privilege; thus a single bit-test instruction can be used to determine a specific privilege's setting.

To elaborate on privilege manipulations performed at image activation and rundown time, consider the following illustration. An unprivileged user can write a program that calls $GETJPI (Get Job/Process Information), but the system will only pass on information about the user's process and subprocesses—nothing about other processes on the system can be requested. The SHOW USER command depends on $GETJPI, too. However, its display lists information about all users logged into the system. How is it that this image can use $GETJPI differently than the user is permitted to do? The system must temporarily elevate the process's privilege in order to perform the SHOW USER function. Figure 7.14 (a duplicate of Figure 2.16) shows how this is done. The elevated privilege for SHOW.EXE, the image activated by the SHOW USER command, is stored in the KFE (Known File Entry) data structure. When the user enters the SHOW command, the image activator locates SHOW.EXE in the KFE, and computes the working privilege by ORing the KFE-entered privilege with the process's authorized privilege. This operation has the effect of increasing the process's privilege while the image is active.

The KFE is maintained by the system manager using the INSTALL utility. For instance, when the system manager INSTALLs SHOW.EXE, the required privileges are specified on the INSTALL command and stored in the KFE.

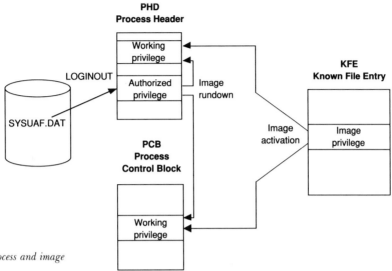

Figure 7.14. Process and image privileges

When the working privilege is computed at image activation time, the privileges to permit execution must be present in the authorized privilege. If a user with insufficient privileges activates an image containing privileged functions, the working privilege will only reflect that user's privilege. When the image begins execution, it will discover that the required privileges have not been granted and will cease execution. INSTALL, SYSGEN (used to set system parameters), and AUTHORIZE (used to maintain the SYSUAF.DAT file) are typical commands that must be restricted.

7.7. Related Issues

Although there are other methods to protect user files from unauthorized access, the access control matrix is the most widely accepted today. However, the implementations vary widely. UNIX only has a UIC-like protection mechanism with three categories, System, Owner, and World, and OS/2 attaches rights to files like Read Only and Deny Writers, but does not support different domains. Even MS-DOS has a primitive solution in which files can take on three protection-related attributes. One, read-only protects them from being deleted or updated. Two, hidden files are not listed when a display of files is requested, nor can they be accessed with any standard command, for example, COPY or ERASE. And three, system files are treated identically to hidden files, except they cannot be accessed by user-written programs either. File protection on a single-user system is intended to protect the user from stupid mistakes rather than from invasions of privacy by other users.

Hardware-supported protection on microcomputers was not introduced into the 80xx series until the 80286. Even so, MS-DOS does not take advantage of the hardware because it was written for the 8088. OS/2 does take advantage of the newer architectural features, and UNIX takes advantage of the hardware protection mechanisms whenever they are available. Since it is a portable operating system, UNIX has been designed to adapt to various hardware features.

File encryption is another protection device. However, although it makes a file indecipherable, it does not prohibit its deletion. Moreover, encryption is only as good as the encrypting key, and judging from common experience with passwords, decrypting should be relatively easy to a dedicated code-breaker. A programmer is likely to encrypt a file with the same password used to enter the account, which is clearly a poor choice; if a hacker has gained access to the account, the account password, or some variation of it, is certain to be the obvious first guess for decrypting a file.

In some cases, it may be vitally important to know if someone is attempting to break into a file or has already gained access to it. To do this, an *audit trail* is necessary. The VMS command, SET AUDIT, traces critical events on the system. For instance, all terminal login failures, execution of the INSTALL utility, modification of the SYSUAF.DAT file, or tape mounts can be displayed on a terminal, stored in a file, or both. This facility is available only to the system manager.

Still another related topic is "erased" disk data. The most convenient form of erasure (for the system) is to simply return the space occupied by a file to a pool of unused space, but this is not true erasure, only a form of "losing" data because it becomes mixed in with all the other deleted files. Depending on the sensitivity of the data, this method may not be adequate, so the VMS system provides an option to overwrite the disk space occupied by a file prior to reassigning the file space, called *high-water marking*.

The area of dial-up users is related to passwords and user authorization. The remote user is becoming more popular for many reasons. For one, computers are quickly permeating every area of our society, and working at home or while traveling is becoming more common. Also, commuting to and from a central workplace in high-technology areas can be difficult, and the supporting communications hardware is becoming faster and less expensive. In view of these facts, the operating system must bear the burden of ensuring that the user on the other end of the communications line is valid, since physical security of the terminal room is not relevant. Dial-back systems work well in some applications; the user's phone number is stored in the operating system and the computer hangs up and dials the user's phone to reconnect. Also, it is essential that the computer disconnect the line as soon as there is any indication that the user is disconnected from the computer.

A final related issue is the amount of resources a user is permitted, although this is related more to ethics than to security or protection. Occasionally, a user program may accidentally or deliberately try to fill up a disk with meaningless garbage. Some operating systems will allow this to happen; others will not. There are other resources that can be "hogged" by a user too—the CPU, for one, can be monopolized by a user with a busy wait program. Another example is the thrashing program illustrated in Chapter 4. As indicated, this happens more often than is generally recognized, and it can drastically reduce system performance. Normally, system accounting will quickly catch this form of abuse, depending on how a computer center charges for its resources, but the problem is much more difficult to solve for institutions like Minnesota State University, whose usage is free. These centers must use an operating system that will protect them from accidental or deliberate resource abuse.

7.8. Summary

The chapter began with a discussion of security as it applies to the physical computer and its peripherals. Protecting the machinery from accidents, vandalism, and natural disasters are all aspects of this topic.

Generalized time-sharing operating systems usually require that users be known before they can log on, so the system manager must enter a user name into some system database. At login, the user must know both the username assigned by the system manager and a password. Password management is largely the responsibility of the user, but the system can provide aids such as password suggestions, multiple passwords, reminders to change passwords, and screenings of potential passwords that may be too easy to guess.

When sharing a computer, the users must be protected not only from their own errors but from the mistakes of others. The time-shared computer can be thought of as a utility, like the electric utility, and as such, it is expected to be reliable in the presence of novices and blatant abusers. The hardware provides several functions that help realize this goal of noninterference. Paging is one, but it only partially fulfills the objective. Virtual memory solves the problems of users interfering with one another, but does nothing to protect users from certain instructions, like I/O controls, that can be disastrous in users' hands.

The operating system itself must be protected from accidental destruction. This problem is different from that of separating users because a user process must interact with the operating system but in a nondestructive way. The user's process must enter the operating system through a narrow gate that is completely protected, and once it is in the operating system, the service it requests must be confirmed to be valid prior to execution.

The next level of security, once the system is functionally reliable, is protection for the user's data. The model for this form of protection is the access matrix, but it is unwieldy in practice and must be modified in order to be implemented. Every resource on the system, not just files, should be brought under the control of this model, but because of the expense it incurs in both time and space, this doesn't usually happen. As a compromise, a secondary, special-purpose access control method is implemented to supersede or accompany the access matrix.

The security and privacy issue is hardly settled, and as computer systems are networked together, more problems will have to be solved.

ACRONYMS

$CHKPRO	Check Access Protection system service
$GETJPI	GET Job and Process Information system service
$QIO	Queue Input/Output operation system service
$RESUME	Resume process system service
$SCHDWK	Schedule Wakeup system service
$SUSPND	Suspend process system service
$WAKE	Wake process system service
ACL	Access Control List
ALTPRI	Alter Priority privilege
ARB	Access Rights Block
BYPASS	Bypass privilege

CHME	Assembly instruction to Change Mode to Execute
CHMK	Assembly instruction to Change Mode to Kernel
CHMS	Assembly instruction to Change Mode to Supervisor
CHMU	Assembly instruction to Change Mode to User
CHMx	Generic assembly instruction to Change Mode
CLI	Command Language Interpreter
CMKRNL	Change Mode to Kernel privilege
CRWED	Control, Read, Write, Execute, Delete
GRPPRV	Group Privilege privilege
MS-DOS	Microsoft Disk Operating System
OPCOM	Operator Communications Manager
OPER	Operator privilege
PC	Program Counter
PROBER	Assembly instruction to PROBE memory for Read access
PROBEW	Assembly instruction to PROBE memory for Write access
PROBEx	Generic assembly instruction to PROBE memory
PSL	Processor Status Longword
PTE	Page Table Entry
READALL	READ ALL files privilege
REI	Assembly instruction to Return from Exception or Interrupt
RMS	Record Management System
SCBB	System Control Block Base register
SCB	System Control Block
SETPRV	Set Privileges privilege
SP	Stack Pointer
SYSPRV	System Privilege privilege
SYSUAF.DAT	System User Authorization file
UIC	User Identification Code

SHORT ANSWER EXERCISES

1. The fencing system of the 1960s did not require a system service instruction. How do you suppose the user made requests to the operating system?

2. What would the ACL look like if there were no provision for grouping users? That is, redraw Figure 7.8 without INTRO_VAX.

3. Summarize the several password features incorporated into the VMS operating system.

4. Why are PHONE and MAIL privileged images? That is, what must PHONE and MAIL do that an unprivileged user is unable to do?

5. Identify other forms of physical identity that various institutions require to grant access.

PROJECTS

1. Use PROBEx to find out what is accessible in P1 and SYS space.

2. Use LINK/MAP to identify shared data—refer to the exercises in Chapter 6.

3. All images in the VMS operating system are stored in the directory SYS$SYSTEM. Attempt to RUN the images and if successful, use the built-in HELP command provided by the image to figure out what it is supposed to do. (Digital provides HELP with every interactive image, so you can get some information about the image that way.) List all of the .EXE files in SYS$SYSTEM, and for each file, specify whether or not an unprivileged user can activate the file and, if the image will activate, what it will do.

4. Design and code a simple assembly program (the simpler, the better) to find out what happens when a user attempts to use an REI to perform the function of a CHMK. How does the VMS system react? What diagnostic is produced? What happens to the process? The image?

PAPERS

1. Explore ACL commands, such as EDIT/ACL, SET ACL, and DIRECTORY. Write a tutorial on the various applications of these commands directed toward a novice user of the VMS system.

2. Explore System, Owner, Group, and World-related commands, such as SET PROT and DIRECTORY. Write a tutorial on the various

applications of these commands directed toward a novice user of the VMS system.

3. Explore Group privileges. Write a tutorial on the various applications of these privileges directed toward a novice user of the VMS system. That is, once a user has Group privilege, what can be done that the unprivileged user cannot do?

4. Explore UIC rights. Write a tutorial on the various application of these rights directed toward a novice user of the VMS system. For instance, how does a user exploit World write privilege of a data file?

Input/Output and Interrupts

GOALS

Interrupt priority level

I/O subsystem design and operation

Asynchronous system trap

I/O transfer methods—PIO and DMA

I/O hardware-software communication

8

Chapter 3 introduced the importance of the I/O subsystem, and Figure 3.2 showed that a program is either executing, performing an I/O operation, or waiting. A time-sharing system gives each user the impression that he or she has exclusive access to the system because the I/O of one user process overlaps the execution of another. Time-sharing is economical when equipment can be distributed among several users, but to effectively time-share, the I/O subsystem must have certain characteristics; in particular, it must be able to preempt a user process in order to react to I/O requests from other users. Even a batch multiprogramming system must have this capability. Furthermore, process preemption implies that the I/O subsystem can even preempt itself when necessary. Another requirement of the I/O subsystem is that it perform its functions as quickly as possible so that the user's program can continue processing. In an interactive system, this is especially important so that the keyboard response time is kept to a minimum. Chapter 3 dealt only with the process scheduling mechanisms inherent in the operating system. This chapter will complete that picture by describing I/O scheduling.

It is difficult to generalize I/O operations independently of operating

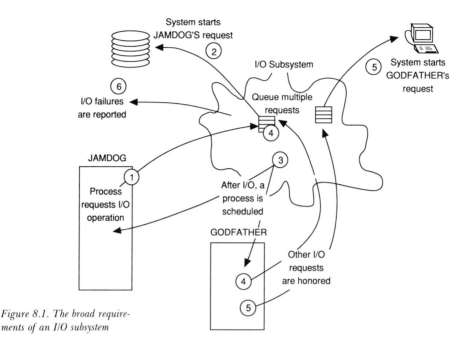

*Figure 8.1. The broad require-
ments of an I/O subsystem*

systems and hardware support because each manufacturer has developed
its own architecture for both the computer and the I/O devices. Nevertheless,
a few generic observations can be made. The user's process should have the
ability to access devices symbolically, without having to refer to a device's
physical name, and the user should be isolated from the intricacies and
idiosyncracies of the hardware devices. For instance, to read data from a
disk takes two operations, one to position the head and one to transfer the
data, but reading data from a terminal takes only a single operation. At a
conceptual level, the input/output subsystem of a time-sharing operating
system must provide minimum services, as shown in Figure 8.1. When a
user requests an I/O operation (circle 1), the operating system does other
useful work while the request is performed (circle 2). This may include
starting another process (circle 3) or continuing the requester's process if
possible; a user should not be penalized because of an I/O operation, nor
should the other users of the system experience performance degradation.
While one operation is being processed, other operations for the same device
should be honored and queued (circle 4) if necessary. Additionally, requests
for other devices (circle 5) should be honored.

Another set of requirements on the I/O subsystem that is usually invisible (as it should be) to the user is handling all error conditions (circle 6), such as the device being off-line, reporting an error condition, or behaving erratically. Error reports should be displayed on the operator's console or recorded in a system file so that when the equipment fails permanently, its error history can aid in failure isolation and proper corrective procedures can be carried out. The error file can also be interrogated periodically to anticipate device failures; usually an I/O device behaves erratically prior to total failure.

To fully comprehend what is required of the I/O subsystem and how the computer architecture can be designed to support the operating system is difficult in the abstract. To aid comprehension, this chapter will feature the interrupt mechanism on the VAX and describe the I/O subsystem that results from the computer's architecture. In the world of high-performance mini- and mainframe computers, the I/O subsystem must be tailored to the host CPU to maximize performance. That is, I/O devices are designed specifically for the host machine and there have been few attempts to standardize a particular interface across the industry. At this time, the only I/O device that is generic in any sense is the dumb terminal.

Most time-sharing systems rely on the concept of the interrupt. The idea of having the I/O hardware interrupt the CPU is very old (relatively speaking in the computer industry), dating to the late 1950s, and throughout operating system and hardware development history, most machines supported the idea in some form. The Control Data Corporation (CDC) 6600 is a notable exception; it was a major machine in its time (the late 1960s) and had no interrupt structure. To compensate, the 6600 operating system periodically polled its I/O devices, and when it found one that needed to be serviced, it did so. If no I/O devices needed servicing, a user process was executed until it was time to poll again.

A machine that supports interrupts requires that the software be able to stack information easily. Actually "requires" is too strong, since several systems were designed with interrupts but no built in stacking instructions. If the computer hardware supports data stacking and has instructions that easily permit it, an I/O subsystem is much easier to implement. Chapters 4 and 7 showed how important VAX stacks are in maintaining the context of processes in conjunction with the CHMx and REI instructions. This chapter will describe how the stack compliments interrupt processing.

Another fundamental idea in an I/O subsystem is interrupt priority levels, which are analogous to process priorities. By assigning an order of importance to various I/O devices, the software can easily decide which interrupt to service first when simultaneous interrupts occur. Interrupt priority designs also define how interrupts preempt one another. This is important because the temporal dynamics of the disk drive, for example, demand that it be serviced faster than a terminal. The disk drive is a shared device, which means that it must service multiple requests. Furthermore, it operates at high data rates, and it is necessary to transfer large volumes of data between the disk and the process. Finally, the basic principle of the rotating disk demands that when data is available, it must be processed within a few microseconds or else there is a considerable penalty in time spent waiting for the disk to rotate. On the other hand, as demonstrated in Chapter 1, the character transfer time of the RS232C protocol is long in comparison to the computer's instruction execution time. Even if character transmission time is shortened, user input is very slow compared to the computer, so the keyboard data volume is low. This means that the operating system can delay its response to terminal interrupts for a relatively longer time.

8.1. Interrupt Priority Level—IPL

The discussion of how the VAX architecture creates a priority environment must precede that of the I/O subsystem to make clear how the I/O subsystem schedules its activities. It is essential for the reader to first grasp the intent of the *interrupt priority level* (IPL) mechanism.

The VAX is designed with 32 interrupt priority levels,[1] divided into two groups: the lower 16, reserved for software, and the upper 16, controlled by I/O devices. Level 0 is the lowest software IPL; user processes run at level 0 and nothing else. All other software running on the computer is considered more important than user processes, which may seem like the tail is wagging the dog, but, viewed another way, all software running on the computer somehow serves the user process, and, normally, I/O must be performed before the process can continue.

Level 31 is the highest hardware IPL. When the computer is running

1. IPLs are not to be confused with the 32 scheduling priorities discussed in Chapter 3; the two concepts are unrelated although easily confused.

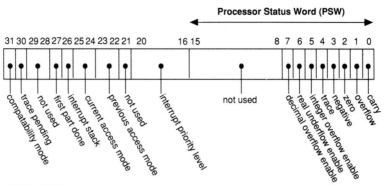

Figure 8.2. The processor status longword (PSL) format

at this priority, nothing can interrupt it; the only way to stop it is to pull the plug. Level 31 is used primarily to prohibit all interrupts during critical I/O operations—specifically, when starting a device. Because this is such a restricted mode of operation, all level-31 code must be designed to execute only a few instructions before the priority is lowered once again.

PROCESSOR STATUS LONGWORD

The current value of the IPL is stored in the processor status longword (PSL), bits 16 through 20 in Figure 8.2. The lower word (bits 0–15) is sometimes called the processor status word (PSW) and can be changed directly with bit-oriented instructions, although bits 8 through 15 are not used. To the assembly language programmer, bits 0 through 3 are the familiar condition codes. Bits 16 through 31, the upper word, cannot be modified directly by any instructions but only indirectly through the use of specific hardware actions and instructions. For example, Chapter 7 showed how the current and previous processor mode is changed as a side effect of the CHMx and REI instructions. As this discussion continues, it should become increasingly apparent how important these 32 bits are to the operation of the machine.

A hardware IPL is associated with each device, and since there are usually several devices with the same priority, the fact that there are 16 levels does not mean that there can only be 16 devices. The hardware is designed to connect many devices to the VAX; the maximum number depends on the particular model. Figure 8.3 summarizes the interrupt priority levels. Eight levels, 16 through 23, are reserved for I/O devices, although only three levels, 21, 22, and 23, are used. Level 20 is normally reserved for the system console, and either 22 or 24 is used for the clock, depending on the VAX model. Levels 25 through 29 are used for system errors such as memory, bus, or processor errors. Lastly, level 30 is reserved for power failures; whenever a hardware sensor detects an input voltage drop below a threshold, this interrupt is activated so that the system can perform an orderly shutdown prior to losing power. Level 31 inhibits all interrupts and is used for starting I/O devices.

INTERRUPT ALGORITHM

When an I/O device signals an interrupt, the control unit examines the interrupt priority level of the signal and compares it to the current IPL stored in the PSL. If the interrupt signal's priority is higher than the IPL, the control unit *grants* the interrupt at the conclusion of the currently executing instruction. If the IPL is the same or lower than the interrupting device, the VAX maintains but otherwise temporarily ignores the signal.

Granting an interrupt request is a three-step procedure as indicated in Figure 8.4: saving the current PC and PSL on a stack (circle 1), obtaining a new value for the PC from the system control block (SCB) (circle 2), and, finally, creating a new PSL that reflects the new IPL and stack location (circle 3). The CHMx instruction performs the same steps, see Figure 7.2, except for the IPL modification. Whenever there is an interrupt, either·the *kernel stack* or the *interrupt stack* is used to store the PC and PSL. When the interrupt stack is used, that fact is recorded in the PSL too, in bit 26. In the VAX hardware, this is a programmable feature; either the interrupt stack or the kernel stack can be used, as declared in the SCB. The stack distinction is important because, although there is only one interrupt stack, there is a kernel stack for each process.

In the IPL logic in the figure (circle 3), prior to the interrupt, the IPL value of 20 indicates that the processor is already executing an interrupt handler. The interrupt at IPL 23 is interrupting code that was processing an interrupt; that is, the new interrupt is preempting a previous interrupt. In effect, an interrupt causes the hardware to perform a context switch from whatever it was doing to the interrupt handler whose entry address is stored in the SCB.

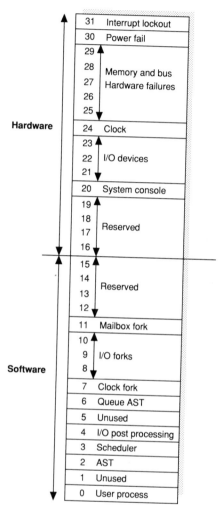

Figure 8.3. Normal IPL assignments

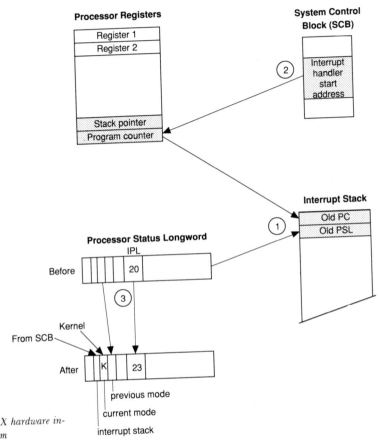

Figure 8.4. VAX hardware in-terrupt algorithm

CONTEXT SWITCHING

Figure 8.5 illustrates a more elaborate example of the context switching operation that occurs after an interrupt. Here, an interrupt handler is executing at an IPL value of 22 (circle 1) when two interrupt requests arrive at the control unit (circle 2), one from an IPL 24 device and one from an IPL 20 device. The control unit will grant the level-24 request, but the level-20 request is deferred. When the currently executing instruction completes at IPL 22, the level-24 interrupt is granted (circle 3); the PC (in the IPL 22 code) and PSL are stacked, a new PSL is created, and the PC is initialized from the SCB, as described in the Figure 8.4. This causes the IPL 24 interrupt handler to begin execution. In the meantime, the IPL 22 handler has

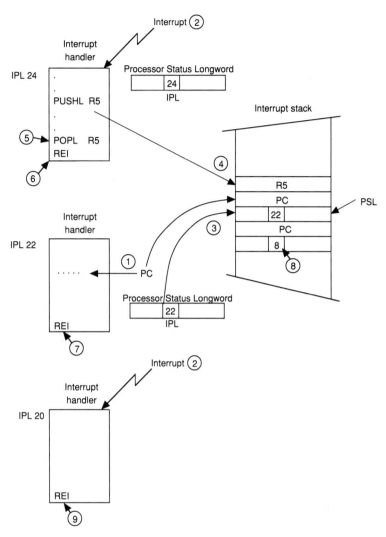

Figure 8.5. An interrupt example

not completed (it was preempted), and there is still a pending interrupt at level 20. The trivial context (the PC and PSL) of the IPL 22 routine is stored on the interrupt stack.

Because interrupts are waiting to be processed, the level-24 handler must not consume too much time. This timing requirement is essential to the efficient operation of the I/O subsystem. When executing, if the level-24 handler requires a register, it is necessary to preserve the context of the interrupt 22 handler, so that the register must be first saved on the stack (circle 4). Later, when the level-24 handler is through with it, prior to returning to the IPL 22 handler, the register is restored (circle 5).

When the IPL 24 interrupt handler is complete, an REI is executed (circle 6). As described in Chapter 7, this instruction causes the PC and PSL to be reset by popping the stack; the REI always pops from the current stack—in this case, the interrupt stack. The REI causes the IPL to be lowered to 22 (that value is stored in the stacked PSL), which causes the interrupted code at level 22 to continue. Thus, executing a single REI instruction, the IPL is lowered and the previous context is restored. Note that the REI instruction can only lower IPL, never raise it. When the REI executes, it checks the IPL field in the PSL on the stack to make sure that the IPL is being lowered.

When the IPL 22 handler is complete, it executes an REI (circle 7), and whatever PC/PSL pair is on the interrupt stack determines where execution will continue. Assume that the PSL on the stack contains an IPL of 8 (circle 8). When that PSL is reloaded, the processor IPL is lowered to 8. Recall, however, that there is an outstanding interrupt waiting at level 20. As soon as the PC and PSL are reloaded, an interrupt for level 20 occurs, which causes the PC and PSL (for level 8) to be stacked again. The net effect is that the PC and PSL on the stack are popped by the REI and then pushed immediately by the hardware because of the interrupt waiting at IPL 20. This level-20 interrupt is processed to completion and its REI (circle 9) finally restores the IPL 8 context.

The purpose of the interrupt handler in the I/O subsystem is to service the interrupt by capturing and saving only time-critical data. Any additional processing should be done at a reduced IPL, thus freeing the interrupt handler to service other interrupts. In other words, the interrupt handler must work as close to real time as possible, in this way ensuring timely responses to interrupts at all levels. The functions performed at the elevated interrupt level must be limited, and the rest of the processing associated with the interrupt is completed later. The high-level IPL logic must somehow reschedule further processing at a lower IPL.

SOFTWARE INTERRUPTS

Having examined the effect that hardware interrupts have on the executing software, we now turn our attention to software interrupts. Interrupt priority levels 1 through 15 are reserved for software interrupts. The VAX gives a program the capability to create an interrupt, just as hardware does. This is accomplished by storing a value of 1 through 15 in an internal processor register (IPR), called the *software interrupt summary register* (SISR). The IPRs can be accessed only in kernel mode by two instructions, move from processor register (MFPR) and move to processor register (MTPR).[2] For example, to create an interrupt at IPL 8, the operating system executes an instruction like this:

```
MTPR #8,#PR$_SIRR
```

A record of outstanding software interrupts is maintained in the software interrupt request status (SIRS) register, which contains one bit per interrupt level. There is no corresponding register for hardware interrupts. In Figure 8.5, if the interrupt handler is running at level 22 and issues the MTPR instruction, the VAX will record (or *arm*) the interrupt. However, as with hardware interrupts, the interrupt will not be granted until the IPL drops below 8.

Figure 8.6 lists the IPRs on the VAX and states how they can be accessed: read only (R), write only (W), or both (R/W). Certain IPRs are automatically reloaded from the hardware PCB whenever the process context is switched; this is indicated in the right-hand column of the figure.

8.2. I/O Subsystem Overview

The I/O subsystem is viewed as an operating system in miniature, having subtle and obvious similarities and differences with the VMS operating system.

---

2. In the case of the SIRR, only the MTPR is valid; use of the MFPR on the SIRR is illegal.

IPR name		Read (MFPR)/ Write(MTPR)	Changed at context switch
KSP	(kernel stack pointer)	R/W	yes
ESP	(executive stack pointer)	R/W	yes
SSP	(supervisor stack pointer)	R/W	yes
USP	(user stack pointer)	R/W	yes
ISP	(interrupt stack pointer)	R/W	no
P0BR	(P0 base register)	R/W	yes
P0LR	(P0 length register)	R/W	yes
P1BR	(P1 base register)	R/W	yes
P1LR	(P1 length register)	R/W	yes
SBR	(system base register)	R/W	no
SLR	(system limit register)	R/W	no
PCBB	(hardware process control block base)	R/W	no*
SCBB	(system control block base)	R/W	no
IPL	(interrupt priority level)	R/W	no
ASTLVL	(AST level)	R/W	yes
SIRR	(software interrupt request register)	W	no
SISR	(software interrupt summary)	R/W	no
MAPEN	(memory management enable)	R/W	no
TBIA	(translation buffer invalidate all)	W	no
TBIS	(translation buffer invalidate single)	W	no
SID	(system identification)	R	no
TBCHK	(translation buffer check)	W	no

* The PCBB is set with an MTPR instruction immediately before the LDPCTX.

Figure 8.6. Internal processor registers (IPRs) on the VAX

The I/O subsystem is driven by process requests and by the I/O hardware itself, not by priorities, states, and time. It is the very heart of the VMS operating system—in mastering it, the rest of VMS is substantiated and harmonized.

- The I/O subsystem has data structures that are analogous to, but simpler than, those already studied; however, the terms have changed. The primary structure is the unit control block (UCB), which is analogous to the PCB.
- The I/O subsystem is preemptive.
- The I/O subsystem is a unit. It executes in kernel mode and is entirely contained in SYS space—it has no access to user virtual memory.
- The I/O subsystem has interrupt handlers and device drivers instead

of processes. The number of handlers and drivers are fixed—they are neither created, deleted, paged, or swapped.

- A handler or driver is always computable—never waiting.
- A handler or driver executes until it is done—there is no time-sharing.
- IPL determines the handler and driver priority.
- Context switches are faster and simpler—there is no scheduler and no process states.

IPL DISPATCHER

In the design of the I/O subsystem, there is usually an interrupt *dispatcher* associated with each IPL, as indicated in Figure 8.7. Since many hardware devices operate at the same IPL, the interrupt IPL dispatchers are required to direct the interrupt to the proper interrupt handler. The interrupt dispatcher gathers information about the interrupt, then locates and starts the appropriate interrupt handler, which signals its completion with an REI instruction, permitting IPLs at lower levels to be granted.

A software interrupt requested with the MTPR instruction signals that a function must be performed at that lower IPL. This function is specified in a data block, which is queued to the dispatcher at the interrupt level. A queue is required because the dispatcher and the code generating the request are running asynchronously, and when the software IPL dispatcher runs, it dequeues a data block, performs the specified function, and loops back to dequeue the next block. When the queue is empty, the dispatcher executes an REI, and the next lowest interrupt is granted.

At some levels, both hardware and software, no dispatcher is necessary—for example, the process scheduler (IPL 3) and hardware clock interrupt handler (IPL 24), which are pictured in Figure 8.8. A clock interrupt has no place to go but to the clock interrupt handler, since no other interrupt can occur at this level. The SCB is directly connected to the clock interrupt handler. The scheduler is executed in response to some part of the VMS system requesting a software interrupt at IPL 3. In Figure 8.8, it is the clock interrupt handler that "calls" the scheduler using the MTPR instruction. Naturally, the VMS code has been simplified to illustrate the point. The clock interrupts every 10 milliseconds. A process quanta is normally 20 interrupts or clicks of the clock (200 milliseconds). If the clock interrupt

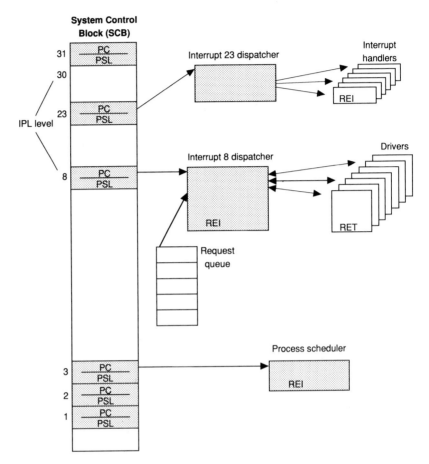

*Figure 8.7. Interrupt dispatchers
control the IPL queues*

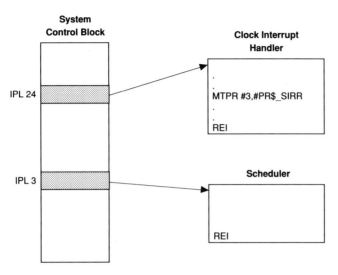

Figure 8.8. The clock interrupt schedules the scheduler

occurs while a process is executing, it raises the IPL to 24, and the clock interrupt handler is entered via the SCB entry for that interrupt.

The clock interrupt routine has two major tasks,[3] to update the system time and to count down the process quantum. When the process quantum expires, the clock interrupt routine requests an interrupt at IPL 3 by executing an MTPR #3,#PR$_SIRR instruction. This creates an interrupt request for the scheduler; then the clock interrupt routine exits using an REI. When no other interrupts are pending above IPL 3, the scheduler interrupt is granted. And it will be granted prior to returning to the process, since processes execute at IPL 0.

SCHEDULER EXECUTION

The scheduler is also directly linked to the SCB, and when it executes, it selects a new process to execute, switches contexts, and performs an REI to lower the IPL to 0, thus starting the new process. If the clock interrupt

3. A third task of the clock interrupt routine is to count down general timer requests. Quantum management is merely a specialized form of the countdown logic. These three tasks are not done at IPL 24 either, but at IPL 7, as indicated by the Clock FORK in Figure 8.3.

handler does not issue the IPL 3 interrupt, then its REI will permit the schedulers to be bypassed and allow the interrupted process to continue.

To perform the context switch, the scheduler saves the current context, selects the new process, and then it needs to switch in the new process's context. The LDPCTX instruction moves the PC and PSL from the hardware PCB to the kernel stack (rather than to the PC and PSL registers) as the rest of the context information is moved from the hardware PCB to the general registers. When the scheduler is finished, the kernel stack is properly set up so that when its REI is executed, as with all the other interrupt processors, the hardware pops the stack as described and starts the newly selected process. Incidentally, the scheduler is the only software in the operating system that uses the LDPCTX instruction.

SYSTEM CONTROL BLOCK

Figure 8.9 is a detailed view of the system control block (SCB). The SCB is contained in a single page frame (512 bytes) and is divided logically into two sections, exceptions and interrupts. Each entry of the SCB is a longword that contains the address of the entry point of the exception or interrupt handler. Most of the exceptions do not have an associated IPL because they retain the current IPL; only kernel stack not valid and machine check exceptions are different. Notice the other exceptions that have been referenced throughout the book: page faults (24) and the 4 change mode entries (40-4C). The 15 software interrupts (84-BC) are near the bottom of the SCB along with the clock interrupt (C0). The 4 hardware interrupts at the bottom (100-1FF) are large enough to specify 16 devices each at each level.

A THIRD WAY TO CHANGE IPL

The hardware and software create interrupt requests, and when the VAX grants that interrupt, it causes the PSL to be changed to the new value. However, there is one instruction that can change the IPL directly, without an interrupt; in other words, software is able to control the IPL value. Another register in the internal processor register (IPR) set, called the IPL register, contains the same value that is stored in the IPL field of the PSL. Changing the IPL register changes the IPL field of the PSL, and, thus, the interrupt priority of the processor is also changed. As an example, the instruction

```
MTPR# #31,#PR$_IPL
```

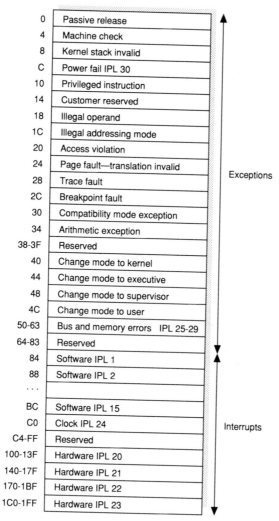

Figure 8.9. The system control block details

will make the corresponding change to the PSL itself, changing the IPL field to 31. The IPL can be either increased or decreased with this instruction because there are no restrictions. This single instruction is provided to make it easier and safer for a program to change priority levels.

8.3. The Primary I/O Database

The primary I/O database is a software reflection of the hardware devices that are attached to the computer. Its primary structure is the unit control block (UCB), and there is one UCB for each hardware device. Thus, a system with 2 disks, 24 terminals, and 4 printers has 30 UCBs. Each UCB is identified by its name; for instance, DUA0 means the first disk drive connected to the "A" disk controller for the DU-type disk. The UCBs form a static framework that is defined when the system is initialized.

Normally, multiple hardware devices are connected to a single hardware controller, so one level up in the database structure, above the UCB, is a device data block (DDB) to correspond to each device controller. Figure 8.10 shows these relationships. The DDBs are linked together to facilitate the operating system's search for a particular device, and each DDB points to a linked list of UCBs that are attached to its controller. The UCBs also point to their driver because the driver code is shared by all identical devices; for example, a system with eight identical disks connected to two controllers shares a single disk driver.

A process must link to this structure when it needs to perform I/O. This is done with the $ASSIGN system service, which will create a channel control block (CCB) in the user's image in P1 space. The CCB contains a link to the UCB that is specified by the $ASSIGN arguments. The CCB is dynamic in that it is created when needed, within a space reserved for it in the process, and destroyed when the process is finished with the device. Figure 8.10 shows two hardware controllers, a terminal controller, and a disk controller, and their corresponding DDBs, labeled TXA and DUA. The terminal controller is connected to four terminal devices, so there are four UCBs labeled TXA0 through TXA3. Likewise, there are two disk devices, DUA0 and DUA1. Notice that the DDBs are threaded together and that each DDB has a list of UCBs connected to it also. But also notice that two UCB lists are not linked. The two processes shown in Figure 8.10 indicate how the channel control blocks are used. ROCKETMAN is connected to

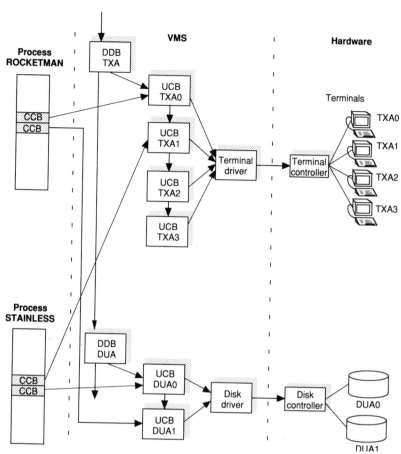

Figure 8.10. The primary I/O
database

TXA0 and DUA1, and STAINLESS is connected to TXA1 and DUA0. Processes link directly to the UCBs, bypassing the DDBs.

LOGICAL NAMES

A user does not refer to his or her terminal by its physical name, for example, "_TTA3:"; instead, it is called TT or SYS$INPUT. Every session has a logical device called TT. To show that TT is a logical name for the terminal, enter the command:

```
$ SHOW LOGICAL TT
```

and the resulting definition will be displayed, for instance:

```
"TT" = "_TXB5:"
```

"TX" is the name of the controller, and "B" means that it is the second terminal controller in the system. This controller is able to direct eight terminals, numbered 0 through 7—the "5" here indicates that this terminal is the sixth. This logical assignment to TT is made by the VMS operating system at the time the process is created, during the LOGIN sequence. The reason for logical names is to permit software independence of the devices. It would be awkward indeed if a program had to be recompiled each time the user changed terminals.

The actual physical terminal used by the program is defined at the time the program is executed. This is a form of *binding*, which is controlled by the operating system. Readers should be familiar with the concept of binding. In Pascal, the CONST declaration binds a constant name to a value at compilation time. Bindings also take place at LINK time—for example, when combining subprograms in two Pascal MODULES. Similarly, when a program is executed, variables and code are dynamically bound to memory in the sense that their virtual addresses must be mapped to physical addresses.

A MAILBOX EXAMPLE

The mailbox example in Chapter 5 is a good way to understand this database. Mailboxes behave like standard I/O devices from the user's point of view except that processes are at both ends of the mailbox connection. Also, the $QIOW mechanism used to access mailboxes is identical to physical I/O operations. Within the I/O system, however, the mailbox is a very different device. First, a mailbox's UCB is created and destroyed by the operating system—it is dynamic, unlike UCBs for physical hardware. Second, the mailbox driver has no interrupt code; it has no need for interrupts, of course, because there is no physical device. Physical hardware is always interrupt-driven in a time-shared system; if it were not, the purpose of sharing the resources would be subverted.

Whenever a mailbox is created, a new UCB must also be created by the $CREMBX system service. At the same time it is created, the mailbox is linked back to the requesting process by the creation of a channel control block (CCB). If, when a process executes $CREMBX, the specified mailbox is already created, only the process's CCB is created. All mailbox names are prefixed with "MBA" and then appended with a unit number no longer than four digits. MBA0, MBA1, and MBA2 are permanently assigned for use by the system. A search of the logical tables using the command below will reveal the names of the active mailbox "devices" that are defined.

```
$ SHOW LOGICAL
```

Just as users do not refer to the physical name of a terminal, they do not refer to a mailbox by its MBA name either. When the mailbox was created in Chapter 5, the programming example assigned it a logical name, CUE. Figure 8.11 illustrates the relationship of the mailbox logical name to the UCB. There is only one mailbox "driver" (corresponding to the DDB labeled MBA) on any VMS system. The DDB points to the string of mailbox UCBs that are currently declared. The figure shows that processes ROCK-ETMAN and STAINLESS are currently sharing MBA17 and that MBA17 has three messages in it. MBA17 is called CUE by the processes, so there is an entry by that name in the logical name table.

It is important to understand in more detail how the mailbox UCB is created. Each time the $CREMBX system service is called, it first searches for the logical name supplied by the user in the logical name table. If there is no match, $CREMBX creates a mailbox UCB by incrementing the last unit number employed and testing the result against 9,999 (the maximum number of mailboxes permitted by the VMS operating system) to determine if it is a valid name. The characters "MBA" and unit number are combined, and the existing mailbox UCBs are searched to make sure there is no duplicated mailbox device name. If there is a duplication, another unit number is created and the search is repeated. When a mailbox is created, an entry is added to the logical name table as well as to the UCB list.

On the other hand, if the logical name supplied is found in the name

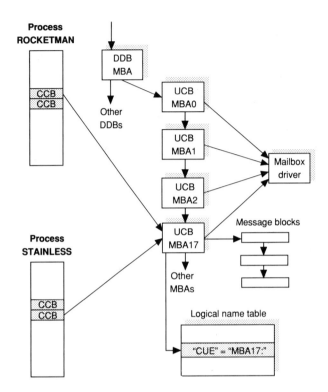

*Figure 8.11. The mailbox
database*

table, $CREMBX recognizes that the UCB has been created already. Whether
or not a UCB existed previously, a CCB is created in user space and linked
to the UCB. The channel number will be used, not the logical name, when
reading and writing mail messages using $QIOW.

THE I/O REQUEST PACKET (IRP)

Figure 8.12 follows a mailbox write operation to show how it involves the
I/O database. The user initiates the write with the $QIOW request (circle
1), and the $QIOW system service (circle 2) first checks the arguments. If
required arguments are missing or illegal, no further action is taken by the
subsystem, and control is returned immediately to the user. If the arguments
are acceptable, an I/O request packet (IRP) is built (circle 3). This data block
is vital because it acts as the interface between the user and the I/O system.

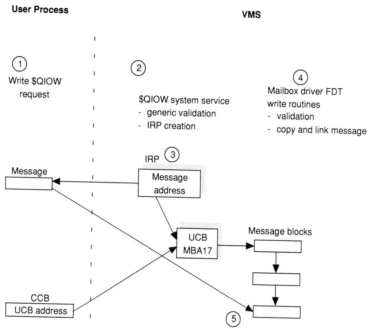

Figure 8.12. The mailbox write operation

In normal I/O operations, data flows between the device and memory asynchronously; that is, the requesting process is not necessarily executing when data is transferred. Therefore, the I/O subsystem must operate in SYS space only, independent of the process. Everything about the request is encapsulated in the IRP because information from the process's context is unavailable. The IRP contains the function code, the address and length of the data buffer, a link to the UCB, and a link to the requesting process.

After the IRP is created and initialized, the mailbox-specific code is executed. These $QIOW operations are taking place in the context of the process, so the process is still in the CUR state.

There is a routine for each possible function supported by the driver; the mailbox write code is part of the device driver and, as such, is referred to as a function decision table (FDT) routine. The mailbox write FDT tests for write access to the mailbox (circle 4), the message size, and its accessibility. The message passed by the process must be *readable*. Notice that the accessibility check is necessary to ensure the security of the system; without it a user could mail any part of memory to a cooperating process, thus accessing normally unreadable sections through a "back door." Finally, the FDT routine allocates a message block, copies the message from the process to the block, and links it onto the UCB message queue (circle 5).

Although the user has several options, the example $QIOW request does not return to the requesting process until the message is delivered to the reader. As a result, the $QIOW mailbox read is much more complex than the write operation. Notice, in particular, that since three messages are already in the message queue, there must be three processes waiting. A single process cannot queue multiple messages using our model, but the VMS system allows for this possibility. The process requesting the mailbox write cannot proceed, so the I/O subsystem causes it to be blocked. A local event flag is used to synchronize process and I/O subsystem operations in much the same way common event flags were used in Chapter 5.

To continue this scenario, trace the mailbox read operation in Figure 8.13. As with the write $QIOW, generic validation tests are performed first and an IRP is created (circle 1). Provided the request is valid, $QIOW transfers to the read FDT routine (circle 2). A message is already available, so it can be copied from the message block connected to the UCB back to the reading process (circle 3). Notice that the message block is used to connect the two processes; it is a shared data region.

The reading process now has the data it requested, but before the reader can continue, the mailbox message database must be "housekept" by the I/O subsystem. This is called *I/O postprocessing*. The delivered message must be dequeued, the IRP deleted, and the corresponding write process scheduled to run again (circle 4); that is, the writer's event flag must be set by the I/O subsystem. Once the event flag is set, the writer becomes computable again. At some point, the writing process becomes the current process and its execution continues. Incidentally, information required to locate the writing process's PCB is recorded in the IRP attached to the message (circle 5).

8.4. A WRITE Example

This section will revisit Chapter 1 and follow a $QIOW write request completely through the operating system, albeit in considerably more detail than was given there. Figure 8.14 contains the $ASSIGN and $QIOW system

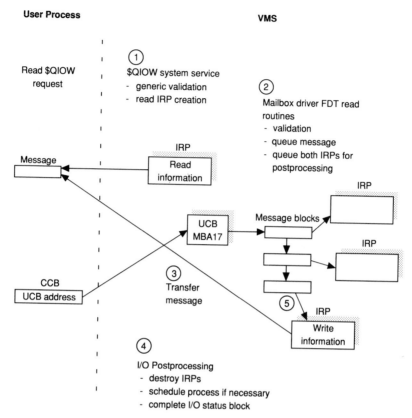

User Process

VMS

Read $QIOW
request

① $QIOW system service
- generic validation
- read IRP creation

② Mailbox driver FDT read
routines
- validation
- queue message
- queue both IRPs for
postprocessing

IRP
Message → Read
information

UCB
MBA17

Message blocks

IRP

IRP

CCB
UCB address

③ Transfer
message

⑤

IRP
Write
information

④ I/O Postprocessing
- destroy IRPs
- schedule process if necessary
- complete I/O status block

Figure 8.13. The mailbox
READ operation

```
ERR := $ASSIGN ( devnam := 'TT',      { in: UCB name }
                 chan := TT_CHAN );    { out: channel number }

ERR := $QIOW ( chan := TT_CHAN,        { in: channel number }
               func := IO$_WRITEVBLK;  { in: function }
               iosb := TT_IOSB,        { out: returned status }
               p1 := BUFFER,           { in: message location }
               p2 := 5 );              { in: message length }
```

Figure 8.14. A typical
$ASSIGN and $QIO write
request pair

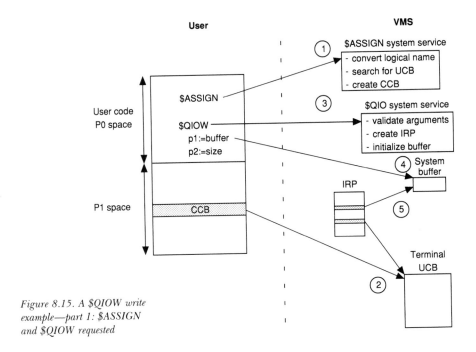

Figure 8.15. A $QIOW write example—part 1: $ASSIGN and $QIOW requested

service calls to be used. Chapter 5 introduced mailboxes, and Figure 5.10 discussed the $QIOW calling sequence. The example that begins in Figure 8.15 will be referring to the Pascal statements in Figure 8.14. The test for service success or failure has been omitted (it was detailed in Chapter 5) to keep the current example less cluttered.

Figure 8.15 begins by executing the two system service calls in Figure 8.14. Although not shown in this figure, the system service requests execute the change mode to kernel (CHMK) instruction and the change mode dispatcher directs each request to the specific service subroutine. This detail was presented in Figure 4.25.

$ASSIGN OPERATION

At circle 1, the $ASSIGN system service creates a direct link to the unit control block (UCB). This is how it is done: the input to $ASSIGN is the logical name of the device; TT is the logical name to the terminal. The output of $ASSIGN is a channel number, stored in TT_CHAN. The $AS-SIGN system service performs an internal logical-to-physical translation before searching the I/O database structure, and so it looks for a device named TXB5, not TT. The device name TXB is used to search the DDBs, and when the proper one is found, the search continues to the specified unit where the UCB is located. Next, $ASSIGN creates a channel control block (CCB) and initializes it to point at the UCB, as indicated by circle 2 in Figure 8.15. The channel number returned by $ASSIGN is the index of the newly created CCB structure.

The $ASSIGN operation is provided to save CPU cycles; future references to the UCB by a $QIOW are performed directly through the CCB (via the "chan" argument), which requires no searching. In most images there are probably many calls to the $QIOW system service, but only one $ASSIGN request is necessary for a given device. Notice that a single $QIOW service call can be in a loop or there can be several $QIOW requests scattered throughout the image, all referring to the same channel number variable (TT_CHAN in Figure 8.14) because they all refer to the same device.

$QIOW VALIDATION

In circle 3 of Figure 8.15, the $QIOW is executed. While the $QIO[4] is executing in kernel mode, the VMS system is permitted to access the process's context. First, the channel number is accessed to check its validity; then, the specified function is verified against the list of possible functions recognized by the driver. The I/O status block is checked to make certain that the user has write access to it. It is always eight bytes long, but both ends must be accessible because it may span a page boundary. When the $QIO operation is complete, data is stored in the status block.

The buffer (the p1 argument) is likewise checked to make certain that the user has read access to the specified array. The buffer length (the p2 argument) is used to ensure that the entire buffer is accessible, not just the first byte. Because the buffer can span pages, just as the status block can, this check is necessary to guarantee the security of the system. The status blocks and buffer checks are performed using the PROBEx instruction discussed in Chapter 7.

If any of these tests fail, an error status is returned to the user in the function's value, ERR. To determine argument validity, the user's program should always check the returned function value. The requested I/O service

---

4. The VMS system service is called $QIO. The distinction between $QIO and $QIOW will be made apparent as this discussion continues.

is not continued if an error is encountered in the arguments. On the other hand, valid arguments do not necessarily mean that the I/O was performed successfully or even that it was started.

I/O REQUEST PACKET

The next step performed by the $QIO system service is the creation and initialization of the I/O request packet (IRP). This structure is required because, once the I/O transfer begins, the I/O subsystem does not have access to the process context for any of the information it needs. The IRP acts as the interface between the process and the I/O subsystem, and it must carry information in both directions.

VMS DYNAMIC DATA POOL

All operating systems need to dynamically allocate data structures, and dynamic memory allocation is fairly straightforward. When applied to an operating system, this important function is carefully optimized for the a priori knowledge of the data structures required by the system. In the case of the VMS operating system, when the system is initialized, a number of blank IRPs are built and linked together in a pool containing dynamically assigned buffers. Collectively, this data area is called the nonpaged pool.

The command:

```
$ SHOW MEMORY
```

will produce a display like Figure 8.16. At the top of the display, physical memory usage is shown; it is similar to the information available with the MONITOR command. The next section, slot usage, shows how the system database is allocated. Since only six balance set slots are used, the example system is lightly loaded. Below the slot usage, the pool area information is presented, and the information about the IRPs is located in the center of this display. In Figure 8.16, 216 packets were created initially, and 62 are currently in use. An IRP is 176 bytes long in Version 5.0 of the VMS operating system. Notice in the figure that two other fixed-size packets are allocated: the small request packet (SRP) is 96 bytes long, and the large request packet (LRP) is 720 bytes long. The SHOW MEMORY display also records the current usage of the page and swap files. The final line on the display shows how much overhead VMS demands; more than 20 percent of the frames (2,059 of 10,240) are permanently allocated to VMS.

```
           System Memory Resources on 11-MAR-1990 14:11:11.95

Physical Memory Usage (pages):   Total      Free      In Use    Modified
   Main Memory (5.00Mb)          10240      6961        3123         156

Slot Usage (slots):              Total      Free      Resident   Swapped
   Process Entry Slots              19        11           8          0
   Balance Set Slots                17        11           6          0

Fixed-Size Pool Areas (packets): Total      Free      In Use       Size
   Small Packet (SRP) List         371       181         190         96
   I/O Request Packet (IRP) List   216       154          62        176
   Large Packet (LRP)                6         6           0        720

Dynamic Memory Usage (bytes):    Total      Free      In Use    Largest
   Nonpaged Dynamic Memory       249856     74304      175552      50848
   Paged Dynamic Memory          152064     54016       98048      53120

Paging File Usage (pages):                Free Reservable       Total
   DISK$VAXVMSRL052:[SYS0.SYSEXE]SWAPFILE.SYS
                                   1696      1696                 1696
   DISK$VAXVMSRL052:[SYS0.SYSEXE]PAGEFILE.SYS
                                   8164      -569                 9600

Of the physical pages in use, 2059 pages are permanently allocated to VMS.
```

Figure 8.16. Typical display
of the command $ SHOW
MEMORY

The pool area display is a fundamental aid in *tuning* VMS data structure sizes to the particular user environment. With SYSGEN, a privileged image, the data structure allocations can be changed to best fit the actual utilization of the system. The tuning topic is too large to be covered in this book, but the point to be made is that operating systems must be adjusted to each environment. As with any complex machine, tuning the VMS operating system is not easy and cannot be approached lightly; it takes an expert. Also, easy-to-understand measurement tools must accompany the on-line tuning capabilities. Digital and third party vendors are starting to provide them.

Dynamic memory is used for most of the data structures we have discussed. Figure 8.17 is a synopsis of data block allocation. Since these blocks are dynamic and threaded together, each one uses header and trailer pointers to enable it to be reached. This collection of pointers is located in the "executive" area in the kernel of the VMS system.

Now, to return to the example in Figure 8.15. Once the IRP is created, it is initialized with the PID, the process priority, the requested I/O function,

Structure name		Allocation
ACL	Access control list	paged
ARB	Access rights block	part of PCB
CCB	Channel control block	part of process
CEB	Common event block	not paged
DDB	Device data block	not paged
FCB	File control block	not paged
FKB	Fork block	part of UCB
IRP	I/O request block	not paged
JIB	Job information block	not paged
LKB	Lock block	not paged
MBX	Mailbox control block	shared memory
PCB	Process control block	not paged
PHB	Process header	part of balance slots
TQE	Timer queue element	not paged
UCB	Unit control block	not paged

Figure 8.17. Synopsis of data block allocation

the address of the I/O status block, the event flag number, the channel number, and other information. Figure 8.18 summarizes the IRP structure. Next, the information to be written to the I/O device (the user's terminal in this example) must be copied from user space into SYS space (circle 4) because the terminal driver will not have access to the process when it eventually gets control. The I/O system executes exclusively in SYS space, so a buffer that is addressable in SYS space must be allocated to save the request's message. The address (the p1 argument) and length (the p2 argument) of the buffer are also stored in the IRP (circle 5).

I/O QUOTAS

Throughout this portion of the $QIO system service, several process quota values must be checked and reduced, such as the quota for the number of buffered I/O operations permitted and the quota regulating the size of the allocated buffer. These quotas are used in maintaining system reliability; they guarantee that a process does not accidentally or deliberately reserve

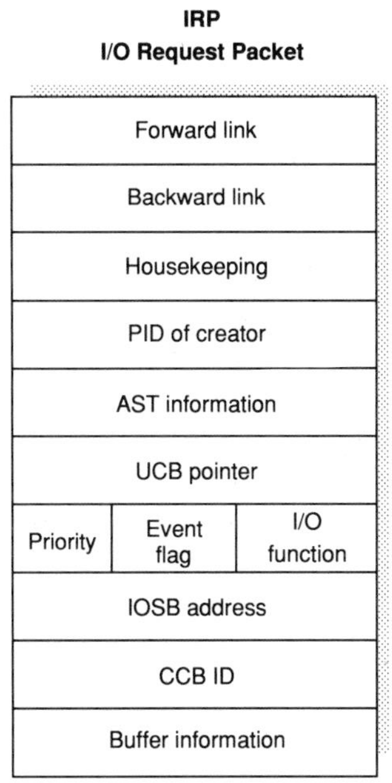

IRP
I/O Request Packet

Forward link
Backward link
Housekeeping
PID of creator
AST information
UCB pointer

Priority	Event flag	I/O function

IOSB address
CCB ID
Buffer information

Figure 8.18. Overview of the
IRP structure

an entire resource to the exclusion of other users. Quota maintenance is one of the primary functions of any general purpose operating system. If any of the quotas are exceeded, $QIO returns to the user with an error status in the ERR variable, and the I/O request is not performed. When an error is discovered, the $QIO routine must restore any allocated storage unique to the operation, such as the IRP and buffer, and must also adjust the quota values.

$QIO AND $QIOW

At this point in the example, all the I/O testing operations are complete. The request has been validated, and the data structures have been allocated and initialized. Now, the $QIO system service has only two more tasks: starting the I/O driver and, optionally, returning to the calling process. This section will elaborate on the optional return logic.

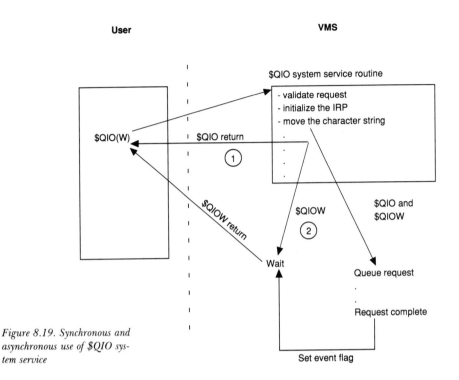

Figure 8.19. Synchronous and asynchronous use of $QIO system service

Figure 8.19 depicts two methods of requesting the $QIO system service, *asynchronously* ($QIO) and *synchronously* ($QIOW). If the user requests a $QIO, the system service returns to the program after initializing the data structures, even though the I/O is only queued (circle 1); I/O has not finished and maybe has not even started. In this case, the process is free to continue execution while the physical I/O is taking place. The process can even issue more $QIOs to the same device, and if it does, the requests are simply FIFO queued. On the other hand, a $QIOW system service request means that the process will be blocked until the I/O transfer is complete (circle 2). In this case, a local event flag is used by the service to signal the process, and the process's state is thus changed to LEF until the I/O operation is complete. The $QIOW request is termed synchronous because the process and I/O subsystem are synchronized the same way ROMEO and JULIET were in Chapter 5. The synchronous/asynchronous information is stored in the IRP and is used after the I/O operation is finished.

Clearly, the advantage of the $QIO is that the process can continue

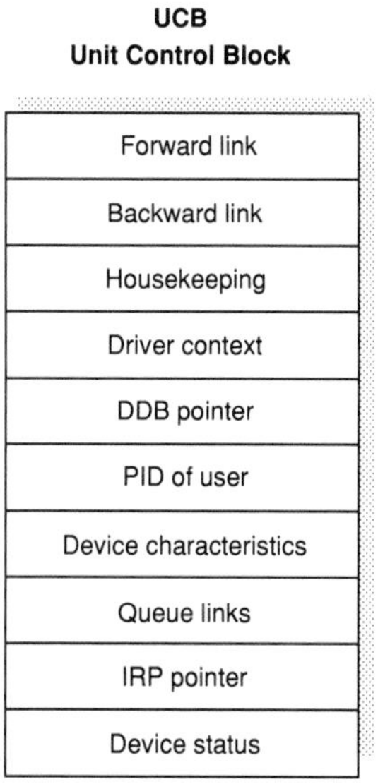

UCB
Unit Control Block

Forward link
Backward link
Housekeeping
Driver context
DDB pointer
PID of user
Device characteristics
Queue links
IRP pointer
Device status

Figure 8.20. Overview of the UCB structure

execution in parallel with I/O operation if doing so makes sense. Generally, a $QIO is used for output and a $QIOW used for input.

UNIT CONTROL BLOCK

In the $QIOW example, the process context is now no longer necessary for the operation to continue because the IRP and system buffer have captured all of the data required to continue the user's request. All remaining operations take place in the context of the I/O subsystem so the final function performed by the $QIO is to add the UCB to the I/O request queue. The UCB contains all the information needed to start the operation, and it points to the IRP and the data buffer. A UCB queue is necessary because it is possible for the terminal to be busy administering a different request. The I/O subsystem permits multiple drivers at an IPL, so, as described, a dispatcher is required to dequeue and start the proper driver.

Figure 8.20 shows the basic structure of a UCB. The position marked "driver context" is a context save area for the driver; it contains information

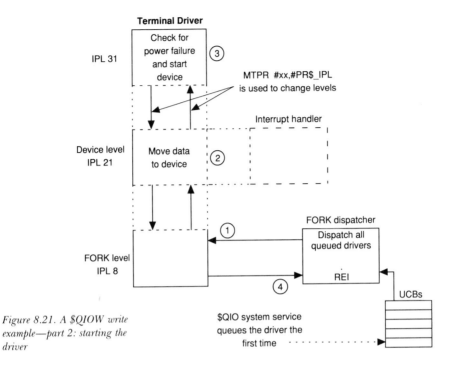

Figure 8.21. A $QIOW write example—part 2: starting the driver

similar to that stored in the hardware PCB. "Device characteristics" vary; the characteristics of a disk are different from those of a terminal. "Queue links" are used to link the UCB to its IPL queue, and "IRP pointer" links the IRPs associated with that unit. "Device status," used in postprocessing, will be discussed later.

FORK DISPATCHING

In part 2 of the write example, depicted in Figure 8.21, the queue at FORK level is shared by all I/O interrupt handlers as well as the $QIO system service. The figure shows the driver split into four sections, one each at the 3 IPL levels and the interrupt handler, each executing at different times and at different IPL levels. The terminal driver operates at the FORK level, the device level, and at level 31. What is accomplished at each of these levels will become more obvious as this discussion continues.

In queuing the unit control block (UCB), the $QIO service must distinguish between a busy terminal and an idle terminal. In the former case, the terminal is already busy and the request will be started when the terminal becomes free, as the entries are removed from the queue. In the latter case, the terminal is idle and can be started immediately. When the FORK dispatcher calls the driver (circle 1), the driver first elevates the IPL to the device level, which prohibits interrupts while it is accessing the device. In this example, at this elevated level (circle 2), the driver moves a single character from the message buffer to the terminal controller. Next, the driver elevates the IPL once again to specifically prohibit a power fail interrupt (circle 3). In this uninterruptable state, the driver checks a bit in the UCB to see if a power failure took place since the controller was initialized with data. If one took place, the character sent to the controller is probably corrupt and must be resent; however, Figure 8.21 does not illustrate this.

Normally, no power failure will be indicated, so the next step is to start the terminal controller at this elevated IPL. The controller (the hardware) is ordered to begin the transfer of data to the terminal, after which the terminal hardware (the controller and terminal) operates independently and the I/O software can continue to do other activities. The driver continues by lowering the IPL and returning control to the FORK dispatcher (circle 4) so it can dequeue the next request. The MTPR instruction is used to raise and lower the IPL throughout this sequence by changing the PR$_IPL register. It is important to know that the three left-hand boxes in Figure 8.21 are code sequences within the terminal driver; they are not separate system services.

At this point, the I/O subsystem has commanded the controller (the hardware) to begin sending the first character of the message, and it is expecting the controller to signal the computer via an interrupt when all the bits in the character have been transmitted.

DRIVER PREEMPTION

However, there is an issue to be cleared up before the example continues, and that is how a driver is preempted by an interrupt from another device controller. It is conceivable that as the IPL is reduced from 31, a pending interrupt will be granted, and Figure 8.22 illustrates this situation: during the time the terminal device is being started at IPL 31 (circle 1), the clock requests an interrupt (circle 2). However, the IPL 24 interrupt is not granted immediately because the IPL is too high. Somewhere in the driver logic

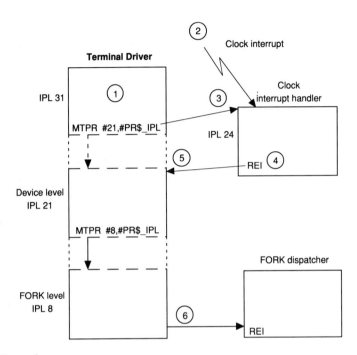

*Figure 8.22. How an interrupt
affects the driver*

executing at IPL 31, an MTPR #21,#PR$_IPL instruction will reduce the IPL to the device level. When the IPL drops below 24 the level-24 interrupt must be granted (circle 3), causing the PC and PSL to be stacked. The PC of the instruction following the MTPR and the PSL indicating IPL 21 are stacked, causing the terminal driver to be suspended and the context to be changed to the clock interrupt handler.

The clock interrupt handler starts, captures essential device data, and performs the rest of its processing as indicated in Figure 8.8. When it is done, it executes an REI (circle 4), which causes the stack containing the saved PC and PSL to be popped. This permits the terminal driver to continue execution (circle 5) as if nothing had happened. It completes its IPL 21 processing, lowers the IPL again, and returns to the FORK dispatcher at IPL 8 (circle 6). The intervening clock interrupt did not disturb the operation of the terminal driver, it merely delayed it in returning to the FORK dispatcher.

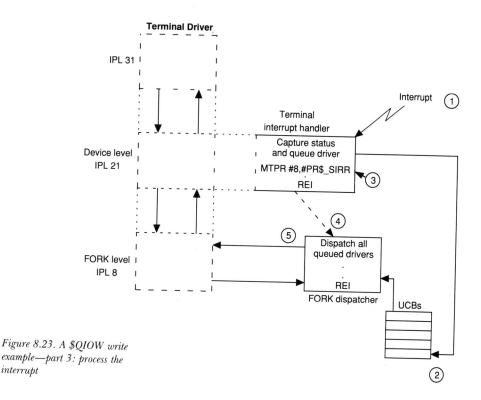

Figure 8.23. A $QIOW write example—part 3: process the interrupt

TERMINAL INTERRUPT PROCESSING

Returning to the example, Figure 8.23, part 3 of the write example illustrates the activity caused by the terminal interrupt. When a terminal interrupt is granted (circle 1) the appropriate portion of the driver is started—the interrupt handler. There is a dispatcher at the device level too, which routes the interrupt appropriately, though it is not shown in this figure. The dispatcher determines which device caused the interrupt and, looking at the corresponding UCB, locates and starts the driver interrupt routine. The interrupt logic must capture the terminal status and queue another request for the driver (circle 2). Finally, the terminal interrupt handler requests a software interrupt at the FORK level (circle 3) with the MTPR #8,#PR$_SIRR instruction. The interrupt handler signals completion with an REI (circle 4).

At some point, the FORK dispatcher is restarted and the queue entry made by the interrupt handler is picked up and passed on to the terminal driver (circle 5) for processing. It is the driver itself, not the interrupt handler portion, that keeps track of which characters have been transmitted to the terminal. Each time the driver is called, it prepares the next character for transmission, so the driver and handler create a loop that is traversed for each character sent to the terminal. The loop starts with the driver sending the first character; then, it waits for an interrupt. The interrupt queues the driver again, and this continues until the driver determines when all the characters have been sent.

POSTPROCESSING

After all the characters have been transmitted, the portion of the terminal driver executing at the FORK level takes on a new responsibility, to record or *post* the completion of the write operation. Figure 8.24, the fourth and last part of the write example, shows the steps that take place to restore control to the process that initiated the request.

The terminal driver removes the IRP (I/O request packet) from the UCB, queues it on the IOPOST queue, and then makes an interrupt request for the IOPOST dispatcher (circle 1). This is done in the same manner as the other requests, by setting the SIRR to 4, indicated by the dashed arrow. Since the IOPOST dispatcher operates at a lower IPL, the queued request is not honored until all FORK requests have been processed and the dispatcher executes an REI (circle 2). Depending on the IPL of the popped PSL, this will cause an interrupt at IPL 4.

Like the generic portion of the $QIO system services described, I/O postprocessing is a VMS function provided to all I/O operations and is not part of the driver; it is called IOC$IOPOST. At this level (circle 3), several operations take place. The message buffer is released, and the IOPOST routine prepares to restart the host process. However, before the process can be allowed to execute, provision for passing information back to it must be made. Returning the I/O status information is an example of data that needs to be passed back. The IOPOST routine cannot do it because it is not executing in the context of the process but in the I/O subsystem. Only the scheduler can ensure that the proper process's context is active.

A scheduler interrupt is requested to switch contexts, as shown by the first dashed arrow out of the IOPOST box. It is also necessary for the IOPOST routine to queue an AST (asynchronous system trap) request at IPL 2 (circle 4). An AST control block (ACB) is built reusing the IRP; in

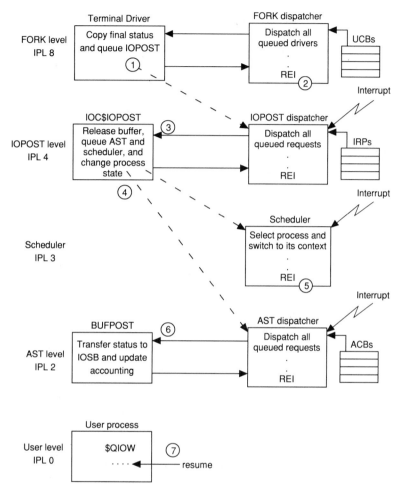

Figure 8.24. A $QIOW write example—part 4: completing the operation

other words, the IRP is redefined and becomes an ACB. Finally, if the process is waiting for the I/O operation to complete, that is, if the original request was a $QIOW, postprocessing also includes setting the process's event flag in its PCB so that the process becomes computable once again.[5] If the user request was a $QIO, no event flag logic is necessary.

AST PROCESSING

When the process is selected by the scheduler, the AST mechanism ensures that the BUFPOST routine will execute before the process is resumed. The value of the AST IPL is very important, and the IPL 2 logic is unlike all other interrupts on the hardware. Since the start of the I/O operation, the context of the requesting process has been out of reach of the I/O subsystem, but during postprocessing, the context must be recalled to complete the operation. For this, an ACB is queued to the process by a link to the PCB of the process that issued the $QIO. This logic is unlike all the other IPL queuing where an arbitrary queue was used. For example, the FORK queue contains all requests without regard to the originating process, but AST requests depend on the process context. An interrupt at IPL 2 may exist for some processes but not for others because not all the processes have an ACB queue.

The scheduler restores the context of the process and transfers control to it via an REI (circle 5). However, before the hardware is able to continue executing at the process level, IPL 0, it must service the interrupt requested at IPL 2, the AST level. The kernel AST routine BUFPOST gains control prior to the process. It is then able to transfer the status from the IRP back to the host process if required,[6] and update system accounting information for the process (circle 6). When all the ASTs for the process have been processed, the AST dispatcher executes its REI and the process resumes execution at the instruction following the $QIOW (circle 7). This action concludes the $QIO write example.

To review, the actual I/O operation consists of:

- Validating the $QIOW arguments.
- Initializing the I/O database with these values.

---

5. The example in Figure 8.14 did not have an event flag indicated, so event flag 0 is used by default.
6. The I/O status block is an optional argument to the $QIO system service routine.

- Queuing this information to the terminal driver.
- Changing the context to the I/O subsystem.
- Starting the terminal driver.
- Receiving an interrupt from the terminal controller and making another terminal driver queue entry.
- Looping between the terminal driver and the interrupt handler until the complete message is transmitted.
- Queuing an ACB to the PCB of the originating process.
- "Calling" the scheduler to switch the context back to the process and starting the AST.
- Resuming the process.

FORK PROCESSING

Now that the example is complete, it is important to discuss the purpose of the FORK level. The IPL 8 processing was included without any supporting explanation. Since drivers are shared—for instance, one terminal driver supports all the terminals—it is important that each part of the I/O request, say, transmit a character, be allowed to complete before another request using the terminal driver is processed. Execution at the FORK level[7] ensures that only one execution thread of a driver is operating and manipulating the I/O database at a time. This could be a problem because there is no scheduler in the I/O subsystem to save and restore the driver's context at arbitrary points; context switches occur only when priority levels are changed with the REI, as illustrated in Figure 8.25. There, the scenario begins with the terminal driver executing for SCOOTER at the FORK level (circle 1). As it is executing, a terminal interrupt for AIRWOLF arrives (circle 2) and is processed, since its IPL is higher than the FORK level. After device status is gathered by the interrupt handler, the rest of the processing executes at the FORK level. The level change is necessary to permit other interrupts. If continued execution at the lower level were allowed to happen immediately, SCOOTER's driver context would have to be saved first, and an interrupt does not do this. To avoid a full context switch, AIRWOLF's request is queued (circle 3), and execution at the lower level continues with SCOOTER's driver (circle 4) when the interrupt handler's REI is executed.

---

7. FORK 8 is shared by all I/O operations, not just terminal operations.

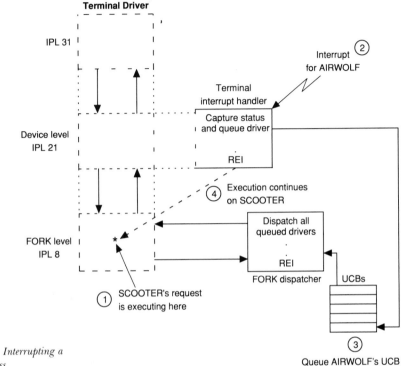

*Figure 8.25. Interrupting a
FORK process*

The reader should be sensitive by now to the fact that the sharing of
any resource carries the risk of nondeterministic operations if the sharing
behavior is not fully considered. Since the FORK queue is shared by code
at various IPLs, a semaphore mechanism must be used to ensure mutual
exclusion when entries are added or removed. The VAX designers considered this problem when designing the instruction set and provided six atomic
instructions for queue manipulation. Once the queuing instruction starts,
the entry will be added or removed from the specified queue, without any
other synchronizing logic,[8] before an interrupt is honored. Since the critical
region is one instruction long, it needs no LOCK and UNLOCK operations.

---

8. Four of the queue manipulation instructions are intended for multiprocessor environments; operating system requirements for multiprocessor environments are not covered
in this book.

8.5. The General AST Mechanism

An AST (asynchronous system trap) is a software-simulated interrupt mechanism provided by the VMS operating system that enables a process to be notified of the occurrence of an event specified in the user's image, asynchronously with respect to process execution. Using system service routines, the user declares an AST subroutine to be executed when the event occurs. When the specified event occurs, the user's process is interrupted and the user-declared AST subroutine is executed. When the AST subroutine exits, the operating system returns control to the interrupted process.

The VAX/VMS designers placed the AST at IPL 2, between the scheduler and the process, for a good reason. The exception caused by the AST executes subroutines in the context of the process rather than in the context of the I/O subsystem. Consider this sequence of events: first, an AST interrupt is requested by any element of the VMS system for a particular process. Next, the scheduler selects that process for execution, sets up the process's context, and then executes its REI instruction. Then, when the REI pops the PSL from the stack, changing the IPL to 0, the AST interrupt is granted, *delivering* the interrupt to an AST subroutine instead of returning to the process execution. When complete, the AST subroutine will execute another REI, thus permitting the process to execute.

The AST interrupt mechanism is activated by the scheduler's REI, otherwise it is very different from other software interrupt activations. Since the AST is process-specific (no other interrupt is), the REI has to determine whether or not to grant the IPL 2 interrupt. It knows that the IPL 2 interrupt belongs to a given process because it has examined an internal processor register called $PR_ASTLVL. A value of 4 means that no AST is pending for the process, 3 that a User mode AST is pending, 2 a supervisor mode AST, 1 an executive mode AST, and 0 a kernel mode AST. This register is loaded from the hardware PCB each time the process's context is loaded, so the act of queuing an ACB at the AST FORK, IPL 6, includes setting $PR_ASTLVL. To do this, the queuing routine must know if the process is CUR or not. If it is, the $PR_ASTLVL must be set; if not, the appropriate field in the hardware PCB must be set.

There is no possibility of interrupts below the AST level,[9] so all the ACBs are dequeued by the dispatcher and executed. An REI from the AST

9. VMS does not use IPL 1 for anything.

dispatcher causes the process to resume. When the AST subroutine is executing, other hardware interrupts are treated no differently. When the interrupt has been processed, the handler's REI permits the AST to continue execution.

AST EXAMPLE

The AST has some user-controlled applications. The user may define his or her own AST subroutine in conjunction with several system services. This special subroutine is executed according to conditions set forth by the particular system service. For instance, an AST subroutine may be declared to execute at the completion of a $QIO system service, in conjunction with a $QIO request, with the timer system service, with the lock system service, and so forth. Another AST system service, $DCLAST, permits the user, not the system, to originate the AST interrupt from anywhere in the image. When the interrupt is granted, the corresponding AST subprogram is executed immediately and behaves almost like a standard call mechanism.

The following example, depicted in Figure 8.26, illustrates a typical scenario using ASTs in conjunction with the $SETIMR (Set Timer) system service. This application is similar to the hibernate example in Chapter 3. The program will set the clock but then, instead of hibernating, continue executing. When the time has expired, the process will be interrupted to report the time. After the time has been reported, the process will resume executing.

The figure assumes that the user's program has called the $SETIMR system service. The $SETIMR call requests that the AST routine execute at a specific time (circle 1), which causes the system service to queue a countdown clock request (circle 2).[10] After this system service call, the program continues executing asynchronously. When the requested time has expired, the clock interrupt handler creates an AST request and queues it to the AST FORK, and the AST FORK adds an AST control block (ACB) on the AST queue of the process's PCB (circle 3). The clock interrupt handler also sets IPL 3 so that the scheduler will be "called."

When the time-out is reached, there is no guarantee that the target process is executing or even executable. The time of the event is not synchronized to process execution. The process may have been stopped in the

---

10. The clock interrupt handler has a FORK at IPL 7 that operates like the I/O FORKs. This detail is suppressed to simplify the example and make it consistent with Figure 8.8 and the accompanying explanation.

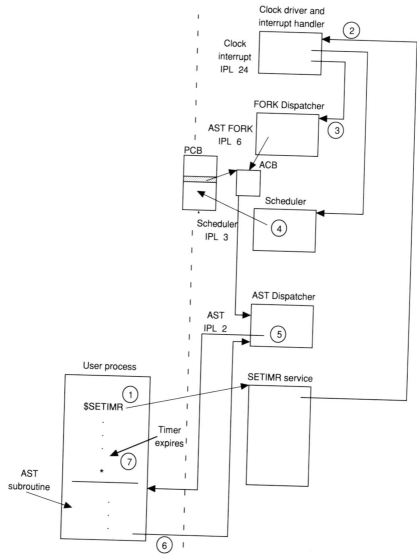

Figure 8.26. The logic of AST
interrupts

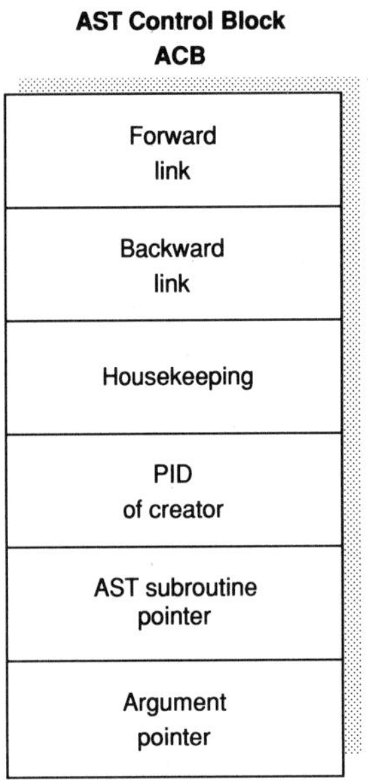

AST Control Block
ACB

Forward link
Backward link
Housekeeping
PID of creator
AST subroutine pointer
Argument pointer

Figure 8.27. Overview of the
ACB structure

meantime, for instance, to perform a $QIOW. If the process is blocked for some reason, the queuing of the ACB will cause the process to be scheduled (circle 4); the process state will change to COM in order to execute the specified AST routine. When selected for execution, the AST dispatcher (circle 5) will transfer into the process at the AST subroutine entry point and run at IPL 2 until the subroutine completes; then it will return to the dispatcher (circle 6). On the other hand, if the process is executing (circle 7) when the timer expires, the user-declared AST routine will preempt the process and the scheduler (circle 4) will continue execution with the AST dispatcher (circle 5). The dispatcher will transfer to the AST subroutine, which will execute and return to the dispatcher (circle 6), and the process will continue from where it was when the interrupt occurred (circle 7).

Figure 8.27 illustrates the format of the AST control block, showing the usual forward and backward links followed by the housekeeping bits. The PID of the creating process is maintained for diagnostic purposes. The two unique entries in this block are the address of the AST subroutine and the address of one argument to be delivered to that subroutine.

8.6. An AST Program

Since they require special knowledge and unrestricted access to the operating system, the design, implementation, and testing of a device driver are not practical on a time-shared computer. Moreover, since the need for device driver programming is so occasional, only one programmer in fifty is sufficiently trained to do it. Nevertheless, by exploiting the AST mechanism, we can investigate a primitive interrupt-like processing subroutine without special privileges and with only a little additional VAX Pascal knowledge. This VMS example, called CONTROL_C_AST, is powerful and often used in an application system.

The example program in Figure 8.28, is easy to understand, and the code is fairly simple to follow. As its name suggests, the program sets up an AST procedure to be executed whenever CTRL-C is struck. Normally, CTRL-C aborts the executing program, but by declaring an AST, the CTRL-C event passes to the process instead, overriding the DCL subsystem default action. CTRL-Y is unaffected by this program; its action remains unchanged. (Incidentally, there are other methods of gaining control of CTRL-C using a $QIO that does not involve an AST procedure.) To make it more interesting, the example is embellished with three other capabilities of the $QIO that were not previously mentioned: unechoed read, read with time-out, and prompt-read. A more extensive use of the I/O status block is required for this example as well.

CONTROL_C_AST DESCRIPTION

The program is designed to prompt, read, and echo a line from the terminal, and if the user does not respond to the prompt in five seconds, it prints a message and issues another prompt-read request. The user may respond with any string of characters or with a CTRL-C. In the former case, the string is echoed by the routine and not the VMS terminal driver; in the latter case, the read request is canceled and a message is displayed. The image loops forever, but CTRL-Y will abort it and return control to DCL.

The source lines in Figure 8.28 have been numbered to make the explanation, which will note only the salient lines of Pascal code, easier to follow.

```
1  [INHERIT ('SYS$LIBRARY:STARLET')]
                                    { Capture CONTROL-C with an AST }
2  PROGRAM CONTROL_C_AST (INPUT, OUTPUT);
     TYPE
3      word_integer = [WORD] 0..65535;
4      io_status = RECORD
                     io_stat, count: word_integer;
                     device_info: integer;
                   END;

     VAR
5      prompt: PACKED ARRAY [1..48] of CHAR :=
              'You have 5 seconds to enter data, or type CTRL/C';
6      buffer: VARYING [80] of CHAR;
7      tt_chan: word_integer;
8      ast_output: [VOLATILE] TEXT;
9      io_func: word_integer;
10     iostat_block: io_status;
11     counter: INTEGER;
12     sys_stat: INTEGER;


13  [ASYNCHRONOUS] PROCEDURE LIB$STOP (%IMMED cond_value: INTEGER);
    EXTERN;


14  [ASYNCHRONOUS, UNBOUND] PROCEDURE c_ast
                                    (channel:word_integer);


      VAR
15    cancel_stat: INTEGER;

      BEGIN {c_ast}
                                    { cancel all I/O on terminal }
16    cancel_stat := $CANCEL (channel);
17    IF NOT ODD (cancel_stat) THEN LIB$STOP (cancel_stat);
                                    { just write a message }
18    WRITELN (ast_output, 'you typed a CTRL/C');
      END;


19  PROCEDURE SET_AST;                        { enable CTRL/C AST }


      BEGIN
20    io_func := IO$_SETMODE + IO$M_CTRLCAST; { set mode for ^C AST }
21    sys_stat := $QIOW (chan := tt_chan,
                          func := io_func,
                          iosb := iostat_block,
                            p1 := %IMMED c_ast, { AST routine ... }
                            p2 := %REF tt_chan);     { called with this
                                                      argument }
22    IF NOT ODD (sys_stat) THEN LIB$STOP (sys_stat);
```

*Figure 8.28. An AST program
to capture CONTROL-C*

```
23  IF NOT ODD (iostat_block.io_stat)
                          THEN LIB$STOP (iostat_block.io_stat);


    END;
      BEGIN {main program}
                       { get output channel for c_ast }
24  OPEN (ast_output, 'TT:');
25  REWRITE (ast_output);
                       { get channel for terminal }
26  sys_stat := $ASSIGN (devnam := 'TT:', chan := tt_chan);
27  IF NOT ODD (sys_stat) THEN LIB$STOP (sys_stat);
28  SET_AST;
                       { loop until control-Y }
29  REPEAT
                       { issue timed prompt-read - no echo }
30    io_func := IO$_READPROMPT + IO$M_NOECHO + IO$M_TIMED;
31    sys_stat := $QIOW ( chan := tt_chan,
                          func := io_func,
                          iosb := iostat_block,
                          p1 := buffer.body,      { place for data }
                          p2 := size(buffer.body),{ data length }
                          p3 := 5,            { 5 second time-out }
                          p5 := %REF prompt,    { prompt message }
                          p6 := size(prompt));{ prompt length }
32    IF NOT ODD (sys_stat) THEN LIB$STOP (sys_stat);
33    buffer.length := iostat_block.count;


                       { check status and leave message }
34    IF iostat_block.io_stat = SS$_NORMAL
35      THEN WRITELN ('You typed: ', buffer)


36    ELSE IF iostat_block.io_stat = SS$_CONTROLC
          THEN BEGIN
37            WRITELN ('Request was canceled');
38            SET_AST;
          END
39    ELSE IF iostat_block.io_stat = SS$_TIMEOUT
40      THEN WRITELN ('You didn"t respond in time')
      ELSE
41        WRITELN ('junk I/O status', iostat_block.io_stat);
42    WRITELN;


43 UNTIL FALSE


    END.
```

Figure 8.28. (cont.)

Line 3.

VAX Pascal has no predefined 16-bit type; all variables are either bytes or 32-bit quantities. This declaration creates a 16-bit data type.

Line 4.

This program needs to access the "io_stat" and "count" fields within the "iostat block" (declared in line 10) in lines 33 through 39. This record is declared so that the program can examine the results returned by the $QIOW call.

Line 5.

This is the prompt message that will be displayed by the read request. The prompt-read operation takes the place of a WRITE-READLN pair. Unlike Pascal, $QIO provides this function with a single call (lines 30–31), which minimizes the number of trips through the $QIO system service and ensures that the response is paired with the prompt. VAX Pascal allows variables to be initialized in this way when they are declared at the PROGRAM (or MODULE) level; these variables are termed "static."

Line 6.

VARYING is like a PACKED ARRAY OF CHAR with the character count appended automatically. Other versions of Pascal use STRING to mean the same thing.

Line 8.

Any global variable referenced by an AST routine (lines 14–18) must have the [VOLATILE] attribute appended to it. This prohibits Pascal from optimizing certain code sequences.

Line 13.

LIB$STOP is a procedure provided in the VMS run-time library. When called, it stops the image and prints the value of the argument, which, in this and most applications, is the error code returned by a system service call. It also produces a traceback, which offers an extremely convenient debug tool. LIB$STOP is called throughout the CONTROL_C_AST program if any system service call returns an error condition. The traceback produced on the user's screen will indicate where the error occurs by the line number. Notice throughout this program that when a system service returns an even number, it is considered an error, whereas an odd number is considered a success. This RSX-11 convention was adopted because only one bit, the low-order bit, has to be tested to determine if an error occurred. The "%IMMED" attribute on the argument forces Pascal to pass the value rather than the value's address as it normally would. LIB$STOP expects a value, not the address of the variable, in its argument.

Line 14.
This is the process's AST routine. Any AST declaration must have the [ASYNCHRONOUS, UNBOUND] attributes. AST routines are different from conventional routines because they can be "called" at any point in the execution of the program. Therefore, the normal assumptions that the Pascal compiler makes about a subroutine's environment must be invalidated using these two attributes. For instance, to optimize the object code, Pascal may assume that a certain variable is stored in a register, not memory. There are two restrictions the user must respect when designing an AST routine. One, there can be, at most, one argument to an AST subroutine, and it must not be a VAR. And two, the AST subroutine must be a PROCEDURE; if data must be returned by the AST routine, a global variable is the only means available. These two broad restrictions distinguish AST subroutines, which otherwise are declared and used as other Pascal subprograms.

Line 15.
Local variables within the AST routine are permitted, and there are no special restrictions or attributes associated with them.

Lines 16–17.
The active I/O is the read request, which is canceled when the user strikes CTRL-C. The $CANCEL system service is designed for this purpose. Once

an AST routine is running, no other AST will interrupt it because all ASTs execute at IPL 2. Even if the programmer declares another AST via $DCLAST, that request will not be honored until the first AST finishes and returns. Other pending ASTs are then delivered one at a time. ACBs are FIFO ordered in the AST dispatcher's queue.

Line 18.

This is the message to the user. The file name, "ast_output," is created in the main program at lines 24 and 25.

Line 19.

This subroutine is called twice in the main program to enable or declare the AST to the I/O handler.

Lines 20–21.

This $QIOW declares the AST routine to be called whenever CTRL-C is struck. In line 20, the desired I/O function is specified. IO$_SETMODE is used to direct the driver to change its operational characteristics. In other words, this $QIOW request does not pass data to the terminal. The IO$_CTRLCAST value indicates to the driver that the information being sent via the $QIOW concerns a CTRL-C AST. In line 21, the address of the AST routine to be used (pl :=) when a CTRL-C is detected is sent to the driver. "%IMMED" means pass the value—in this case, the address of the routine. The argument to the AST routine is identified by the p2 := argument; in this case, the channel number (line 26) is passed to the AST. "%REF" means to pass the address. All Pascal subprogram arguments are assumed to be addresses, and there is no way to override this. When declared in Pascal, as on line 14, the "channel" argument must be an address or the procedure will not execute correctly.

Lines 22–23.

Two checks must be made on this $QIOW service. Line 22 is checking to see that the arguments are correct or if any other error occurred. And, line

23 is testing the result of the $QIOW operation to see that the AST has been properly declared and is functional. Notice that the two IF statements are testing different variables to determine that the service operated correctly.

Now the main program begins. Lines 24 through 28 are initialization logic, and lines 29 through 43 constitute the body of the example.

Lines 24–25.
If an AST is to do writing, it must have its own channel. Normally, the channel allocation takes place outside of the AST routine because of the amount of time it takes. AST routines should be kept as short as possible, since all other ASTs are blocked when one is executing. I/O in the AST can be performed either by OPEN-REWRITE-WRITE, as in this example, or by using $ASSIGN-$QIO, as shown further on in the program. Both methods have advantages and disadvantages.

Lines 26–27.
The $ASSIGN service is required because $QIOWs are used in the body of the program, and $QIOWs need channel numbers, not file names. The $QIOW in this example (line 31) is necessary because Pascal does not offer the specific functions required. Pascal READLN and WRITELN are used whenever possible, since the $QIOW is laborious and error-prone to use. The program consistently checks all VMS system service calls to be sure that the arguments are valid.

Line 28.
The AST is declared.

Line 29.
A never-ending REPEAT loop is entered, and a CTRL-C will not terminate it, since the image is coded to intercept that keystroke. The remainder of the main program is an infinite loop because the condition of the UNTIL (line 43) will never be satisfied. The program has no provision to exit the loop, so the user must resort to CTRL-Y to terminate the program.

Lines 30–31.

This is the fundamental unechoed, timed, prompt-read $QIOW request. Line 30 defines the function with the three attributes, and the function is used in line 31. The two lines are unnecessary, but it is more readable this way. The arguments "p1" and "p2" specify the location of the buffer that is to receive the keyboard line and its length. The "p3" argument specifies the time-out value in seconds. And the arguments "p5" and "p6" specify the prompt message and its length. The $QIOW will block the process until one of three events happen: the user enters data followed by a RETURN, the time-out takes place, or CTRL-C is struck.

Line 33.

The actual number of characters entered by the user is stored by the driver (actually by I/O postprocessing, as previously seen) in the I/O status block; it must be retrieved so that the "buffer" can be displayed in line 35 without trailing garbage. Line 33 initializes the variable "buffer" so the WRITELN will present the data nicely in line 35.

Lines 34–42.

Three things can happen to terminate the I/O request: a CTRL-C is entered, nothing is entered within five seconds, or a valid string is entered. The three cases of I/O status are treated differently in the program. The final ELSE is included because it is always good coding practice to expect every condition when dealing with system services; never say, "That case will never happen" because it will.

Lines 34–35.

These lines echo the user's keystrokes.

Lines 36–38.

These lines are executed when CTRL-C is entered. The program arrives at this point after the AST PROCEDURE has executed. Whenever a CTRL-C is keyed, the $QIOW is canceled, so the final line redeclares the CTRL-C AST.

Lines 39–40.

This code is executed when the user fails to respond after five seconds.

Line 42.

The extra WRITELN is necessary to advance the cursor to the next line prior to the read-prompt $QIO because there is no carriage control associated with the prompt message. It can be included in the string that contains the prompt message.

8.7. Direct Memory Access

The terminal I/O described in the examples so far is a typical application of PIO (Programmed I/O) operations. In contrast, by reducing software intervention, direct memory access (DMA) provides vastly enhanced data transfer, because data moves to and from memory faster than PIO by several orders of magnitude. As shown in the example, PIO operations typically transfer only one character at a time, and there is a considerable amount of software processing associated with each transfer. In DMA I/O, the transfer is executed not by the operating system but by the device controller. As the term DMA implies, data is transferred to or from memory by the controller without benefit of multiple interrupts. Thus, many thousands of characters, potentially, can be transferred without operating system intervention. This scheme frees the operating system from housekeeping tasks and ultimately means that the user process receives more CPU cycles per second.

Figure 8.29 schematically summarizes the two read operations, PIO and DMA. It represents the CPU, a single device controller, memory, and a bus that connects these units. (Without elaborating on Digital architecture, consider the bus a bidirectional data path.) In Figure 8.29a, the PIO operation requires that each character be transferred first from the device to the CPU and then from the CPU to memory. In Figure 8.29b, the DMA operations totally circumvent the CPU, and data is transferred directly from the device to memory.

The DMA controller is more complex than the PIO controller. Likewise, the software driver that controls the DMA controller is different from

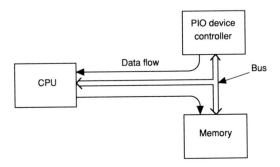

a) Programmed I/O (read)

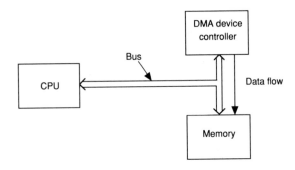

b) Direct Memory Access (read)

Figure 8.29. A comparison of a read operation using direct memory access (DMA) and programmed I/O (PIO)

the PIO driver. For one thing, it is more complicated—the DMA driver must provide several additional pieces of information to the controller and then start it. Typical information required for a read operation includes:

- A source address, for example, a disk address of the data to be read
- A count of the number of bytes to transfer
- A memory address for the first byte

Once the controller is started, it transfers data sequentially from the source to the memory, counting and incrementing source and destination addresses as the data is passed. When all the data has been moved, the controller interrupts the CPU in the manner described earlier. This interrupt is used by the operating system to post the I/O operation and, if necessary, to start another on the device.

Thus, the controller itself has assumed most of the I/O responsibility and runs asynchronously to the CPU; several units[11] of data may be transferred while a single instruction is executing, and data may be passed in bursts because of the particular characteristics of the device. For instance, a disk may have to rotate several degrees before the data is located, and then data streams from the disk to memory for several more degrees.

The operating system, although excused from the actual data transfer responsibilities, must be aware of the details of the operation. For instance, the area of memory dedicated to the DMA transfer is normally considered inaccessible by the rest of the system; two DMA devices should not be writing to the same locations in memory simultaneously, and simultaneous DMA and CPU access should be prohibited. Another detail the operating system must keep track of is making sure a page frame of memory is made ineligible for reuse during the DMA operation. The demand paging algorithm must include a frame "lock down" bit for the duration of the transfer. In this context, "locked" means it must remain in the process's working set, which will prohibit the operating system from selecting that frame for any other purpose.

Since the operating system is not involved, DMA transfers free the CPU for other tasks, such as executing programs. However, in order for the CPU to execute any program, the instructions and data must be read from memory into the CPU, and data must be stored back in memory. This

---

11. Depending on the device and the bus, bytes, words, longwords, or quadwords may be moved as a unit. It is not unusual to transfer tens of megabits per second.

means that in a system that supports DMA devices, memory must be designed to accept data simultaneously from two (or more) sources, the CPU and any of the DMA devices attached to the bus. There are various solutions to this problem. One is to alternate or *interleave* CPU and DMA accesses. A second is to provide multiple buses, thereby providing multiple entry ports into memory; say, the CPU has a private bus to memory and the I/O devices share another bus. Various manufacturers have implemented these and other solutions.

8.8. Accessing Hardware Devices

Many times this book refers to the device driver "telling" the device controller what to do, by accessing registers within the controller. Now is the time to explain what this means. There are two ways to approach this explanation, and each revolves around a different concept of mainframe I/O. IBM's concept centers on a *channel*, which is a very intelligent device controller—in fact, a small computer. Digital's concept centers on direct addressing of devices.

The IBM channel must be programmed in a language unrelated to the computer's language. This program, called a channel program, is transferred to the channel by a special host instruction, execute I/O (XIO). The channel uses DMA to transfer the channel program from the computer's memory to its own memory, and then it executes the program from there, relieving the CPU to do other things.

Figure 8.30 illustrates channel-directed I/O. First, the device driver must build the channel program (circle 1)—including the necessary parameters such as destination address, source address, and length of data to be transferred—into the body of the program. Next, the driver executes the XIO instruction, directing the channel to the program it just created (circle 2). Using DMA, the channel then copies the channel program (circle 3) into its memory and begins to execute it. In the meantime, after issuing the XIO, the host computer continues execution on some other activity. When the channel reaches the end of its channel program (circle 4), it interrupts the host, which must post I/O completion and (possibly) prepare another channel program (circle 5). Data transfers implied by the channel program are DMA, under control of the channel.

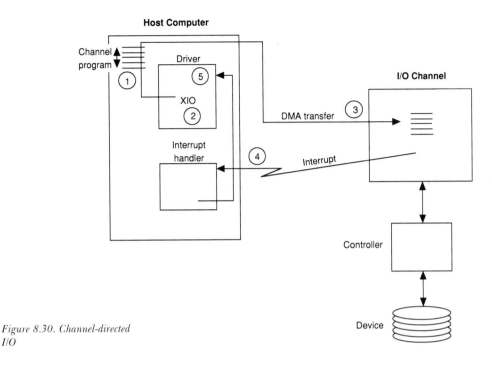

Figure 8.30. Channel-directed I/O

UNIBUS ADDRESSING

Digital's concept of device accessing is different. Instead of a channel, it uses normal instructions (not an XIO) with special addresses. For instance, to transfer data to a register within a controller, a MOV{B,W,L} instruction can be used, or to test if a particular bit is set in the controller's register, the BIT{B,W,L} instruction can be used. No special instructions are provided in the VAX architecture that pertain only to controllers, but there are restrictions. For one, not all instructions can be used on controllers, and for another, some addressing modes are prohibited when addressing I/O controllers (floating and quadword instructions, for example, are not supported). However, even though the instruction set is limited in this way, many instructions remain, and this restricted subset does not limit the software engineer in the design of device drivers. This uniform method of addressing both memory and I/O devices using a single bus was developed for the PDP-11 and is called *UNIBUS addressing*.

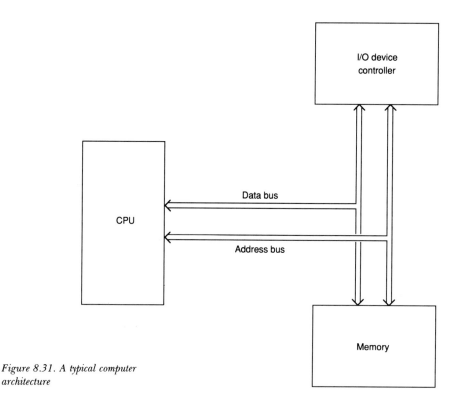

Figure 8.31. A typical computer architecture

To understand how the computer knows the difference between a MOVL to a memory address and MOVL to an I/O device, refer to Figure 8.31. This figure embellishes the VAX architecture diagram in Figure 8.29, and separates the bus into two components: one to carry an address and the other to carry the data. This is a very simple model of how the hardware operates as the CPU reads data:

- The CPU sends the address to the *address bus.*
- Either the I/O controller or memory responds by sending the corresponding data back to the CPU on the data bus. If neither responds within a certain amount of time, a *bus time-out error* occurs.
- The CPU receives the data from the *data bus,* not knowing how it got there.

Thus, there can be no overlap between memory addresses and I/O device addresses, but the designers must decide the address or group of addresses to be assigned to specific devices. By convention, memory starts at address 0 and increases, and I/O address space begins well above the last memory location. Typically, there is an address "hole" between the largest memory address and the smallest I/O address. The starting point of I/O space varies with the VAX model; an 11/750 begins at 00,F00,000 (hexadecimal), while an 8600 begins at 20,000,000 (hexadecimal) because of the maximum memory permitted on the various machines.

Addressing is much more complicated than this, however. Hardware automatically converts a virtual address to a physical address, but it is the physical address that rides the bus, since memory and I/O controllers are physical address devices.[12] Addressing the device is not the problem; the problem is that when dealing with DMA transfers, a physical memory buffer address is needed, because the data to be transferred are either located in a buffer (write operation) or are going to be moved into a buffer (read operation). When the process and the device driver operate, they are dealing strictly with virtual addresses, and physical address translation is transparent to the software.

There are three ways to solve this virtural to physical address translation problem. The first is to include a hardware instruction to perform virtual-to-physical translation by accepting an input virtual address and producing a physical address. With such an instruction, the device driver could do the translation itself prior to sending the buffer address to the controller. However, there is no such instruction, although the PROBEx instruction comes close. The other two solutions, used by the VMS operating system, put the total addressing burden on the controller. The philosophy embodied in the VAX is that the DMA controller is designed to be "smart," relieving the CPU from as much of the I/O task as possible; the I/O hardware must do the translations itself.

The first VMS method is to pass the buffer's page frame number (PFN) to the I/O controller along with the virtual address. If the buffer spans multiple frames, a PFN for each frame must be passed because, as Chapter 4 illustrated, a contiguous virtual buffer is not necessarily contiguous in physical space. Using the PFNs, the controller can construct the required physical address.

The other VMS method is the more intelligent solution: pass the virtual address of the process's page table to the controller. Then the I/O hardware can look up the PFNs it needs, and the entire translation problem

---

12. In this model, memory can be thought of as simply one more device.

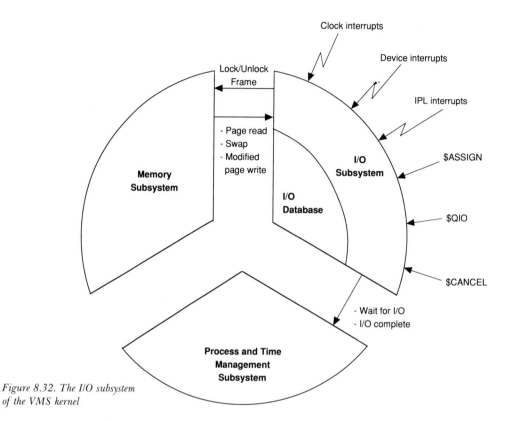

Figure 8.32. The I/O subsystem of the VMS kernel

must be solved by the I/O controller. Recall that the page tables are located in SYS space, so the device controller also needs the system page table to find the process's page table in physical space in both VMS solutions. Furthermore, since the page tables are pageable, the operating system must "lock down" the process's page tables for the same reason that the buffer must be locked down.

8.9. I/O Subsystem Design

Figure 8.32 illustrates the final third of the VMS kernel, the I/O subsystem. This subsystem must service clock and device interrupts as well as various software interrupts it creates. It also supports several system services, including $ASSIGN, $QIO, and $CANCEL. The I/O database reflects the physical hardware; that is, there is one UCB for every device connected to the system. Except for mailboxes and I/O request packets (IRPs), the majority of the database is static and built when the system is created. IRPs are created in response to user and system requests and are dynamically assigned and released.

The subsystem must also interface with the other two-thirds of the kernel to signal the scheduler to wait for change states for I/O completion and then signal it again when the I/O is complete. The VMS operating system is designed so that the I/O subsystem has no direct access to the scheduler database and must signal the change to a process's state. This design isolates the subsystems better, making them easier to maintain. Consistent with that philosophy, the I/O subsystem does all of the page I/O for the memory management subsystem. This interface is a special $QIO request that bypasses much of the checking to improve system performance. Reading process pages and writing the modified pages, as well as process swap logic, are supported by the I/O subsystem, which also signals that frames are to be locked down during DMA processing and makes these requests to the memory management subsystem.

8.10. Related Issues

The organization of I/O subsystems varies as widely as the computer architecture does; an IBM mainframe and an IBM PS/2, for example, have no software in common, even though they are made by the same company. In fact, memory-mapped video found on IBM personal computers is a concept that more closely matches the VAX I/O architecture than it does IBM mainframes. VAX architecture varies too, but it has enough commonality so that the VMS software will run on all models. The VAX was originally designed with this goal in mind—to permit all software to be completely compatible—and that goal has been faithfully respected from model to model.

The I/O architecture is the major reason for differences and incompatibilities between computers, such as the bus structure and how the I/O devices communicate with the CPU and memory. Other variations in the I/O hardware show up across the various computer architectures in how interrupts are implemented. Many machines reserve a portion of memory to receive and route interrupts; on the PDP-11, the first 1,000 bytes of memory are reserved for this purpose. Other machines use the uppermost part of memory to locate the interrupt vector, and some computers make no attempt to localize interrupt locations in a contiguous portion of memory.

The VAX is unique in that its interrupt vector is not fixed in memory; instead, a single register contains the vector's base location. From a software viewpoint, this makes excellent sense because it allows the operating system to select the "best" location.

The difficulty of supporting a single operating system across a combination of architectures and configurations (such as the amount of installed memory and number and type of attached I/O devices) is immense. The operating system must tailor itself to the specific installation by loading the proper I/O drivers and adjusting its buffers and data structures to be consistent with the expected user load. It would be ridiculous to size the operating system to run on a microVAX II and then run it on an 8600. At the very least, the maximum number of users (processes) is considerably different on the two machines. Conversely, if the microVAX operating system was sized to meet the 8600 needs, it would have no memory left for legitimate users because of the operating system's data structure size. The operating system must have the freedom to assign data structure sizes, so the interrupt vector itself cannot be static.

Digital has enhanced VAX Pascal and other high-level languages so that programmers can take full advantage of VMS system services and features (such as ASTs) without resorting to assembly language routines. This philosophy permits programs to be more understandable because they are written in a high-level language. However, to accommodate these extended capabilities, the language must become more complex, which makes it harder to learn and use properly. The application system designers must make a trade-off: complicate the Pascal code with the extensions, or use assembly language routines to access the required operating system features.

It was stated that hardware interfaces for I/O devices are not standard within the industry but there are some exceptions. In the personal computer marketplace, interfaces to components such as hard disk drives and graphics support are becoming standardized by the manufacturers for their own benefit. In the minicomputer marketplace, Digital has been instrumental in defining the VT100 terminal hardware interface to the RS232C standard as well as the software interface's use of escape sequences to control certain logical functions, such as cursor movement and character enhancements. This software interface is now called the ASCII interface and is recognized by both terminal hardware and terminal software companies.

It is interesting to note that in personal computer software, drivers are not considered the responsibility of the operating system. For instance, when buying a word processor, the printer driver is included in it. Then, if a spreadsheet application is added later, it too includes a printer driver. But the user has to be careful that the application he or she is buying supports the printer. Likewise, there is no guarantee that all the drivers needed to run a particular application will fit into memory—this form of memory management is the user's problem.

Even though many I/O topics were covered, several were omitted to simplify the presentation. The information omitted is not trivial or unimportant, but the added detail it would have provided would not have enhanced overall understanding of the complexity of the subsystem.

The major topic left out was error handling in the I/O devices. Not only must the software be made aware when the hardware fails, it is the software's responsibility to report on the failure and attempt to recover from it. Error recovery is not a generic issue; different hardware requires different treatment. However, reporting has a common solution. In the VMS system, all hardware errors are passed to a standard process called ERRFMT, which records the failure in a disk file for later investigation. The only difficulty with this solution is that it presents further complications if the disk itself fails. ERRFMT provides data for a summary display with the following unprivileged command:

```
$ SHOW ERROR
```

Error reporting has three forms: the hardware diagnoses itself and reports the error, the hardware reports an impossible or ridiculous condition, or the hardware refuses to respond to a request. The last case is handled in a uniform way in the VMS system. Whenever an I/O request is made to a device controller, a timer is started. If the time limit is reached before the controller responds, the assumption is made that the hardware failed in some mysterious way, and it is reported accordingly. The next step in this error scenario is for the driver to either try again or to abandon the attempt. Of course, successful I/O operations must cancel the timer request. Clearly this is a large responsibility for the clock logic.

A side benefit of this hardware error reporting logic is that errors discovered by the operating system within itself (for instance, the discovery of inconsistent data structures) can be similarly reported. Normally, when the operating system discovers an internal error, it stops itself after reporting it. This is so Digital engineers can examine the current conditions of the operating system databases before the error is masked or compounded by other errors related to or caused by the first one.

Another major function of the I/O subsystem is recovery after a power failure. The consequences of a power failure are felt most strongly in this area of the system. If one results in the loss of the contents of memory, clearly no simple graceful recovery can take place; however, monetary power fluctuations are often completely recoverable. If main memory is not lost, only currently active I/O operations may be affected. Some operations, such as reading a disk, can simply be restarted: others, such as reading from a keyboard, are ignored.

8.11. Summary

Just as I/O architectures vary across the industry, so do the I/O subsystems that support them. Because meaningful generalities about I/O subsystems are difficult to make, this chapter elaborated on the VMS implementation in order to give the reader an appreciation of the complexity of the subject. In addition, we limited our examples to VAX/VMS in order to delve deeply into the subject. Since I/O comprises one-third of the VMS operating system, the I/O third of the VMS kernel was examined in some detail, although certainly not enough to permit the reader to write a driver (this is a feature the VMS operating system supports, however). The emphasis was on understanding the entire subsystem by dissecting it, so that the relationships between the hardware architecture and the software design can be thoroughly appreciated and understood.

The I/O subsystem design cannot be developed without knowledge of the interrupt priority level hardware, and the IPL is closely related to the operation of the REI (Return from Exception or Interrupt) instruction. This chapter looked at how the hardware devices interrupt and set the priority level and how software can do the same by manipulating processor registers. We showed how the interrupt handlers can preempt one another and compared the I/O subsystem to a miniature version of the operating system by drawing parallels whenever possible.

This chapter then explained the steps taken during a write $QIOW. In examining these steps, we saw that the AST logic plays an important role in communicating with the process. However, the AST has a broader application and an example was presented to illustrate both the AST and the interrupt concept. While investigating the $QIOW, several related issues were mentioned, namely logical names, VMS memory utilization, and synchronous and asynchronous system services.

To round out the I/O discussion, we introduced other hardware issues to show, generally, how a program communicates with a device controller. First, both programmed I/O (PIO) and direct memory access (DMA) were examined and compared. Secondly, the discussion of the DMA concept raised other questions about the treatment of virtual addresses. Finally, we discussed how a program accesses a device, either by direct addressing or through channel programs.

ACRONYMS

$ASSIGN	Assign channel system service
$CANCEL	Cancel I/O system service
$CREMBX	Create Mailbox system service
$DCLAST	Declare Asynchronous System Trap system service
$QIOW	Queue Input/Output operation and Wait system service
$SETIMR	Set Timer system service
ACB	AST Control Block
ANSI	American National Standards Institute
AST	Asynchronous System Trap
CCB	Channel Control Block
CHMK	Assembly instruction to Change Mode to Kernel
CHMx	Generic assembly instruction to Change Mode
CPU	Central Processing Unit
DMA	Direct Memory Access
ERRLOG	Error Log
FIFO	First In First Out
HOL	Higher-Order Language
IPL	Interrupt Priority Level
IPR	Internal Processor Register
IRP	I/O Request Packet
LDPCTX	Assembly instruction to Load Process Context
LIB$STOP	RTL routine to stop an image
LRP	Large Request Packet
MFPR	Assembly instruction to Move From Processor Register

MTPR	Assembly instruction to Move To Processor Register
PC	Program Counter
PFN	Page Frame Number
PID	Process Identification
PIO	Programmed I/O
PROBEx	Generic assembly instruction to PROBE memory
PSL	Processor Status Longword
PSW	Processor Status Word
REI	Assembly instruction to Return from Exception or Interrupt
SCB	System Control Block
SIRR	Software Interrupt Request Register
SIRS	Software Interrupt Request Status register
SRP	Small Request Packet
UCB	Unit Control Block
XIO	Execute I/O

SHORT ANSWER EXERCISES

1. Why must both the process's page tables and the DMA buffer be "locked down" in order to perform DMA transfers?

2. Suppose the $QIOW example was a read instead of a write. When does the read buffer get allocated? When does it get transferred to the process?

3. Suppose you were to design the "read ahead" logic for the VMS operating system. How would the example change with the inclusion of the read ahead buffer? Is the buffer permanently allocated? Are there two buffers or one? Is the read ahead buffer bypassed when a read is in progress and used only when there is no read outstanding?

4. Suppose the buffer address of a $QIOW write operation is some location in the VMS system. Now, assume that the $QIOW does not validate your arguments. What happens? How does this invalidate system security?

5. Why is $QIO a FUNCTION instead of a PROCEDURE? Or, stated another way, why does $QIO report argument errors via the function's value instead of via the I/O status block argument?

6. You must have access to a VAX assembly language textbook that includes a description of the PROBEx instruction, or to the VAX

architecture handbook, to do this exercise. The PROBEx instruction only checks two locations. In checking a $QIO request, the PROBEx is used to check both ends of the status block. The PROBEx test of the buffer must be somewhat smarter; outline that algorithm.

7. What is the consequence of stacked clock interrupts? What happens if a clock interrupt is not granted within 10 milliseconds?

8. This chapter alluded to the fact that I/O interrupt routines may request a scheduler interrupt. Outline a scenario to describe such a case.

9. Rewrite the hardware steps required to write data using the style of the three-step algorithm in Section 8.8.

10. Why does interrupt priority level 0 not need a software interrupt, as stated in Section 8.1?

PROJECTS

1. Write a program that writes 20 lines to the terminal using $QIOWs. Then make a copy of the program that uses $QIOs instead. Compare the execution time of the two programs. There are two execution times to consider: the elapsed time (or wall time) and the CPU time (or time consumed by the CPU). Can you draw any performance conclusions about the two methods? Is one better than the other? Why or why not? If your terminals are very fast, you may have to write more than 20 lines to the screen before you can draw any conclusions.

2. Explain why a $QIOW is generally necessary when reading data. Fabricate and test a simple program that fails to execute correctly with a $QIO.

3. Design a program with an AST subroutine that is entered via CTRL-C. Show how it becomes like an interrupt processor. Modifying Figure 8.28 is a good approach to this project.

4. Use $QIOW on a terminal to perform
   • "Read-pass-all"
   • No echo
   • One-character-at-a-time input
   • Display of the character

Design your program to interpret unprintable characters like TAB, ESC, and BACKSPACE and print an appropriate symbol instead of the character.

5. Code the CONTROL_C_AST program and execute it enough to decide how the five-second time-out is treated by the VMS operating system. For instance, if you respond with at least one character in five seconds, does the time-out logic terminate? Does it mean that you must hit the carriage return in five seconds? Or does it mean that you can type one character every five seconds and still correctly terminate? Are there other interpretations? Design and perform a series of tests to determine empirically how VMS works. Then write a paper describing your assumptions, approach, test results, and conclusions.

6. Design and code the $SETIMR program suggested in Section 8.5.

PAPERS

1. Prepare a paper outlining the advantages and disadvantages of the two I/O methods developed in this chapter: $ASSIGN-$QIO and OPEN-RESET-READ.

2. Discuss the pros and cons of the addition of the attribute constructs such as VOLATILE, ASYNCHRONOUS, and so forth to the Pascal language. What advantage is there to such a philosophy? What is the cost?

3. Illustrate a $QIOW read operation to the same level of detail presented in the write example. The answer to this is not in the text; educated guesses and intuition must be the guide. Accompany your figure with the necessary narrative.

4. Compare and contrast the hardware PCB and the software PCB.

Disks and Disk Files

9

Before learning about files and file structures, it is necessary to understand the *physical* structure of the common *secondary*[1] storage medium, the magnetic disk. In large measure, the disk's physical structure and its limitations dictate how it is used to store data files. To be specific, a *disk* is the magnetic medium on which the data are stored. A *disk drive* is a larger hardware system that includes the disk and its supporting machinery—record-playback (or read-write) heads, the arm that holds them, the positioner (or actuator) that moves them, the motor that spins the disk, and the electronics that control these components. To this end, the characteristics of disks and disk drives are presented first.

After describing the hardware, we will turn to the logical organization of the data on the disk. The *logical* file structure is maintained by the file subsystem, a subset of the operating system. No general purpose operating system is functional unless it has file system capabilities, no matter how

---

1. The *primary* storage medium is memory Tape is normally considered a *tertiary* storage medium. This ordering is based on access time.

primitive. The only exception to this observation is an embedded real-time operating system in which the entire application, its data, and the operating system are permanently memory-resident, for instance, a weapons control system on a tactical fighter plane or the software in an automobile. Typical of these real-time systems are RSX-11S for the PDP-11 and some operating systems for microcomputers, like the 68000 family.

9.1. Physical Characteristics of a Disk

The first file[2] medium used for program and data storage was inch-wide paper tape in which round holes represented the data. Paper tape was popular long before the computer revolution and dates to the turn of the century. It was used primarily in the news industry and military community for recording and transmitting messages. Paper tape reading and writing is very slow, and the tape is difficult to handle and store. Today, data stored on paper tape would be called a sequential file. The next file medium to be developed was the IBM card[3]—a deck of cards represented a file to which the user was permitted random access but the computer regarded as a sequential file. For the most part, paper tape and IBM cards are no longer used.

Magnetic media was introduced to the computer industry in the early 1950s. This technology grew out of the sound recording industry. The first magnetic storage device was a drum,[4] but it had very limited capacity. The IBM 650 employed a drum for main memory as did several small computers. However, it was so expensive that paper tape and cards were the I/O media and no data was permanently stored on drum. Drums are random access devices but are rarely used today because disks are less expensive. In the late 1950s, magnetic tape was perfected and used for long-term storage of sequential files. This has proven to be the most popular magnetic medium developed. In the middle 1960s, disks become generally available, and with them, random file accessibility became practical.

Figure 9.1 presents some of the important characteristics of the file

---

2. The term "file" did not come into use until the late 1950s with the advent of magnetic tape. File names were introduced with multiprogramming systems.
3. The IBM card predated paper tape, but in the 1950s, paper tape dominated the programming industry because the KSR 33 teletype unit was used on many computers.
4. A drum is now referred to as a fixed head (immovable) disk.

Device	Read-write	Access	Speed
Paper tape	Read only	Sequential	10 bytes/sec
IBM cards	Read only	Sequential	1.5 kilobytes/sec
Magnetic tape	Read and destructive write	Sequential	3 megabytes/sec
Disk	Read and write	Sequential and random	3 megabyte/sec

Figure 9.1. File medium characteristics

media. Both paper tape and IBM cards are write-once media; however, the card reader is a much faster device than paper tape primarily because 80 characters[5] can be stored on a single card. On the other hand, magnetic tape can be rewritten. In order to change a single item in the middle of the tape, however, all data from that point to the end must be rewritten. The audio cassette has the same property; there is no way to replace a single "cut" in the middle of a tape. However, it is easy to extend a data file on tape by first positioning the tape to the end of the existing data and then adding the new data. Since magnetic data is packed densely on the tape, high data rates are possible. A disk has all the properties of tape; additionally, it can be randomly accessed for both read and write operations.

A disk is logically divided into *tracks* and *sectors*.[6] Tracks are concentric magnetic paths, and each track is divided into sectors, as shown in Figure 9.2. The tracks and sectors are defined when the disk is formatted, not in the factory; there are no physical marks on the disk that reveal these structures. As each sector is defined during the format operation, its track and sector numbers are written on the disk so the hardware can, repeatedly and reliably, find its way back to a specific disk location. The normal configuration of a large capacity disk drive, called a hard drive in personal computer nomenclature, contains a stack of several double-sided disks on a single spindle. Several surfaces, or sides, are available for data storage. Three

5. Incidentally, when the terminal was developed, the number of characters on an IBM card determined the number of characters presented on a terminal screen.
6. *Physical record* and *block* are synonyms for sector.

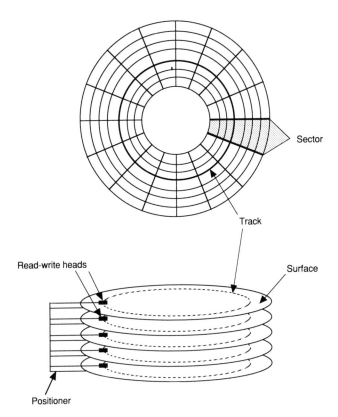

*Figure 9.2. The components of a
disk*

numbers, surface, track, and sector, are required to identify a specific sector
on such a disk system. Most disks define a sector as 512 bytes. Unlike memory, which can be addressed to a specific byte, a disk can be addressed only
to a sector; any smaller granularity must be supported in software, as will
be explained.

Figure 9.2 indicates that there is a *read-write head* for each surface of
the disk. To minimize the hardware requirements, all the read-write heads
travel together on a mechanism called the *positioner*. The hardware moves,
or *actuates*, the positioner in a radial direction from the outer edge to a point
near the center. Reading or writing a data sector requires several steps to
be taken by the disk hardware. First, to position the head to the specified

track, the read-write head assembly is moved to locate, or seek, approximately the track number. Then, as the disk spins, the track-sector addresses are read from it. The beginning of a sector is identified with a particular bit pattern followed by the address. Once each address is located and interpreted, the hardware can determine if it has reached the specified track, and if not, it readjusts the read-write head position. When the head is positioned to the proper track, the hardware must wait until the specified sector rotates under the read-write head. Finally, when the sector arrives, the data is transferred to the controller and then to the CPU at the rate the disk surface passes by the read-write head.

The time, or *latency*, to read or write a sector has three components. The *seek* time is the time required to position the head to the desired track. The *rotation time* is the time spent waiting for the disk to revolve to the desired sector. The average rotational time is one-half the rotation period; that is, on average, the disk must turn halfway around before the specific sector is reached. The third component is the data *transfer time*, the time required for the sector to pass under the read-write head. Figure 9.3 summarizes typical disk drive characteristics, in particular, two Digital disks and two representative personal computer disks—two floppies and two hard disk systems.

The seek time is a complicated quantity; it is discontinuous because the head positioner speed is limited, as shown in Figure 9.4. To move "x" tracks, it must accelerate for half the distance and then decelerate the rest of the way, unless the maximum velocity is reached. This profile is a result of hardware limitations—for instance, the RA90 tracks are approximately $\frac{1}{1000}$-inch wide. The head mechanism must be able to move accurately over about a 2½-inch range and remain fixed over the desired track indefinitely. The positioner can move from one track to an adjacent one in 5 milliseconds and from the inner track to the outer track in 40. These times are limited by the mass of both the heads and the positioner. Scaled up, the acceleration required is equivalent to an automobile going from 0 to 100 mph in less than half a second.

The term *cylinder* is also used when discussing disk characteristics. It refers to the vertical collection of corresponding tracks on each *surface*. For example, cylinder 5 represents all tracks numbered 5 on each of the surfaces. In this sense, a cylinder and a track are the same thing—the cylinder is a three-dimensional extension of the track. This results in the two addressing nomenclatures depicted in Figure 9.5: [cylinder, track, sector] (top); and

Characteristic	RX23 floppy*	RA90*	Typical PC 360K floppy	Typical PC hard drive
Platter size (diameter, inches)	3.5	9	5.25	5.25
Capacity (megabytes)	1.4	1216	0.36	42
Number of surfaces	2	13	2	5
Tracks per surface	80	2648	40	973
Sectors per track	18	69	9	17
Bytes per sector	512	512	512	512
Average seek delay (milliseconds)	94	18.5	77	28
Average rotation delay (milliseconds)	100	8.3	100	8.3
Transfer rate (megabytes per second)	0.05	2.8	0.03	0.6

* Digital products

Figure 9.3. Representative disk drive characteristics

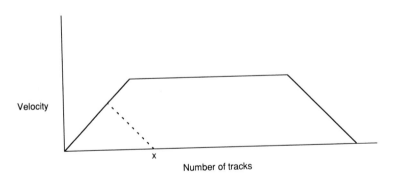

Figure 9.4. Disk positioner velocity profile

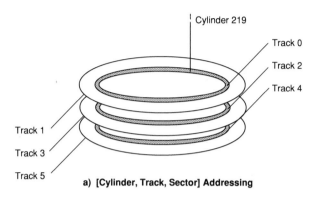

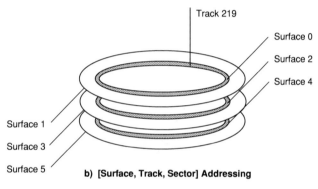

Figure 9.5. Alternate disk address nomenclature

[surface, track, sector] (bottom).[7] In both cases, the geometry and capacity of the disk are the same; the only difference is the terminology.

Because of the geometry of the disk, a large percentage of it is unused. This is a result of the fact that the sector length (in inches, not bit capacity) grows as the radius increases, yet the number of bits in the sector remains constant. Therefore, the bit density is highest at the inner radius. At the rim, the bit density may be half the innermost density, and this represents a problem of wasted space on the disk. There are two ways to solve this problem: either vary the speed of the disk as a function of head position or

7. This chapter will use the [surface, track, sector] notation throughout.

vary the data write rate as a function of head position. Both methods involve considerably more hardware than is currently available, and changing the disk speed would drastically reduce performance because of the time required for acceleration or deceleration. In either case, the number of sectors per track would have to vary, which, as we will see, would have software implications. A third way to solve the problem of wasted space is to vary the capacity of the sectors, but since this complicates the software so much, it is not even considered.

Hard disks are rigid, not flexible (floppy). Historically, these were made with a mixture of magnetic oxide and a plastic material that was bonded to a substantial aluminum disk. The current technology electroplates a magnetic medium on a nonmagnetic disk to produce a thin magnetic surface and permit high bit densities.

The rigid disk construction allows the disk assembly to be rotated at a high rate, 3,600 rpm or higher, without deformation. However, at this speed, if the read-write head were to touch the surface of the disk, the heat caused by the friction would cause both to melt or burn. On the other hand, to be most effective and to keep the tracks narrow, the read-write head must be kept as close to the surface as possible, about 10 microinches—less than the diameter of a human hair. To achieve this, the read-write head is attached to a *slider*, which provides the aerodynamic stability for it to literally fly, or glide safely, over the surface of the disk.

Scaled up, the flying disk head and slider assembly is like a 747 flying a foot above the ground. So, if the read-write head touches the surface, *crashing* is a most appropriate term. The more precise term, however, is *contamination-induced touchdown*. To reduce the possibility of contamination, a hard disk is hermetically sealed in a dust-free environment. An assembly composed of two heads[8] and a slider attached to its positioner arm is compared to a mechanical pencil in Figure 9.6. The heads are fastened to the back of the slider, which constitutes the majority of the mass.

Floppy disks do not have an aerodynamic problem. At 300 rpm, they spin much more slowly than a rigid disk, so the head can safely ride in contact with the disk surface without creating destructive friction. However, because of this constant contact between the heads and the surface, both components suffer deterioration and wear.

The disk controller is a direct memory access (DMA) device. (The

8. This is an RA90 disk head; it has two heads per surface to enhance performance.

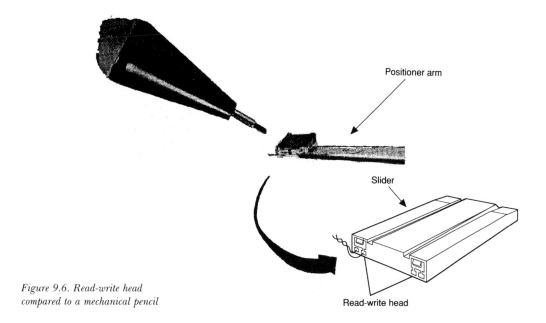

Positioner arm

Slider

Figure 9.6. Read-write head
compared to a mechanical pencil

Read-write head

operation of DMA and programmed I/O (PIO) was treated in Chapter 8.) After the head is positioned to the proper track, and when the required sector rotates under the head, the movement of the disk's surface determines the rate at which data is transferred from the disk to the controller. This rate is determined by the physical aspects of the system, not by software. The controller has an internal buffer to store the data as it streams to or from the disk. Then, for instance, after the sector read operation is complete, the buffered data is transferred into memory. Figure 9.7 illustrates this two-step operation. Notice that, on average, the transfer to memory must keep up with the transfer from disk because, generally, the controller is tasked to read another sector while a DMA transfer is taking place. Therefore, the buffers must be freed up as soon as possible.

More advanced controllers have several buffers in which to store the data so that disk performance is maximized. Multiple buffers are required when consecutive sectors will be read because there is not enough time to empty the buffer before it is needed again. Once the sector is reached, there can be no delays because the disk is spinning; the data must be transferred from the read head at exactly the proper time. If a buffer is unavailable to receive the data, the disk must rotate a full revolution while the buffer is

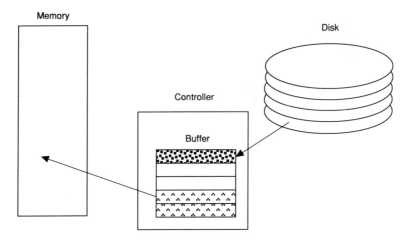

*Figure 9.7. A disk read
operation*

emptied and released. A similar scenario takes place for writing data onto a disk; the data must be available in the controller's buffer prior to the specified sector being located.

In some cases, particularly in minicomputer applications, the controller buffer is absent. This is seen as a way to reduce the disk hardware cost. However, this design adversely affects performance. When adjacent sectors are to be transferred, the software must send the I/O request for the second sector to the controller within a few microseconds of the receipt of the first sector, which is an impossible timing requirement. As a consequence, the disk controller must wait nearly a full revolution for the desired sector to reach the read-write head, thus significantly reducing the effective disk data transfer rate. To compensate for this hardware deficiency, the sectors are staggered or *interleaved,* as illustrated in Figure 9.8. Unknown to the software file manager, the disk controller considers sectors n and n + 1 to be separated by one or more sectors; thus, logically, consecutive sectors are physically separated by one, two, or more sectors on the disk. This separation gives the software enough time to formulate and send an I/O request to the controller before the data reaches the head.

Sector numbering is performed when the disk is formatted, and the interleave *gap* is defined at that time. Once the disk is formatted with a specific interleave assignment, it cannot be changed without causing the data to be destroyed. The disadvantage of interleaving is that when all the sectors

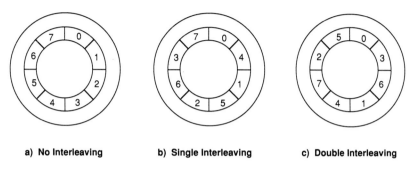

a) No Interleaving   b) Single Interleaving   c) Double Interleaving

Figure 9.8. Disk sector interleaving

of a given track must be read, it can be done in one revolution only when there is no interleaving; it takes two revolutions if the disk is arranged for single interleaving, three revolutions for double interleaving, and so forth. Of course, the alternative is undesirable too: if the controller is unable to keep up, eight revolutions are required to read the track when the disk is formatted without interleaving in the example.

The primary characteristic that makes the disk randomly accessible is that a specific sector can be repeatedly and reliably located. Another factor is that to move from one sector on the disk to any other one takes, at most, a few milliseconds, and most of this time is spent in positioning the read-write head. In contrast, randomly positioning a tape takes approximately a thousand times longer; it takes several minutes to move from the beginning of a tape to the end. A third favorable characteristic of a disk is that once the head is properly positioned, the sector contains a fixed number of bytes; this allows writing, reading, and rewriting of specific information without regard to the other information adjacent to the sector or anywhere else on the disk. With tape, on the other hand, even if it is properly positioned, it is impossible without extraordinary precautions to replace an existing data block with a new one. However, blocks may vary in size on a tape.

9.2. Disk File Management

Designing a system for storing data on disk involves a set of tradeoffs. First, the designer must decide how the data is to be stored in the sector, since

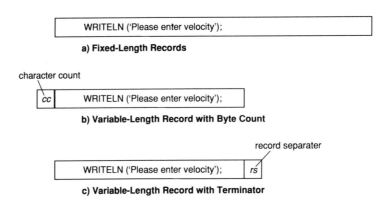

*Figure 9.9. Three methods of rec-
ord representation*

the number of bytes of data is not necessarily the same as the sector capacity. Then, the designer must decide how the sectors are to be associated to form the file; somehow, the sector numbers that contain the data must be saved. In a time-sharing system, these decisions are complicated by the fact that many users will need access to the disk and so the data must be protected and shared in the ways considered in Chapter 7. It must be secure, private, and protected from both accidental or deliberate abuses, and if required, it must be shared under user control. Finally, since file operations are frequent, the file system must be efficient and fast—efficient in the use of memory and disk space and fast in processing a user's request.

A file is composed of records. A *record* is a user-defined collection of related data items or *fields* that are to be treated as a unit. The record concept originated in tape nomenclature. Originally, tapes were copies of IBM card decks; one card became a record on tape, and the deck became a file. Today, instead of an IBM card, each record is a line of the program.

Storage of the record on disk can be achieved in three ways: fixed-length records, variable-length records with a byte count, and variable-length records with a terminator—all illustrated in Figure 9.9. The first method, fixed-length, shown in Figure 9.9a, stores exactly 80 characters, including blanks, in a record. But this is not very space efficient because most lines are only partially filled. So, to conserve disk space, the trailing (or rightmost) blanks are deleted but leading blanks are retained. This results in a variable-length record. There are two ways to store the variable-length record. The first method, illustrated in Figure 9.9b, counts the number of characters in the record and stores that count as the first byte of the record. The second method, shown in Figure 9.9c, terminates each record with a special, unprintable character such as 1E (hexadecimal), called a *record separator*. If all three methods cannot be supported, the file subsystem designer must make a tradeoff of disk space and execution time when deciding to append (method 1) or remove (method 2 and 3) trailing blanks. Fixed-length records require more space on disk but are easier to place and locate on it. On the other hand, variable-length records take less room on disk, but, as explained below, require more software to place and locate.

Once the record storage scheme has been decided, the next decision is how the record is to be stored in the sector. Storing one record per sector leads to poor utilization of the disk, since a normal record is less than 80 bytes whereas sectors are usually several hundred bytes. So, multiple records must be stored together or *blocked* in each sector; and the designer must decide if records can span sectors or if unused space will be left intact. Figure 9.10 illustrates these two alternatives. In the first scheme, the records are completely contained in the sector, which means that some amount of wasted space in each sector is inevitable. In the second scheme, the records extend across sectors. Here, multiple sector accesses will occasionally be required to read or write a record.

DIRECTORY AND FREE SPACE MANAGEMENT

No matter which record storage method is selected, a file will be stored over several sectors of the disk. This means that the file subsystem of the operating system must manage two more disk file properties: first, the location or directory of user and system files, and, second, the disk's unused space. Free space must be managed so that when a user process needs to create or extend a file, it can readily be supplied.

FILE ADDRESSING

Normally, a process refers to a file symbolically by name, not by an absolute disk address. In fact, a process has no information concerning a file's location because the disk surface, track, and sector are unknown to the user program. Consequently, the file subsystem must maintain a *directory* that associates the file's name to its location. This location is expressed as a series of ordered sector addresses that contain the file. Further, by relegating the task of sector assignments to the file subsystem, this not only relieves the user process from

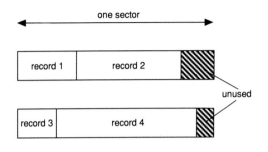

a) Records Do Not Span Sectors

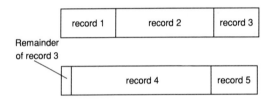

b) Records Span Sectors

Figure 9.10. Two record alloca-
tion schemes

tedious detail, but permits convenient sharing of the disk resource. If users chose sectors for their files themselves, some method of ensuring that multiple users did not choose the same sector would have to be devised.

There are several schemes for linking sectors to form a file. The most obvious is *contiguously,* in adjacent sectors, so that the directory need contain only the address of the initial sector and a count of sectors that contain the file. This method works well for certain trivial applications, but some provision must be made to extend the file; for example, when the file is lengthened, it may have to be copied to a larger empty portion of the disk. A way to avoid this complication is to augment the contiguous scheme by leaving the initial allocation in place and storing the *extension* in some other contiguous area of the disk. Then a thread between the original and the extension must be saved in the directory. This creates a file containing one or more collections of contiguous sectors, and, in time, may result in a disk with many small contiguous empty sectors, none of which are large enough to contain the extension of any file. It also puts a burden on the file subsystem to identify and coalesce adjacent groups of contiguous empty sectors whenever possible—a nontrivial and time-consuming problem that we introduced in Chapter 4.

A better solution assigns one sector at a time to the file. This is termed linked or *threaded* allocation. With this algorithm, the file's sectors can be anywhere on the disk, and the problem of unusable space disappears. One method of implementing threaded allocation is by recording the first sector's address in the directory, the second sector's address in a reserved field within the first sector, and so forth, as Figure 9.11 indicates. The final sector can have a special code in the link field to signify the end-of-file. The problem with the threaded allocation is that it does not permit random access to the file—and that, after all, is one of the major advantages of storing a file on disk. To reach the last record of the file, for instance, every sector, but not necessarily every record, must be accessed sequentially.

A far better way to permit random access to the file is to store all of the sector addresses in the directory itself, as shown in the bottom of Figure 9.11. This is called *indexed* allocation. To find the xth sector of a file, the file system merely indexes to the file's x^{th} sector address. Indexed allocation requires that the directory be much larger than the threaded algorithm, but the total space consumed by the two methods is the same. An added benefit of indexed allocation is that there are no inherent timing disadvantages. Suppose a user needs to read the nth sector of a file. Further suppose the $n-1^{th}$ sector is located at [4,927,14] and the nth is at [5,927,14], directly "below" its predecessor. If the file is threaded, after reading the $n-1^{th}$ sector, the system has to wait one disk revolution to read the nth sector, but there is no such limitation in indexed allocation because the $n-1^{th}$ sector does not have to be accessed at all.

The issues of privacy and reliability enter into the file allocation algorithm. If the allocation thread is stored with the data, it could be subjected to either accidental or deliberate modification, thus compromising the entire file structure. From a security standpoint, it is far better to store the allocation information in a restricted structure such as the directory. The VMS operating system takes this approach one step further by maintaining a separate, system-private structure called the Index File apart from the directory.

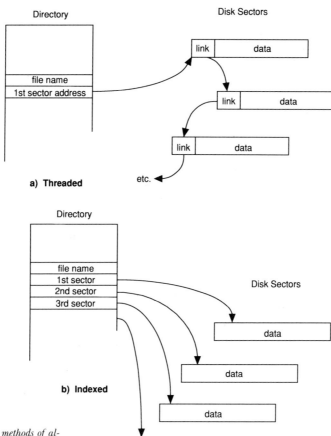

Figure 9.11. Two methods of allocating sectors to a file

FREE SPACE MANAGEMENT

The second major responsibility of the file management subsystem is maintaining a record of empty sectors. Because of privacy and security issues, this algorithm and structure must be entirely separated from the user. When the user releases or deletes a file, the data is not erased from the disk because of the time involved. (Some high security systems offer this additional step when deleting files as an option, however.) In most file subsystems, all the sectors of the deleted file are merely returned to a pool of empty sectors. If this pool were public, the dedicated hacker could reconstruct the file contents and thus invalidate most of the system's security features.

The database for empty sector administration can be part of the data file management, or it can be held separately, for example, in a special system file. Although intuitively appealing, however, the latter scheme is rarely implemented because it is costly in time and space.

BITMAP

First, look at a design involving the maintenance of an independent sector utilization map, in which a single bit is designated for each sector and signifies whether or not the sector is allocated. Suppose a 512-megabyte disk is organized in 512-byte sectors, that is, into 1 million sectors. The *bitmap* of the disk is considered a three-dimensional array, one dimension for each ordinal, [surface, track, sector]. (Three-dimensional linear mapping is well known; it is also used to map a three-dimensional matrix into memory.) At one bit per sector, 1 million bits occupies 125,000 bytes. If this bitmap were to reside in memory, it would represent a significant overhead in most systems. The bitmap scheme becomes more complex if there are a variable number of sectors per track because the function that maps the three dimensions of the disk address into a linear address is much more complicated. The VMS operating system uses a bitmap scheme that will be investigated in depth.

One method used to reduce the overhead of this housekeeping information is to group or *cluster* the sectors.[9] Then, a bitmap entry represents a cluster of sectors rather than only one. The justification for clustering sectors is that normal files are typically much larger than 512 bytes. In reducing the bitmap overhead, another problem arises: wasted disk space at the end of every file. For example, when clustering four 512-byte sectors (2,048 byte clusters), if only one byte is written in the cluster, 2,047 bytes are unused and unusable by others. On the average, half of the last cluster, or two sectors (1,024 bytes), will be unused in each file on the disk; however, the bitmap is reduced by a factor of four to 31,250 (125,000 ÷ 4) bytes in this example. The tradeoff is this: to reduce the resident bitmap size causes an increase in the unusable disk space. The wasted disk space is a form of *internal fragmentation*, which Chapter 4 introduced in its discussion of paging.

Even so, the tradeoff picture is incomplete. When a file is created, the system does not normally know in advance how large it will be. When a user

---

9. The remainder of the discussion will use the more general term, cluster, rather than sector.

creates or updates a file with an editor, there is no possible way to determine its eventual size; the file subsystem assigns clusters to the file one at a time, as needed. Because the disk is shared by others doing the same thing, there is no reason to expect that the file's clusters will be contiguous on the disk. More likely, each extension of the file will occupy a noncontiguous cluster. This condition is termed *external fragmentation.* Commonly, internal fragmentation is simply ignored, and when someone refers to "fragmentation" alone, external fragmentation is meant. When a file is said to be fragmented, it means that it is assigned discontiguous clusters on disk.

The disadvantage of a fragmented file is that file access time can be greatly increased because the disk head must be moved several times when the entire file is being accessed—as much as once for each cluster. To minimize fragmentation, the clusters must be *physically contiguous,* which means that cluster 1 of the file is physically adjacent to cluster 2, and so forth. One method used to reduce fragmentation is to allocate several contiguous clusters when the file is created. If the file is completed before all the clusters are used, the unused clusters are returned to the free cluster pool. If additional clusters are needed, another contiguous group of clusters is logically appended to the first. This second group is probably fragmented from the first, but the file itself is less fragmented overall.

COMBINING FREE SPACE AND DATA MANAGEMENT

If free disk space is to be maintained in conjunction with used space, a more elaborate scheme of threading clusters, typified by MS-DOS version 3, can be used. This scheme implements a composite of threading and linking clusters. A structure called the file allocation table (FAT) replaces both the bitmap and the cluster links as Figure 9.12 indicates, but a directory is still required. The FAT is indexed by the cluster number, which is stored in the directory; each entry in the FAT contains the next cluster number in the file. For historical reasons, the first FAT entry is cluster 2; 0 and 1 are reserved for system files. Figure 9.12 also indicates the meaning of the link value in a FAT entry: unusable clusters are specifically indicated in the FAT. As with the bitmap method, clustering saves FAT memory space. A FAT entry is 2 bytes;[10] hence, an unsigned hexadecimal value between 0 and

---

10. MS-DOS 2 maintained a 1.5-byte-per-entry FAT. MS-DOS 3 uses a 2-byte-per-entry FAT.

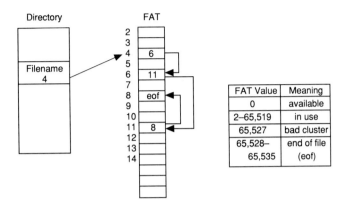

*Figure 9.12. MS-DOS file allo-
cation table*

FFFF, or 64K (65,536), value can be stored. This would require 128K bytes
to be stored in memory, which is considered too large for a 640K machine.
Depending on disk capacity, sectors are clustered and the FAT is made
smaller. For instance, on a 32 megabyte disk, each entry of the FAT points
to a 4-sector cluster. Even with this compression, the FAT requires 64 sectors
to store on the disk.

Consider an example that outlines the steps required to read a particular record, r, from an MS-DOS disk. The user thinks of his or her file
as a collection of uniform records numbered from 0, but the system has
gathered several records together in a cluster of sectors to reduce housekeeping overhead. The hardware treats each sector separately and does not
maintain either file or cluster information. Figure 9.13 shows how a particular record is logically located within a sector that is part of a cluster. For
the rth record of the file to be read, its cluster number and sector within the
cluster must be computed. The integer division quotient and remainder
yield these two values.

Returning to the FAT scheme for this example, assume the length of
all the records in the file is uniform. The record length and sector size
determine how many records are stored in a cluster, R. The desired record
will be located in relative cluster number, C, of the file by performing integer
division according to

```
C := r DIV R
```

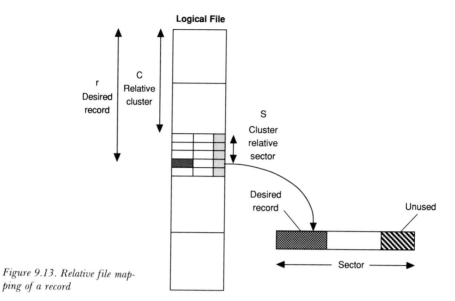

Figure 9.13. Relative file mapping of a record

Assuming there are K records per sector, the relative sector number, S, within the cluster, C, is

    S := (r MOD R) DIV K

and the relative record within that sector, rr, is

    rr := (r MOD R) MOD K

Throughout, the notation assumes that all numbering begins with 0; that is, the first record in the file, (r = 0), is in relative cluster 0, (C = 0), relative sector 0, (S = 0). These equations are evaluated for Figure 9.13, assuming r = 26, with R = 10. The first equation locates the third cluster, that is, C is 2. In the next two equations, using K = 2, S is found to be 3 and rr is 0.

Once the variables have been calculated, the search algorithm must thread through the FAT C times to determine the physical sector number of the first sector of the Cth cluster in the file. Adding S to this sector number yields the physical sector number containing the desired record. Figure 9.14 illustrates the transformation from logical to physical disk address, [surface, track, sector]. Finally, when the physical sector is read, the record must be located within the sector and delivered to the requesting program.

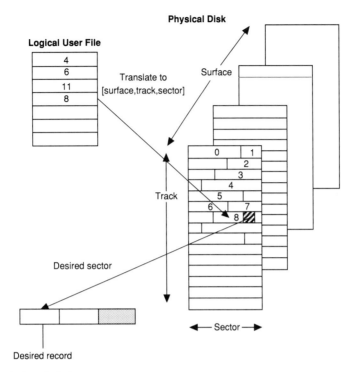

Figure 9.14. Logical to physical disk mapping

9.3. Disk Scheduling

The disk and the user files contained on it are shared and managed by the file subsystem. In order to minimize the impact of the file subsystem on process execution time, the disk must be managed just as the other system resources are. The previous section introduced file management. This section discusses time management.

Disk head movement contributes the greatest part of the three components of the timing equation. Thus, the first level of time management, seek latency, orders the disk access requests in a way that minimizes overall head movement. The second level of time management, rotational latency, is at the sector level; the current position of the disk determines the request processing order. This level of scheduling takes place only when there are

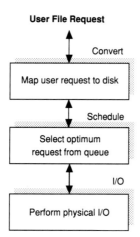

User File Request

Convert

Map user request to disk

Schedule

Select optimum
request from queue

I/O

Perform physical I/O

*Figure 9.15. Three abstraction
levels of the file subsystem*

multiple requests for the same track. The rotational delay also becomes important when several disks are involved. By minimizing head movement and rotation delay, the file subsystem will delay some requests. FIFO is not the optimum solution to this scheduling problem, although it is the most obvious one.

In the following algorithms, suppose there is a queue of disk requests. This is not so unusual because the disk scheduler operates in a time-sharing environment. To further complicate the situation, queued requests may also result from file fragmentation and may require several I/O requests to transfer completely. Figure 9.15 depicts a three-level file subsystem design. The top level maps the user's file request into a series of disk requests. Mapping was discussed in the previous section. The middle and lowest levels schedule and perform the I/O requests, respectively. These are the topics discussed next.

Although the simplest disk scheduling is FIFO, it is not the best for overall system performance. This point was argued in the discussion of CPU and memory management; the time-sharing operating system schedules for the best response time in a community setting, which may result in unfair treatment at the individual level. The same is true of disk scheduling. For instance, if the next request in the queue requires a large head movement, it means a delay to all the remaining requests in the queue. If one of the other requests can be serviced faster, it will be performed at the expense of the first request.

The four scheduling algorithms to be described scan the disk request queue to determine which request to honor next. Thus, a disk request to read several records from a fragmented file may not be processed sequentially; instead, the last fragment may be the first one read.

The first disk scheduling algorithm, called *shortest seek time first* (SSTF), must be cognizant of the current head position and then search the queue for the request nearest to the current position, which it services first by moving the head in either forward or backward. SSTF has a serious flaw, although it may not be obvious—since the request queue is not static, some requests may never be served without special attention because the head never gets close enough to them. To be certain that every request is honored eventually, three variations of SSTF have been developed, called scan, c-scan, and n-scan.

The second scheduling algorithm is called *scan* because it moves the head in one direction only until no more requests in that direction remain in the queue; then, it reverses itself, and all the requests in the opposite direction are serviced. This is also called the *elevator algorithm.*

The third algorithm is called *c-scan* (circular scan). It services requests in one direction only—for instance, toward the disk's center—until no more requests remain in the queue. It then returns the head to the outer edge without processing any requests and again scans toward the center. This is essentially a unidirectional scan algorithm in which the inner track is logically considered to be next to the outer track.

The fourth algorithm is called *n-scan*. This is another scan-derived algorithm, which does not permit additions to the queue until the head is reversed. New requests are ignored until the present requests are all serviced.

There is no best disk scheduling algorithm, and variations of the four presented are under investigation. All have subtle disadvantages. Figure 9.16 illustrates the behavior of three of these algorithms in a particular example. The FIFO, SSTF, and scan algorithms are applied to a static disk queue containing requests for data in tracks 112, 681, 907, 442, and 1,091 in that order. The initial position of the head is assumed to be track 711. In all three cases, the total distance the head must travel to service the queue has been computed. The disadvantage of FIFO is quite apparent, but the advantage of scan over SSTF is not obvious. In the scan example, the head was initially moved to the left. This is arbitrary, and the results might be altered by moving the head initially to the right.

The three abstraction levels presented in Figure 9.15 are a convenient subdivision of functions, but they are not necessarily the only solution.

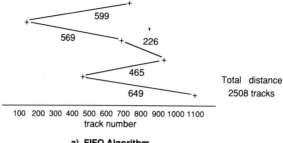

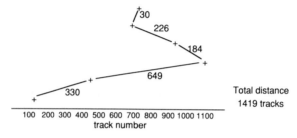

a) **FIFO Algorithm**

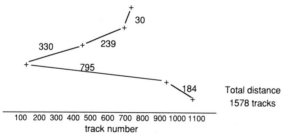

b) **SSTF Algorithm**

c) **Scan Algorithm**

Figure 9.16. Three disk schedul-
ing algorithms

Access method	Major characteristics
Sequential	Consecutive access, forward only
Direct	Sequential or random access by record number
Indexed	Random access by key within record then random or sequential thereafter

Figure 9.17. Comparison of file access methods

Controllers are becoming more intelligent because the scheduling responsibility is migrating from the file subsystem to the controller; the last two abstraction levels are interchanged in newer systems. This is especially true in personal computer networks, where the disk *server* (the computer dedicated to processing disk requests) optimizes system throughput, not individual requests. This is also true of Digital's clusters of computers where a collection of CPUs share a pool of disks.

9.4. File Organization

To this point, the file has been regarded as simply containing records, and very little has been said about how it is internally logically organized. This section will examine three file access methods: sequential, direct, and indexed, at two abstraction levels: the user's view and the file subsystem's view. Most readers will have had some experience with sequential file structure, and many have also dealt with direct files. However, probably few have worked with indexed files.

This section also discusses file operations; the functions the user is permitted to perform on a file organized in a particular manner. The two file access methods normally found in all file subsystems are sequential and direct. The third, indexed, is found in only the more robust systems. Figure 9.17 summarizes the dominant characteristics of the three types of file organizations. These characteristics are general, and a given system may implement some operations on these files differently. For instance, the VMS operating system will allow direct access to sequential files (with restrictions), while other systems will not.

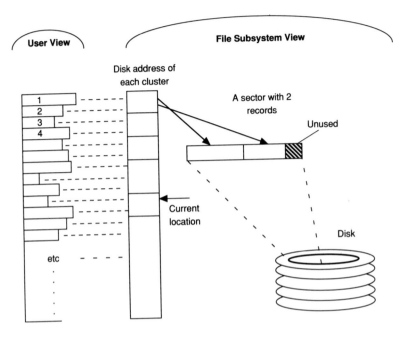

Figure 9.18. Two views of a sequential file

SEQUENTIAL FILES

Looked at in more detail, Figure 9.17 shows that a *sequential* file on disk mimics what can be done on tape; variable- or fixed-length records are accessed consecutively and only in one direction, from beginning to end. The records are not numbered, but simply follow one another. When records are being read, the end-of-file must be treated specially because there is no way to anticipate it. The rewind[11] operation logically resets a pointer that is internal to the file subsystem to the first record, but no physical motion takes place.

Figure 9.18 illustrates the user and subsystem views of sequential files. On the left, the user views the file as an ordered collection of variable-length records. On the right, the file subsystem maintains a corresponding list of disk sector addresses and a pointer to the currently accessed record. As the user works through the file, the file subsystem advances this pointer to locate

11. Rewind is a term historically associated with tape files.

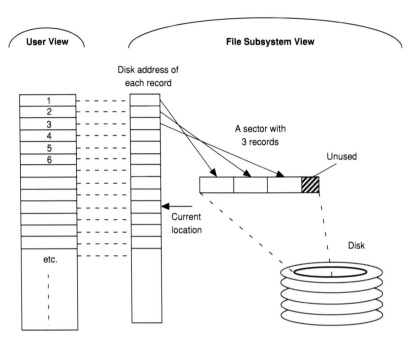

Figure 9.19. Two views of a direct file

(when reading) or position (when writing) records. The records are likely to be blocked within the sector, but the user does not have to account for this. Records cannot be deleted from the file or inserted: they can only be added to the end. Sequential files do not normally permit shared access because there is only one pointer.

DIRECT FILES

A *direct* file can be accessed randomly by record number. This implies that the file subsystem must maintain additional, more detailed information to locate a record, as Figure 9.19 indicates. Moreover, to allow for speed in the location algorithm, the records must all be the same length. When a direct file is accessed, a record number must accompany the request for a read or a write operation. This requires that the user's process maintain some information that relates the content of the record to the record number—say the user program hashes a social security number to transform it into a record number. The rewind operation is generally not required, since the user process can just as easily position the file to the first record.

With direct files, the file subsystem may permit a read of a particular record before a write. Depending on the implementation details, this unusual operation may result in undefined data because there is no data to read. That is why, for the sake of security, a read before a write is normally prohibited. The user must initially declare the size of a direct file so that the file subsystem can initialize the index. A read or write operation beyond this declared limit results in an end-of-file or error condition. Direct files can usually be accessed sequentially as well as randomly, but the file subsystem must be notified of this usage, since a pointer is required. A record in a direct file can be deleted or rewritten, but the file cannot be extended; thus, there is no way to insert a record between existing records in a direct file. An important characteristic of a direct file is that several processes may share it simultaneously because they can access different records in the same file. Only one process at a time can access a given record, however.

INDEXED FILES

With the advent of database applications, more advanced file access methods were needed as records became further subdivided into *fields*. The field concept should be clear to Pascal, C, and COBOL programmers who have studied record structures. An employee record, for example, is divided into one field for name, another for address, a third for social security number, and so forth.

Thus, with the addition of fields, the record number is a rather coarse retrieval key when a program requests the record for a specific "employee number." Furthermore, multiple keys are necessary. To handle fields, a complex intermediate structure, a *key index,* replaces the direct file's simple indexing scheme. Figure 9.20 illustrates the two views of an *indexed* file.

In the file subsystem, a key index structure is maintained in which the keys' values are sorted. Associated with each key value is the disk address of the corresponding data record. In general, there is no need to keep the file arranged in any particular order because the key index itself is ordered. Besides, there may be multiple keys within the file and therefore multiple index structures, but there is only one data file.

In the center of Figure 9.20, a second key structure is suggested in the background. On the left, the user is unaware of the indexing structure and views the file as a series of ordered records. Each record contains an

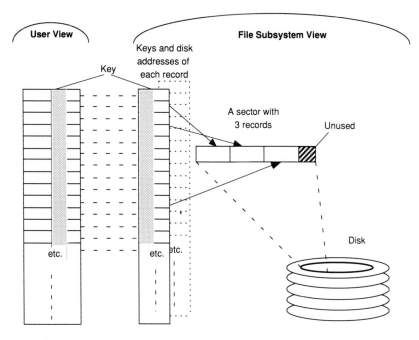

Figure 9.20. Two views of an
indexed file

embedded key and can be stored or retrieved randomly. As each record is written, it will appear to be inserted in the proper position according to the key's value.

These three file access methods are implemented by adding a fourth abstraction level to Figure 9.15, shown in Figure 9.21—the identification level. In this level, the user process's request is translated by means of an auxiliary data structure into a cluster number and record position within the cluster before mapping the request, scheduling, and performing the physical operation.

9.5. Maintaining Disk Integrity

There are three levels of integrity the file subsystem must provide beyond the normal privacy and security required:

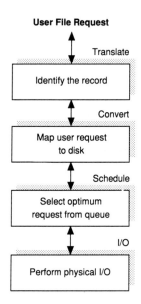

User File Request

Translate

Identify the record

Convert

Map user request
to disk

Schedule

Select optimum
request from queue

I/O

Perform physical I/O

*Figure 9.21. Four abstraction
levels of the file subsystem*

- Maintaining the disk structure in case the computer suddenly stops
- Coping with physical errors in the disk media without losing user data
- Providing for copies or backups of the disk data in case the disk fails

The stability of the disk data is extremely important in any system, but it is especially so in a time-shared system where many users are dependent on that single resource.

If the computer stops because of a power failure or operating system error, the files on disk should not be subjected to corruption. In MS-DOS, the FAT is the essential data structure used to locate all files in the system; if MS-DOS updated the FAT in memory only and not on disk, a system failure could result in the loss of the correct FAT and with it all the file threads and data locations on the disk. Every time the FAT is changed, the MS-DOS file system must change both its memory and disk versions. For added protection, MS-DOS keeps two copies of the FAT on disk in case the primary one becomes unreadable. MS-DOS does not protect against power loss during the FAT write operation. This is one reason a user is warned against turning the computer off while the disk motor is running.

The FAT was designed for small capacity disks, and since the advent of larger disk systems, it is no longer adequate. The bitmap has become the universal approach to maintaining disk structure. Normally, only a portion of the bitmap is copied to memory by the file subsystem. This is because, as explained earlier, the entire bitmap is large and probably not all of it is required in memory simultaneously. As the bitmap is changed in memory, the corresponding change must take place on disk as insurance against computer failure. If the disk copy is not properly maintained and the system stops for any reason, an out-of-date bitmap on disk will not reflect the disk's true condition when the system is restarted. To aid error recovery attempts, an operating system tool is usually provided to read through the files on disk and recreate a bitmap. The only problem this tool has is finding the files or, rather, the beginning of each file, in the system. First it is necessary to find the root directory. Therefore most hierarchical file systems save the root directory in a specific location on disk. VERIFY is the VMS operating system tool used for disk recovery.

PHYSICAL ERRORS ON DISK

The disk is not a perfect device. Although the electronics are reasonably reliable and usually replaceable, the recording medium has occasional unusable areas, and in today's technology, a single platter on a disk drive cannot be easily replaced. Normally, the unusable portions of the disk are found during the formatting step, which occurs when the disk is initially put into service. In formatting, the system tests every track and byte of the disk by writing a known data pattern and then attempting to read it back to confirm the stability of the media. It reports any bad sectors to the file system. Clearly, it will not do to mark the bad sector itself, since it is known to be unreliable; instead, the common recording method is to write the bad sector addresses on a portion of the disk known to be good. After the formatting operation is complete, the file system reads that special track and marks its bitmap (or the equivalent FAT) according to the results of the formatting.

Once a disk has been successfully formatted, its recording surface can deteriorate because of usage. However, this is a gradual process that can be detected by the hardware before data is lost. When data is written into a sector, a checksum of the data (or some more elaborate computation) is made and recorded with it. When the data is read, the checksum is recomputed and compared against the checksum value recorded on disk. If the checksum values do not match, the sector is marginal and should be removed from service. The sector may be reread, and usually the data can be extracted correctly, but occasionally, the corrupted data must be accepted. When a marginal sector is detected, it must be marked as bad by the file subsystem. This part of the disk integrity function is built into the disk controller. It reports the checksum status to the driver. Then, if the controller reports read difficulties, it is the file subsystem's responsibility to logically remove the sector from service. It can simply mark it "used" in the bitmap or "bad" in the FAT or take some other appropriate action.

On more advanced disk systems, spare (or hidden) tracks are available to replace the ones that fail to format correctly or that have deteriorated with use. An adaptive file subsystem can make use of these extra tracks so that the total capacity of the disk is constant over time.

DISK BACKUP

In a personal computer environment, the user is solely responsible for disk backup, but in a time-sharing environment, the user usually relies on the system manager to perform the required backup functions. The convenience of a large-capacity disk in a time-sharing environment is that it holds a great deal of data, but that convenience is also a danger. If, for any reason, the data on the disk cannot be read, many users are going to be disappointed, and a large amount of data will be lost. Thus, the file management subsystem must guarantee the readability of the disk as much as possible. Of course, it is the system manager's responsibility to regularly back up the data from disk to tape to protect the data in the event that the disk becomes unreadable, but beyond providing the backup tool, there is nothing the subsystem can do to ensure the responsible use of the program.

Many data centers regularly back up disk data to tape, but often no thought is given to restoring the tapes to disk if the need arises. Sometimes, the system manager makes incremental[12] backups nightly and cycles through his tape supply once a month. But if a full disk backup is never performed, files that have not changed will never be saved. Thus, a restore from the backup tapes brings back only those files that changed during the current month; but unchanged files are lost entirely.

---

12. An incremental backup is one that copies only those files that have changed since the last backup to tape. A full backup copies all files onto tape.

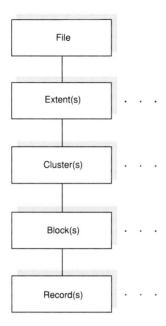

Figure 9.22. VMS file nomenclature

9.6. Files in the VMS Operating System

The remainder of this chapter will look at the VMS file subsystem, called Files-11, using several commands for illustration. Files-11 has its origins in the VMS predecessor, RSX, which runs on the PDP-11 hardware series. RSX files are horizontal, meaning they are all at the same level. RSX does not support a hierarchical file system with subdirectories. Even so, these files were adapted to and are still supported by the VMS operating system. That is, an RSX-generated file can be written on disk and then transported and read by a VMS system.

Figure 9.22 clarifies the VMS file nomenclature used here and in the following sections. A file is made up of one or more *extents*, each of which contains one or more contiguous clusters. A *cluster* is a contiguous collection of blocks (sectors), thus extents are contiguous blocks also. Multiple records are normally contained in a block, but the record length is not necessarily limited by the block size.

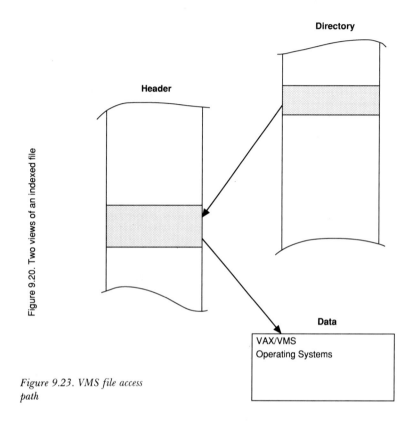

Figure 9.20. Two views of an indexed file

Figure 9.23. VMS file access path

A VMS file is composed of three parts: the directory, the header, and the data, as shown in Figure 9.23. The directory points to the header and the header locates the data. The header is invisible to the user, but the directory is a special user file with the extension .DIR. The header is located in the top-level file called $DISK1:[000000]INDEXF.SYS, which is inaccessible to the user. This and other system files will be discussed later.

The command that allows directory exploration is:

```
DIR/FULL
```

It produces a display like Figure 9.24, showing the complete directory entry. The "File ID" field links the directory to the header. The *File ID* may appear to be a [cylinder, track, sector] address, but it is not. Instead, the leftmost number is an index into the header file, INDEXF.SYS, and the middle number is a sequence number used to ensure that the INDEXF.SYS index

```
Directory SYS$SYSDEVICE:[GRP5A]

X.X;1
Size:                    1/3          File ID: (1150,1,0)
Created: 11-MAR-1990 15:03:31.61     Owner:    [GRP5A]
Revised: 11-MAR-1990 15:03:32.22 (2)
Expires:    <None specified>
Backup:     <No backup recorded>
File organization:  Sequential
File attributes:    Allocation: 3, Extend: 0, Global buffer count: 0
                    No version limit
Record format:      Variable length, maximum 17 bytes
Record attributes:  Carriage return carriage control
RMS attributes:     None
Journaling enabled: None
File protection:    System:RWED, Owner:RWED, Group:RE, World:
Access Cntrl List:  None

Total of 1 file, 1/3 blocks..
```

*Figure 9.24. A typical display of
the command $ DIR /FULL*

is up to date. In this case, the 1 indicates that the file X.X is the first file to
occupy slot 1150 of the INDEXF.SYS. The rightmost number has to do with
linking multiple disks together logically. Most of the time, there is only a
single disk in the volume set, so that number is usually 0. As for other
information in the directory, the Size field indicates the number of blocks
used (1) and the number of blocks allocated to the file (3). The reason these
two numbers are different is that a cluster contains three blocks on this disk,
but only one of the blocks contains data. This illustrates internal fragmentation of the disk file. The display also shows that the file is sequential and
has variable-length records; the longest is 17 bytes. Other information in
the directory is the security data—the protection and access control list.

The INDEXF.SYS structure is more complex and can be displayed
with the command:

```
DUMP/HEADER/BLOCK=COUNT:0
```

as in Figure 9.25. This display is divided into four categories: Header area,
Identification area, Map area, and Checksum. Notice that the VMS designers
have allowed for modification to this structure: the location of the Identification area and Map area is carried as data in the Header area. This permits future expansion of the structure without changing the code that
accesses it.

Much of this data is a restatement of the directory information, main-

```
Dump of file SYS$SYSDEVICE:[GRP5A]X.X;1 on 11-MAR-1990 15:47:30.71
File ID (1150,1,0)   End of file block 1 / Allocated 3
```

                              File Header

```
Header area
     Identification area offset:         40
     Map area offset:                    100
     Access control area offset:         255
     Reserved area offset:               255
     Extension segment number:           0
     Structure level and version:        2, 1
     File identification:                (1150,1,0)
     Extension file identification:      (0,0,0)
     VAX-11 RMS attributes
          Record type:                   Variable
          File organization:             Sequential
          Record attributes:             Implied carriage control
          Record size:                   17
          Highest block:                 3
          End of file block:             1
          End of file byte:              30
          Bucket size:                   0
          Fixed control area size:       0
          Maximum record size:           255
          Default extension size:        0
          Global buffer count:           0
          Directory version limit:       0
     File characteristics:               <none specified>
     Map area words in use:              2
     Access mode:                        0
     File owner UIC:                     [GRP5A]
     File protection:                    S:RWED, O:RWED, G:RE, W:
     Back link file identification:      (1027,5,0)
     Journal control flags:              <none specified>
     Active recovery units:              None
     Highest block written:              1

  Identification area
     File name:                          X.X;1
     Revision number:                    2
     Creation date:                      11-MAR-1990 15:03:31.61
     Revision date:                      11-MAR-1990 15:03:32.22
     Expiration date:                    <none specified>
     Backup date:                        <none specified>

  Map area
     Retrieval pointers
          Count:            3       LBN:      75708

  Checksum:                                 18699
```

Figure 9.25. A typical display of the command $ DUMP/ HEADER/BLOCK = COUNT:0

tained for system unity and directory reconstruction. This discussion will focus on some of the unduplicated data. Looking first at the bottom of the listing, a Checksum is maintained for every header to preserve its integrity. The Checksum pertains to the header itself, not the data. Located under the "VAX-11 RMS attributes" section, labeled "End of file block" and "End of file byte," is information that locates the logical data termination point. This is necessary because a file can end anywhere in the cluster, and the application must be kept from reading beyond the end of the file.

The Map area contains the LBN (logical block number) used to locate the data on disk. This is a linear sector address of the data that must be converted to [surface, track, sector] prior to a physical read or write operation. In the figure, the file is three sectors long, beginning at 75,708. There is one entry in the Map area for each fragment so, when a file is fragmented, multiple Retrieval pointers are displayed here. A highly fragmented file could conceivably exceed the maximum of allowable entries in the map area. When this condition occurs, another INDEXF.SYS entry is assigned to the file. This extends the file header and provides room for additional LBNs; the index of the second header entry is recorded in the "Extension file identification." This example, however, contains no extensions and only a single fragment.

Since fragmentation increases file access time, and therefore program execution time, the user should be on guard for this condition. It is easily corrected with the command:

```
$ COPY/CONTIGUOUS input output
```

This command determines the number of clusters occupied by the *input* file from its file header and then locates the required number of contiguous clusters on the disk. It then copies all the blocks from the input file to these new clusters and names the new file according to the *output* parameter. The output file name need not be the same as the input file name.

There is one danger in defragmenting large files: there may not be enough contiguous blocks to contain the file, even when the disk is not particularly full. If the disk does not have a contiguous group of clusters, COPY makes a best-fit decision.

At this time, there is no VMS tool available to indicate the degree of disk fragmentation or the size of the largest contiguous block, but Digital does offer a defragmentation tool that will run on the VMS operating system.

```
Dump of file SYS$SYSDEVICE:[GRP5A]X.X;1 on 11-MAR-1990 15:05:47.08
File ID (1150,1,0)   End of file block 1 / Allocated 3

Virtual block number 1 (00000001), 512 (0200) bytes

7265704F 00110053 4D562F58 41560007  ..VAX/VMS...Oper  000000
FFFF0073 6D657473 79532067 6E697461  ating Systems...  000010
00000000 00000000 00000000 00000000  ................  000020
00000000 00000000 00000000 00000000  ................  000030
........ ........ ........ ........  ................

00000000 00000000 00000000 00000000  ................  0001D0
00000000 00000000 00000000 00000000  ................  0001E0
00000000 00000000 00000000 00000000  ................  0001F0
```

*Figure 9.26. A partial display
of the command DUMP X.X
output*

SEQUENTIAL FILES

Sequential files are the most common files found on any system. They can be easily created with any of the editors in the VMS operating system. To examine the detailed structure of any *file*, the following command can be used:

    $ DUMP *file*

Figure 9.26 illustrates the typical output of this command. The file X.X contains two lines and would appear like the following if displayed with a TYPE command.

    VAX/VMS
    Operating Systems

The figure itself has been modified to shorten it. Normally, all blocks in the file are dumped with the DUMP command, but this figure shows only the first block; the other two contain only 0s. The default display format of the dump is arranged 16 bytes to a line and presented in both hexadecimal and ASCII format. The byte number of the first byte on the line is displayed in hexadecimal in the right column.

Reading the dump is a bit difficult, so this discussion will interpret several bytes. The first four are found on the top line, in the rightmost longword of the dump. The first byte, numbered 000000, is 07 hexadecimal, which is an unprintable character, and so the corresponding ASCII character is printed as a ".". Byte 1 is 00 hexadecimal and also unprintable. These first two bytes contain the length of the line. Byte 2 is 56, a "V" in ASCII, and byte 3 is 41, an "A." Notice that the hexadecimal portion reads from right to left and the ASCII from left to right. This is because bytes are numbered from right to left so that the least significant digit appears on the right. However, since this makes the ASCII unreadable, the ASCII characters are displayed from left to right instead.

This dump is an example of a variable-length record format. Byte 9 is a 0 to indicate the end of the record, and bytes 10 and 11 contain the length of the second line. The second line ends at byte 29, and bytes 30 and 31 contain FFFF to indicate the end-of-file. The address of FF corresponds to the end-of-file byte in Figure 9.25. The remainder of the block is zeroed. DUMP will print every line, but repetition is indicated with the line of periods in the figure.

The DUMP command has several other options; only two have been demonstrated here.

DIRECT FILES

The VMS operating system also supports *direct* files, which Digital documentation refers to as *relative* files, the term used here. Unlike sequential files, the software engineer must make a special effort to create relative files. The most obvious way to do this is to write a program. However, Digital considers direct files to be common enough to provide three tools for the task: one to create the file definition, one to populate the file, and one to analyze the file to optimize the definition. In general, this section will not go into great detail about these tools, but will only present the results of using them.

The first step is to create a definition for the relative file with the following command.

```
$ EDIT/FDL defn
```

This command invokes an interactive editor that presents the user with a series of menus used to create a file definition. The file definition is stored in the *defn* file specified in the command. FDL is an acronym for file definition language. The default *defn* file extension is .FDL. The exact steps in the edit dialog are not presented, but Figure 9.27 shows how a user displays the result of an edit session. This figure shows two pages. The top-level menu, part a, lists the options available. When "View" is selected, the definition,

```
                    Parsing Definition File
                    Definition Parse Complete

                    VAX-11 FDL Editor
Add            to insert one line into the FDL definition
Delete         to remove one line from the FDL definition
Exit           to leave the FDL Editor after creating the FDL file
Help           to obtain information about the FDL Editor
Invoke         to initiate a script of related questions
Modify         to change an existing line in the FDL definition
Quit           to abort the FDL Editor with no FDL file creation
Set            to specify FDL Editor characteristics
View           to display the current FDL Definition

Main Editor Function                  (Keyword)[Help]     : view
```

a) page 1

```
IDENT          "24-MAR-1990 14:21:20   VAX-11 FDL Editor"

FILE
               MAX_RECORD_NUMBER        10
               ORGANIZATION             relative

RECORD
               BLOCK_SPAN               yes
               CONTROL_FIELD_SIZE       2
               FORMAT                   variable
               SIZE                     80

ACCESS
               DELETE

Press RETURN to continue (^Z for Main Menu)
```

b) page 2

Figure 9.27. A typical two-page display of a file definition

part b, is displayed. The definition in the figure describes a relative file with 10 80-character records.

The next step is to create and populate the data file, using the newly formulated definition. This is done with the command,

```
$ CONVERT/CREATE/FDL=defn input output
```

Conveniently, the CONVERT command builds the *output* file using a sequential *input* file. The format of the output file is defined in the *defn* file, which is a product of the EDIT/FDL command. The power of the CONVERT command is that source data can be entered into the file subsystem

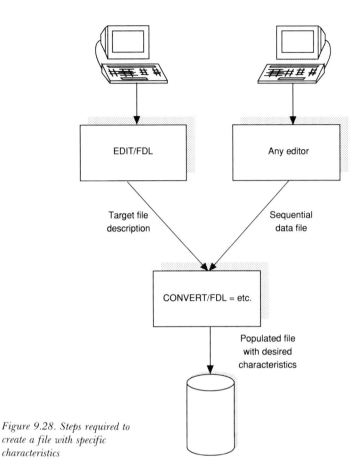

Figure 9.28. Steps required to create a file with specific characteristics

with an editor without regard to its final form. Figure 9.28 illustrates this process.

The CONVERT command was performed on a sequential file with the definition illustrated in Figure 9.27, and the resulting relative file was dumped in Figure 9.29. This dump should be compared to the sequential file dumped in Figure 9.26. Three blocks have been allocated to contain the relative file rather than only one for the sequential file. The first block has changed dramatically; it now contains several integers that aid in defining the file and locating the data. The data is now placed in block 2 and it has also been augmented. The first byte contains an 8; then, each 80-character record is prefixed with the record length. The records have been *padded* (filled with trailing characters) with 0s.

```
Dump of file SYS$SYSDEVICE:[GRP5A]X.REL;1 on 24-MAR-1990 14:10:17.91
File ID (1024,6,0)   End of file block 3 / Allocated 3

Virtual block number 1 (00000001), 512 (0200) bytes

   00000000 00000000 00000000 00000000 ................   000000
   00000000 00000000 00000000 00000000 ................   000010
   00000000 00000000 00000000 00000000 ................   000020
   00000000 00000000 00000000 00000000 ................   000030
   00000000 00000000 00000000 00000000 ................   000040
   00000000 00000000 00000000 00000000 ................   000050
   0000000A 00000002 00000000 00000000 ................   000060
   00000000 00000000 00000001 00000004 ................   000070
   00000000 00000000 00000000 00000000 ................   000080
   ........ ........ ........ ........ ................   ......
   00000000 00000000 00000000 00000000 ................   0001D0
   00000000 00000000 00000000 00000000 ................   0001E0
   00110000 00000000 00000000 00000000 ................   0001F0

Dump of file SYS$SYSDEVICE:[GRP5A]X.REL;1 on 24-MAR-1990 14:10:17.91
File ID (1024,6,0)   End of file block 3 / Allocated 3

Virtual block number 2 (00000002), 512 (0200) bytes

   00000000 0000534D 562F5841 56000708 ...VAX/VMS......   000000
   00000000 00000000 00000000 00000000 ................   000010
   00000000 00000000 00000000 00000000 ................   000020
   00000000 00000000 00000000 00000000 ................   000030
   00000000 00000000 00000000 00000000 ................   000040
   20676E69 74617265 704F0011 08000000 ......Operating   000050
   00000000 00000000 00736D65 74737953 Systems.........  000060
   00000000 00000000 00000000 00000000 ................   000070
   00000000 00000000 00000000 00000000 ................   000080
   00000000 00000000 00000000 00000000 ................   000090
   4D206469 76614400 0C080000 00000000 ........David M   0000A0
   00000000 00000000 00000072 656C6C69 iller..........   0000B0
   00000000 00000000 00000000 00000000 ................   0000C0
   ........ ........ ........ ........ ................   ......
   00000000 00000000 00000000 00000000 ................   0001E0
   00000000 00000000 00000000 00000000 ................   0001F0

Dump of file SYS$SYSDEVICE:[GRP5A]X.REL;1 on 24-MAR-1990 14:10:17.91
File ID (1024,6,0)   End of file block 3 / Allocated 3

Virtual block number 3 (00000003), 512 (0200) bytes

   00000000 00000000 00000000 00000000 ................   000000
   00000000 00000000 00000000 00000000 ................   000010
   ........ ........ ........ ........ ................   ......
   00000000 00000000 00000000 00000000 ................   0001E0
   00000000 00000000 00000000 00000000 ................   0001F0
```

*Figure 9.29. Typical output of
the command DUMP X.REL,
a relative file*

INDEXED FILES

The same tools, EDIT/FDL and CONVERT, are used to create, populate, and display *indexed* or, as Digital calls them, *keyed* files. EDIT/FDL is executed to create the definition, and this time, the definition must specify characteristics about the key, for instance, its location and size in the data record. Figure 9.30 shows a portion of a definition for a file with two keys. The file represents a phone book containing the name (in KEY 1), extension (in KEY 0), and title of university employees. Again, CONVERT is used to populate the file from a sequential file. A sample of the data looks like this:

```
        Beck                  Prof emertia phy ed
2060    Schultz               General repair work
2825    Miller                Prof of comp science
2916    Picket                Prof of physics
2933    Alberti               Asst prof of edu
3756    Geisen                Room assignments
```

The composition of a keyed file is much more complex than that of sequential or direct files, primarily because the data is sorted according to the key's value. Sorting the key allows random access to the data, using a key's value, to be accomplished quickly. In the VMS operating system, the complete data record is separated from the key and not stored in any particular order; it is sorted and stored in another structure. Each key is then linked to the corresponding data record. If the data requires multiple keys, a sorted key and link structure is created for each key defined, but there is still only one copy of the full data record. This is depicted in Figure 9.31.

To further illustrate the complexity of keyed files, a dump of the second key, the name (stored in block 7 of the file), is shown in Figure 9.32. In the dump, note that the first letter of each name is missing. This is to facilitate the search technique and reduce the storage requirements of the key. The sorted keys are stored in *buckets*, and the prefix of the first key in the bucket is stored with each bucket. When searching for a key, the file subsystem only has to examine the prefix of the bucket to determine if the key is in that bucket or another one. This is analogous to the binary search technique and saves examining every key in the file during a search.

A common use for keyed files is database applications. Users can write high-level language programs that create, populate, and display the contents of a keyed file. These programs can be tailored to the end-user who might

```
FILE
        ALLOCATION                  12
        BEST_TRY_CONTIGUOUS         yes
        BUCKET_SIZE                 1
        CLUSTER_SIZE                3
        CONTIGUOUS                  no
        EXTENSION                   1
        FILE_MONITORING             no
        GLOBAL_BUFFER_COUNT         0
        NAME                        "DUA1:[FACULTY.DMILLER.OS_BOOK]
                                    PHONE_BOOK.INX;1"
        ORGANIZATION                indexed
        OWNER                       [FACULTY,DMILLER]
        PROTECTION                  (system:RWED,owner:RWED,group:,world:)

RECORD
        BLOCK_SPAN                  yes
        CARRIAGE_CONTROL            carriage_return
        FORMAT                      fixed
        SIZE                        50

KEY 0
        CHANGES                     no
        DATA_AREA                   0
        DATA_FILL                   100
        DATA_KEY_COMPRESSION        no
        DATA_RECORD_COMPRESSION     no
        DUPLICATES                  yes
        INDEX_AREA                  1
        INDEX_COMPRESSION           no
        INDEX_FILL                  100
        LEVEL1_INDEX_AREA           1
        NAME                        "Ext"
        NULL_KEY                    no
        PROLOG                      3
        SEG0_LENGTH                 4
        SEG0_POSITION               0
        TYPE                        string

KEY 1
        CHANGES                     yes
        DATA_AREA                   2
        DATA_FILL                   100
        DATA_KEY_COMPRESSION        no
        DUPLICATES                  yes
        INDEX_AREA                  2
        INDEX_COMPRESSION           no
        INDEX_FILL                  100
        LEVEL1_INDEX_AREA           2
        NAME                        "Name"
        NULL_KEY                    no
        SEG0_LENGTH                 20
        SEG0_POSITION               9
        TYPE                        string
```

Figure 9.30. A typical display of
a keyed file definition

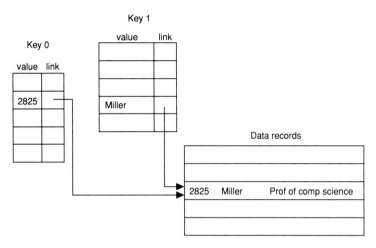

Figure 9.31. A representation of
a keyed data file

```
Dump of file DUA1:[FACULTY.DMILLER.OS_BOOK]PHONE_BOOK.INX;2
File ID (15907,36,2)   End of file block 10 / Allocated 12

Virtual block number 7 (00000007), 512 (0200) bytes

001B0100 00000007 000100BC 00070100 ....<.......... 000000
20202020 20202020 20207A74 6C756863 chultz          000010
6B636500 1B000000 0A000282 47202020    G........eck 000020
20202020 20202020 20202020 20202020                 000030
206E6573 6965001B 0000000A 00018250 P.........eisen 000040
06825220 20202020 20202020 20202020               R.. 000050
20202020 74656B63 69001B00 00000A00 .......icket    000060
000A0004 82502020 20202020 20202020          P..... 000070
20202020 20202072 656C6C69 001B0000 ....iller       000080
1B000000 0A000382 50202020 20202020          P....... 000090
20202020 20202020 20697472 656B6C00 .lberti         0000A0
00000000 0000000A 00058241 20202020     A.......... 0000B0
00000000 00000000 00000000 00000000 .............. 0000C0
00000000 00000000 00000000 00000000 .............. 0000D0
```

Figure 9.32. A partial display
resulting from the command
DUMP PHONE_BOOK.INX

```
Disk DUAD:, device type RD54, is online, mounted, file-oriented device,
    shareable, available to cluster, error logging is enabled.

    Error count                   0    Operations completed       2194
    Owner process                ""    Owner UIC                 [1,1]
    Owner process ID       00000000    Dev Prot  S:RWED,O:RWED,G:RWED,W:RWED
    Reference count              13    Default buffer size         512
    Total blocks             311200    Sectors per track            17
    Total cylinders            1221    Tracks per cylinder          15

    Volume label     "VAXVMSRL052"    Relative volume number        0
    Cluster size                  3    Transaction count           110
    Free blocks              205746    Maximum files allowed      38900
    Extend quantity               5    Mount count                   1
    Mount status             System    Cache name      "_DUAD:XQPCACHE"
    Extent cache size            64    Maximum blocks in extent cache  20574
    File ID cache size           64    Blocks currently in extent cache 1428
    Quota cache size              0    Maximum buffers in FCP cache   84

    Volume status: subject to mount verification, file high-water marking, write
    through caching enabled.
```

Figure 9.33. A typical display
of the command $ SHOW
DEVICE DUA0 /FULL

require a user-friendly interface allowing him or her to modify and display data.

Many VMS "standard" utilities, like PRINT and the editors, will accept both relative and indexed files as input. This capability is useful because these common functions are often necessary, and the user should not be limited to only sequential files when performing them. The CONVERT utility will also produce a sequential file from a relative or indexed file.

9.7. VMS Disk Structure

This section examines in some detail the physical arrangement of data on the disk using a typical small disk drive, an RD54, as the example. Figure 9.33 contains sample output from the following command.

```
$ SHOW DEVICE DUA0 /FULL
```

remaining free blocks are displayed. Blocks are clustered in groups of three on this device. This is a system disk, so the protection is RWED for every category. The maximum number of files on this disk is limited to 38,900; because the number of file headers is fixed however, the actual current value is not displayed. This is an unfortunate omission, since the system manager needs that information to regulate the disk usage.[13] Disk capacity is determined by either of two nearly independent values: the number of blocks used and the number of files declared.

Every disk supported by the VMS operating system has a similar physical structure. There are four essential categories of information defining the disk, and they are located at the same place on the disk no matter what the disk model. These are summarized below:

1. Boot block—bootstrap program if a system disk
2. Home block—volume control information
3. Index bitmap—bitmap for file header index
4. File headers—file information

The *primary bootstrap program* (VMB.EXE) is located in read-only memory (ROM), the console media, or on the system disk depending on the CPU type. If stored on the system disk, it is located by information contained in the *boot block*. The primary bootstrap program performs many preliminary functions and then locates and reads the *secondary bootstrap program* (SYSBOOT.EXE) in from the system disk. SYSBOOT.EXE then continues the system initialization and reads VMS into memory. The primary boot is not designed with the specifics of the VMS system in mind, and this leaves the designers free to put VMS at any convenient location on disk.

The second category, the *home block,* contains all the information necessary to locate the remaining data on the disk; in particular, it locates the index bitmap and file headers. Like the boot block, this information is repeated several times on the disk to guarantee data integrity.

The next category is the *index bitmap,* which indicates the usage of each file header slot defined on the disk. Part of the disk initialization process allocates enough room in the index bitmap for a specific number of files; this is a fixed value. The bitmap must be contiguous on disk, because there is a one-to-one correspondence between the index bitmap and the file headers.

Figure 9.34 illustrates the relationship between the physical block

---

13. The DIRECTORY command has the capability of counting files using the TOTAL qualifier, but it is a time-consuming operation.

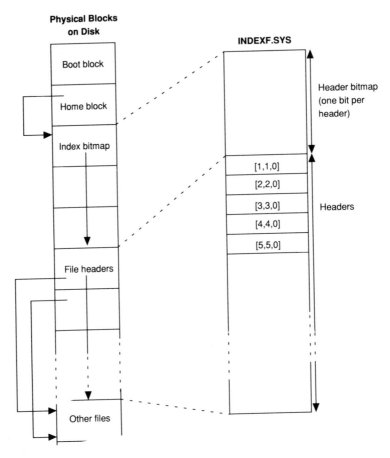

Figure 9.34. Relationship between physical disk assignment
and the index file INDEXF.SYS

assignments and the index file. Nine files[14] are created when the disk is initialized; they are listed below together with their file IDs.

[1,1,0]. INDEXF.SYS—file description and disk location
[2,2,0]. BITMAP.SYS—cluster utilization
[3,3,0]. BADBLK.SYS—lists unusable clusters
[4,4,0]. 000000.DIR—top-level or master file directory
[5,5,0]. CORIMG.SYS—RSX file; core image
[6,6,0]. VOLSET.SYS—volume set list
[7,7,0]. CONTIN.SYS—continuation file
[8,8,0]. BACKUP.SYS—backup log
[9,9,0]. BADLOG.SYS—pending bad blocks

The six-letter name and three-letter extension are the result of restrictions on RSX file names. INDEXF.SYS contains the file header bitmap and headers. BITMAP.SYS indicates whether or not a cluster of blocks is used. Notice that there is no information in this file to link utilization to a particular file. That information is contained only in the header. The BADBLK.SYS file lists unusable blocks on the disk that were discovered during disk initialization or during normal operations. The primary or *root* directory is 000000.DIR, and all files lie logically below it.

The CORIMG.SYS file is supported only by RSX and is maintained by the VMS system for consistency. A VMS file is not restricted to a single disk. Similarly, a logical volume may involve several physical devices. VOLSET.SYS lists the physical volumes that are part of the logical set. The CONTIN.SYS file has to do with files that span volumes. The BACKUP.SYS file is not currently used by the VMS system but is reserved for future use. The bad block algorithm attempts to recover data stored on a suspicious block. During recovery, the block numbers are temporarily stored in BADLOG.SYS to permit access to them. The algorithm cannot be permitted to reuse the bad blocks when looking for good blocks; at the same time, it cannot be prohibited from accessing the blocks altogether, so an intermediate file is required.

These files can be found in the top-level directory, $DISK1:[000000]. A user may enter the command[15]

---

14. The first five are carried over from RSX and constitute Files-11 level 1. The set of nine are called Files-11 level 2.
15. The disk name may be spelled differently depending on system configuration. DISK$DISK1 is used also.

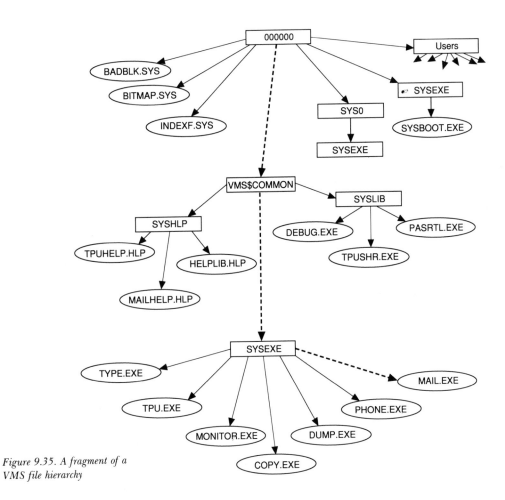

*Figure 9.35. A fragment of a
VMS file hierarchy*

```
$ DIR $DISK1:[000000]INDEXF.SYS
```

to see that the file does exist, but no further user query can be made concerning this file because it is "world" protected and belongs to a system account.

Figure 9.35 summarizes the top-level disk structure. All VMS files are rooted in $DISK1:[000000], and the as-delivered VMS file structure is partially outlined in the figure. User files are normally rooted in [000000] also. The figure uses rectangles to indicate directories and ellipses to indicate files. The figure locates some familiar files, such as MAIL.EXE; it resides in the SYSEXE directory. Notice that there are three SYSEXE directories, but the commonly used one is shown in the bottom of the figure.

9.8. The VMS File Subsystem

This section will integrate several topics in outlining the structure of the VMS file subsystem and specifically show how the various functions are assigned. In summary, the VMS file subsystem is distributed across the several subsystems, as illustrated in Figure 9.36. This makes it different from the models previously introduced because the focus is on disk files, not terminal I/O. Normally, the user makes disk requests directly or indirectly through RMS (record management system). Since $QIO operates only at the block level, it is RMS that defines and supports the structure within the block. Hence, it turns the user's request for a record into a request for a block and then makes a $QIO request. This transformation is supported by ancillary information like record length, which is stored in the directory and file header database. This database is too massive for anything more than a brief overview here.

XQP (eXtended QIO program) supports Files-11 level 2 data structures through file control primitives (FCPs) executed by the $QIO system service. Every file that is open on a disk is kept in a structure called the file control block (FCB). This contains a very large number of files because all the utility files, for example, PASCAL.EXE, DIRECTORY.EXE, and SHOW.EXE, are kept open at all times to reduce system overhead. The command:

```
$ SHOW DEVICE /FILES DUA0:
```

will list all the files that are open and the responsible process, if any. But even a nominal system has hundreds of open files; additionally, to reduce search time, a cache of the most active files is maintained by XQP. The system manager and user should be provided with metrics (such as those generated by the VMS MONITOR command) to make rational decisions about performance issues. They must understand what the metrics mean and what changing them will do to the system.

To make this point clearer, Figure 9.37 shows the file caching statistics produced by MONITOR. There are seven caches listed in that display, with

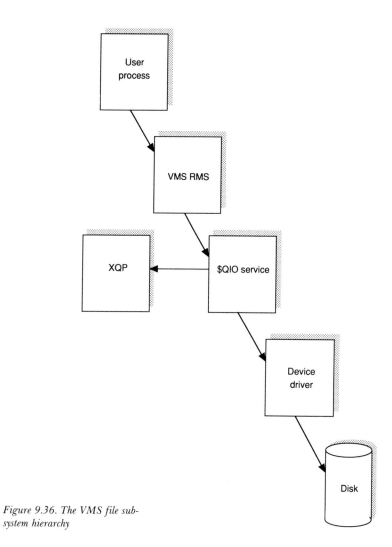

Figure 9.36. The VMS file sub-system hierarchy

```
                        VAX/VMS Monitor Utility
                     FILE SYSTEM CACHING STATISTICS
                            on node BSU::
                        21-OCT-1990 12:54:17

                                 CUR        AVE        MIN        MAX

        Dir FCB     (Hit %)     100.00     100.00      0.00      100.00
                    (Attempt Rate)  4.91      1.11      0.00        5.24
        Dir Data    (Hit %)     100.00      94.44      0.00      100.00
                    (Attempt Rate)  4.91      1.17      0.00        5.24
        File Hdr    (Hit %)     100.00     100.00      0.00      100.00
                    (Attempt Rate)  0.65      0.52      0.00        3.26
        File ID     (Hit %)       0.00     100.00      0.00      100.00
                    (Attempt Rate)  0.00      0.06      0.00        0.65

        Extent      (Hit %)       0.00     100.00      0.00      100.00
                    (Attempt Rate)  0.00      0.08      0.00        0.65
        Quota       (Hit %)       0.00     100.00      0.00      100.00
                    (Attempt Rate)  0.00      0.19      0.00        1.30
        Bitmap      (Hit %)       0.00       0.00      0.00        0.00
                    (Attempt Rate)  0.00      0.00      0.00        0.00
```

Figure 9.37. A typical display of
MONITOR FILE—CACHE
command

two lines provided for each. The "Attempt Rate" shows how many times a request for the corresponding data structure was made. The "Hit %" shows the percentage of those requests satisfied by data already in the cache. When data is not in the cache, additional disk accesses must be made, increasing user response time. To understand this, look at the last cache, the bitmap. The entire bitmap for a multi-gigabyte disk system cannot be kept in memory; only enough of it to satisfy current requests is necessary. The questions the system manager must ask are "How much is enough?" and "When is it too much?" Examining this display will provide some feeling for cache behavior. If necessary, a cache can be reduced or extended and the MONITOR display reexamined in an effort to satisfy the user community.

9.9. Related Issues

This chapter was purposely limited to the subject of disk files, but tape files are a subject that is nearly as complex. As with disks, the storage of data on tapes is unique, and very little about disk files carries over to tape files.

Historically, tapes were used before disks, but their primary importance today is as a means to archive disk data. A second use is to move large data files from one computer to another, but this application is losing its importance as networks become more common.

Tape files are efficient in only one form—sequential. Random access is out of the question because the transport mechanism and the rotating mass of the tapes take a significantly longer time to start and stop than do disk heads. Moreover, moving the tape faster is not a solution to the access time because of the friction generated. These factors make tape a poor substitute for a disk.

However, properly used, tapes can store large amounts of data for a long time, and they require very little maintenance. "Refreshing" or rewriting data is unnecessary. Furthermore, since tapes are less expensive than disk, the cost per megabyte is very low.

In the early 1970s, prior to the advent of inexpensive disks, Digital tried to emulate the operation of a disk with a small tape drive called DECtape. Like a disk, DECtape had to be formatted before it was used so that its "sectors" could be labeled, and only fixed-length records could be transferred. To enhance its operation, it was made bi-directional—it could read and write as the tape traveled backward and forward. A block on the DECtape was 128 36-bit words, and one tape had a capacity of 450K 6-bit characters. DECtape was very slow by today's standards, but at the time, users were happy to have any sort of random access device when using a minicomputer.

A second subject deliberately avoided in this chapter is compact disks (CDs), a medium very much like magnetic disks in that it is easily adapted to random access methods. Compact disks are the newest of the mass storage techniques, and they have a promising future. This is in spite of the fact that, as yet, they are much slower than magnetic disks and are primarily read-only devices (write capabilities are currently very expensive). Unlike magnetic disk's data storage technology, which is starting to reach its physical limits, CD technology is in its infancy and should see significant breakthroughs over the years. CDs will probably replace magnetic disks eventually because they have greater storage capacity, they are more portable, and they are less sensitive to the environment.

Because of their very large capacity, CDs will offer new applications as well. For instance, both audio data and video images will reside along with the digital data on these disks, and this additional capability will require new methods of logically structuring the disk "files." Even the terminology will have to change to fully encompass these new forms.

9.10. Summary

In this chapter we discussed disks and how they are used to store data, notably, user files. We basically ignored other secondary storage media, not because they are uninteresting, but because disks provide such rich and varied material and are at the center of our present technology and systems.

A disk is subdivided into tracks and sectors when it is formatted and carries the track and sector addresses with the data so that a given sector, the smallest addressable unit, can be reliably reaccessed. It is this reaccessibility that makes the disk a convenient storage medium. The design of the hardware read-write mechanism makes the time to reach any sector on the disk quite fast, and this too is a heavily exploited feature of the disk drive.

Several platters can be stacked to increase the overall capacity of the disk drive and reduce its cost per bit, but there are physical limitations to this scheme resulting from the precision construction of the disk drive components; for instance, thermal differences between the top platter and the bottom platter can distort the configuration of the disk surfaces so that the read-write head on the bottom is on a different track than the read-write head on the top.

Because a sector is the smallest addressable element on the disk, there are several methods of storing records on the disk. Blocking, or packing the records into sectors, leads to efficient use of the sector but burdens the file subsystem with having to separate them again. Usually, the individual records are identified in one of two ways: by prefixing each record with a byte count or by suffixing each record with a special record separator.

The file subsystem is also responsible for maintaining a directory of files residing on the disk, which means that it must also manage the disk's unused space. When a user requests disk space, a pool of empty sectors is used to satisfy the request. And when a user process deletes a file, the now-unoccupied sectors that file needed return to the public pool. However, the disk is a shared resource within the system, so the file subsystem must supply some form of protection from unauthorized file access (either accidental or deliberate) of these discarded sectors.

Since the disk is a shared resource, file access must infringe on the user's response time as little as possible. Disk head movement accounts for the majority of time required to access data, so the primary technique used to reduce file access time is global scheduling of disk requests to minimize head movement. Although head movement is measured in milliseconds on disk units, in an environment of many simultaneous users, this can result in significant delays.

On time-sharing systems, the user does not have to keep track of several small-capacity floppy disks and try to organize data to fit on them. Instead, disk space is allocated from a large capacity disk system. This is a relief in some ways and a concern in others. Data on a floppy disk is as secure as the user wants it to be; data in a shared resource may be compromised. On the other hand, floppy users are notorious for not making copies of important data, but in a time-shared system, file backup is normally offered at no additional cost to the user. As a further benefit, time-sharing systems are designed to maintain disk files even when power fails. A PC user must purchase an uninterruptable power source (UPS) to solve this problem.

In closing the chapter, we briefly examined the database that supports the file subsystem in the VMS operating system, using the standard commands DUMP and DIRECTORY for illustration. We also delved into a few of the file-support features of the VMS system provided by EDIT/FDL and CONVERT, and applied these tools to a sequential file to transform it into a relative file.

Finally, we introduced the file structure of the disk itself and provided an overview of the file subsystem. A measurement tool available under MONITOR gives some insight into the subsystem design as well as an inkling of how it can be tuned to optimize performance.

ACRONYMS

ASCII	American Standard Code for Information Interchange
CD	Compact Disk
CPU	Central Processing Unit
DMA	Direct Memory Access
FAT	File Allocation Table
FCB	File Control Block

FCP	File Control Primitive
FDL	File Description Language
FIFO	First In First Out
MS-DOS	Disk Operating System
PIO	Programmed I/O
RMS	Record Management System
ROM	Read Only Memory
RPM	Revolutions Per Minute
RSX	Resource Sharing Executive operating system
RWED	Read, Write, Execute, and Delete protection
SSTF	Shortest Seek Time First
XQP	Extended QIO Program

SHORT ANSWER EXERCISES

1. Name three disadvantages of maintaining a system file of disk free space.

2. In the discussion of variable records, the statement was made that trailing (rightmost) blanks on a line do not have to be restored. Why is that?

3. This chapter discussed two bitmaps on a VMS disk; define them.

4. Explain why the number of blocks used and the number of files used on a disk are nearly independent.

5. Refer to the disk scheduling algorithms in Figure 9.16. Draw the path and compute the track distance for the scan case in which the head is initially traveling to the right (rather than to the left).

6. Rewrite and detail the read algorithm, outlined at the end of Section 9.2, which is required to read the rth record of a file.

7. What is the maximum linear velocity of a 5.25-inch floppy disk spinning at 300 rpm? What is the maximum linear velocity of a 14-inch hard disk spinning at 3,600 rpm? For comparison, compute the linear velocity of the tape in a cassette tape recorder. Express all your answers in miles per hour and inches per second.

8. What is the protection code of $DISK1:[000000]INDEXF.SYS?

9. Find a file in your directory that is fragmented. Use COPY to defragment it. Provide hardcopies of the two DIR/FULL displays that show the map before and after defragmentation.

PROJECTS

1. Since users are permitted to easily reconstruct contiguous files, the advantage of contiguous files will be demonstrated by working in the area of I/O timing. This is an excellent location for a discussion of benchmarking and the difficulties of timing on a multiprocessing system.

2. Repeat the illustration, of Section 9.6, concerning relative files; create a relative file definition, populate it (that is, fill it with one of your source programs), and then perform "standard" commands on the resulting file. Which commands still work (for example, PRINT, EDIT, SEARCH, DIRECTORY, SORT, PASCAL, TYPE, DIFFERENCE, etc.)? Does the file remain relative after performing each command?

3. Develop an algorithm that maps a [surface, track, sector] address to a linear address if the number of sectors per track varies according to the following scheme: the inner track, number 2,499, contains 60 sectors and one sector is added as the circumference increases, that is, every 100 tracks. Thus, tracks 2,301 through 2,399 have 61 tracks, and so forth, to the outside of the disk where tracks 0 through 99 have 84 sectors.

4. Develop an inverse algorithm of the previous project that maps the linear address to [surface, track, sector].

5. What is the general form of the mapping function used to convert the physical sector address [surface, track, sector] expression to a logical sector number? Prove your equation works by applying it to the following example:

   Assume a disk system with 8 surfaces, 500 tracks per surface, and 19 sectors per track. What is the logical sector of physical [2,147,11]? Draw a picture of the disk system, properly and unambiguously labeled, showing the sector in question. Assume all three dimensions of the physical address are numbered from 0.

6. What is the general form of the mapping function used to convert physical sector number [surface, track, sector] to logical sector number. Prove your equations by reversing the previous project.

7. In the previous project, the logical sector number could also be considered the bit number in the bitmap. This value may not be as useful to know as the word number and bit within the word, depending on the machine instruction set. Derive a general pair of equations that

convert bit number to word and bit-within-word number for a machine with "b" bits per word. Show that your equation is correct by converting bit number 11,247 to word and bit-within-word assuming that the words are 32 bits long. Draw a picture of the bitmap showing this bit, clearly and unambiguously.

8. Under the supervision of the computer center staff, load a tape on a drive, BACKUP your files, DIR the tape to show that the files were properly saved, and, finally, unload the tape. The tapes should be initialized beforehand by the staff because this is a privileged operation. The commands to do that are:

```
$ ALLOCATE unit
$ INITIALIZE unit label
$ DEALLOCATE unit
```

Then, to back up your files, you will need to execute the following commands of the form:

```
$ ALLOCATE unit
$ MOUNT unit label
$ BACKUP etc
$ DISMOUNT unit
$ DEALLOCATE unit
```

"Unit" is specific to your installation and refers to the tape drive. "Label" can be chosen by the user. You must research the BACKUP command line in the VMS documentation.

PAPERS

1. Investigate the DUMP command fully and prepare a presentation that succinctly describes it. Examples of each capability are expected. The Digital documentation should not be copied, but extended.

2. Research the history of the paper tape character code called Baudot. For instance, how many bits were required to represent a character? What character set could be represented? When was it invented and for what purpose? How did paper tape find its way into the computer

field? Are there other paper tape codes besides Baudot? Where did that term come from? If possible, locate a sample of paper tape or arrange for a teletype demonstration.

3. Research the history of the IBM card. For instance, how were characters represented? What character set could be represented? When was it invented and for what purpose? How did IBM cards find their way into the computer field? If possible, locate an IBM card or arrange for a keypunch demonstration for the class.

4. IBM cards could be manipulated mechanically by "sorters," "duplicators," and "tabulators" that could be "programmed" to some extent through the use of plug-in boards. Certain trivial computations could be performed also. Research the capabilities and uses of these machines.

5. Review the literature for defragmentation algorithms. What are the basic issues involved? What are the apparent, common, current solutions and unresolved problems?

6. Research the history of bubble memory. This medium was a favorite of the 1970s and 1980s but has largely disappeared as a viable technology. This topic can be approached from several different angles:
   • How bubble memory works
   • Why it was thought to be so promising and what were the promises
   • Why bubble memory failed as a commercial product

History of Digital
Operating Systems

GOALS

Hardware—software symbiosis

Hardware technology shapes software concepts

Evolution of the importance of the operating system

Growth of the VAX strategy

10

Most operating systems texts present a chapter on the broad history of operating systems. We deviate from this practice by looking at this history as it took shape in a single company, Digital Equipment Corporation. This approach is justified because the flow of computer history is similar either way. For instance, the development of time-sharing operating systems was taking place on four machines simultaneously in the middle 1960s: Digital's PDP-1, IBM's 7090, Burrough's B5000, and SDC's AN/FSQ-32V. Concentrating on a specific company, rather than simply marking the stages of that development, we can, perhaps, lend some insight into the reasoning behind certain decisions made and directions taken by the company's management and engineers. Incidentally, because this chapter comes after all the technical material has been presented, we can use the correct terminology in describing the evolution of the various operating systems concepts.

It should be obvious that the history of operating systems is also the history of hardware systems; for example, paging and interrupts are software concepts that must be supported by hardware. As stated, the hardware is designed to support the requirements of the operating system and the customer, as well as the technology. Although early computers did not emphasize this philosophy, it gained acceptance over time, reaching its epitome in the VAX and RISC (Reduced Instruction Set Computer) designs. These two machine classes were jointly designed by hardware engineers, operating system designers, compiler designers, and so forth, to optimize total system performance.

From the outset, Digital wanted to provide computer access at an engineer's desk. This philosophy ran counter to the rest of the industry of the late 1950s, for three reasons. First, most computers available at that time were running only batch operating systems that provided job turnaround measured in hours, not minutes. Attempting to put computing power on a desk was not seriously considered outside the academic community, but Digital was founded by MIT researchers.

Second, the computer industry was split between business and engineering applications. For instance, IBM had two product lines, one for each segment of the industry. But, throughout its history, Digital concentrated on the engineering market. Today, the business-engineering differences are almost entirely gone. Most users can customize their desk-top computer to meet the needs of their job with easily obtainable software and hardware, but the basic hardware architecture is fixed throughout a large segment of the industry. Even so, there are still requirements for special-purpose, high-performance machines for such tasks as computer aided design and technical illustrating.

Third, Digital realized from the outset that any computer that sits on the user's desk must be connected to other computers for the purpose of sharing data and user communications. However, from the advent of personal computing in the middle 1970s, it took the industry almost 10 years to discover networks, and even today's PC networks are still overshadowed by DECnet's capabilities in the areas of privacy and flexibility.

Computer history has been repeated three times: once by mainframes, a second time by minicomputers, and, finally, by microcomputers. Figure 10.1 illustrates this progression. They all began the same way, by offering a "bare bones" computer—just the hardware with no supporting software. Next, assembly languages became available and then rudimentary operating systems consisting only of device drivers. Finally, more sophisticated operating systems were developed—first batch operating systems and, later, time-sharing operating systems using paging. An example illustrates this replication: time-sharing on IBM mainframes was available in the middle 1960s

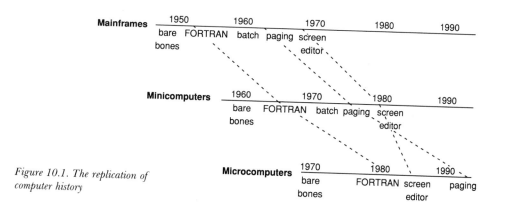

Figure 10.1. The replication of computer history

and on minicomputers a little later, but it has only become available on microcomputers in recent years.

Three milestones can be easily identified on Figure 10.1: FORTRAN, screen editors, and paging. Tracing these milestones across the computer types leads to the conclusion that development time compresses as a concept migrates from the mainframe to the microcomputer. For instance, it took nearly ten years for compilers to appear on mainframes, but they were available on microcomputers only a couple of years after the first ones appeared. The reason for this time compression is that software engineers did not know anything about compilers in the 1950s, but they learned a lot in the intervening 20 years. By the 1970s, writing a new compiler had become a graduate student project. This observation is true for the other concepts depicted as well.

Another way to express this migration is to say that only a few concepts have been introduced uniquely into minicomputers or microcomputers; most have been explored on mainframes first and then transported to "smaller" machines. WYSIWYG (What You See Is What You Get) word processors and spreadsheets are notable exceptions, appearing first on microcomputers.

As the industry matures, the distinction between the three computer classes narrows. Ten years ago, it was easy to compare a mini and a micro by price alone; today one is hard-pressed to define a minicomputer in terms of cost, memory capacity, physical size, speed, or any of the other traditional measurements. Thus, Figure 10.1 will soon give way to a single timeline and hold only historical significance.

10.1. Digital's Founding

Digital was founded in August 1957 by two members of the Whirlwind project at MIT. The Whirlwind computer was designed to be an interactive, real-time cockpit simulator for the Navy. This explains the vision of interactive computing that has been the single thread woven throughout Digital's history.

Digital did not begin by making computers. Their first product was called a Digital Laboratory Module—a digital building block about the size of a thin paperback (1¾ inches by 4½ inches by 7 inches) that was intended to sit on an engineer's workbench with other instruments. A module contained what would be considered trivial logic components today: for example, six inverters, one flip-flop, or a crystal clock. Modules were designed to connect to form logic circuits.

In 1958, Digital Systems Modules were introduced, which were identical to Laboratory Modules but packaged to be rack-mounted and interconnected with pins in the back. Digital engineers built their first three computers, the PDP-1, PDP-4, and PDP-5 using Systems Modules. By 1964, the Systems Module was repackaged into the Flip Chip Module to make the interconnection even cheaper. This module used what is today called "edge connectors." The PDP-7 and PDP-8 computers were built initially with Flip Chip Modules, but integrated circuit chips—dual inline packages (DIPs)—introduced by the semiconductor industry, put an end to the Flip Chip Module product line.

Figure 10.2 illustrates the progression of Digital's computers. In this figure, the life span of the family is indicated along with the introduction of the most important machines in the class. The numbers in parentheses are the number of computers manufactured. Each of the classes will be discussed in more detail in the following sections. Notice that there are 5 classes defined by the primary memory word size. 12-bit, 18-bit, and 36-bit words seem like strange choices today, but at that time, the industry was based on a 6-bit character code called BCD (Binary Coded Decimal) and the 5-bit Baudot code. Notice too that the product lines overlap in time. As a result, both hardware and software ideas developed on one line were transferred to another line as personnel moved from one part of the company to another.

Digital computer models were simply named, starting with the PDP-1. PDP is an acronym for programmed data processor, a term coined to avoid

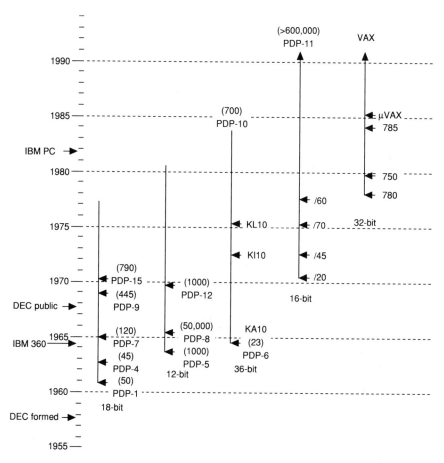

Figure 10.2. The Digital
product overview

the word "computer," and on the face plate of the PDP-1 console, the full name, not the acronym, was used. There is a story that Digital's venture capitalists thought the word "computer" had a negative connotation because too many companies were losing money making these machines. Even Digital's original name, Digital Computer Corporation, was scrapped in favor of something more ambiguous.

As each model was proposed, the number in the name was incremented, regardless of the machine's designed capabilities. There are model number gaps in Figure 10.2 that will not be discussed. Let it suffice that the PDP-2 (a 24-bit design) and the PDP-3 (a 36-bit design) were never built and that others, like the PDP-14 and PDP-16, were special-purpose machines that were not widely produced.

Initially, Digital was an "ironmaker"; it sold only the "bare" hardware, making the customer responsible for all of the software. As customers designed and debugged the software, it was shared—for instance, RSX-11A, the distant ancestor of the VMS operating system, was designed at Du Pont. Other software, notably FORTRAN, was designed and built by Digital as customer and marketing pressures for software products grew.

10.2. The 18-Bit Family

The first Digital computer, the PDP-1, was less expensive than an I/O channel attached to the top-of-the-line IBM 7090. It was an 18-bit machine, which may seem like a very curious choice today, but it made good sense at the time. Because of IBM's influence, primarily its keypunch, the most popular character code, BCD, was 6 bits. However, the 64-character set did not contain any lower-case letters and offered only a few special characters. A second reason for designing an 18-bit machine was that the large IBM machines were based on 36-bit words. This factor-of-two philosophy undoubtedly contributed to the unprecedented success of the PDP-11 as well. The PDP-11 was a 16-bit machine, which was half the size of the popular IBM 360 word. A third reason for the factor-of-two PDP-1 word size was that the most ubiquitous electronic keyboard/printer at the time was the teletype machine, used worldwide by news and telegraph companies. The teletype used a 5-bit code called Baudot, and it was the user's primary input/output device until the late 1960s, when Digital designed its own 8-bit devices.

Figure 10.3 shows the 18-bit family. It indicates the five models built,

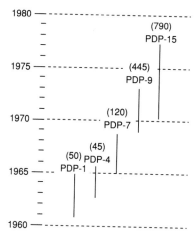

Figure 10.3. The 18-bit timeline

the production time span, and the total number of each model built. Notice that each new model outsold the sum of its ancestors. The first PDP-1 was sold in November 1960. It was manufactured with Digital's primary product, System Modules, which contained flip-flops, inverters, gates, amplifiers, and so forth. It was intended to be used as a small scientific computer. Similar machines, for example, the Bendix G-15 and the Librascope LGP-30, were cheaper but slower than the PDP-1 because they used a drum for primary memory. The original PDP-1 had a 4K-word core memory. Nearly half of the 50 produced were purchased by International Telephone and Telegraph (ITT) for use in a message switching system.

Of more importance to the computer industry than the PDP itself were the first time-sharing experiments being carried out on PDP-1s at MIT and BBN (Bolt, Beranek and Newman) in the early 1960s. At about the same time, another MIT time-sharing experiment was taking place on an IBM 7090. This was called the compatible time sharing system (CTSS) and was the forerunner of MULTIC (Multiplex Information and Computing Service). It was during these studies that the minimum requirements for a time-sharing system were identified:

- Memory protection
- An operating system
- I/O interrupts
- Time quanta applied to user processes

The BBN time-sharing system began operating in September 1962 on a modified PDP-1. It supported five teleprinters[1] and occupied 4K words of memory. Since each user had 4K of memory also, only one user resided in core memory at a time. Stanford and MIT were also developing time-sharing systems at this time. This work eventually led to a time-sharing system for the PDP-6, a 36-bit machine.

The PDP-4 was the PDP-1's successor. The PDP-1 performed one's complement arithmetic, whereas the PDP-4 was designed as a two's complement computer. Multiple precision had been discovered to be easier to implement in two's complement. The PDP-4 doubled the PDP-1 address space to 8K words, but its primary goal was to take advantage of the emerging silicon technology to become a faster, smaller machine than its predecessor.

The user community wanted more than iron, however, and Digital decided to provide a FORTRAN II compiler with the PDP-4. ALGOL-60 was briefly considered as well, but FORTRAN won out because of its popularity in the scientific community. Then too, at this time, ALGOL was available only on a Burroughs mainframe. Apparently, there were severe restrictions with the FORTRAN compiler because most users continued to code in assembly language. Probably, on such a small machine, useful FORTRAN programs exceeded memory too often to be practical. MIT contributed the assembler, the linker, and the debugger called DDT (Digital Diagnostic Technique) to the PDP-4 community.

In the early 1960s, Digital engineers were not concerned with software or its related costs because the company could change computer architecture at will. These changes were justified with the reasoning that the user software, when rewritten, would run faster and occupy less memory. Now, this philosophy would put the company out of business, since customers expect and demand "upward compatibility"; whatever programs used to execute on the old machine must also execute on the new one.

Machine compatibility is taken for granted today. In fact, the compatibility philosophy has been extended to the operating system; whenever the operating system is changed, users expect previously functioning applications to continue to execute without being recoded. They also expect purchased applications like word processors and spreadsheets to behave consistently from the old version to the new. Of course, users look forward to new features in the upgraded products, but they expect existing features to remain. And this expectation means that the operating system (or appli-

---

1. CRT terminals as they are known today were not used until the middle 1960s.

cation) forever grows and becomes increasingly complex; software entropy escalates.

The PDP-7 was a repackaged PDP-4 with enhanced performance. This time, the instruction set was compatible, and the software base, including the operating system and FORTRAN from the PDP-4, was moved to the new machine. Notice in Figure 10.3 that the PDP-7 outsold the sum of PDP-1s and PDP-4s, which means that Digital management must have understood its market. One interesting I/O feature was incorporated into the PDP-7: the industry at this time (middle 1960s) was changing over to the ASCII character standard, so the PDP-7 was designed to recognize either ASCII or the older Baudot code.

But even while the PDP-7 was in the late design stage, requirements for the PDP-9 were starting to develop. Again, the new machine was upward compatible but with packaging and performance enhancements; the PDP-9 was the first of the microprogrammed Digital machines. It should be noted that the 18-bit family was evolving in parallel with the other four families, so hardware and software design concepts were transferred between different family branches. For instance, the 2-$\frac{1}{2}$-D memory design developed in the PDP-8 family was transported to the PDP-9. As Figure 10.3 shows, more PDP-9 computers were built than the sum of their predecessors.

The PDP-15 soon replaced the PDP-9. This was a family of seven closely related models that represented a concept evolving in both the 12-bit and 16-bit branches. The PDP-15 was one of the first Digital machines to use integrated circuits instead of system modules. It had a floating point processor that enabled it to perform better in the FORTRAN environment, and with the addition of a special processor, a decrease of a factor of 10 in floating point execution time was realized. Once again, the PDP-15 sold more than the sum of its predecessors. In 1973, it was available in a dual processor configuration. The PDP-15 software suite included an assembler, an editor, a debugger, FORTRAN IV, a background/foreground monitor, and an assortment of utilities. The later versions of the PDP-15 supported disk drives.

10.3. The 12-Bit Family

Digital engineers realized that a computer smaller than the 18-bit family would have a place in the market, which was still viewed as an engineer's

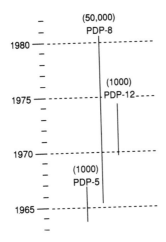

Figure 10.4. The 12-bit timeline

laboratory, not as monster computers behind a window-wall. Thus, the 12-bit computer was oriented toward data collection and process control. Figure 10.4 shows the major machines in this class. The PDP-5, introduced in 1963, was designed as a 4K-word machine and eventually grew to support 32K words. The concepts that most influenced the PDP-5 were developed at MIT on a device called the Laboratory Instrument Computer (LINC) that was developed in 1962 and 1963 from Digital modules. Over time, the LINC and the PDP-8 were integrated in two ways, as a two-processor system (LINC-8) and as a single-processor system (PDP-12).

Market pressures demanded a faster machine, so Digital engineers developed the PDP-8 at the same time as the PDP-7. One significant performance improvement was realized by moving the program counter (PC) from memory to a dedicated register, which could be done because of the reduction in flip-flop costs. The PDP-8 was the first "desk-top" computer; it was only a half-cabinet high and could be placed on the top of a laboratory workbench. It was also the first machine that took on a "family" status, since 10 implementations of the same architecture were developed over its 15-year production lifetime. The PDP-8 was so popular that in 1976, two manufacturers offered the processor on a chip, which was incorporated into the production of PDP-8s later that year. Digital engineers were more careful

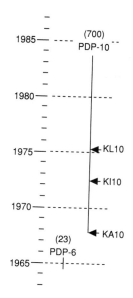

Figure 10.5. The 36-bit timeline

to maintain compatibility in the PDP-8 family, having learned their lesson in the 18-bit design.

From an operating systems standpoint, the most interesting application of the PDP-8 was the TSS/8, built at Carnegie-Mellon University in 1968. TSS/8 was built to show that time-sharing was not restricted to mainframes like the IBM 360/67. The TSS/8 system became the basis of RSTS, a time-sharing system that was available for the PDP-11.

10.4. The 36-Bit Family

Several nontraditional naming conventions were introduced with the 36-bit family. For example, two machines, the PDP-6 and the PDP-10, are collectively called DECsystem-10. And one rarely hears the PDP-10 referred to specifically; it goes by its three model's names: the KA10, KI10, and KL10. Figure 10.5 shows the DECsystem-10 timeline.

From a profit standpoint, the 36-bit family was the least successful, but from a technical standpoint, it paved the way for the PDP-11 and VAX family and significantly contributed to the knowledge base of the entire computer industry. The PDP-6 was the fourth machine designed by Digital engineers (the PDP-1 was marketed in 1960, the PDP-4 in 1962, and the PDP-5 in 1963). It represented an opportunity to correct past mistakes, both hardware and software, and to build on the successes of the earlier machines.

As initially conceived, the PDP-6 was to be a powerful time-shared machine targeted at the scientific community. It was designed with the primary goal of supporting a time-sharing operating system that would give each user the illusion that he or she owned a large computer. A 36-bit machine was a logical extension of the 18-bit PDP-4. It also meant that address space could be extended to 256K 36-bit words. However, this dream was not implemented until later on the PDP-10 in the early 1970s, when paging was introduced.

From the beginning, Digital engineers decided that FORTRAN would be supported on the PDP-6, but it was not clear at the time that FORTRAN would be an important language. Also, because of the MIT influence at Digital, the machine was designed to support LISP. There was no interest in supporting business applications, so COBOL was not considered in the initial design, although COBOL support was added in the early 1970s.

At the inception of the 36-bit computer, the computer design community had not yet settled on the value of stack-oriented architecture (like the Burroughs 5000) and general register-oriented architecture (like the IBM 360). However, it had become clear that the special-purpose register architecture (used in IBM 70xx machines) was not optimal from a software standpoint. Digital engineers decided to incorporate both general registers and stacks in their new machine. The general register could be used for accumulations, multiplier-quotients, subroutine linkage, temporary variables, stack pointers, and cache-like storage of very small programs. The stack could be used for implementing compilers (even today the theory of compilers is based on a stack model).

On the software side, Digital hardware designers had learned an important lesson from previous projects: software development is very costly; therefore, programming ease should be seriously considered, even if it means added expense to the hardware. The PDP-6 included hardware support for integer, real, and Boolean data for FORTRAN, and to support LISP, it included instructions for address arithmetic and character manipulation. The hardware also included support for recursive and reentrant subroutines because of the stack architecture, which was required by LISP. The instruction set was designed to be orthogonal and complete. For instance, all six comparisons would be included: three ADD instructions, one for each data type—integer, real, and double—and three subtract, three multiply, and three divide instructions. Thus, the PDP-6 turned out to be a CISC (Complex Instruction Set Computer) with 365 instructions.

This lesson of ease in programming can be observed in the VAX. In it, certain instructions like POLY (to evaluate a polynomial), CASE (to implement the case language construct), and INDEX (to compute a linear subscript) were obviously added to help the programmer. One measure of the usefulness of the instruction set is how many of the computer's instructions are used in code generated by the compiler. A study of the FORTRAN compiler on the KL10 revealed that of the 222 instructions related to FOR-TRAN data types, 212 of them appeared in user code—a very good score.

In the middle 1960s, the PDP-6 machine was trespassing into traditional mainframe territory because of its performance, but the computer's application was different from the traditional batch system application. In fact, it did not have batch capabilities at all; batch was to be supported as if it had originated from a virtual terminal. As described earlier, several universities were experimenting with time-sharing in the middle 1960s, and the PDP-6 was one of the first to come out of the laboratory and on-line for daily use.

Not much was known about time-sharing operating systems when the PDP-6 was designed, but it was clear that in order to support time-sharing, certain hardware facilities were prerequisite:

- Two modes (user and executive)
- Support for communication between user and operating system
- Separation and protection of users from one another

It was also clear that users would need to share the operating system and other software, such as editors, compilers, and utilities.

The goal of the primary PDP-6 operating system was to provide general-purpose time-sharing. This operating system was called Monitor,[2] and its first version, released in 1965, was memory-resident. Monitor was termed a "gentlemen's time-sharing" system because system resource allocation was not protected from deadlocks. Initially, it did not include any utilities, languages, or run-time support libraries. It supported a console and two DEC-tapes, but did not support a file system, and it was smaller than 6K words.

---

2. The operating system was later named TOPS-10 (Time-share Operating System).

The first PDP-6s had only 16K words of memory, which meant that they could reasonably support two users at a time. By 1978, Monitor had approximately 100K words because of increased support for files, spooling for more I/O devices and options, paging, a sophisticated scheduler, command language support, batch support, support of more users, reliability, and networking capabilities.

As time went on, Monitor and the DECsystem-10 advanced until the final CPU model (the KL10) was introduced, which could support over 70 users. Eventually, Monitor supported a loader, an interactive calculator, an assembler, several editors (EDIT, TECO, SOS), and several languages (APL, BASIC, BLISS, FORTRAN, LISP, and COBOL). Much of this software was distributed to the users through DECUS (DEC Users Society) and written primarily by the university programmers. The lessons learned on Monitor were incorporated in TSS/8, the PDP-8 time-sharing system previously mentioned, which was migrated to the PDP-11.

10.5. The 16-Bit Family

Like the successful PDP-8, the PDP-11 family had multiple models, 12 of which were defined by 1978. Figure 10.6 includes four of these models. In the first eight years, 50,000 PDP-11s were sold—a record that the PDP-8 took 15 years to achieve. The PDP-11 is still manufactured, and over 600,000 have been built.

The most important design concept of the PDP-11 was its Unibus: all system components, CPU, memory, and I/O devices are connected to a single, uniform bus. This architecture permits address mapping of I/O devices using exactly the same mechanism by which memory is addressed; it also permits the programmer to use the same instructions to access memory data and device data. Another notable feature of the PDP-11 is that it was the first Digital machine to implement the general register concept, first introduced in the PEGASUS computer in the middle 1950s.

Early in the PDP-11's life span, the 16-bit address space was recognized as too small. 16-bits means that an address can have only a 64K-byte range, which was too small for the class of problems the PDP-11 was expected to solve. This range was further restricted because the Unibus structure required that the last 8K of memory be reserved for I/O devices, so only 56K bytes of memory could be used for instructions and data. To partly overcome

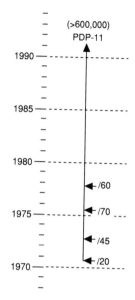

Figure 10.6. The 16-bit timeline

this limitation, the PDP-11/45, introduced in 1972, included a primitive virtual address mechanism. In today's terms, it possessed 8 virtual-to-physical registers.[3] Additionally, the Unibus was designed as an 18-bit structure, so physical memory could be increased to 256K bytes, permitting several 64K-byte processes to reside in memory simultaneously. If an application became too large, the designer made smaller processes out of it, and the memory management registers would be used to switch between processes. The operating system switched from process to process by reloading the paging registers at each context switch. Later, in the PDP-11/70, the Unibus was increased to 22 bits, permitting 2-megabyte memories. This had the effect of lengthening the effective product lifetime because the machine was able to perform well as application programs grew larger and larger. Furthermore, as the PDP-11 series's performance improved, the systems could handle more and more simultaneous time-sharing users.

3. Actually, there were 16 paging registers, 8 for instructions (read-only, called I-space) and 8 for data (read-write, called D-space). This meant that each process could address 64K words of instructions and 64K words of data, but Digital software did not take advantage of this design until much later.

The advent of the PDP-11 was a turning point in Digital's attitude toward software. The design of the PDP-11 incorporated several software issues, among them interrupt response time, debugging aids, compiler-generated code, program loading, and relocation. As with the 18-bit family, FORTRAN was the primary language for the PDP-11, a decision influenced undoubtedly by the IBM 1130 competition. The first PDP-11, the PDP-11/20, had only 16K bytes of physical memory, and 4K of those were dedicated to the operating system, DOS. The user code had to reside in the remaining 12K and therefore had to be used effectively by the application.

But this was a problem; typical compiler-generated code relies on a "run-time environment" to do data conversion, I/O support, and so forth. The PDP-11/20 had no floating point hardware, so the emulation of REAL arithmetic was carried out in run-time routines, too, and this was true of COMPLEX and DOUBLE PRECISION data types also. Thus, the run-time environment further reduced the application size. Digital engineers feared that a compiler would generate an inordinate number of subroutine calls. One subroutine call, a JSR instruction, takes four bytes on the PDP-11: two for the instruction and two for the address. Figure 10.7, part a, illustrates one method of FORTRAN execution using the JSR instruction. The user program makes calls to the FORTRAN service routines, often many calls to the same routine.

An interpreter was considered also in the FORTRAN design because it has the advantage of making all its FORTRAN service calls from a central location within the interpreter, as seen in part b of Figure 10.7. This reduces the number of JSR instructions. The user program size shrinks because two-byte operation codes replace the subroutine calls. The disadvantage of an interpreter is that the maximum run-time environment must reside in memory at all times; there is no way it can be tailored to the application. For instance, the COMPLEX service routines must reside in memory, even though they are not used, because the interpreter references them.

A third scheme, threaded code, was devised to combine the advantages of the two former methods. Native code limits the service routines to those actually referenced by the code, and interpreted code is smaller. The composite scheme is called *threaded code*. The user program consists of a series of addresses of the service routines. The service routines execute and, then, taking advantage of the PDP-11 architecture, jump to the next service routine. This is done with the JMP instruction, as Figure 10.7, part c, indicates. Register 4 is dedicated as a location counter for the user program. The program points to the next service routine, so an indirect jump is used to

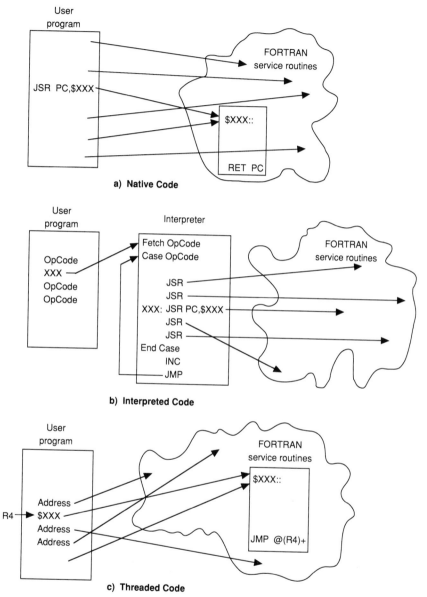

Figure 10.7. Three methods of
FORTRAN execution

enter each routine. At the same time, using auto-incrementing, register 4 is advanced to the next instruction. Thus, the threaded compiler created a program roughly half the size of a native code compiler.

Because hardware performance improved and memories grew bigger, the threaded compiler was replaced, in early 1975, by FORTRAN IV-PLUS, which generated native PDP-11 code. It is interesting to note that Digital engineers considered developing a computer that would execute threaded FORTRAN directly, but such a computer proved to be no faster than native code, so the project was abandoned.

In part, the PDP-11/60 was a response to the market. The majority of potential users were coding in FORTRAN IV and computing with integers, so an optimizing compiler that Digital officials called FORTRAN IV-PLUS was developed to take advantage of the PDP-11/60 architecture. The result was that FORTRAN program performance increased by a factor of 3.

Curiously, it was the PDP-11 that caused the Digital philosophy to deviate from the FORTRAN and scientific emphasis. Later in the lifetime of this machine, Digital decided to explicitly support COBOL, and in 1976, the PDP-11/03 added a Commercial Instruction Set (CIS) composed of instructions specifically designed for processing character strings, a decimal data type, and conversions between data types.

The first operating system, DOS (Disk Operating System), for the PDP-11 was transported from the PDP-8. This was a single-user batch system, the entire documentation set for which was contained in a Sears catalog-like bound manual. Another early system, based on a tape drive and called CAPS-11 (Cassette Programming System), was ported from the PDP-8. The first time-sharing system was written by a user and carried to Digital when he joined the company as an employee. This was RSX-11A (Resource-Sharing Executive). Initially, the system was memory-resident, and it had to be modified to make use of the disk drive. Since a disk was involved, a file system, Files-11, had to be added. By the time RSX-11A was running well, it had advanced to RSX-11D and was released to Digital customers.

Unfortunately, RSX-11D was too big for the smaller PDP-11 systems, so a scaled-down version, RSX-11M, was developed for them. (There were no systems between RSX-11D and RSX-11M; a naming philosophy change accounted for the jump in sequence ("M" meant medium).) In the early days of the PDP-11, computers had operator consoles equipped with LEDs and switches for reading and writing memory mechanically. It was not unusual for programmers to debug their code from the front panel of the computer by single-stepping through the program and modifying the assembly language as necessary. Single-stepping could not be tolerated in a time-sharing environment, but the lights still remained on the consoles and the system programmers continued to use them. The Null process (RSX called it a Null task) displayed a pattern in the console lights that appeared to circulate. The speed at which it circulated indicated how often Null was executing. This was the first performance monitor supported by Digital. In RSX-11D, the lights rotated from left to right and RSX-11M from right to left.

RSX-11M continued to be improved until the newer, larger, and more capable hardware made using it impractical. RSX-11M +[4] was invented to support the high-end of the product line, notably the large memory PDP-11/70s.

Several spin-off operating systems were developed by Digital in the PDP-11's 20-year history, but most had only a limited life. IAS (Interactive Application System) was derived from RSX-11D. Although it was never very popular, some of its concepts were incorporated in the VMS operating system. RSX-11S was a diskless system intended for very small CPUs that would be called embedded application systems today. TRAX was a transaction operating system. CTS-300 was a commercial time-sharing system. RSTS (Resource-Sharing Time-Sharing) was based on BASIC and carried forward from TSS/8; it is still a popular second choice to RSX. RT-11 (Real-Time) was intended as a small real-time system. Parts of it influenced CP/M (Control Program for Microcomputers), a system developed for the Intel 8080 and floppy disk drives in the middle 1970s.

In the early 1970s, experimental multiprocessor systems constructed with the PDP-11 were developed. At Carnegie-Mellon University, one called C.mmp contained 16 processors sharing a 5-million-byte memory. Although multiprocessor systems have not been discussed in this text, the argument for their development is appealing. Without being precise, through the combination of many relatively inexpensive computers, the performance of large, expensive computers can be easily realized at a fraction of the cost. But combining computers in this way is by no means trivial, in terms of hardware or software, and programming the resulting system is even more difficult. Software, especially compilers, that automatically subdivide an

---

4. It is interesting to see how system names are spelled: FORTRAN-IV PLUS, not FORTRAN-IV +, and RSX-11M +, not RSX-11M PLUS.

application across several processors, has yet to be developed. In the case of C.mmp, these difficulties were somewhat minimized. As mentioned, since the address space was small, PDP-11 processes tended to be small. Further, if the processes were independent, running them on a multiprocessor system was a natural extension to time-sharing—for instance, an editor could run on one processor, a compiler on another, and so forth. The operating system developed to support these experiments was named Hydra. Work on this system and other variations of hardware and software continued throughout the 1970s.

10.6. The 32-Bit Family

The fundamental weakness of the PDP-11 was its small addressing capability, as defined by the 16-bit address. Luckily, its design permitted a limited workaround for many years through a memory management scheme introduced on the PDP-11/45. However, as the computing need grew, it became apparent that the addressing capability needed to be extended. For instance, a FORTRAN program containing an 8,000 entry DOUBLE PRECISION array completely filled the address space. So the target audience (scientific users) was restricted by the PDP-11 architecture to a class of problems users could conveniently solve. The PDP-11 needed to be extended, and for this purpose, the term and the concept Virtual Address Extension—VAX—were formulated. Work on the VAX began in April 1975.

After much internal agonizing, Digital engineers decided to make a quantum leap from the successful PDP-11 but to maintain compatibility with it. Much of the PDP-11's instruction set was emulated on the VAX; the PDP-11 user instructions (not the privileged ones) were implemented. This permitted Digital designers to change the architecture without worrying about PDP-11 compatibility. The lessons learned on the PDP-11 were not forgotten on the VAX; for instance, since it was found that PDP-11 literals were six bits or less 98 percent of the time, the VAX instruction set was designed to accommodate various-size literals, and the 6-bit literal was the most efficiently implemented. Figure 10.8 presents the VAX family history.

Another lesson was learned from the PDP-11 experience: limit the number of operating systems. Each operating system requires a team of software engineers to maintain and extend it, which is expensive. Very early in the VAX development, this duplication of effort was articulated in what

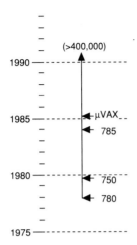

Figure 10.8. The 32-bit timeline

has become known as the *VAX strategy*: one architecture and one operating system. This is the foundation on which Digital continues to build.

Although this goal makes sense by itself, it also led to distributed computing, which is more difficult if the VAX strategy is not in place. The huge proliferation of networking solutions for microcomputers today attests to the complexity of distributed computing, and Digital engineers saved untold manpower by adhering to the VAX strategy for almost 15 years. On the other hand, the PDP-11 is still a viable and profitable product.

The first VAX, the VAX-11/780, was demonstrated to have comparable performance to the top-of-the-line PDP-11/70. In maintaining performance capability, Digital management hoped to migrate its PDP customers into the VAX family. Even the name, VAX-11, was a suggestion that the two machines were closely related. Digital's marketing philosophy was in high contrast to IBM's when it introduced the 360 series 10 years earlier. In IBM's case, the new machine bore no relation to the popular 70xx series it was intended to replace, either in function or in name. Even the word size was incompatible: the 70xx was a 36-bit machine, and the 360 was a 32-bit machine; thus, every program, even FORTRAN and COBOL programs, had to be reconsidered because the word sizes had shrunk.

Digital had decided that the VAX would actually execute PDP-11 instructions in what was called the *compatibility mode*. Offering this mode ensured that user applications that included assembly code could be moved from the PDP-11 to the VAX-11 with little effort. Furthermore, the VAX instruction set, the *native mode* instructions, was heavily influenced by the experience gained on the PDP-11. Several PDP-11 features were carried into the VAX:

1. The PDP-11 data types: byte, integer, and real.
2. The instructions and addressing modes. This made the VAX assembler an extension of the PDP-11 assembler.
3. The same bus structure, so PDP-11 peripherals could be used on the VAX.
4. System services, command languages, the utilities, security features, and file management carried over from the PDP-11 and simply extended—the operating system, VMS, was an extension of RSX-11M+.

In the move from the PDP-11 to the VAX, a total operating system rewrite was out of the question; such an effort would have been resource consuming, requiring the full Digital software staff and more calendar time than the hardware design would have allowed. Not just the operating system but also all of the support software—compilers, file support routines, and so forth—would have to have been rebuilt. So another reason to provide the VAX with a PDP-11 compatibility mode was that only the nucleus of the operating system would have to be written. Other parts, for instance, the compilers, would not need drastic modification; they could be moved into the VMS operating system with only minor changes.

There were three compilers initially available. The FORTRAN compiler was rewritten in VAX native instructions, and it created native VAX instructions, but there was no time to rewrite the other two. COBOL and BASIC executed PDP-11 instructions on the VAX and produced PDP-11 instructions, so both the compilers and the application programs had to run in compatibility mode. If the user called the COBOL or BASIC compiler, it would switch to the PDP-11 mode, compile the program, and then, when finished, switch back to VAX native mode. By structuring the compilers this way, Digital engineers gave themselves time to rewrite them, but in the meantime, the users had use of their full software capabilities. It was only after several years that these two compilers were rewritten in native code to generate native VAX instructions.

Other utilities were treated the same way; initially, they were not recoded except to switch into compatibility mode to execute, but on later releases of the VMS operating system, native versions of these utilities were included. The compatibility philosophy was carried to the limit: originally, a version of RSX-11 was available to execute on the VAX to ease the customer migration effort.

By providing both hardware and software upward compatibility, the VAX family was allowed to evolve without causing any customer interruptions. As newer models of the computer and the operating system were introduced, the user's applications were at most recompiled and relinked before they ran again. Of course, new features were added to the VMS operating system over time, and the user could take advantage of them whenever it was convenient. Another benefit of PDP-11 compatibility was that using existing operating system code resulted in VMS being quite reliable. Normally the first version of an operating system is not very stable because it contains many latent errors. By borrowing heavily from RSX-11, an operating system used for many years, the VMS code avoided much of the trouble normally associated with initial releases.

10.7. Summary

Here we have presented a brief history of Digital Equipment Corporation, starting with its first product, laboratory modules. We then examined each of its five computer families. The computer industry as a whole and its customers shaped Digital's design philosophy; for instance, the company followed IBM in selecting the word size of its machines. However, Digital also contributed to the industry's knowledge base—for instance, in its vigorous support of time-sharing systems.

The story is not over. The DECsystem-10 was discontinued over the strong objections of a loyal customer base. The VAX was supposed to replace and put an end to the PDP-11, but customers' objections prevailed, and the PDP-11 remains a manufactured and supported product. The VAX was designed to be the last of the families, but technology has a way of dealing with absolutes. The VAX operating system was thought to possess an extensible architecture too, but AT&T's UNIX, which, ironically, was developed on a PDP-7 and later moved to a PDP-11, is a serious contender for use on the VAX. An interesting benefit of the AT&T breakup is that UNIX is in the hands of the public, whereas VMS is a proprietary product.

ACRONYMS

ALGOL	International ALGOrithmic Language
AT&T	American Telephone and Telegraph
BCD	Binary Coded Decimal
BBN	Bolt, Beranek and Newman
CISC	Complex Instruction Set Computer
CP/M	Control Program for Microcomputers
CTSS	Compatible Time-Sharing System
DDT	Digital Diagnostic Technique
FORTRAN	Formula Translator
ITT	International Telephone and Telegraph
LED	Light Emitting Diode
LINC	Laboratory Instrument Computer
LISP	List Processor
PDP	Programmed Data Processor
RISC	Reduced Instruction Set Computer
RSTS	Resource-Sharing Time-Sharing
RSX	Resource Sharing Executive
RT	Real Time operating system
TSS	Time-Shared System
VAX	Virtual Address Extension

PAPERS

1. Refer to Bell. Chapter 1, "The Practice of Design," can be applied to software also. For instance, what are the objectives and costs of software (page 22), and what are the software equivalents to Vonada's Engineering Maxims (page 24)?

2. Superimpose the lifespan (date of first delivered unit to date of last delivered) of the following machines on Figure 10.2: IBM 650, IBM 709, IBM 360, CDC 160, CDC 6600, Cray 1, Apple I, and HP 35. Use other operating systems texts for resources and state the exact reference, including page number. Warning: several of these machines are rather obscure, and data will be difficult to find.

3. Why was the HP 35 considered to be a milestone in hand-held calculators?

4. Compare and contrast interpreted code, threaded code, and compiled code for the following characteristics:

- Compilation time
- Execution time
- Incremental execution
- Symbolic debugging
- Execution memory requirements
- Portability

There are numerous references for compilers and interpreters, but the only references I know for threaded codes are:

Bell, J. R., "Threaded Code," *Communications of the ACM,* 16(6), June 1973.

Bell, C. G. et al., eds., *Computer Engineering* (Chapter 15, "Turning Cousins into Sisters: An Example of Software Smoothing of Hardware Differences"), Bedford, Mass.: Digital Press.

5. Compare and contrast the PDP-11/45 "paging" scheme with the VAX paging mechanism.

6. Add the following milestones to the three timelines in Figure 10.1. Defend your findings with specific references and dates: for example, state the date BASIC appeared on a minicomputer, and quote the reference in which you found that information.

- BASIC
- COBOL
- Relational database
- Hierarchical database
- Symbolic debuggers
- Word processing (by embedded commands—e.g., RUNOFF)
- WYSIWYG word processors

7. Research various definitions of micro-, mini-, and mainframe computers. The attributes that form the definitions as well as the definitions themselves have changed drastically over time. Carefully present a picture of these definitions and their changes over time.

8. Outline the development of OS/2, which is an operating system similar in function to the VMS operating system and is designed to run on hardware functionally similar to the VAX.

Appendix A

Answers to Short
Answer Exercises

CHAPTER 1

1. CTRL-Y and CTRL-C produce a reverse video 'Interrupt.'
   CTRL-T produces a status line, if enabled.
   CTRL-M or Return echoes both CTRL-M and CTRL-J (line feed).
   Left and right arrows move the cursor.
   Up and down arrow display previously entered commands.
   CTRL-J or Line feed deletes characters to a delimiter.
   CTRL-I or Tab echoes spaces until the next tab mark is reached.
   ESCAPE echoes nothing.
2. The print head will then be positioned over the 'bad' character. And
   when the correct character is struck, it will overwrite the previous one,
   making both characters illegible.
3. A blinking checkerboard is displayed instead of the character on the
   Microterm Ergo 301. Other terminals will respond differently.
4. See Figure A.1.
5. See Figure A.2. The second character's start bit can immediately follow

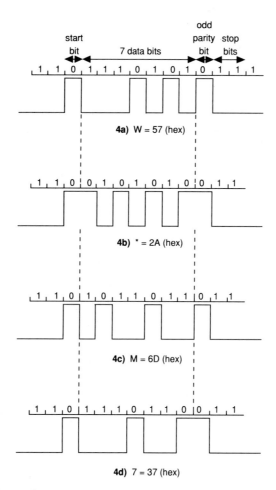

Figure A.1. Answers for question 4 (Chapter 1)

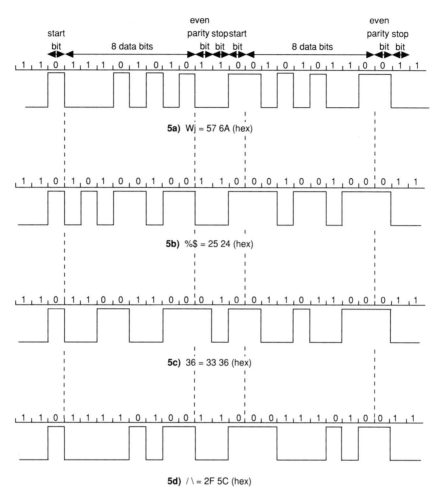

Figure A.2. Answers for question 5 (Chapter 1)

the first character's stop bit, although that is not a requirement; this is why this is an asynchronous protocol.

6. • DELETE echoes a backstroke (\) and the deleted character.
   • ∧U starts a new line.
   • ∧Y and ∧C display *INTERRUPT*.
   • ∧Z displays *EXIT*.

7. At least 10/4800 × 80 = 0.167 seconds. It can be longer if there are any delays between characters.

8. 100 × 6 = 600 characters/minute = 10 characters/second.
   10 characters/second = 90 bits/second = 90 baud. Not too fast.

9. A process can change its *own state* only when it is executing. Notice that a process may change states when it is not 'current,' for instance from 'waiting' to 'computable,' but the system is performing that change, not the process itself.

10. • Any of the interactive utilities are possible candidates; EDT, TPU, MAIL, PHONE, HELP, and DEBUG are the most common. These utilities also use the keypad, and although the user can create keypad commands at the command level, there are no default definitions. ∧Y and ∧Z generally behave differently in these utilities.
    • HELP, DEBUG, and CREATE are identical to command level editing.
    • The editors cause the up and down arrows to scroll the file. EDT LF has some subtle differences. EDT ∧Z brings the user to a different editor.
    • PHONE echos characters in the proper window, not necessarily where the cursor is located. ∧L clears the entire window.
    • MAIL treats ∧Y and ∧C differently.

11. The keys you enter are not echoed, but the system responses are displayed as usual.

12. 'Type_ahead' is a terminal driver feature not described in the book. It permits the user to type even though data is being actively written on the screen. The command turns off this feature.

CHAPTER 2

1. Depending on SYSGEN selection, either BREAK or one of the following:
   a. RETURN
   b. CTRL-Y

2. The sum of the 'CPU' column should be less than the 'Uptime' value because users have logged on, used some CPU time, and then logged off again. These users are not accounted for in the display—only current processes are recorded there.

3. `$ SPAWN`

   `$ LOGOUT/FULL`

   will be approximate. Assuming that the LOGOUT time is a constant (which is a valid assumption), the result from Exercise 5 can be subtracted from the 'Charged CPU time' value in the logout message.

   A second method is to use ∧T inside the subprocess. The command SET CONTROL = T entered in the parent process is automatically carried into the subprocess, so the sequence:

   `$ SPAWN`

   `$ ∧T`

   `$ LOGOUT`

   can be executed several times to determine an average value. The 11/785 time in this case is 0.56 seconds.

4. The most exact method is to use the ACCOUNTING utility, but since students are probably not privileged enough to use it, the SHOW SYSTEM command can be used in the following way: LOGIN, SHOW SYSTEM (and record the JOB_CONTROL CPU time), and LOGOUT. Perform this a number of times to determine an average value. Care must be taken to discount multiple JOB_CONTROL runs because of two (or more) simultaneous LOGINs. It would be best to run this experiment during 'off' hours when it is likely that only a few users will be logged in to the system. On our 11/785, the time ranged from 0.03 to 0.09 seconds in the five tries I made.

5. Use the technique outlined in Exercise 4 for the SWAPPER process CPU time. On an 11/785, the time is uniformly 0.01 seconds in five tries.

6. Use the technique outlined in Exercise 4 for your process. To eliminate LOGIN.COM processing to get a more accurate value, the user should login without the command file, that is

   `Username: DMILLER/NOCOMMAND`

A more accurate technique is to LOGIN without a command file, e.g., DMILLER/NOCOMMAND, and then set (SET CONT=T) and use CTRL-T to record the CPU time. ∧T is much faster than SHOW SYS and produces only one line. Using the ∧T method on an 11/785, the average LOGIN time is 1.28 seconds.

7. The command LOGOUT/FULL displays 'Charged CPU time'. This value must be reduced by the LOGIN time that was determined in Exercise 3. With the ∧T method in Exercise 4, the average LOGOUT time on an 11/785 is 0.07 seconds.

8. RUN does not verify the file's extension. Attempting to RUN a .OBJ file, for instance, results in an error message. On older versions of the VMS operating system, this message is followed by a register dump.

9. SHOW PROCESS/QUOTA displays the remaining quota. One experiment to show this is to start several subprocesses to see what happens to that quota value. Another is to simply observe the various values to see that they are changing. The job quota is an anomaly. The number of jobs one user has active must be kept in some other, more global data structure.

10. The (*) indicates which (sub)process is executing the SHOW PROCESS command.

CHAPTER 3

1. There is a discrepancy between the defaults; entering time from the keyboard makes different assumptions from those the system service makes.

2. The formal definition in HELP contains two more optional arguments. Since they are not specified, they default to the values specified in STARLET.

3. $ASCTIM has two modes of operation. The one indicated in Figure 3.9 gives the current date/time. The other mode translates an arbitrary binary time to ASCII.

4. LIB$ADDX and LIB$SUBX are the two arbitrary precision add and subtract routines that can be used for this purpose.

5. This question is intended to get the reader into the code.

6. The key to this exercise is the WAIT command. Apparently, $HIBER is used by WAIT; SHOW PROCESS/CONTINUOUS shows the event

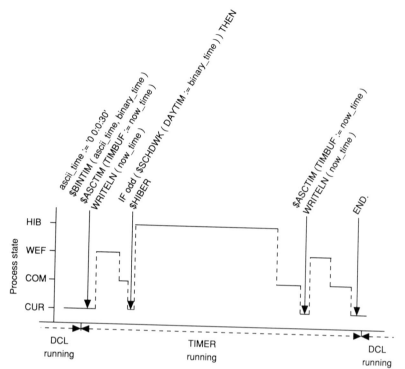

Figure A.3. Answer for question 7 (Chapter 3)

flags changing. Event flags are unnecessary with $SUSPEND/$WAKE logic.

7. Refer to Figure A.3. All Pascal executable statements should be associated with the CUR state. The other state changes are caused by the VMS operating system itself.

8. It is extremely convenient for users to be able to develop software and run it on the same machine. Editing, compiling, linking, and then moving to another machine for test and check-out is awkward and time-consuming.

    A second reason can be strictly financial. Why buy two machines when one, with twice the capacity (presumably at less than twice the cost), is available.

9. As the time quantum increases, less time-sharing between processes is done. This causes the response time to increase and the system begins

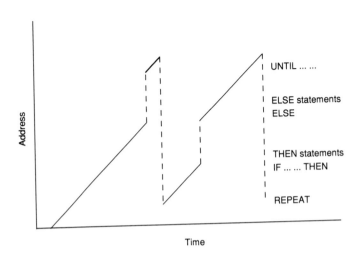

*Figure A.4. Answer for question
3 (Chapter 4)*

to exhibit batch system characteristics. On the other hand, when the quantum is increased, the overhead drops. Therefore, there is an optimum value for the quantum when the response time is acceptable for a given overhead.

CHAPTER 4

	Region	Page	Offset
1.			
a.	2(SYS)	1AD,1A5	102
b.	0(P0)	007,000	1FF
c.	1(P1)	0A8,01D	0A9
d.	3(illegal)	152,24D	1B2
e.	2(SYS)	094,017	0D3

2. A page length violation causes an access-control violation fault, which is distinct from a page fault (Digital calls this a translation not valid fault). That is, there are two SCB addresses associated with paging. Since the image contains an error, a traceback is produced and the image is rundown. Control returns to DCL and the process is not deleted.

3. See Figure A.4. It depicts the IF . . . THEN clause executing first.

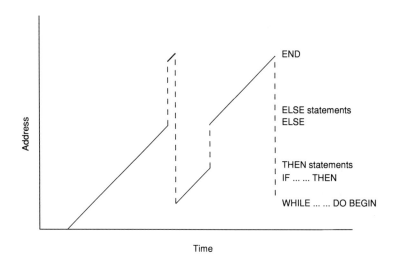

Figure A.5. Answer for question
4 (Chapter 4)

Next, the UNTIL is evaluated and the loop is repeated. This time, assume the IF condition is not met and the ELSE clause is executed instead.

4. See Figure A.5. It depicts the IF . . . THEN clause executing first, skipping the ELSE clause and executing the bottom of the WHILE loop. Then the WHILE condition is tested and the loop continues. This time, the IF condition is not met and the ELSE clause is executed instead.

5. If the page replacement is demanded immediately after the reference bits are all cleared, it will appear as if all pages are eligible for replacement. Another difficulty arises in deciding which unreferenced page to use; presumably, there is more than one. However, a third difficulty might occur when, near the end of the time limit, all pages have been referenced.

6. One reason is that the page tables of a large process occupy a large percentage of physical memory, denying this resource to other users. A second, more subtle reason is that page tables must be contiguous. Refer to the Papers section for a related question.

7. The following hexadecimal arithmetic is performed:

$$8,70A = 43 \times 200 + 10A$$

Partial Display of Memory

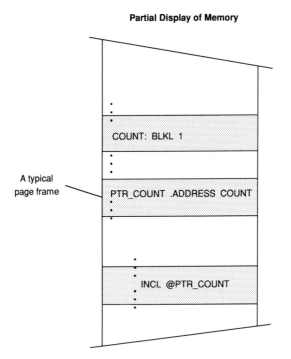

Figure A.6. Answer for question 10 (Chapter 4)

The multiplication by 200 is needed to shift the frame value 9 bits, then the offset is added. In other words, to compute physical address from virtual address, the frame number replaces the page number.

8. The SLR contains a count of the number of SYS page table entries. Multiply this value by 4; the result is 3F,800 or about 260K bytes.

9. The solid lines are positive because the PC is incremented; it is never decremented. A JUMP instruction causes either a negative or a positive discontinuity in the figure, never a sloped line.

10. See Figure A.6. The first fault happens when PTR_COUNT, which contains COUNT's address, is being located. The second fault occurs when the address in PTR_COUNT is being used to locate the value to be incremented, COUNT.

11. Two megabytes is not 2,000,000 bytes, as newspaper columnists some-

times state. A megabyte is a kilobyte squared. A kilobyte is 1,024 bytes thus 2 megabytes is

$$2 \times 1,024 \times 1,024 = 2,097,152$$

Another way to compute this is knowing a megabyte is 2^{20}

$$2 \times 2^{20} = 2,097,152.$$

12. Two mega-pages is $2 \times 1,024 \times 1,024 \times 512$ bytes as stated above. (A page is 512 bytes.) This results in 1,073,741,824. A gigabyte is a thousand million bytes (1024^3), the same value.

CHAPTER 5

1. Here are some possibilities, but they are not the only ones:
   - Traffic lights and stop signs synchronize vehicles.
   - Drawbridges synchronize boat and vehicular traffic.
   - A "line" (or queue) of customers at a cash register.
   - The baton used in relay races synchronizes the runners.
   - A referee's whistle or starter's gun signals that play is to begin.
   - The quarterback calling out signals synchronizes team movement.
   - The conductor of an orchestra synchronizes the players.

2. Process A   Process B

```
$SETEF (65);

                        $WAITFR (65);
                        logic
                        $SETEF (64);
                        $CLREF (65)
                        $WAITFR (65);
$CLREF (64);
$WAITFR (64);
```

In the example above, the $SETEF in "A" starts "B," which runs to its next WAIT. Then when "A" runs again, the $CLREF permanently clears the flag. This is another form of a deadly embrace.

3. The first process needs four mailboxes, the second needs three additional mailboxes (it already has a mailbox between itself and the first), and so forth. Ten mailboxes are needed in all. This is shown in Figure A.7.

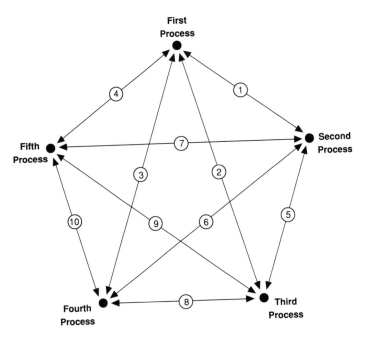

Figure A.7. Answer for question
3 (Chapter 5)

4. The VMS designers decided not to incorporate the priority logic within the event flag logic. In other words, rather than including priority logic in the event flag system service, all processes are changed to COM, and the scheduler decides which one is to execute first.

5. Over time, the mailbox number may exceed its maximum value and begin again at MBA1. However, as described, there are always permanent mailboxes in the system, like MBA1, and so "x" must be incremented until an unused mailbox name is located.

6. The $QIOW for the write will not complete until the message is received by another process. The sender will wait until its message has been received and, therefore, cannot receive its own message.

7. Only one $WAIT request can be queued because the PCB only has a single bit to record the request. If the bit was replaced by a counter, queuing could be supported.

8. See Figure 3.12. The only change is that the process moves to CEF (Common Event Flag) state instead of HIB (Hibernate).

CHAPTER 6

1. Besides the two listed in Figure 6.3, there are two others:

```
(FIRST)    COUNT := 5;
(SECOND)   COUNT := COUNT + 2;
(FIRST)    COUNT := COUNT + 1;
(FIRST)    WRITELN (COUNT);

(FIRST)    COUNT := 5;
(FIRST)    COUNT := COUNT + 1;
(SECOND)   COUNT := COUNT + 2;
(FIRST)    WRITELN (COUNT);
```

Note, particularly, that the following is not possible because the instructions within a process cannot be rearranged:

```
(FIRST)    COUNT := COUNT + 1;
(SECOND)   COUNT := COUNT + 2;
(FIRST)    COUNT := 5;
(FIRST)    WRITELN (COUNT);
```

2. There are 20 possible threads—four are shown below—and two possible results: either 1 or 2.

   a. Process B runs to completion before A starts:

```
TempB := X;
TempB := TempB + 1;
X := TempB;
TempA := X;
TempA := TempA + 1;
X := TempA;              result = 2
```

   b. The first line of Process A is executed, and then all of Process B:

```
TempA := X;
TempB := X;
TempB := TempB + 1;
X := TempB;
TempA := TempA + 1;
X := TempA;              result = 1
```

   c. The first two lines of Process A are executed, and then all of Process B executes:

```
TempA := X;
TempA := TempA + 1;
TempB := X;
TempB := TempB + 1;
X := TempB;
X := TempA;              result = 1
```

d. Process A runs to completion before B starts:

```
TempA := X;
TempA := TempA + 1;
X := TempA;
TempB := X;
TempB := TempB + 1;
X := TempB;            result = 2
```

3. There are many possible threads—four are shown below yielding three possible results: 1, 2, or 3.

a. Process C runs completely, then B runs to completion, and finally A starts:

```
TempC := X;
TempC := TempC + 1;
X := TempC;
TempB := X;
TempB := TempB + 1;
X := TempB;
TempA := X;
TempA := TempA + 1;
X := TempA;            result = 3
```

b. The first line of Process A is executed, and then all of Process C, followed by all of Process B; then A finishes:

```
TempA := X;
TempC := X;
TempC := TempC + 1;
X := TempC;
TempB := X;
TempB := TempB + 1;
X := TempB;
TempA := TempA + 1;
X := TempA;            result = 1
```

c. The first two lines of Process A are executed, and then all of Processes C and B execute:

```
TempA := X;
TempA := TempA + 1;
TempC := X;
TempC := TempC + 1;
X := TempC;
TempB := X;
TempB := TempB + 1;
X := TempB;
X := TempA;            result = 1
```

d. Process A runs to completion before B starts and executes two lines before C. C runs to completion; then B executes its final line:

```
TempA := X;
TempA := TempA + 1;
X := TempA;
TempB := X;
TempB := TempB + 1;
TempC := X;
TempC := TempC + 1;
X := TempC;
X := TempB;                    result = 2
```

4. a. This is nearly identical to the chapter's example. The thread:

```
Q := VARIB;
LIB$WAIT ( 0.5 );
VARIB := Q + 1;
```

   is critical. The two WRITELNs are "read only" uses of VARIB.

   b. This is the more normal form of the code exhibited in part a. The single line:

```
VARIB := VARIB + 1;
```

   is critical.

5. Assume that both processes are waiting for the event flag to be set. When it is, both begin executing. It does not matter which clears the event flag first because they both enter the critical region. Likewise, the order of setting the event flag is immaterial, since neither are waiting for it.

Process A	Process B

`$WAITFR (flag_number);`
`$CLREF (flag_number);`
.
.
.
`$SETEF (flag_number);`
	`$WAITFR (flag_number);`
	
	`$CLREF (flag_number);`
	.
	.
	.
	`$SETEF (flag_number);`

6. See Figure A.8. The resource hash table (RHT) contains three entries, one for each resource block (RSB). Likewise the lock ID table (LID) has six entries in it, one for each lock block (LKB). Process ONE is linked to its three LKBs, and Process TWO links to its three. Since Resources Y and Z are currently inactive, their states are NULL and the LKBs are linked into the granted queue. Process ONE's LKB is linked to the granted queue of the RSB for Resource X while Process TWO's LKB is linked to the queue.

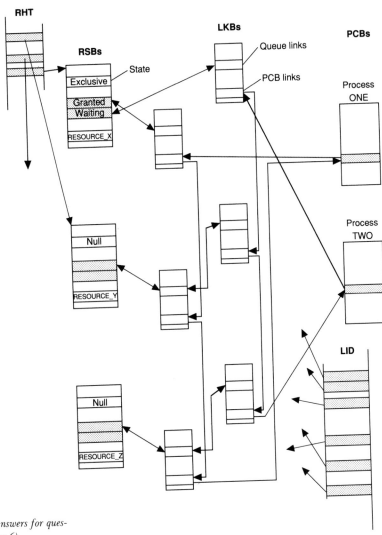

Figure A.8. Answers for question 6 (Chapter 6)

7. The code would look like this:

```
CONDITION := $CLREF (flag_number)        { Lock critical region }
WHILE (CONDITION <> SS$_WASSET) DO BEGIN
  $WAITFR (flag_number);
  CONDITION := $CLREF (flag_number)
END;
.
.
.
                                         { Critical region }

$SETEF (flag_number);                    { Unlock critical region }
```

8. In Chapter 5, the basic problem was to ensure that only one process was executing at a time. Now, in this application, multiple processes must execute in parallel except during certain times. $HIBER-$WAKE prohibits parallel execution; $ENQW conditionally prohibits parallel execution.

9. The VMS operating system does not make a test for spelling errors. If the resource is declared and used consistently, VMS can only assume you have set up two resources. A mix-up can also occur if the lock status blocks are confused.

10. There are two cases to consider, depending on the relative positions of W_INDEX and R_INDEX, that is, depending on whether the data is contiguous or split. Looking at Figure 6.21 aids in understanding the following code.

```
IF (R_INDEX <= W_INDEX) THEN      { data contiguous }
      DATA_ENTRIES := W_INDEX - R_INDEX
ELSE                               { data discontiguous }
      DATA_ENTRIES := max_size + 1 - (R_INDEX - W_INDEX);
```

11. See Figure A.9. It shows two processes sharing a resource block through their respective lock blocks. One of the processes also has declared two common event flag clusters.

CHAPTER 7

1. Whenever the fence boundary was violated, the operating system examined the offending instruction to see that it was a subroutine call and that the desired destination address was the entry point to a system service. If these two conditions were met, the instruction was permitted to execute. Otherwise, the user's process was aborted.

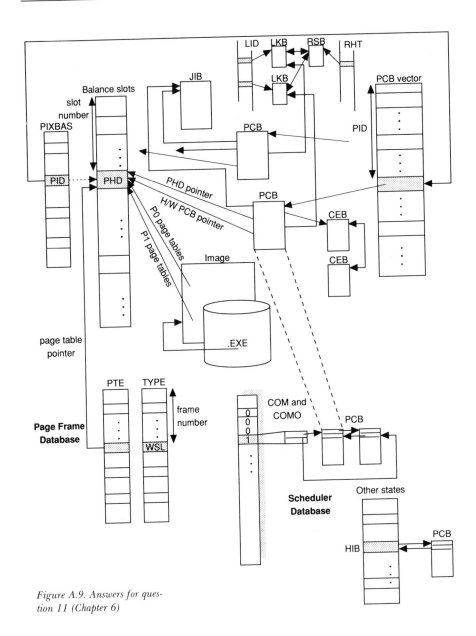

Figure A.9. Answers for question 11 (Chapter 6)

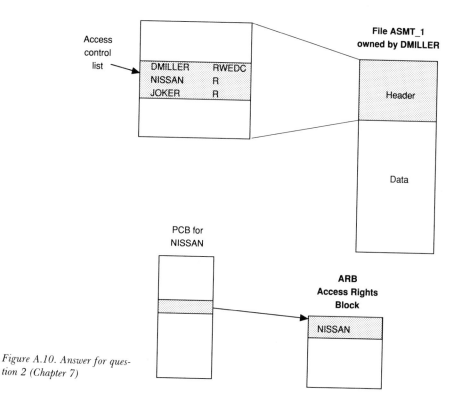

Figure A.10. Answer for question 2 (Chapter 7)

2. See Figure A.10. If the INTRO_VAX group were removed, every member of that group would have to be added to the access control list in the file.

3. This summary was not included in the text of Chapter 7. The interested reader will be curious enough to read the summary below, which contains some new material.

   • The system manager may disable passwords.

   • The user may require two passwords to access the account.

   • The system requires that passwords be reset periodically, usually every 180 days.

   • On VMS Version 5.4 and beyond, a password may not be reused for some period of time. Earlier versions did not keep a password history.

   • The VMS system will generate passwords for the user. This is either optional or mandatory as determined by the system manager.

- The VMS system will audit legal or illegal account entries, or both.
- The VMS system will optionally prohibit certain passwords.
- Passwords cannot be displayed by anyone, including the system manager.
- Passwords are required to be a minimum length, usually six characters.

4. MAIL must be able to write into the destination user's account. The SYSTEM UIC is used to determine account availability, and the user can prohibit mail by clearing the system field of the root directory. The required PHONE privilege is not so obvious. An unprivileged user is not permitted to write data on any other terminal. In the system's view, terminals are treated like files. Just as MAIL requires system privilege to enter data in specific files, PHONE requires system privilege to enter data on another user's terminal.

5. Our society is bursting with security examples: I can remember when my mother's maiden name and my account number were all I needed to gain telephone access to my savings balance. Some banks will accept a passbook and signature as proof of ownership. A signature and a key are normally all that is required to access my safe deposit box. To check out a library book, all I need is a card. To get a job, I have to produce my social security card and a birth certificate. To travel abroad, I need a U.S. passport and, sometimes, a visa from the destination country. To unlock my safe (or bicycle), I need a combination, which, normally, the lock manufacturer selects for me. At one time, there was a proposal to integrate a sobriety test with an automobile ignition lock.

CHAPTER 8

1. The page tables must be locked down so that the hardware can do the necessary virtual-to-physical translations at any time. The buffers must be locked down to be available throughout the I/O transfer. If they are not locked, the VMS system may remove a page from the working set because it appears unreferenced during I/O operations.

2. The read buffer is allocated by the system and linked to the UCB just as the write buffer is. Data is transferred from this buffer to the user area during postprocessing and then released.

3. In the VMS operating system, the read ahead buffer is allocated as part of the process creation activity. All read data is routed through that buffer into a second buffer within the I/O system as described in Exercise 2. This is necessary because the read ahead buffer may contain carriage returns, whereas the I/O buffer usually does not.

4. If the VMS system did not check the $QIO arguments, any arbitrary portion of memory can be copied to a disk file and later analyzed. This is possible because the I/O system operates in privileged mode only; no privilege checking, so no violations, can occur during an I/O operation.

5. All system services are FUNCTIONS for historical reasons (RSX-11 did it that way). Most services do not have a status block, so the most consistent design is to report errors via the function-return mechanism. This is a design decision more than a technical decision.

6. The problem here is that the $QIO service must check to be certain that every page represented by the request is accessible to the user. The IO status block is only two words long, so it can span across one page boundary at most. The buffer, depending on its length, can span many pages, so testing the accessibility of its first and last location does not ensure that the intermediate pages are also accessible. The PROBER test has to "touch" every page in the buffer by checking every 512 bytes—the PROBER tests bytes, not longwords.

7. Stacking interrupts is not possible. If the hardware requests a second interrupt before the first is granted, the second one is lost. In particular, if a clock interrupt is lost in this manner, the internal clock value falls 10 milliseconds behind. To ensure that this does not happen, the clock interrupt is higher (see Figure 8.8, which is typical of most VAX models) than any I/O interrupt; hence, I/O interrupts cannot block the clock.

8. See Figure A.11. When a device interrupt occurs (circle 1), the appropriate interrupt handler receives it and executes. During that execution process, it ascertains that the scheduler must be called, presumably because a process must preempt other processes. This scenario is likely to occur in a real-time system; thus, the interrupt handler requests a software interrupt at level 3 using the MTPR instruction, (circle 2). At some later time, when the IPL drops below 3, the scheduler will be started (circle 3), to reevaluate and select the highest available process to execute.

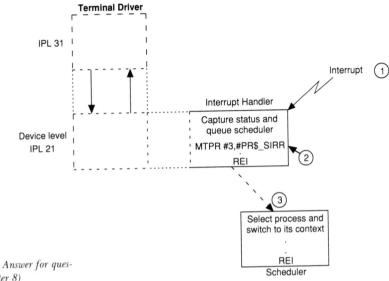

Figure A.11. Answer for question 8 (Chapter 8)

9. These are the major steps required:
    - The CPU puts the address on the address bus.
    - The CPU puts the data on the data bus, not knowing where it goes.
    - Either an I/O controller or memory responds to the address by removing and "processing" the corresponding data on the data bus. The other devices on the bus ignore the data because the address is out of their range.
10. The REI mechanism that grants an interrupt (as described in Figure 8.5) operates when the IPL in the PSL drops below the level of the pending interrupt. Since there is no way to drop below IPL 0, there is no provision to set an interrupt at IPL 0.

CHAPTER 9

1. There are certainly more than three, but the following list comprises the ones that occur to me. Assume that the "free space" file connects all the free clusters of the disk together in a file. As a consequence,

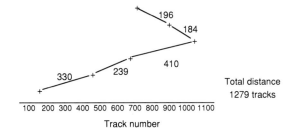

Figure A.12. Answer for question 5 (Chapter 9)

- The file would have to be arranged so that "data" clusters can be removed from within it in order to accommodate a user data allocation request. This function would be required nowhere else in the file subsystem.
- Upon a user "delete" request, that data file would be added to the "free" file. Adding to the front of the "free" file is not a standard file operation, and adding to the end of the file would be time-consuming, unless some special provision for locating the file's end is provided.
- The file location information could conceivably consume a large fraction of the disk, especially if the disk had many small "holes" on it, which is quite likely. A defragmentation operation would eliminate this plethora of holes, but the operation is time-consuming.

2. In the printing, displaying, or editing of the text, right-hand blanks (or tabs) are unnecessary and, therefore, do not have to be carried onto the disk. Left-hand blanks are essential to position the text properly.

3. This is a review question. One bitmap indicates the status of each cluster on disk, whether it is used or not. The second bitmap indicates whether or not the corresponding file header is used.

4. There is no reason to assume that each file consumes exactly the same number of blocks on the disk. Files vary in size in an unpredictable way. As a result, a disk will become full either because the file headers are all used up or because all the disk space is used up. It is unlikely that these two conditions will occur simultaneously.

5. See Figure A.12. The results are not dramatically different.

6. The algorithm to read the rth record of a fragmented file on an MS-DOS disk follows these steps:
   - Compute the proper logical cluster number.
   - Starting at the beginning of the file, thread through the FAT the required number of clusters.
   - Convert the resulting cluster number to the physical disk [track, sector] address.
   - Compute the required sector number within that cluster.
   - Compute the target [track, sector].
   - Read that sector of the disk.
   - Compute the logical record number within the sector.
   - Extract the bytes corresponding to the rth record and deliver them to the requesting process.

7. The edge of a 5.25 inch floppy is moving at:

   $$(300 \text{ rev/min}) \times (5.25 \times \pi \text{ in/rev}) = 4,948 \text{ in/min.}$$

   The edge of a 14-inch hard disk is moving at:

   $$(3,600 \text{ rev/min}) \times (14 \times \pi \text{ in/rev}) = 158,336 \text{ in/min.}$$

   A cassette tape moves at 1.875 in/sec = 112.5 in/min.
   To convert from inches per minute to miles per hour multiply by:

   $$\frac{\text{in}}{\text{min}} \times \frac{\text{ft}}{12 \text{ in}} \times \frac{\text{mile}}{5,280 \text{ ft}} \times \frac{60 \text{ min}}{\text{hour}} = 0.0009469 \frac{\text{miles}}{\text{hour}}$$

   This means that the edge of a 14-inch hard disk is moving at almost 150 mph.

8. Locating INDEXF.SYS is probably the biggest headache. Try

   ```
   DIR/SEC SYS$SYSDEVICE:[000000]INDEXF.SYS
   ```

   or perhaps you should use the physical device name, such as

   ```
   DIR/SEC DUA0:[000000]INDEXF.SYS
   ```

   In any case, you will quickly find that it is completely locked out from the unprivileged user. You will receive the following message in response to the command:

   ```
   No privilege for attempted operation
   ```

This is as it should be, since INDEXF.SYS corruption means that all data on the disk is lost. This message implies that the UIC protection code is most likely [RWED,,,], accessible only to SYSTEM.

9. The proof of defragmented file is that there is only one map entry in the file header.

Appendix B

Selected System Service and Run-time Library Descriptions

Each description that follows is divided into four sections. The first is an English explanation of the routine. Next is the Pascal calling sequence, with optional arguments shown in square brackets. Third is a discussion of each argument. And, finally, the Pascal declaration is given. This information is extracted from either STARLET.PAS (for system services) or PASCAL$LIB.PAS (for run-time library routines).

The following list contains all the descriptions given in this appendix.

$ADJWSL	$DCLAST	$SETIMR
$ASCEFC	$DELPRC	$SETPRN
$ASCTIM	$DELTVA	$SUSPND
$ASSIGN	$ENQ(W)	$WAITFR
$BINTIM	$GETJPI(W)	$WAKE
$CANCEL	$GETTIM	$WFLAND
$CLREF	$HIBER	LIB$SIGNAL
$CREMBX	$QIO(W)	LIB$SPAWN
$CREPRC	$RESUME	LIB$STOP
$CRETVA	$SCHDWK	LIB$WAIT
$CRMPSC	$SETEF	

$ADJWSL

ADJUST WORKING SET LIMIT

The Adjust Working Set Limit service adjusts a process's current working set limit by the specified number of pages and returns the new value to the caller. The working set limit specifies the maximum number of process pages that may be resident in physical memory.

```
$ADJWSL ( [pagcnt] ,[wsetlm] )
```

pagcnt. Signed adjustment value specifying the number of pages to add (if positive) or to subtract (if negative) from the current working set limit. The pagcnt argument is this signed longword value.

wsetlm. Value of the working set limit, returned by $ADJWSL. The wsetlm argument is the address of this longword value. The wsetlm argument specifies the newly adjusted value if pagcnt was specified, and it specifies the old, unadjusted value if pagcnt was not specified.

```
FUNCTION $ADJWSL ( %IMMED PAGCNT : INTEGER := %IMMED 0;
    VAR WSETLM : [VOLATILE] UNSIGNED := %IMMED 0) : INTEGER; EXTERNAL;
```

$ASCEFC

ASSOCIATE COMMON EVENT FLAG CLUSTER

The Associate Common Event Flag Cluster service causes a named common event flag cluster to be associated with a process for the execution of the current image and to be assigned a process-local cluster number for use with other event flag services. If the named cluster does not exist, but the process has suitable privilege, the service creates the cluster.

```
$ASCEFC ( efn ,name ,[prot] ,[perm] )
```

efn. Number of any event flag contained within the desired common event flag cluster. The efn argument is a longword value specifying this number.

name. Name of the common event flag cluster with which to associate. The name argument is the address of a character string descriptor pointing to this name string.

prot. Protection specifier that allows or disallows access to the common event flag cluster by processes with the same UIC group number as the creating process. The prot argument is a longword value, which is interpreted as Boolean.

0 -> default, any process in group
1 -> only owner's UIC

perm. Permanent specifier that marks a common event flag cluster as either permanent or temporary. The perm argument is a longword value, which is interpreted as Boolean.

0 -> temporary cluster
1 -> permanent cluster

```
FUNCTION $ASCEFC ( %IMMED EFN : UNSIGNED;
     NAME : [CLASS_S] PACKED ARRAY [$12..$u2:INTEGER] OF CHAR;
     %IMMED PROT : INTEGER := %IMMED 0;
     %IMMED PERM : INTEGER := %IMMED 0) : INTEGER; EXTERNAL;
```

$ASCTIM

CONVERT BINARY TIME TO ASCII STRING

The Convert Binary Time to ASCII String service converts an absolute or delta time from 64-bit system time format to an ASCII string.

```
$ASCTIM ( [timlen] ,timbuf ,[timadr] ,[cvtflg] )
```

timlen. Length (in bytes) of the ASCII string returned by $ASCTIM. The timlen argument is the address of a word containing this length.

timbuf. Buffer into which $ASCTIM writes the ASCII string. The timbuf argument is the address of a character string descriptor pointing to the buffer.

timadr. Time value that $ASCTIM is to convert. The timadr argument is the address of this 64-bit time value. A positive time value represents an absolute time. A negative time value represents a delta time. If a delta time is specified, it must be less than 10,000 days.

cvtflg. Conversion indicator specifying which date and time fields $ASCTIM should return. The cvtflg argument is a longword value, which is interpreted as Boolean. A value of 1 specifies that $ASCTIM should return only the hour, minute, second, and hundredth of second fields. A value of 0 (the default) specifies that $ASCTIM should return the full date and time.

0 -> return full date and time

1 -> return converted time only

```
FUNCTION $ASCTIM (
    VAR TIMLEN : [VOLATILE] $UWORD := %IMMED 0;
    VAR TIMBUF : [CLASS_S,VOLATILE] PACKED ARRAY [$12..$u2:INTEGER] OF CHAR;
    TIMADR : $UQUAD := %IMMED 0;
    %IMMED CVTFLG : INTEGER := %IMMED 0) : INTEGER; EXTERNAL;
```

$ASSIGN

ASSIGN I/O CHANNEL

The Assign I/O Channel service (1) provides a process with an I/O channel so that input/output operations can be performed on a device or (2) establishes a logical link with a remote node on a network.

```
$ASSIGN ( devnam ,chan ,[acmode] ,[mbxnam] )
```

devnam. Name of the device to which $ASSIGN is to assign a channel. The devnam argument is the address of a character string descriptor pointing to the device name string.

chan. Number of the channel that is assigned. The chan argument is the address of a word into which $ASSIGN writes the channel number.

acmode. Access mode to be associated with the channel. The acmode argument specifies the access mode. The most privileged access mode used is the access mode of the caller. I/O operations on the channel can only be performed from equal and more privileged access modes.

mbxnam. Logical name of the mailbox to be associated with the device. The mbxnam argument is the address of a character string descriptor pointing to the logical name string.

```
FUNCTION $ASSIGN (
    DEVNAM : [CLASS_S] PACKED ARRAY [$l1..$u1:INTEGER] OF CHAR;
    VAR CHAN : [VOLATILE] $UWORD;
    %IMMED ACMODE : UNSIGNED := %IMMED 0;
    MBXNAM : [CLASS_S] PACKED ARRAY [$l4..$u4:INTEGER] OF CHAR:= %IMMED 0)
    : INTEGER; EXTERNAL;
```

$BINTIM

CONVERT ASCII STRING TO BINARY TIME

The Convert ASCII String to Binary Time service converts an ASCII string to an absolute or delta time value in the system 64-bit time format suitable for input to the Set Timer ($SETIMR) or Schedule Wakeup ($SCHDWK) services.

```
$BINTIM ( timbuf ,timadr )
```

timbuf. The timbuf argument specifies the address of a character string descriptor pointing to the VMS time string. The VMS time string specifies the absolute or delta time to be converted by $BINTIM. The VMS Data Type Table describes the VMS time string.

timadr. The timadr argument is the address of the VMS quadword system time, which receives the converted time. Absolute time strings are specified in the format:

dd-mmm-yyyy hh:mm:ss.cc

Delta time strings are specified in the format:

dddd hh:mm:ss.cc

```
FUNCTION $BINTIM (
    TIMBUF : [CLASS_S] PACKED ARRAY [$l1..$u1:INTEGER] OF CHAR;
    VAR TIMADR : [VOLATILE] $UQUAD ) : INTEGER; EXTERNAL;
```

$CANCEL

CANCEL I/O ON CHANNEL

The Cancel I/O On Channel service cancels all pending I/O requests on a specified channel. In general, this includes all I/O requests that are queued as well as the request currently in progress.

```
$CANCEL ( chan )
```

chan. I/O channel on which I/O is to be canceled. The chan argument is a longword containing the channel number.

```
FUNCTION $CANCEL ( %IMMED CHAN : INTEGER ) : INTEGER; EXTERNAL;
```

$CLREF

CLEAR EVENT FLAG

The Clear Event Flag service clears (sets to 0) an event flag in a local or common event flag cluster.

```
$CLREF ( efn )
```

efn. Number of the event flag to be cleared. The efn argument is a longword containing this number.

```
FUNCTION $CLREF ( %IMMED EFN : UNSIGNED ) : INTEGER; EXTERNAL;
```

$CREMBX

CREATE MAILBOX AND ASSIGN CHANNEL

The Create Mailbox and Assign Channel service creates a virtual mailbox device named MBAn: and assigns an I/O channel to it. The system provides the unit number, n, when it creates the mailbox. If a mailbox with the specified name already exists, the $CREMBX service assigns a channel to the existing mailbox.

```
$CREMBX ( [prmflg] ,chan ,[maxmsg] ,[bufquo]
        ,[promsk] ,[acmode] ,[lognam] )
```

prmflg. Indicator specifying whether the created mailbox is to be permanent or temporary. The prmflg argument is a byte value. A value of 1 specifies a permanent mailbox; a value of 0, which is the default, specifies a temporary mailbox. Any other values result in an error.

0 -> temporary (default)
1 -> permanent

chan. Channel number assigned by $CREMBX to the mailbox. The chan argument is the address of a word into which $CREMBX writes the channel number.

maxmsg. Maximum size (in bytes) of a message that can be sent to the mailbox. The maxmsg argument is a longword value containing this size. If maxmsg is not specified or is specified as 0, VMS provides a default value.

bufquo. Number of bytes of system dynamic memory that can be used to buffer messages sent to the mailbox. The bufquo argument is a longword value containing this number. If bufquo is not specified or is specified as 0, VMS provides a default value.

promsk. Protection mask to be associated with the created mailbox. The promsk argument is a longword value that is the combined value of the bits set in the protection mask. Cleared bits grant access, and set bits deny access to each of the four classes of user: world, group, owner, and system.

acmode. Access mode to be associated with the channel to which the mailbox is assigned. The acmode argument is a longword containing the access mode.

lognam. Logical name to be assigned to the mailbox. The lognam argument is the address of a character string descriptor pointing to the logical name string.

```
FUNCTION $CREMBX (
    %IMMED PRMFLG : INTEGER := %IMMED 0;
    VAR CHAN : [VOLATILE] $UWORD;
    %IMMED MAXMSG : UNSIGNED := %IMMED 0;
    %IMMED BUFQUO : UNSIGNED := %IMMED 0;
    %IMMED PROMSK : UNSIGNED := %IMMED 0;
    %IMMED ACMODE : UNSIGNED := %IMMED 0;
    LOGNAM : [CLASS_S] PACKED ARRAY [$17..$u7:INTEGER] OF CHAR:= %IMMED 0)
    : INTEGER; EXTERNAL;
```

$CREPRC

CREATE PROCESS

The Create Process service creates a subprocess or detached process on behalf of the calling process.

```
$CREPRC ( [pidadr] ,[image] ,[input] ,[output] ,[error] ,[prvadr]
    ,[quota] ,[prcnam] ,[baspri] ,[uic] ,[mbxunt] ,[stsflg] )
```

pidadr. Process identification (PID) of the newly created process. The pidadr argument is the address of a longword into which $CREPRC writes the PID.

image. Name of the image to be activated in the newly created process. The image argument is the address of a character string descriptor pointing to the file specification of the image.

input. Equivalence name to be associated with the logical name SYS$INPUT in the logical name table of the created process. The input argument is the address of a character string descriptor pointing to the equivalence name string.

output. Equivalence name to be associated with the logical name SYS$OUTPUT in the logical name table of the created process. The output argument is the address of a character string descriptor pointing to the equivalence name string.

error. Equivalence name to be associated with the logical name SYS$ERROR in the logical name table of the created process. The error argument is the address of a character string descriptor pointing to the equivalence name string.

prvadr. Privileges to be given to the created process. The prvadr argument is the address of a quadword bit vector wherein each bit corresponds to a privilege; setting a bit gives the privilege.

quota. Process quotas to be established for the created process; these quotas limit the created process's use of system resources. The quota argument is the address of a list of quota descriptors, where each quota descriptor consists of a 1-byte quota name followed by a longword that specifies the desired value for that quota. The list of quota descriptors is terminated by the symbolic name PQL$_LISTEND.

prcnam. Process name to be assigned to the created process. The prcnam is the address of a character string descriptor pointing to a 1- to 15-character process name string.

baspri. Base priority to be assigned to the created process. The baspri argument is a longword value in the range 0 to 31, where 31 is the highest possible priority and 0 is the lowest. Normal priorities are in the range 0 through 15, and real-time priorities are in the range 16 through 31.

uic. User identification code (UIC) to be assigned to the created process. The uic argument is a longword value containing the UIC. If 0, create a subprocess.

mbxunt. Unit number of a mailbox to receive a termination message when the created process is deleted. The mbxunt argument is a word containing this number.

stsflg. Options selected for the created process. The stsflg argument is a longword bit vector wherein a bit corresponds to an option. Only bits 0 to 10 are used; bits 11 to 31 are reserved and must be 0.

Bit	Meaning
0	disable resource wait mode
1	enable system service failure exception mode
2	inhibit process swapping
3	disable accounting messages
4	batch process
5	cause created process to hibernate
6	allow login without authorization file check
7	process is a network connect object

```
FUNCTION $CREPRC (
    VAR PIDADR : [VOLATILE] UNSIGNED := %IMMED 0;
    IMAGE : [CLASS_S] PACKED ARRAY [$12..$u2:INTEGER] OF CHAR :=%IMMED 0;
    INPUT : [CLASS_S] PACKED ARRAY [$13..$u3:INTEGER] OF CHAR :=%IMMED 0;
    OUTPUT : [CLASS_S] PACKED ARRAY [$14..$u4:INTEGER] OF CHAR:= %IMMED 0;
    ERROR : [CLASS_S] PACKED ARRAY [$15..$u5:INTEGER] OF CHAR :=%IMMED 0;
    PRVADR : $UQUAD := %IMMED 0;
    %REF QUOTA : [UNSAFE] ARRAY [$17..$u7: INTEGER] OF $UBYTE :=%IMMED 0;
```

```
PRCNAM : [CLASS_S] PACKED ARRAY [$18..$u8:INTEGER] OF CHAR:= %IMMED 0;
%IMMED BASPRI : UNSIGNED := %IMMED 2; %IMMED UIC : UNSIGNED := %IMMED 0;
%IMMED MBXUNT : INTEGER := %IMMED 0; %IMMED STSFLG : UNSIGNED := %IMMED 0;
%REF ITMLST : [UNSAFE] ARRAY [$113..$u13: INTEGER] OF $UBYTE:= %IMMED 0)
: INTEGER; EXTERNAL;
```

$CRETVA

CREATE VIRTUAL ADDRESS SPACE

The Create Virtual Address Space service adds a range of demand-zero allocation pages to a process's virtual address space for the execution of the current image.

$CRETVA (inadr ,[retadr] ,[acmode])

inadr. Address of a two-longword array containing the starting and ending virtual addresses of the pages to be created. If the starting and ending virtual addresses are the same, a single page is created. Only the virtual page number portion of the virtual addresses is used; the low-order 9 bits are ignored.

retadr. Address of a two-longword array to receive the starting and ending virtual addresses of the pages actually created.

acmode. Access mode and protection for the new pages. The acmode argument is a longword containing the access mode.

```
FUNCTION $CRETVA (
    INADR : STARLET$$TYP2;
    VAR RETADR : [VOLATILE] STARLET$$TYP3 := %IMMED 0;
    %IMMED ACMODE : UNSIGNED := %IMMED 0) : INTEGER; EXTERNAL;
```

$CRMPSC

CREATE AND MAP SECTION

The Create and Map Section service allows a process to associate (map) a section of its address space with (1) a specified section of a file (a disk file section) or (2) with specified physical addresses represented by page frame numbers (a page frame section).

This service also allows the process to create either type of section, and to specify that that section be available only to the creating process (private section) or to all processes that map to it (global section).

```
$CRMPSC ( [inadr] ,[retadr] ,[acmode] ,[flags] ,[gsdnam]
    ,[ident] ,[relpag] ,[chan] ,[pagcnt] ,[vbn] ,[prot] ,[pfc] )
```

inadr. Starting and ending virtual addresses into which the section is to be mapped. The inadr is the address of a two-longword array containing, in order, the starting and the ending process virtual addresses. Only the virtual page number portion of each virtual address is used; the low-order 9 bits are ignored.

retadr. Starting and ending process virtual addresses into which the section was actually mapped by $CRMPSC. The retadr is the address of a two-longword array containing, in order, the starting and ending process virtual addresses.

acmode. Access mode that is to be the owner of the pages created during the mapping. The acmode argument is a longword containing the access mode.

flags. Flag mask specifying the type of section to be created or mapped to, as well as its characteristics. The flags argument is a longword bit vector wherein each bit corresponds to a flag. The flags argument is constructed by performing a logical OR operation on the symbol names for all desired flags.

Flag	Meaning
SEC$M_GBL	Global section
SEC$M_CRF	Copy-on-reference pages
SEC$M_DZRO	Demand zero pages
SEC$M_EXPREG	Find first available space
SEC$M_PERM	Permanent section
SEC$M_PFNMAP	Physical page frame section
SEC$M_SYSGBL	System global section
SEC$M_WRT	Read-write section

gsdnam. Name of the global section. The gsdnam is the address of a character string descriptor pointing to this name string.

ident. Identification value specifying the version number of a global section and, for processes mapping to an existing global section, the criteria for matching the identification. The ident argument is the address of a quadword structure containing three fields.

relpag. Relative page number within the global section of the first page in the section to be mapped. The relpag argument is a longword containing this page number.

chan. Number of the channel on which the file has been accessed. The chan argument is a word containing this number.

pagcnt. Number of pages in the section. The pagcnt argument is a longword containing this number.

vbn. Virtual block number in the file that marks the beginning of the section. The vbn argument is a longword containing this number. If vbn is not specified or is specified as 0 (the default), the section is created beginning with the first virtual block in the file.

prot. Numeric value representing the protection mask to be applied to the global section. This value is ORed with the protection mask associated with the file; if the file protection does not allow access to a particular category of user and the protection mask allows access, access is denied.

pfc. Page fault cluster size. If specified, the cluster size indicates how many pages are to be brought into memory when a page fault occurs for a single page. This argument is not used for physical page frame sections or for global sections in memory shared by multiple processors.

```
FUNCTION $CRMPSC (
     INADR : STARLET$$TYP4 := %IMMED 0;
     VAR RETADR : [VOLATILE] STARLET$$TYP5 := %IMMED 0;
     %IMMED ACMODE : UNSIGNED := %IMMED 0;
     %IMMED FLAGS : UNSIGNED := %IMMED 0;
     GSDNAM : [CLASS_S] PACKED ARRAY [$l5..$u5:INTEGER] OF CHAR:= %IMMED 0;
     IDENT : $UQUAD := %IMMED 0;
     %IMMED RELPAG : UNSIGNED := %IMMED 0;
     %IMMED CHAN : INTEGER := %IMMED 0;
     %IMMED PAGCNT : UNSIGNED := %IMMED 0;
     %IMMED VBN : UNSIGNED := %IMMED 0;
     %IMMED PROT : UNSIGNED := %IMMED 0;
     %IMMED PFC : UNSIGNED := %IMMED 0) : INTEGER; EXTERNAL;
```

$DCLAST

DECLARE AST

The Declare AST service queues an AST for the calling access mode or for a less privileged access mode. For example, a routine executing in supervisor mode can declare an AST for either supervisor or user mode.

```
$DCLAST ( astadr ,[astprm] ,[acmode] )
```

astadr. AST service routine to be executed. The astadr argument is the address of the entry mask of this routine.

astprm. AST parameter to be passed to the AST routine specified by the astadr argument. The astprm argument is a longword containing this parameter.

acmode. Access mode for which the AST is to be declared. The most privileged access mode used is the access mode of the caller. The resultant mode is the access mode for which the AST is declared.

```
FUNCTION $DCLAST (
    %IMMED [UNBOUND, ASYNCHRONOUS] PROCEDURE ASTADR;
    %IMMED ASTPRM : UNSIGNED := %IMMED 0;
    %IMMED ACMODE : UNSIGNED := %IMMED 0) : INTEGER; EXTERNAL;
```

$DELPRC

DELETE PROCESS

The Delete Process service allows a process to delete itself or another process.

```
$DELPRC ( [pidadr] ,[prcnam] )
```

pidadr. Process identification (PID) of the process to be deleted. The pidadr argument is the address of a longword that contains the PID.

prcnam. Process name of the process to be deleted. The prcnam is the address of a character string descriptor pointing to a 1- to 15-character process name string.

```
FUNCTION $DELPRC (
    VAR PIDADR : [VOLATILE] UNSIGNED := %IMMED 0;
    PRCNAM : [CLASS_S] PACKED ARRAY [$12..$u2:INTEGER] OF CHAR:= %IMMED 0)
    : INTEGER; EXTERNAL;
```

$DELTVA

DELETE VIRTUAL ADDRESS SPACE

The Delete Virtual Address Space service deletes a range of addresses from a process's virtual address space. Upon successful completion of the service, the deleted pages are inaccessible, and references to them cause access violations.

$DELTVA (inadr ,[retadr] ,[acmode])

inadr. tarting and ending virtual addresses of the pages to be deleted. The inadr argument is the address of a two-longword array containing, in order, the starting and the ending process virtual addresses. If the starting and ending virtual addresses are the same, a single page is deleted. Only the virtual page number portion of each virtual address is used; the low-order 9 bits are ignored.

retadr. Starting and ending process virtual addresses of the pages that $DELTVA has actually deleted. The retadr is the address of a two-longword array containing, in order, the starting and ending process virtual addresses.

acmode. Access mode on behalf of which the service is to be performed. The acmode argument is a longword containing the access mode.

```
FUNCTION $DELTVA (
    INADR : STARLET$$TYP6;
    VAR RETADR : [VOLATILE] STARLET$$TYP7 := %IMMED 0;
    %IMMED ACMODE : UNSIGNED := %IMMED 0) : INTEGER; EXTERNAL;
```

$ENQ

ENQUEUE LOCK REQUEST

The Enqueue Lock Request (and Wait) service queues a new lock or lock conversion on a resource.

The $ENQ service completes asynchronously; that is, it returns to the caller after queuing the lock request, without waiting for the lock to be either granted or converted.

For synchronous completion, use the Enqueue Lock Request and Wait ($ENQW) service. The $ENQW service is identical to the $ENQ service in every way except that $ENQW returns to the caller when the lock is either granted or converted.

The $ENQ, $ENQW, $DEQ (Dequeue Lock Request), and $GETLKI (Get Lock Information) services together provide the user interface to the VMS lock management facility.

```
$ENQ[W] ( [efn] ,lkmode ,lksb ,[flags] ,[resnam] ,[parid]
   ,[astadr] ,[astprm] ,[blkast] ,[acmode], [nullarg] )
```

efn. Number of the event flag to be set when the lock request has been granted. The efn argument is a longword containing this number.

lkmode. Lock mode requested. The lkmode argument is a longword specifying this lock mode. The values of lkmode are:

Value	Meaning
LCK$K_NLMODE	null lock
LCK$K_CRMODE	concurrent read
LCK$K_CWMODE	concurrent write
LCK$K_PRMODE	protected read
LCK$K_PWMODE	protected write
LCK$K_EXMODE	exclusive lock

lksb. Lock status block in which $ENQ writes the final completion status of the operation. The lksb argument is the address of the 8-byte lock status block.

flags. Flags specifying options for the $ENQ operation. The flags argument is a longword bit mask that is the logical OR of each bit set, where each bit corresponds to an option. The values permitted are:

LCK$M_NOQUEUE
LCK$M_SYNCSTS
LCK$M_SYSTEM
LCK$M_VALBLK
LCK$M_CONVERT

resnam. Name of the resource to be locked by this lock. The resnam argument is the address of a character string descriptor pointing to this name. The name string may be from 1 to 31 bytes in length.

parid. Lock identification of the parent lock. The parid argument is a longword containing this identification value.

astadr. AST service routine to be executed when the lock is either granted or converted. The astadr argument is the address of the entry mask of this routine.

astprm. AST parameter to be passed to the AST routine specified by the astadr argument. The astprm argument specifies this longword parameter.

blkast. Blocking AST routine to be called whenever this lock is granted and is blocking any other lock requests. The blkast argument is the address of the entry mask to this routine.

acmode. Access mode to be associated with the lock. The acmode argument is a longword containing the access mode.

nullarg. Place-holding argument. This argument is reserved to Digital.

```
FUNCTION $ENQ (
    %IMMED EFN : UNSIGNED := %IMMED 0;
    %IMMED LKMODE : UNSIGNED;
    %REF LKSB : [VOLATILE,UNSAFE] ARRAY [$13..$u3: INTEGER] OF $UBYTE;
    %IMMED FLAGS : UNSIGNED := %IMMED 0;
    RESNAM : [CLASS_S] PACKED ARRAY [$15..$u5:INTEGER] OF CHAR:= %IMMED 0;
    %IMMED PARID : UNSIGNED := %IMMED 0;
    %IMMED [UNBOUND, ASYNCHRONOUS] PROCEDURE ASTADR := %IMMED 0;
    %IMMED ASTPRM : UNSIGNED := %IMMED 0;
    %IMMED [UNBOUND, ASYNCHRONOUS] PROCEDURE BLKAST := %IMMED 0;
    %IMMED ACMODE : UNSIGNED := %IMMED 0;
    %IMMED NULLARG : UNSIGNED := %IMMED 0) : INTEGER; EXTERNAL;
```

$GETJPI

GET JOB/PROCESS INFORMATION

The Get Job/Process Information service returns information about one or more processes on the system.

The $GETJPI service completes asynchronously; that is, it returns to the caller after queuing the information request, without waiting for the requested information to be returned.

For synchronous completion, use the Get Job/Process Information and Wait ($GETJPIW) service. The $GETJPIW service is identical to the $GETJPI service in every way except that $GETJPIW returns to the caller with the requested information.

```
$GETJPI[W] ( [efn] ,[pidadr] ,[prcnam] ,itmlst
        ,[iosb], [astadr], [astprm] )
```

efn. Number of the event flag to be set when $GETJPI returns the requested information. The efn argument is a longword containing this number.

pidadr. Process identification (PID) of the process about which $GETJPI is to return information. The pidadr argument is the address of a longword containing the PID.

prcnam. Name of the process about which $GETJPI is to return information. The prcnam argument is the address of a character string descriptor pointing to this name string.

itmlst. Item list specifying which information about the process(es) is to be returned. The itmlst argument is the address of a list of item descriptors, each of which describes an item of information. The list of item descriptors is terminated by a longword of 0.

iosb. I/O status block that is to receive the final completion status. The iosb is the address of the quadword I/O status block.

astadr. AST service routine to be executed when $GETJPI completes. The astadr is the address of the entry mask of this routine.

astprm. AST parameter to be passed to the AST service routine specified by the astadr argument. The astprm argument is the longword parameter.

```
FUNCTION $GETJPI (
    %IMMED EFN : UNSIGNED := %IMMED 0;
    VAR PIDADR : [VOLATILE] UNSIGNED := %IMMED 0;
    PRCNAM : [CLASS_S] PACKED ARRAY [$13..$u3:INTEGER] OF CHAR:= %IMMED 0;
    %REF ITMLST : [UNSAFE] ARRAY [$14..$u4: INTEGER] OF $UBYTE;
    VAR IOSB : [VOLATILE] $UQUAD := %IMMED 0;
    %IMMED [UNBOUND, ASYNCHRONOUS] PROCEDURE ASTADR := %IMMED 0;
    %IMMED ASTPRM : UNSIGNED := %IMMED 0) : INTEGER; EXTERNAL;
```

$GETTIM

GET TIME

The Get Time service returns the current system time in 64-bit format.

```
$GETTIM ( timadr )
```

timadr. Address of a quadword that is to receive the current time in 64- bit format.

```
FUNCTION $GETTIM (
      VAR TIMADR : [VOLATILE] $UQUAD) : INTEGER; EXTERNAL;
```

$HIBER

HIBERNATE

The Hibernate service allows a process to make itself inactive but to remain known to the system so that it can be interrupted, for example, to receive ASTs. A hibernate request is a wait-for-wake-event request. When the Wake Process from Hibernation ($WAKE) service is called, or when a Schedule Wakeup ($SCHDWK) service comes due,the process continues execution at the instruction following the Hibernate call.

```
$HIBER

FUNCTION $HIBER : INTEGER; EXTERNAL;
```

$QIO

QUEUE I/O REQUEST

The Queue I/O Request service queues an I/O request to a channel associated with a device.

The $QIO service completes asynchronously; that is, it returns to the caller immediately after queuing the I/O request, without waiting for the I/O operation to complete.

For synchronous completion, use the Queue I/O Request and Wait

($QIOW) service. The $QIOW service is identical to the $QIO service in every way except that $QIOW returns to the caller after the I/O operation has completed.

```
$QIO[W] ( [efn] ,chan ,func ,[iosb] ,[astadr] ,[astprm]
         ,[p1] ,[p2] ,[p3] ,[p4] ,[p5] ,[p6] )
```

efn. Event flag that $QIO is to set when the I/O operation actually completes. The efn argument is a longword value containing the number of the event flag.

chan. I/O channel that is assigned to the device to which the request is directed. The chan argument is a word value containing the number of the I/O channel; however, $QIO uses only the low-order word.

func. Device-specific function codes and function modifiers specifying the operation to be performed. The func is a longword value containing the function code.

iosb. I/O status block to receive the final completion status of the I/O operation. The iosb is the address of the quadword I/O status block.

astadr. AST service routine to be executed when the I/O completes. The astadr argument is the address of a longword value that is the entry mask to the AST routine.

astprm. AST parameter to be passed to the AST service routine. The astprm argument is a longword value containing the AST parameter.

p1 to p6. Optional device- and function-specific I/O request parameters.

```
FUNCTION $QIO (
    %IMMED EFN : UNSIGNED := %IMMED 0;
    %IMMED CHAN : INTEGER;
    %IMMED FUNC : INTEGER;
    VAR IOSB : [VOLATILE] $UQUAD := %IMMED 0;
    %IMMED [UNBOUND, ASYNCHRONOUS] PROCEDURE ASTADR := %IMMED 0;
    %IMMED ASTPRM : UNSIGNED := %IMMED 0;
    %REF P1 : [UNSAFE] ARRAY [$17..$u7: INTEGER] OF $UBYTE := %IMMED 0;
    %IMMED P2 : INTEGER := %IMMED 0;
    %IMMED P3 : INTEGER := %IMMED 0;
    %IMMED P4 : INTEGER := %IMMED 0;
    %IMMED P5 : INTEGER := %IMMED 0;
    %IMMED P6 : INTEGER := %IMMED 0) : INTEGER; EXTERNAL;
```

$RESUME

RESUME SUSPENDED PROCESS

The Resume Process service (1) causes a process previously suspended by the Suspend Process ($SUSPND) service to resume execution or (2) cancels the effect of a subsequent suspend request.

$RESUME ([pidadr] ,[prcnam])

pidadr. Process identification (PID) of the process that is to be resumed. The pidadr argument is the address of a longword containing the PID.

prcnam. Name of the process to be resumed. The prcnam is the address of a character string descriptor pointing to the process name, which is a character string of from 1 to 15 characters.

```
FUNCTION $RESUME (
    VAR PIDADR : [VOLATILE] UNSIGNED := %IMMED 0;
    PRCNAM : [CLASS_S] PACKED ARRAY [$12..$u2:INTEGER] OF CHAR:= %IMMED 0)
    : INTEGER; EXTERNAL;
```

$SCHDWK

SCHEDULE WAKEUP

The Schedule Wakeup service schedules the awakening of a process that has placed itself in a state of hibernation with the Hibernate ($HIBER) service. A wakeup can be scheduled for a specified absolute time or for a delta time, and can be repeated at fixed intervals.

$SCHDWK ([pidadr] ,[prcnam] ,daytim ,[reptim])

pidadr. Process identification (PID) of the process that is to be awakened. The pidadr argument is the address of a longword containing the PID.

prcnam. Name of the process to be awakened. The prcnam is the address of a character string descriptor pointing to the process name, which is a character string of from 1 to 15 characters.

daytim. Time at which the process is to be awakened. The daytim argument is the address of a quadword containing this time in the system 64-bit time format. A positive time value specifies an absolute time at which the specified process is to be awakened. A negative time value specifies an offset (delta time) from the current time.

reptim. Time interval at which the wakeup request is to be repeated. The reptim argument is the address of a quadword containing this time interval. The time interval must be expressed in delta time format.

```
FUNCTION $SCHDWK (
    VAR PIDADR : [VOLATILE] UNSIGNED := %IMMED 0;
    PRCNAM : [CLASS_S] PACKED ARRAY [$12..$u2:INTEGER] OF CHAR:= %IMMED 0;
    DAYTIM : $UQUAD;
    REPTIM : $UQUAD := %IMMED 0) : INTEGER; EXTERNAL;
```

$SETEF

SET EVENT FLAG

The Set Event Flag service sets an event flag in a local or common event flag cluster. The condition value returned by $SETEF indicates whether the specified flag was previously set or clear. Once the event flag is set, processes waiting for the event flag to be set resume execution.

```
$SETEF ( efn )
```

efn. Number of the event flag to be set. The efn argument is a longword containing this number.

```
FUNCTION $SETEF (
    %IMMED EFN : UNSIGNED) : INTEGER; EXTERNAL;
```

$SETIMR

SET TIMER

The Set Timer service sets the timer to expire at a specified time. When the timer expires, an event flag is set and (optionally) an AST routine executes.

```
$SETIMR ( [efn] ,daytim ,[astadr] ,[reqidt] ,[flags] )
```

efn. Event flag to be set when the timer expires. The efn argument is a longword value containing the number of the event flag. If efn is not specified, event flag 0 is set.

daytim. Time at which the timer expires. The daytim argument is the address of a quadword time value. A positive time value specifies an absolute time at which the timer expires; a negative time value specifies an offset (delta time) from the current time.

astadr. AST service routine that is to execute when the timer expires. The astadr is the address of the entry mask of this routine. If astadr is not specified or is specified as 0 (the default), no AST routine executes.

reqidt. Identification of the timer request. The reqidt is a longword value containing a number that uniquely identifies the timer request. If reqidt is not specified, the value 0 is used.

flags. If bit 0 is set, then this timer request is in terms of CPU time.

```
FUNCTION $SETIMR (
    %IMMED EFN : UNSIGNED := %IMMED 0;
    DAYTIM : $UQUAD;
    %IMMED [UNBOUND, ASYNCHRONOUS] PROCEDURE ASTADR := %IMMED 0;
    %IMMED REQIDT : UNSIGNED := %IMMED 0;
    %IMMED FLAGS : UNSIGNED := %IMMED 0) : INTEGER; EXTERNAL;
```

$SETPRN

SET PROCESS NAME

The Set Process Name service allows a process to establish or to change its own process name.

```
$SETPRN ( [prcnam] )
```

prcnam. Process name to be given to the calling process. The prcnam argument is the address of a character string descriptor pointing to a 1- to 15-character process name string. If prcnam is not specified, the calling process is given no name.

```
FUNCTION $SETPRN (
    PRCNAM : [CLASS_S] PACKED ARRAY [$l1..$u1:INTEGER] OF CHAR:= %IMMED 0)
    : INTEGER; EXTERNAL;
```

$SUSPND

SUSPEND PROCESS

The Suspend Process service allows a process to suspend itself or another process. A suspended process cannot receive ASTs or otherwise be executed until another process resumes or deletes it.

```
$SUSPND ( [pidadr] ,[prcnam], [flags] )
```

pidadr. Process identification (PID) of the process to be suspended. The pidadr argument is the address of the longword PID.

prcnam. Name of the process to be suspended. The prcnam argument is the address of a character string descriptor pointing to a 1- to 15-character process name string.

flags. If bit 0 is set, then this is a hard suspend request; if clear, this is a soft suspend request.

```
FUNCTION $SUSPND (
    VAR PIDADR : [VOLATILE] UNSIGNED := %IMMED 0;
    PRCNAM : [CLASS_S] PACKED ARRAY [$l2..$u2:INTEGER] OF CHAR:= %IMMED 0;
    %IMMED FLAGS : UNSIGNED := %IMMED 0) : INTEGER; EXTERNAL;
```

$WAITFR

WAIT FOR SINGLE EVENT FLAG

The Wait for Single Event Flag service tests a specific event flag and returns immediately if the flag is set. Otherwise, the process is placed in a wait state until the event flag is set.

```
$WAITFR ( efn )
```

efn. Number of the event flag for which to wait. The efn argument is a longword containing this number.

```
FUNCTION $WAITFR (
     %IMMED EFN : UNSIGNED) : INTEGER; EXTERNAL;
```

$WAKE

WAKE FROM HIBERNATION

The Wake Process from Hibernation service activates a process that has placed itself in a state of hibernation with the Hibernate ($HIBER) service.

```
$WAKE ( [pidadr] ,[prcnam] )
```

pidadr. Process identification (PID) of the process to be awakened. The pidadr argument is the address of a longword containing the PID.

prcnam. Process name of the process to be awakened. The prcnam argument is the address of a character string descriptor pointing to a 1- to 15-character process name string.

```
FUNCTION $WAKE (
     VAR PIDADR : [VOLATILE] UNSIGNED := %IMMED 0;
     PRCNAM : [CLASS_S] PACKED ARRAY [$l2..$u2:INTEGER] OF CHAR:= %IMMED 0)
     : INTEGER; EXTERNAL;
```

$WFLAND

WAIT FOR LOGICAL AND OF EVENT FLAGS

The Wait for Logical AND of Event Flags service allows a process to specify a set of event flags for which it wishes to wait. The process is put in a wait state until all specified event flags are set, at which time $WFLAND returns to the caller, and execution resumes.

```
$WFLAND ( efn ,mask )
```

efn. Number of any event flag within the event flag cluster that is to be used. The efn argument is a longword containing this number. Specifying the number of an event flag within the cluster serves to identify the event flag cluster.

mask. Event flags for which the process is to wait. The mask argument is a longword bit vector wherein a bit, when set, selects the corresponding event flag for which to wait.

```
FUNCTION $WFLAND (
    %IMMED EFN : UNSIGNED;
    %IMMED MASK : UNSIGNED) : INTEGER; EXTERNAL;
```

LIB$SIGNAL

SIGNAL EXCEPTION CONDITION

The Signal Exception Condition routine generates a signal that indicates that an exception condition has occurred in your program. If a condition handler does not take corrective action and the condition is severe, your program will exit.

Only the condition-value1 argument must be specified; other arguments are optional. The number-of-arguments1 argument, if specified, contains the number of FAO arguments that will be associated with condition-value1. The condition-value2 argument is optional; it may be specified with or without the number-of-arguments2 or FAO-argument2 arguments. The number-of-arguments2 argument, if specified, contains the number of FAO arguments that will be associated with condition-value2. You may specify condition-value3, condition-value4, condition-value5, and so on, along with their corresponding number-of-arguments and FAO arguments.

```
LIB$SIGNAL ( condition-value1 ,[number-of-arguments1]
    ,[FAO-argument1. . .] ,[condition-value2]
  ,[number-of-arguments2] ,[FAO-argument2. . .] )
```

condition-value1. VAX 32-bit condition value. The condition-value1 argument is an unsigned longword that contains this condition value.

number-of-arguments1. Number of FAO arguments associated with the condition value. The optional number-of-arguments1 argument is a signed longword integer that contains this number. If omitted or specified as 0, no FAO arguments follow.

FAO-argument1. Optional FAO (formatted ASCII output) argument that is associated with the specified condition value.

condition-value2. VAX 32-bit condition value. The optional condition-value2 argument is an unsigned longword that contains this condition value.

number-of-arguments2. Number of FAO arguments associated with the condition value. The optional number-of-arguments2 argument is a signed longword integer that contains this number. If omitted or specified as 0, no FAO arguments follow.

FAO-argument2. Optional FAO (formatted ASCII output) argument that is associated with the specified condition value.

```
PROCEDURE lib$signal (
       %IMMED condition_value : UNSIGNED;
       %IMMED number_of_arguments : INTEGER := %IMMED 0;
       %IMMED FAO_argument : [LIST,UNSAFE] INTEGER); EXTERNAL;
```

LIB$SPAWN

SPAWN SUBPROCESS

The Spawn Subprocess routine requests the command language interpreter (CLI) of the calling process to spawn a subprocess for executing CLI commands. LIB$SPAWN provides the same function as the DCL SPAWN command.

```
LIB$SPAWN ( [command-string] ,[input-file] ,[output-file]
,[flags] ,[process-name] ,[process-id] ,[completion-status]
        ,[byte-integer-event-flag-num] ,[AST-address]
        ,[varying-AST-argument] ,[prompt-string] ,[cli] )
```

command-string. CLI command to be executed by the spawned subprocess. The command-string argument is the address of a descriptor pointing to this CLI command string. If omitted, commands are taken from the file specified by input-file.

input-file. Equivalence name to be associated with the logical name SYS$INPUT in the logical name table for the subprocess. The input-file argument is the address of a descriptor pointing to this equivalence string. If omitted, the default is the caller's SYS$INPUT.

output-file. Equivalence name to be associated with the logical names SYS$OUTPUT and SYS$ERROR in the logical name table for the subprocess. The output-file argument is the address of a descriptor pointing to this equivalence string. If omitted, the default is the caller's SYS$OUTPUT.

flags. Flag bits that designate optional behavior. The flags argument is the address of an unsigned longword that contains these flag bits. By default, all flags are clear.

process-name. Name defined for the subprocess. The process-name argument is the address of a descriptor pointing to this name string. If omitted, a unique process name will be generated. If you supply a name and it is not unique, LIB$SPAWN will return the condition value SS$_DUPLNAM.

process-id. Process identification of the spawned subprocess. The process-id argument is the address of an unsigned longword that contains this process identification value.

completion-status. The final completion status of the subprocess. The completion-status argument is the address of an unsigned longword. LIB$SPAWN writes the address of the final completion status of the subprocess into completion-status.

byte-integer-event-flag-num. The number of a local event flag to be set when the spawned subprocess completes. The byte-integer-event-flag-num argument is the address of an unsigned byte that contains this event flag number. If omitted, no event flag is set.

AST-address. Entry mask of a procedure to be called by means of an AST when the subprocess completes. The AST-address argument is the address of this procedure entry mask.

varying-AST-argument. A value to be passed to the AST procedure. Typically, the varying-AST-argument argument is the address of a block of storage the AST procedure will use.

prompt-string. Prompt string to use in the subprocess. The prompt-string argument is the address of a descriptor pointing to this prompt string. If omitted, the subprocess will use the same prompt string that the parent process uses.

cli. File specification for the command language interpreter (CLI) to be run in the subprocess. The cli argument is the address of this file specification string's descriptor. The CLI specified must reside in SYS$SYSTEM with a file type of EXE, and it must be installed. No directory or file type may be specified.

```
FUNCTION lib$spawn (
        command_string : [CLASS_S] PACKED ARRAY [$l1..$u1:INTEGER] OF CHAR := %IMMED 0
        ;input_file : [CLASS_S] PACKED ARRAY [$l2..$u2:INTEGER] OF CHAR := %IMMED 0;
        output_file : [CLASS_S] PACKED ARRAY [$l3..$u3:INTEGER] OF CHAR := %IMMED 0;
        flags : UNSIGNED := %IMMED 0;
        process_name : [CLASS_S] PACKED ARRAY [$l5..$u5:INTEGER] OF CHAR := %IMMED 0;
        VAR process_id : [VOLATILE] UNSIGNED := %IMMED 0;
        %IMMED completion_status_address : $DEFPTR := %IMMED 0;
        byte_integer_event_flag_num : $UBYTE := %IMMED 0;
        %IMMED [UNBOUND, ASYNCHRONOUS] PROCEDURE AST_address := %IMMED 0;
        %IMMED varying_AST_argument : [UNSAFE] INTEGER := %IMMED 0;
        prompt_string : [CLASS_S] PACKED ARRAY [$l11..$u11:INTEGER] OF CHAR := % IMMED 0;
        cli : [CLASS_S] PACKED ARRAY [$l12..$u12:INTEGER] OF CHAR := %IMMED 0) :
        UNSIGNED; EXTERNAL;
```

LIB$STOP

STOP EXECUTION AND SIGNAL THE CONDITION

The Stop Execution and Signal the Condition routine generates a signal that indicates that an exception condition has occurred in your program. Exception conditions signaled by LIB$STOP cannot be continued from the point of the signal.

Only the condition-value1 argument must be specified; other arguments are optional. The number-of-arguments1 argument, if specified, contains the number of FAO arguments that will be associated with condition-value1. The condition-value2 argument is optional; it may be specified with or without the number-of-arguments2 or FAO-argument2 arguments. The number-of-arguments2 argument, if specified, contains the number of FAO arguments that will be associated with condition-value2. You may specify condition-value3, condition-value4, condition-value5, and so on, along with their corresponding number-of-arguments and FAO arguments.

```
LIB$STOP ( condition-value1 , [number-of-arguments1]
    ,[FAO-argument1. . .] ,[condition-value2]
    ,[number-of-arguments2] ,[FAO-argument2. . .] )
```

condition-value1. VAX 32-bit condition value. The condition-value1 argument is an unsigned longword that contains this condition value.

number-of-arguments1. Number of FAO arguments associated with the condition value. The optional number-of-arguments1 argument is a signed longword integer that contains this number. If omitted or specified as 0, no FAO arguments follow.

FAO-argument1. Optional FAO (formatted ASCII output) argument that is associated with the specified condition value.

condition-value2. VAX 32-bit condition value. The optional condition-value2 argument is an unsigned longword that contains this condition value.

number-of-arguments2. Optional FAO argument associated with the condition value. The number-of-arguments2 argument is a signed longword integer that contains this number. If omitted or specified as 0, no FAO arguments follow. FAO-argument2 FAO (formatted ASCII output) argument that is associated with the specified condition value.

```
PROCEDURE lib$stop (
    %IMMED condition_value : UNSIGNED;
    %IMMED number_of_arguments : INTEGER := %IMMED 0;
    %IMMED FAO_argument : [LIST,UNSAFE] INTEGER); EXTERNAL;
```

LIB$WAIT

WAIT A SPECIFIED PERIOD OF TIME

The Wait a Specified Period of Time routine places the current process into hibernation for the number of seconds specified in its argument.

```
LIB$WAIT ( seconds )
```

seconds. The number of seconds to wait. The seconds argument contains the address of an F_floating number that is this number.

```
FUNCTION lib$wait (
     seconds : SINGLE) : UNSIGNED; EXTERNAL;
```

Appendix C
Acronym List

$ADJWSL	Adjust Working Set Limits system service
$ASCEFC	Associate to Common Event Flag Cluster system service
$ASCTIM	ASCII time conversion system service
$ASSIGN	ASSIGN channel system service
$BINTIM	Binary Time conversion system service
$CANCEL	CANCEL I/O system service
$CHKPRO	Check Access Protection system service
$CLREF	Clear Event Flag system service
$CREMBX	Create Mailbox system service
$CREPRC	Create Process system service
$CRETVA	Create Virtual Address Space system service
$CRMPSC	Create and Map a Section system service
$DACEFC	Disassociate Common Event Flag Cluster system service
$DCLAST	Declare Asynchronous System Trap system service
$DELPRC	Delete Process system service
$DELTVA	Delete Virtual Address Space system service
$ENQW	Enqueue lock request and Wait system service

$EXIT	Terminate image system service
$GETJPIW	Get Job/Process Information and Wait system service
$HIBER	Hibernate system service
$IMGACT	Image Activator system service
$QIOW	Queue I/O and Wait system service
$RESUME	RESUME process system service
$SCHDWK	Schedule wakeup system service
$SETEF	SET Event Flag system service
$SETIMR	SET Timer system service
$SETPRN	Set Process Name system service
$SUSPND	Suspend process system service
$WAITFR	Wait for Event Flag set system service
$WAKE	Wakeup system service
$WFLAND	Wait for Logical AND of Event Flags system service
ACB	AST Control Block
ACL	Access Control List
ALGOL	International ALGOrithmic Language
ALTPRI	Alter Priority privilege
ANSI	American National Standards Institute
AP	Argument Pointer register
ARB	Access Rights Block
ASCII	American Standard Code for Information Interchange
AST	Asynchronous System Trap
ATM	Automatic Teller Machine
BBN	Bolt, Beranek and Newman
BCD	Binary Coded Decimal
BLINK	Backward Link in PFN data base
BYPASS	Bypass privilege
CALLG	Assembly instruction for subroutine call
CALLS	Assembly instruction for subroutine call
CCB	Channel Control Block
CDC	Control Data Corporation
CD	Compact Disk
CEB	Common Event Flag Block
CEF	Common Event Flag wait process state
CHME	Assembly instruction to Change Mode to Executive
CHMK	Assembly instruction to Change Mode to Kernel
CHMS	Assembly instruction to Change Mode to Supervisor
CHMU	Assembly instruction to Change Mode to User

CHMx	Generic assembly instruction to Change Mode
CISC	Complex Instruction Set Computer
CLI	Command Language Interpreter
CMKRNL	Change Mode to Kernel privilege
CMPL	Assembly instruction to Compare Longwords
COM	Computable process state
COMO	Computable Outswapped process state
CP/M	Control Program for Microprocessors
CPU	Central Processing Unit
CRC	Cyclic Redundancy Check
CRWED	Control, Read, Write, Execute, Delete
CTSS	Compatible Time-Sharing System
CUR	Currently executing process state
DAT	Digital Audio Tape
DCL	Digital Command Language
DDB	Device Data Block
DDT	Digital Diagnostic Technique
DEC	Digital Equipment Corporation
DMA	Direct Memory Access
DOS	Disk Operating System
EBCDIC	Extended Binary Coded Decimal Information Code
EDIV	Assembly instruction to perform Extended integer Divide
ERRLOG	Error LOG
FAT	File Allocation Table
FCB	File Control Block
FCP	File Control Primitive
FDL	File Description Language
FDT	Function Decision Table
FFS	Assembly instruction to Find First Set bit in a long word
FIFO	First In, First Out
FLINK	Forward Link in PFN data base
FORTRAN	Formula Translator
FP	Frame Pointer register
GRPPRV	Group Privilege privilege
HIB	Hibernate process state
HIBO	Hibernate Outswapped process state
HOL	Higher Order Language
I/O	Input/Output

IBM	International Business Machines
INCL	Assembly instruction to increment a value by one
INSQUE	Assembly instruction to insert a queue entry
IPL	Interrupt Priority Level
IPR	Internal Processor Register
IRP	I/O Request Packet
ISR	Interrupt Service Routine
ITT	International Telephone and Telegraph
JCL	Job Control Language
JIB	Job Information Block
KESU	Kernel, Executive, Supervisor, User
LAN	Local Area Network
LDPCTX	Assembly instruction to load process context
LED	Light Emitting Diode
LEF	Local Event Flag wait process state
LIB$SIGNAL	An RTL routine to terminate an image
LIB$STOP	RTL routine to stop an image
LIB$WAIT	An RTL routine to hibernate a specific time
LID	Lock Identification Table
LINC	Laboratory Instrument Computer
LISP	List Processor
LKB	Lock Block
LKSB	Lock Status Block
LOGIN.COM	User LOGIN file
LRP	Large Request Packet
LRU	Least Recently Used
M-bit	Modify bit
MFLOPS	Million Floating Point Operations Per Second
MFPR	Assembly instruction to Move From Processor Register
MFT	Multiprogramming with a Fixed number of Tasks
MHz	Megahertz
MIPS	Million Instructions Per Second
MS	Microsecond
MS-DOS	MicroSoft Disk Operating System
MTPR	Assembly instruction to Move To Processor Register
MUTEX	Mutual Exclusion
MVT	Multiprogramming with a Variable number of Tasks
OPCOM	Operator Communications Manager
OPER	Operator privilege

P0LR	P0 Length Register
P0	Region 0 of virtual memory
P1LR	P1 Length Register
P1	Region 1 of virtual memory
PA	Physical Address
PCBB	PCB Base register
PCB	Process Control Block
PC	Personal Computer; Program Counter
PDP	Programmed Data Processor
PFN	Page Frame Number
PF	Page Fault
PFW	Page Fault Wait process state
PHD	Process Header
PID	Process Identification
PIO	Programmed I/O
PIXBAS	PHD index base
PRMGBL	Permanent Global Privilege
PROBER	Assembly instruction to PROBE memory for Read access
PROBEW	Assembly instruction to PROBE memory for Write access
PROBEx	Generic assembly instruction to PROBE memory
PSL	Processor Status Longword
PSW	Processor Status Word
PTE	Page Table Entry; Array in the PFN data base
READALL	READ ALL files privilege
REFCNT	Reference Count array in the PFN data base
REI	Assembly instruction to Return from Exception or Interrupt
REMQUE	Assembly instruction to remove a queue entry
RET	Assembly instruction to Return from subroutine
RHT	Resource Hash Table
RISC	Reduced Instruction Set Computer
RMS	Record Management System
RMS	Record Management Services
ROM	Read Only Memory
RPM	Revolutions Per Minute
RSB	Resource Block
RSTS	Resource Sharing Time-Sharing

RSX	Resource Sharing Executive operating system
RT	Real Time operating system
RTL	Run-time Library
RWED	Read, Write, Execute, Delete protection
SBR	SYS Base Register
SCBB	System Control Block Base register
SCB	System Control Block
SETPRV	Set Privileges privilege
SIRR	Software Interrupt Request Register
SIRS	Software Interrupt Request Status register
SLR	SYS Length Register
SP	Stack Pointer
SRP	Small Request Packet
SS$_ACCVIO	A system service return code
SS$_NORMAL	A system service return code
SSTF	Shortest Seek Time First
SVPCTX	Assembly instruction to save process context
SYSPRV	System Privilege privilege
SYS	System region of virtual memory
SYSUAF.DAT	System User Authorization File
TSS	Time-Shared System
UCB	Unit Control Block
UIC	User Identification Code
ULTRIX	A UNIX-like operating system that runs on the VAX
V-bit	Valid bit
VA	Virtual Address
VAX	Virtual Address Extension
VMS	Virtual Memory System
WSLX	Working Set Link index
XIO	Execute I/O
XQP	Extended QIO Program

Index

Also from Digital Press

These books may be purchased from technical reference bookstores or by calling 1-800-DIGITAL.

VAX/VMS: Writing Real Programs in DCL

PAUL C. ANAGNOSTOPOULOS

Taking up where the VAX/VMS documentation leaves off, this book describes how to write applications using Digital Command Language as a general purpose programming language. EY-C168E-DP.

UNIX for VMS Users

PHILIP E. BOURNE

The only book on UNIX for VMS users, this volume is invaluable for those making the transition between the two operating systems. It does not assume too high or low a level of knowledge and uses prior experience as a teaching tool. EY-C177E-DP.

VAX Architecture Reference Manual, Second Edition

EDITED BY RICHARD A. BRUNNER

Covering every VAX instruction addressing mode, instruction, and register, this reference is essential for the computer professional using any VAX from the MicroVAX II to the VAX 9000. EY-F576E-DP.

Writing VAX/VMS Applications Using Pascal

THEO DE KLERK

Programmers will appreciate this book's methodology for producing high-quality applications by focusing on the most important aspects of VMS. It provides numerous working program examples and coverage of the VAX calling standard, System Services, and Run Time Library routines and their implementations. EY-F592E-DP.

VAX/VMS Internals and Data Structures: Version 5.2

RUTH E. GOLDENBERG AND LAWRENCE J. KENAH

This authoritative description of the VMS operating system sets a new standard for completeness, accuracy, and accessibility. EY-C171E-DP.

RDb/VMS: A Comprehensive Guide

LILIAN HOBBS AND KEN ENGLAND

The authors have drawn on their extensive experience to introduce and discuss the functionality of this relational database product. EY-H873E-DP.

Computer Programming and Architecture
The VAX, Second Edition

HENRY M. LEVY AND RICHARD H. ECKHOUSE, JR.

The authors' unique systems approach uses the VAX to teach assembly language programming and computer architecture. They cover higher-level concepts and other architectures such as RISC and the Intel 80386 for comparison. EY-6740E-DP.

VMS File System Internals

KIRBY MCCOY

This comprehensive study of the VMS file system examines the components, interfaces, and basic synchronization mechanisms needed to store and manage files and information. EY-F575E-DP

The VMS User's Guide

JAMES F. PETERS AND PATRICK HOLMAY

Up to date with VMS Version 5.0, this volume provides hands-on experience in customizing a working environment through step-by-step instructions, exercises, and review questions. EY-6739E-DP.